HISTORICAL SKETCHES
OF THE
SOUTH OF INDIA

HISTORICAL SKETCHES

OF THE

SOUTH OF INDIA,

IN AN ATTEMPT TO TRACE THE

HISTORY OF MYSOOR;

FROM THE
ORIGIN OF THE HINDOO GOVERNMENT OF THAT STATE TO THE
EXTINCTION OF THE MOHAMMEDAN DYNASTY IN 1799.

LIEUT. COLONEL MARK WILKS

IN THREE VOLUMES
VOL. III

GYAN

Published by

Gyan Publishing House
5, Ansari Road
Daryaganj, New Delhi-110002
Phone: 011-47034999, 9811692060
E-mail: books@gyanbooks.com

Distribution Network
gyanbooks.com
India, USA, Canada, UK, Australia, France

ISBN: 978-81-212-8763-0 (Set)
978-81-212-8760-9 (PB)
First Published, 1817

2nd Impression 2023

Printed at: Gyan Press, Delhi.

HISTORICAL SKETCHES OF THE SOUTH OF INDIA (VOL. III)
Author: Mark Wilks

HISTORICAL SKETCHES

OF THE

SOUTH OF INDIA,

IN AN ATTEMPT TO TRACE THE

HISTORY OF MYSOOR;

FROM THE

ORIGIN OF THE HINDOO GOVERNMENT OF THAT STATE, TO THE EXTINCTION OF THE MAHOMMEDAN DYNASTY IN 1799.

FOUNDED CHIEFLY ON INDIAN AUTHORITIES COLLECTED BY THE AUTHOR WHILE OFFICIATING FOR SEVERAL YEARS AS

POLITICAL RESIDENT AT THE COURT OF MYSOOR.

BY COLONEL MARK WILKS.

VOL. III.

LONDON:

PRINTED FOR LONGMAN, HURST, REES, ORME, AND BROWN, PATERNOSTER-ROW.

1817.

CONTENTS

OF

THE THIRD VOLUME.

CHAPTER XXXII.

CHAPTER XXXIII.

CHAPTER XXXIV.

CHAPTER XXXV.

CHAPTER XXXVI.

CHAPTER XXXVII.

CHAPTER XXXVIII.

CHAPTER XXXIX.

CHAPTER XL.

CHAPTER XLI.

CHAPTER XLII.

CHAPTER XLIII.

CHAPTER XLIV.

CHAPTER XLV.

CHAPTER XLVI.

CHAPTER XLVII.

CHAPTER XLVIII.

CHAPTER XXXII.

The Sultaun destroys Mysoor — Curious example of vicissitude — Descends to Malabar — Extract from his own work, descriptive of the singular habits of the women — Discussion of that subject — Habits of the ancient Britons — Impolitic demolition of Calicut — The monsoon — Impious pretensions — The word prophet — Arrival at Coimbetoor — Suspected madness — French physician — Influence of European politics — Visits Dindigul — Alarm of the Raja of Travancore — Tippoo returns to Seringapatam — Arrangements — Coorg and Malabar in general rebellion — caused by the supercession of Arshed Beg Khân, and the crude measures of his successor — That respectable man disgraced — Died of grief — Tippoo proceeds to Malabar — hunts the Nairs — Alternative of circumcision or deportation — Opinion of the spontaneous appearance of small-pox without contagion — examined and discussed — Nair Raja Chercul is received with distinction — Reciprocal suspicions of treachery — Killed — The corpse treated with base indignity — Destruction of the temples — Marriage of the Sultaun's second son, to the daughter of the Beebee of Cannanore — Astrology — Arrangements for forcible and universal conversion — Reconnoissance of the Travancorean frontier — Returns to Coimbetoor — End of the King of histories — and specimen in its concluding page — Embassador from Nizam Ali received — proposes a strict and solemn alliance — rejected except on condition of a previous intermarriage in the families — which Nizam Ali declined.

WHATEVER may have been the Sultaun's motives for concluding the late peace, they had certainly no influence in diminishing the arrogance of his subsequent pretensions. On returning to his capital, some months were employed in the enlargement of those numerous innovations in the interior, which will be most conve- CHAP. XXXII. 1787.

CHAP. XXXII. niently described in a subsequent part of this work. The town and fort of Mysoor, the ancient residence of the rajas, and the

1787. capital from which the whole country derived its name, was an offensive memorial of the deposed family, and he determined

Nov. that the existence, and if possible the remembrance of such a place, should be extinguished. The fort was levelled with the ground, and the materials were employed in the erection of another fortress on a neighbouring height, which he named Nezerbâr *: and it is a curious example of that vicissitude in human affairs, which history so often preaches in vain, that the very same stones were re-conveyed to rebuild the same old fort of Mysoor, in 1799. The town was utterly destroyed, and the inhabitants were ordered to remove at their option, to Gunj-aum on the island of Seringapatam, or to the Agrâr (bramin village) of Bumboor, now to be named Sultaun-pet, a little to the southward of that island.

When the season was sufficiently advanced to make the

1788. Jan. march convenient, the Sultaun, at the head of his army, proceeded by the route of Tamburcherry, to visit and reform his possessions in Calicut. "The country of Calicut," as he informs us, "is situated on the coast of the ocean, and is named Malabar: its breadth does not exceed twenty-three coss, and its length is nearly two hundred. The Mahommedan inhabitants are called Pilla (Mapilla) and the infidels Naimârs; and as the rainy season lasts six months, and mud continues throughout

* I have been assured by two of his secretaries, that he meant to intimate by this name, "the place visited by the eye of the Almighty;" an evidence, as I apprehend, of his imperfect knowledge of the language in which he wrote. The name, however, gives the date, and the numerical power of the words may have been considered more than their grammatical import.

the year, the roads are excessively difficult, and the inhabitants prone to resistance, dividing their time between agriculture and arms. Such is the excess of infidelity, that if a Mussulman touch the exterior wall of a house, the dwelling can only be purified by setting it on fire. From the origin of Islâm in Hind, to the present day, no person had interfered with these practices, excepting the revered *, who is in paradise, after the conquest of the country, in the manner which has been narrated †; and during the twenty-five years that the country of Calicut had belonged to this dynasty, in as much as twenty thousand troops were maintained for its occupation, and the revenues never equalled their monthly pay; the balance, to a large amount, was uniformly discharged from the general treasury. Notwithstanding all this, the actual circumstances of the country were never properly investigated, until his Majesty, the shadow of God, directed his propitious steps, &c. &c. and remained three months in that country. He observed that the cultivators (instead of being collected in villages as in other parts of India) have each his separate dwelling and garden adjoining his field; these solitary dwellings he classed into groupes of forty-houses, with a local chief and an accountant to each, an establishment which was to watch over the morals and realize the revenue; and a Sheickh-ul-Islâm ‡ to each district for religious purposes alone; and addressed to the principal inhabitants a proclamation to the

* Hyder Ali.

† It will be recollected, that this part of the Sultaun-u-Towareekh, although referred to, was never written; see preface.

‡ This is the title of the chief of Medina.

CHAP. XXXII. 1788. following effect. From the period of the conquest until this day, during twenty-four years, you have been a turbulent and refractory people, and in the wars waged during your rainy season, you have caused numbers of our warriors to taste the draught * of martyrdom. Be it so. What is past is past. Hereafter you must proceed in an opposite manner; dwell quietly, and pay your dues like good subjects; and since it is a practice with you, for one woman to associate with ten men, and you leave your mothers and sisters unconstrained in their obscene practices, and are thence all born in adultery, and are more shameless in your connexions than the beasts of the field; I hereby require you to forsake these sinful practices, and live like the rest of mankind. And if you are disobedient to these commands, I have made repeated vows, to honour the whole of you with Islâm, and to march all the chief persons to the seat of empire. Other moral inferences, and religious instruction, applicable to spiritual and temporal concerns, were also written with his own hand, and graciously bestowed upon them."

The account here given of the manners of the women of Malabar, corresponds in its principal features, with the narratives of all the voyagers, and this inversion of the usual acceptation of polygamy, has produced strange theories, founded on very questionable facts. In hot climates, according to Montesquieu, females are marriageable at eight, nine, or ten years of age, and they are old at twenty: when beauty demands the empire, the want of reason forbids the claim; when reason is obtained, beauty is no more: polygamy is there-

* "Sherbet;" literally drink.

fore the natural effect of the climate: this enlightened author does not seem to have been aware that the great mass of the Indian population are monogamists; with the modification of being enjoined a second marriage after the first has ceased to augment population. "That the law of polygamy is an affair that depends on calculation," is the title of one of his chapters. According to the calculations which he quotes, in some countries there are born more boys than girls *, as in Thibet, where there is a plurality of husbands, and in others the proportion is inverted; and with a lubricity and reserve which shews the weakness of his ground, he treads lightly on a theory which would make the will of God to depend on the vices of man. In a work which professes to deliver the theory of every fact, and generally, it must be admitted, with eminent success, we must expect to find some failures; and in the very next chapter, forgetting the theory of the last, he explains the plurality of husbands in Malabar, by adverting to the military spirit of the Nairs, which makes it inconvenient to be shackled with a wife. The facts without theory, are described in the official report of the first commissioners for Malabar, after its cession to the English Government in 1792, to the following effect. The rajas are generally of the second Hindoo cast, some are of the fourth: but in all, the line of succession is not (as in other countries) in favour of their own sons, but those of their sisters; who do not marry according to the acceptation of that term in other countries, but form connections of a longer or shorter duration, with a race of bramins named Nambouries; who

* Ten women to one man in Bantam. In Meaco, according to Kempfer, 182,072 males, and 223,573 females. — Spirit of Laws, book xvi. chap. 4.

CHAP. XXXII. 1788. thus provide heirs for all the principalities of Malabar.—The same line of succession prevails among the Nairs, (soldiers and husbandmen of the fourth class); and their women (in the southern parts, however, more than in the north,) indulge with more or less freedom in fugitive connexions with various men of their own or of higher casts; and strange to tell, the same rule of succession extends to the Mapillas, the descendants of Arabs, settled in Malabar, long before even the Christian æra, and converted by their countrymen to the new religion of Mahommed, after these domestic habits had been so fixed, as not to be shaken even by the positive law of the Korân. The rule of direct filiation is only observed by foreign Hindoos, and by the indigenous tribes, inferior to that of Nair, among whom prevails the custom, as if to discredit the influence of climate, common to the two extremes of Coorg and Thibet, of several brothers having one and the same wife. The account, thus officially rendered, of which the above is an imperfect abstract, is however qualified by the explanations of several highly enlightened correspondents, who have favoured the author with the result of their personal observations, after a long residence in Malabar, and who bear honourable testimony to the respectable conduct of the Nair ladies of Northern Malabar; it is however admitted, that the wife, if such she may be named, usually continues to reside in the paternal mansion, where she is visited by her lord, or sallies forth to visit him; and that the natural marks of tenderness and affection to children, are lavished by the men on nephews and nieces, and scarcely ever on reputed sons and daughters; the statement indeed which most strenuously denies a plurality of husbands, admits the occasional prevalence of lax morals, and a tendency to various intercourse, but states the practice to be deemed disreputable. Not so, however, in the south, the parties are betrothed in childhood, and united at the age of puberty, but if after a short cohabitation, the lady disapproves the choice of her parents, she is at liberty to make her own, by accepting a cloth (a dress) from the man of her own selection, and declaring in the presence of four witnesses that she discards her husband, and accepts the donor of the cloth; and this she may repeat as often as the donor of a new cloth can be found, but never without the declared dismission of her old companion, *who of course must be deemed equally free to form a new connection.* In a condition of morals which acknowledges so wide a licence, it must be inferred, that the privileged line is frequently overstepped: but, however this may be, it is obvious that no departure from those general laws of nature, which regulate population, is necessary for the production or continuance of a state of society, which, as far as regards the question of relative numbers, may as correctly be deemed a plurality of wives, as a plurality of husbands. With regard to the marriage of one wife to a family of brothers, an ingenious friend long resident in Malabar, whose attention had been drawn, after answering my first enquiries, to Cæsar's description of the manners of Britain, at the period of the Roman conquest, declares his belief in their general coincidence with the actual practice of Malabar *, not

* Uxores habent deni duodenique inter se communes, et maxime fratres cum fratribus, et patres cum liberis. Sed qui sunt ex his nati eorum habentur liberi a quibus primum virgines quæque ductæ sunt. — Cæsar, lib. v. cap. 14.

Sir William Temple deviates a little from the sense of the original, which he probably referred to from memory. Henry doubts Cæsar's accuracy.

only in the lower, but the higher classes, with the exceptions regarding filiation, which have been recited; the original passage is inserted at the bottom of the page, and Sir William Temple *, who has some curious observations on these associations of ten or twelve families as practised by our ancestors, relates the apology made on the subject by a British lady, who had been admitted to some intimacy with Julia Augusta in the time of Severus. "We do that openly with the best of our men, which you do secretly with the worst of yours."

For a similar reason to that which induced the demolition of Mysoor, the Sultaun ordered the entire destruction of Calicut, and the erection at a few miles distance of another fortress, with the new name of Ferruckhee, a fancy which afterwards nearly proved fatal to his troops, by leaving them the choice of a ruin, or an unfinished work, as points of retreat and rendezvous; and while loitering over these and other equally fruitless projects, and rioting in imagination over bigoted schemes of converting the infidels, he was apprised by men of cooler heads, that the monsoon had commenced: he determined to march through the depth of it to Coimbetoor, answering those who attempted to dissuade him, that he would *order the clouds to cease discharging their waters, until he should have passed.* It may be difficult to determine whether this was intended as an impious jest, or a blasphemous pretension; but it is certain, that about this period, he frequently placed his own exploits in the cause of religion, particularly in the number of his converts, above those of Mahommed; the word *Peighâmber* he said signified no more

* Temple's Works, vol. ii. page 532, folio edition, 1720.

than a bearer of tidings (to the uninstructed,) and that Mahommed was but such a man as Tippoo Sultaun: on which subject it may not be out of place to remark, that neither this nor any other term by which Mahommed is distinguished in Mahommedan writings conveys any meaning approaching our word *prophet*, the customary translation * of those terms. But pretensions of this nature gave great offence to the orthodox, and if the Sultaun's arrogance had not been checked by the subsequent English war, there is abundant reason to conjecture, that, drunk with flattery, and uncontrolled dominion, he would have openly claimed the apostolic character, and as his followers believe, a still more impious assumption. However this may be, the clouds were not controlled, and the army suffered the greatest hardships, in their tedious march through the swamps, the floods, and the unceasing torrents of rain, until their arrival at Coimbetoor.

A variety of incidents occurred in this and the succeeding year, which confirmed in general opinion the inference that an intellect too weak for such a giddy height occasionally tottered on the verge of insanity; and among them a tale is related, the accuracy or incorrectness of which may possibly be ascertained by persons still living in France. The Sultaun's letters shew that he had written to Louis XVI. to send him three medical persons, a physician, a surgeon, and an apothecary, and on the return of his embassy, which we shall presently notice, two of these gentlemen were presented to him at Coimbetoor. The physician

* "Russool," an apostle: — "nubbee," a person who awakes or admonishes: — "peighâmber," — a bearer of tidings, but nothing approaching *prophet*, a person who predicts future events.

CHAP. XXXII. 1788.

after being introduced, demanded his dismission, but however strongly vouched, I cannot venture to determine whether the tale be founded, of his having assigned as his reason, to Heckeem Wâsil, the native physician in waiting, that he perceived in the Sultaun symptoms of incipient madness, nor whether it be an embellishment of Heckeem Wâsil, that the Sultaun overheard some of the conversation which ensued, and called a council to deliberate on the case, which council gravely and unanimously determined that it was the physician, and not the patient, who was mad.

Among the causes which had influenced the Sultaun in the decided measures which he had executed, and was preparing in Malabar, was a combination of European politics, deeply and deliberately planned, but ultimately never executed.

The faction in Holland, inimical to the house of Orange, and leaning on France for support, had, as the price of that support, and the means of effecting their own objects, secretly consented to a plan suggested by the French for their own aggrandizement, for surrendering to that power the port and fortresses of Trincomalee, to be employed as a naval station, in furtherance of those operations necessary for the restoration of the affairs of France, on the continent of India; and the combined and determined efforts of France and Holland, were at a proper time, and immediately, if necessary, to give effect to these projects, which were studiously concealed from the knowledge of the Orange party.

General Conway, Governor of Pondicherry, was charged with the execution of this measure, and sailed from Pondicherry, ostensibly for the Isle of France, with a suitable armament, comprising nearly the whole of his garrison; in the confidence of obtaining the unresisted possession of the place, and occupying it in force, before the English, who were expected to consider the transaction as little short of a declaration of hostility, should have any intimation of the design.

The original machination, however, did not entirely escape the vigilance of the Government of Holland. Secret instructions were sent to the Governor of Ceylon, to provide against the attempt; and when General Conway arrived at Trincomalee, he found the means of defence so perfectly prepared, by a staunch adherent of the house of Orange, that he felt the necessity of desisting from the attempt, and returned to Pondicherry.

Sir Archibald Campbell, on receiving the first intelligence of the object of General Conway's departure, determined, without waiting for any authority, to counteract a proceeding so decidedly hostile, by immediate preparations for the siege of Pondicherry; but General Conway's failure at Trincomalee, caused the whole of these designs reciprocally to subside. The Sultaun was for the present left to his own measures on the continent of India, without the co-operation of his French allies; and the interior distractions of the Government of Holland, of which the affairs of India formed no more than a subordinate branch, had in the meanwhile assumed a new aspect, through the co-operation of Prussia and England; and the celebrated expedition of the Duke of Brunswick into Holland; and an amicable explanation between the courts of France and England, produced the abandonment of those preparations, by sea and land, which appeared to threaten an early and general war in every part of their respective possessions.

CHAP. XXXII. 1788. From Coimbetoor the Sultaun made a progress to visit Dindigul, a jageer conferred by himself on his relation Seyed Saheb, (Moyeen-u-Deen), by whom he was splendidly entertained, and it was soon after this period, that the raja of Travancore entertained the first serious alarm, which he communicated to the Government of Madras, of being invaded at one and the same time from the east and the north, in consequence of the minute investigation of routes on each of these frontiers. * Before leaving this quarter, he laid waste with fire and sword, the countries of such of the poligars dependent on Dindigul and Coimbetoor, as had recently failed in obedience, and returned
August. by the route of Gujelhutty to Seringapatam, where, according to his own statement, four months were exclusively devoted to the operation of embodying all the seyeds of his infantry into separate brigades, and the sheicks into others, leaving for the present the Patâns and Moguls † to be intermixed with the Hindoos. He had scarcely accomplished these separations before he received intelligence, that all Coorg and Malabar had risen in simultaneous rebellion, and even, according to his own statement, were every where pressing his troops with the most desperate valour.

Arshed Beg Khân, as we have seen, had been appointed

* The difficult pass of Goodaloor, at the bottom of the vale of Dindigul, and the access by the coast of Malabar.

† A stranger, on making enquiries, will find the four divisions of Mahommedans mentioned in the text, considered by the multitude as so many sects. In fact, Patan and Moghul are merely national appellations. The only original distinction of a general nature, being that of Seyeds, descendants of Mahommed, and men of Arabian family, not so descended, who, in India, are usually named *Sheickhs*. The numerous religious sectaries, who have subsequently arisen, are to be found in every country and every race.

by Hyder, shortly before his death to the office of civil and military governor of Malabar; he was a Mussulman of rare talents, humanity, and probity, and by adapting the scheme of his government to the actual circumstances of the country, had brought the province into a state of comparative tranquillity and contentment. But the Sultaun had composed rules and regulations, to which all circumstances must bend, and they must be equally applied to all his dominions. Among these was the separation of authorities, and the consequent supercession of Arshed Beg Khân in the civil, while he retained the military powers. On the arrival of his new coadjutor, (Meer Ibraheem, a relation of the secretary for the department of innovation,) this excellent servant distinctly perceiving the inevitable consequences of the new system, wished to retire; and in 1786, requested that permission to make the pilgrimage to Mecca, which in Kirkpatrick's notes on Tippoo's letters is ascribed to another cause. The new Asoph (civil and fiscal governor) broke through all his cowles, (written engagements,) substituted new exactions, and set the inhabitants in a flame. Arshed Beg Khân employed the influence which his virtues had commanded, in the maintenance of quiet, and attempted in vain to impress on his colleague the duty of maintaining inviolate the public faith. His urgent intreaties to his master to avert the destruction of Malabar by his own presence had caused the Sultaun's visit to that country in the beginning of 1788. He found the conduct of Meer Ibrahim to have really placed the province on the verge of rebellion, and he removed and confined him; but he also removed and disgraced Arshed Beg Khân, and invented other novelties for the misgovernment of Malabar. The

CHAP. XXXII. 1788. Sultaun's arrogance could not contemplate the possibility of his having himself created the rebellion by changing the order of things which was already as successful as could reasonably be expected, for in spite of his assertion, Arshed Beg Khân had uniformly realized a surplus revenue. This venerable man, whose name alone would have commanded the tranquillity which an army could not achieve, was still in prison, not with the hope of extorting money, for calumny acknowledged he was poor, but because calumny and injury, when inflicted by a tyrant, constitute in the sufferer an unpardonable crime; and he soon afterwards died of grief and disgust.

1789. Jan. The Sultaun, however, who simply observes, that the infidels of Malabar had disregarded his preaching, and had risen in rebellion, pitched his tents, and marched with his whole army, and after some delay in traversing Coorg, and restoring a temporary quiet, descended by the pass of Tambercherry into Malabar. The report of the arrival of the whole army, caused the Nairs to retire as usual into their woods and mountains; and Tippoo divided his troops into numerous detachments for the purpose of apprehending them. While the detached divisions were conducted with various success, his own took the direction of a place named *Gootipoor*, where about two thousand Nairs with their families, occupied an old fortified position, which they defended for some days, but finding it untenable against the superior number and means by which they were invested, they were ultimately compelled to surrender at discretion. The alternative was signified to them of a voluntary profession of the Mahommedan faith, or a forcible conversion, with deportation from their native land. The unhappy captives gave a forced assent, and on the next day the rite of circumcision was performed on all the males, every individual of both sexes being compelled to close the ceremony by eating beef. This achievement being completed, it was held out as an example to the other detachments of the army, and it is certain that great numbers of Nairs incessantly hunted out of their places of concealment, at length came forth to be circumcised, as the only mode which remained to them of avoiding a more cruel fate.

It has been stated, that this alternative presented to the imaginations of the Nairs, the apprehension of death as well as banishment; and it is necessary to explain, that the very singular opinion was entertained at that period, and prevails in Mysoor at the present day, that small-pox is generated without contagion, by the mere act of a crowded deportation from Malabar to the upper countries. The fact appears to be incontestable, that former emigrations were followed by the appearance of small-pox, and the death of a large portion of the population, and in some instances of nearly the whole. The earlier could not be traced by the same means of personal enquiry, as some of the later deportations, in which the precaution is stated to have been taken, of moving in smaller divisions, with express orders to avoid all possible communication which could risk the conveyance of infection. Officers who have been charged with this service, have assured the author, of the exact execution of these precautions, and of the spontaneous appearance of the disease, soon after passing from the summits of the hills into the plain table land. It is not intended to attach importance to the opinions and inferences of men, who are confessedly careless observers, and frequently inaccurate narrators: but it does appear of importance to the human race, that a fact, which can scarcey be deemed an unfit subject of philosophical enquiry, should be watched and examined by more competent observers, in that country where the disease is stated to have originated: not only as the investigation may regard small-pox, (whose destructive powers have been happily arrested in every part of the habitable globe,) but as it may relate to all those diseases, which are referred by general opinion to contagion alone.

It is evident that small-pox was either coeval with the creation, or had a subsequent beginning; and it is an inference deducible from the first principles of reasoning, that *the same causes which originally produced may re-produce it without contagion.* A late author * who has combined the most profound and interesting historical research, with the story of a loathsome disease, thinks that it has been known in China and India for at least three thousand years: there are reasons which shall presently be discussed for assigning to it a more modern origin, but the general proposition is not affected by comparative antiquity. It is now familiarly known that the small-pox was without a name in the ancient languages of Europe; and Mr. Moore has established, in the most satisfactory manner, that it was equally unknown in Arabia, in Persia, and in those Asiatic countries which are deemed to be the cradle of the human race, before A. D. 569 †, when it was first introduced into Arabia by vessels trading with India. During the latter part of the 6th and the whole of the 7th century, it was spread over the remaining

* Moore's History of the Small-pox.

† Ibid, p. 110.

portions of Asia, and all that part of Africa which is washed by the Mediterranean sea. In the 8th century it accompanied the conquests of the Arabs into Spain, Sicily, Italy, and France; Saxony, Switzerland and England received it certainly in the 10th and probably in the 9th century; and lastly it travelled into Hispaniola, and soon afterwards to Mexico, in the beginning of the 16th century.*

The early antiquities of China and India have become nearly synonimous with fable. In China † the first appearance of small-pox, is fixed by one authority with suspicious accuracy, at 1122 years anterior to the Christian æra, before which period it was unknown; and at least as remote an origin is claimed by the legends of India. In that country, we find apparent indications of long experience in the treatment, rather than the legendary history of the disease. That the presiding deity is a low bred goddess, whose temples are never approached by a bramin, and are frequented exclusively by the outcasts, furnishes little ground of inference; but the immemorial practice of the bramins of Orissa near Ganjâm, of inoculation by means of a sharp steel instrument, of exposure to the cool open air, to prevent the confluent disease, and even of the cold ‡ affusion for a day or two before the eruptive fever is expected — although indicative of successful experience, affords no evidence of antiquity beyond the 6th century.

Mr. Moore ascribes to the deserts, which separate India from Persia, the long exemption of the latter country from infection; and assigns satisfactory reasons, why contagious diseases should

* Moore, passim. † Moore, page 22. ‡ Doctor Ainslie.

CHAP. XXXII. 1789. rather follow the irruption of an invading army than its return. He seems, however, to lean to the opinion, that the eruptive disease mentioned by Quintus Curtius, which carried off great numbers of Alexander's army, at the mouths of the Indus, may have been an ill described small-pox; and was prevented by the intervening deserts from making its way into Persia. Now the fleet, with which Nearchus navigated the Persian gulf, was not built by Alexander, but chiefly found * upon the Indus; the facts of the voyage shew, that these vessels were equal to the coasting trade, and even to a communication with the opposite and not distant shores of Arabia; a country which, from the earliest periods of history or tradition, possessed the productions of India. The neighbourhood of the Indus near its mouths, and particularly the northern vicinity, is shewn by the historians of Alexander to have possessed a considerable population; which must have received from Alexander's fleet and army, the contagious disease described by Quintius Curtius; or the small-pox, at an earlier date, if it had previously existed in the interior. And it is difficult to conceive its being arrested at that spot without extending northwards into Persia by land, or coastwise, by means of the Arabian trade. The hardships sustained by the army of Alexander in its march through Gedrosia were unquestionably severe, but the daring travels of Lieutenant Pottinger have recently established the existence in that route of the ruins of cities and palaces, which now half-covered by the encroaching sands, must in the days of Alexander have sustained a population at least sufficient to receive and transmit a contagious disease, by its shores, or in-

* Vincent's Voyage of Nearchus, page 11.

land, although producing too little surplus food to meet the wants of the Grecian army. The Arabian trade is described by the earliest authors as a coasting * voyage, more likely perhaps than a direct one to afford the means of successive infection ; and other authorities supply the intermediate links of an unbroken chain, extending from the earliest to the latest periods of authentic history, to support the uninterrupted existence of an intercourse between India and Arabia, sufficient for the propagation of an infectious disease. Moses † specifies the appropriation to religious uses, and in large quantities too, of cinnamon and cassia, the productions of Ceylon and Malabar; which shews that a communication of some kind or other was open between India and Egypt, even in that early age. From that period until about two centuries before the Christian æra, the aromatic productions of India were supposed in the west to grow in Arabia; whether the chintz and other fabrics introduced into Media may have been referred to their proper country before the age of Alexander does not distinctly appear ‡; after that period the information becomes more precise. Agatharcides, who wrote 146 years after the death of Alexander, and 177 A. C. tells us, not only that the Sabeans possessed the trade from India to Arabia, as the Egyptians monopolized the same trade from Arabia to Europe; but is the first to relate that ships from India were met with in the ports of § Sabea, that the mariners of Sabea sail in very large vessels to the country where the odoriferous productions grow‖, *and plant colonies*

* Vincent's Periplus, page 45. † 30th Exodus, verse 23, 24.
‡ Vincent's Periplus, page 17. § Ibid, 35. ‖ Ibid. 32.

CHAP. XXXII. 1789. *there* (the progenitors of the Mapillas of Malabar). The embassies of Porus and Pandion to Augustus; the incident of the freedman of Plocamus being blown off the coast and carried by the monsoon to Ceylon; his return from that island accompanied by embassadors from its king to Claudius: the voyage of Hyppalus consequent on that discovery, in the first century of the Christian æra, and the more direct communication which ensued, are so many links in a chain of incessant and immemorial intercourse: and even before the discovery of Hyppalus, the direct proof of the arrival at Rome of bales of muslin from Bengal in the earliest part of the first century, (and probably long before) is furnished by the reproaches of a licentious poet addressed to the Roman matrons for their public semi-nudity in garments of "woven * wind," or "a texture of cloud." Excluding then the abundant proofs of

* Quo Margarita cara tribacca Indica?
An ut matrona ornata phaleris pelagiis,
Tollat pedes indomita in strato extraneo,
Smaragdum ad quem rem viridem pretiosum vitrum?
Quo Carchedonias optas ignes lapideos
Nisi ut scintillent? Probitas est carbunculus.
Æquum est induere nuptam *ventum textilem?*
Palam prostrare nudam in *nebula linea?*

Petronius, page 53. London, 1711.

This is the true muslin, *the shebnum*, the dewy vesture, the gossamer of Dacca. That cotton, and not flaxen is intended, is evident from the following description, in the same century of the plant which produced the *Xylina lina*. "Superior pars Egypti in Arabiam vergens gignit fruticem, quem aliqui Gossipium vocant, plures *Xylon*, et ideo *lina* inde facta *Xylina*. Parvus est, similemque barbatæ nucis defert fructum, cujus ex interiore nuce lanugo netur, nec ulla *lina* sunt iis candore mollitiâve preferenda." Pliny. Hist. Mund. 19. 1. The term *Xylon*, was certainly not derived from the Arabs, who name it *Kuttun*, cotton, but it bears a close resemblance to the common Indian pronunciation of Ceylon, (*Cýlon*, with the accent on the first syllable,) as muslin from *Moosul*, and calico from *Calicut*, the emporia earlier date, we find that for seven centuries at the least before the introduction of the small-pox into Arabia from India, the ships of each country were received into the ports of the other; and for upwards of five centuries before that period, we have testimonies of an intercourse in its first stage, exclusively between India and Arabia, which brought into Italy the productions of Bengal: the whole exhibiting authentic evidence of an unceasing intercourse apparently sufficient for the transmission of infectious disease. The inference therefore appears to rest on something more than probability, that in the 6th century the small-pox was a new disease in India, and according to a similar chain of probability in China also: and in reverting to our first proposition, that *the causes which originally produced, may reproduce it without contagion,* I am persuaded that the members of a liberal and estimable profession will distinguish between the suggestion of a new and interesting subject of research, and those dreams of planetary * influence, or medical theory equally visionary, which disgraced the literature even of the 17th century.

Although the particular condition and change of atmosphere, supposed to generate small-pox, be vaguely indicated in the apprehensions of the Nairs, the opinion of its spontaneous

from which these substances became known in the west. The above passage, in the feast of Trimalcion was pointed out to me for purposes totally unconnected with the present subject, by Doctor Kay, one of the most enlightened men, and accomplished scholars of the age in which he lives; whose elegant mind has been lost to the literature of his country, by a residence of nearly half a century in the island of St. Helena.

* Moore's History of the Small-pox, page 198, and passim.

CHAP. XXXII. 1789. appearance is not peculiar to Malabar and Mysoor, but may be traced in many provinces of Decan and the south. Its periodical disappearance and return would seem to be the necessary consequence of the periodical exhaustion and accumulation of subjects, but its sudden appearance in the centre of a district, without introduction from abroad, although an impression on minds little distinguished by habits of accurate investigation, will not be treated with levity by men who really possess those habits; and who will at least find an apology for the error, if such it be, of men habituated to observe the disease named *the hill* (*or jungle*) *fever* invariably contracted by the inhabitants of the shore who visit particular hills, and the very same disease contracted by the inhabitants of those same hills, in consequence of visiting the shore, and named by them the *sea fever:* an error, of men accustomed (with whatever inferiority of science) to consider in these reciprocal predispositions to a fatal endemic, not only the quality of the air to be breathed, but the previous condition of the person who is to breathe it.

The Nair raja of Chercul had been induced, by the most sacred promises, to pay his personal respects to the Sultaun, and was, for several days, treated with considerable distinction, and dismissed wtih costly presents to his little principality. Immediately after his departure, real or pretended information was received, of his being engaged in a secret conspiracy to revenge the cruel indignities of his countrymen; and Tippoo detached two brigades to effect his destruction, or ascertain his obedience, by directing him instantly to return to camp. His attendants, justly alarmed at these appearances, prepared for defence, and before any explanation could be given, a skirmish ensued, in which the raja and some of his attendants were killed, and a few prisoners secured: and Tippoo, considering the accusation to be established, ordered the most base and unmanly indignities to be offered to the corpse *, and that the dead and the living should afterwards be hanged on the same tree. These indignities recounted by the Sultaun himself, although free from his usual obscenity, are too brutal for translation; and he relates, among the incidents pertaining to this raja, that he had, during their personal intercourse, offered 400,000 rupees, and the plates of gold with which a particular temple was roofed, on condition of sparing the temple itself; to which proposition the Sultaun is made to reply, that he would not spare it for all the treasures of the earth and the sea. He states the destruction in the course of this holy war, of eight thousand idol temples, many of them roofed with gold, silver, or copper, and all containing treasures buried at the feet of the idol, the whole of which was royal plunder: but when crimes are deemed to be virtues, we may infer that their amount is much exaggerated. Before leaving Malabar, he paid a visit to Cannanore, and solemnized the first ceremonies of a marriage between the daughter of the dowager chief, and one of his sons, Abd-ul-Khâlic. A minute detail is given of the fortunate conjunctions of the planets, and

* Another account says, that he was accompanied by a detachment, to aid in seizing the insurgents, under the command of a confidential officer, charged with instructions to use the raja as an instrument, till the purpose was accomplished, and then to seize himself; and that the raja having obtained information of this design, sent forward secret instructions to his family to escape by Tellicherry; when he heard of their safety, he attempted his own escape, and finding that impossible, shot himself.

CHAP. XXXII. 1789.

the astrologers unanimously pronounce, that such an auspicious hour would not return for 120 years. From this place, he made a progress along the coast, as far south as Chawgaut, for the purpose of making the local investigations, and instituting the intrigues, necessary to the attack on Travancore in the ensuing season; and in returning to Coimbetoor for the rains, made yet another change in his plans for propagating the faith and plundering the country. Six divisions, consisting of two brigades each, were left in Malabar, with distinct establishments of officers, spiritual, civil, and military, charged with the three-fold duty of surveying the lands, numbering the productive trees, and seizing and instructing the remaining Nairs. All that related to the fiscal management was put into bad hands, and was ill executed; the joint duties of the spiritual and military officers were performed with horrible precision.* The Sultaun had, during the two last years, been gradually encreasing his infantry, and in preparation for the war which he now evidently contemplated as near, made a further augmentation, while at Coimbetoor, of two cutcherries † of infantry,

* Palgaut was captured by the English in the ensuing year, and an officer of the staff, in searching the records of the place, for military intelligence, found one of the circular orders for conversion under the Sultaun's seal and signature, which was at that time deemed a curiosity of the highest order. It directed, "that every being in the district, without distinction, should be honoured with Islâm, that the houses of such as fled to avoid that honour should be burned, that they should be traced to their lurking-places, and that all means of truth and falsehood, fraud or force, should be employed to effect their universal conversion."

† Four appears to have been the fortunate number; four companies, (yeuz,) one battalion, (teep,) four teeps, one cushoon, (which I have generally rendered brigade,) four cushoons, one cutcherry. The establishment of these cushoons, with their artillery, was only 1422, and a cutcherry of course 5688; but these numbers fluctuated with the Sultaun's caprices, and at one time a cushoon with its cavalry attached, was a legion of about 3000.

amounting to 11,376 men. At the same place he employed himself, as he informs us, in a profusion of "new inventions and creations of the mind," among which the example which he selects, closes all that was written of the King of histories *, and as it affords a fair specimen of the subjects which occupied his thoughts, and exhibits his ostentatious lore in judicial astrology, we take leave of a guide which has demanded incessant suspicion, by presenting an abstract of his concluding page. — "Aurengzebe, from the commencement of his reign, which happened on a Sunday, ordered the sounding of the noobut (royal band) five times on that day of the week; and for want of due consideration, the practice had since continued. His Majesty, the shadow of God reflecting on this subject, ordered the substitution of Friday for this ceremonial. Because, Sunday is appropriated by the Nazarenes; Saturday, by the Jews; and Friday is the festival of the Mussulmans; and the excellence of that day is impressed on every mind by numerous traditionary

* The memoirs of the Sultaun's reign found in the palace, and written in the first person, is supposed by Colonel Kirkpatrick to be the rough draft from which the Sultaun-u-Towareekh was prepared by Zein-ul-ab-u-Deen by the Sultaun's command: but if his opinion (page 32, preface) be correct, that the rough draft bears internal evidence of having been composed subsequently to the peace of Seringapatam in 1792, the supposed relation of the manuscripts is more than doubtful, as the last page of the Sultaun-u-Towareekh appears to me to have been written in 1789, and it contains no allusion throughout to any subsequent event. I am not aware of the nature of the internal evidence relied upon; and if it had not been so strongly stated, I should have been disposed to conjecture that Colonel Kirkpatrick's manuscript which terminates in 1787 was put into Zein-ul-ab-u-Deen's hands at that date, from which period he became the historian instead of the Sultaun, who, although an incessant writer, was an exceedingly bad scribe; however this may be, they entirely coincide in substance in those portions which have been published by Colonel Kirkpatrick. I find on referring to my notes, that one of my copies was in the hand writing of Zein-ul-ab-u-Deen.

CHAP. XXXII. 1789. texts. The Almighty, on that day created the heavens; on that day occurred the martyrdom of the heads of the church; on that day commenced the flood of Noah; besides other holy coincidences. Therefore, in a propitious hour, when the moon was in the mansion of Taurus, Mercury and Venus in the mansion of Virgo, the Sun in Leo, Saturn in Aquarius, and Venus in opposition to Libra; — the royal mandate descended, directing the noobut to be performed in the royal hall, and by all Mussulmans entitled to that distinction, five times on every Friday."

It is evident, from the insolent letters of the Sultaun to Nizam Ali, shortly after the peace of Mangalore, in 1784, that he contemplated the early subjugation of that chief. The termination of the war of 1786-7 had induced some amicable communications, in consequence of which Nizam Ali had dispatched an embassador, named Hâfiz Fereed-u-Deen Khân, who, in conformity to directions previously sent to Seringapatam, waited the Sultaun's arrival at Coimbetoor. This envoy was charged with the proposal of a strict and indissoluble union between these only remaining Mahommedan powers of Decan and the South. A splendid Korân was sent for the Sultaun's acceptance; and the return of a similar pledge, was to establish the most sacred and solemn obligations of friendship and alliance. To this proposition, the Sultaun distinctly replied, that he was ready to return the pledge, and establish an offensive and defensive treaty, on the condition of an intermarriage in the families, but not without this preliminary alliance; but on this subject the envoy had no orders, and could give no reply. The forms of ordinary courtesy did not admit of his suggesting objections from himself; and the Sultaun, foreseeing no impediment, sent an embassy in return, consisting of Kuttub-u-Deen and Ali Reza, who accompanied the envoy in his return to Hyderabad. Nizam Ali, however, distinguished between political union, and the degradation which he attached to the proposed alliance; and it seems extraordinary, that so acute a courtier as Ali Reza should not have been able to ascertain Nizam Ali's intentions, and save his master the awkwardness of a public refusal. "We are desirous," said Ali Reza, "of partaking of the Sheker-Bhât," the dish of rice and sugar sent as the first preliminary ceremonial of marriage; to which intimation Nizam Ali made no sort of reply, and there the negotiation and the embassy terminated.

CHAPTER XXXIII.

Tippoo's designs for indirectly conquering Travancore, through the instrumentality of the Samorin, had failed through his own persecutions — He now attempts to employ the raja of Cochin — this also fails — Threatens to seize him in Cochin — Intervention of the Travancorean lines — History of transactions which led to the disputed question regarding these lines, and produced the war of 1790 *— Geographical position of Travancore — to the north-east fixed — in Malabar fluctuating — Notices of these variations — chiefly from Valentyn — Anquetil-de-Peron — and Stavorinus — Records — and other manuscript authorities — Hyder's designs — his war with the Dutch in* 1776 *— State of the Travancorean lines — Peace with the Dutch — Guarantee of* 1784 *— Tippoo nevertheless pursues his father's designs — Representation by Sir Archibald Campbell — His own grounds of apprehension in* 1788 *— Lord Cornwallis's demand and occupation of Guntoor, in virtue of the treaty of* 1768 *— Nizam Ali's demand of the execution of the other conditions, involving the conquest of Mysoor — Barbarous incident in elephant hunting — Previous correspondence with Sir Archibald Campbell — Purchase of Cranganore and Ayacota by the raja, with his concurrence as asserted by the raja — denied by the Government — discussed — Tippoo's complaint of protection given to his rebellious subjects, by the raja and by the English at Tellicherry — discussed — Governor of Madras proposes to send commissioners — Tippoo attacks the lines — turns the flank, and had apparently carried his point, when he is repulsed with great loss, and personal danger — Sends for reinforcements and guns — Pause of three months and a half of preparation — Notice of embassies received at that period.*

CHAP. XXXIII. 1789.

THE measures of conversion in Malabar had been obstructed in the north by the escape of the Nairs to the English settlement of Tellicherry, whence they embarked for Travancore, and in the south by the connivance for a similar purpose of the raja of Cochin, the acknowledged tributary * of Hyder and Tippoo, although bound by more ancient ties to the Dutch and the raja of Travancore. Tippoo was particularly anxious to achieve the conquest of Travancore, without appearing himself as a principal in the war; and in 1788 had actually adjusted with the Samorin of Calicut, the restoration of a part of his former territories, on the condition of his acting for the Sultaun, but in his own name, in rendering some antiquated claims the ground of the conquest of Travancore. These projects, like many others, were foiled by the Sultaun's precipitation in beginning the work of general circumcision, which the Samorin resented, and joined in the general insurrection; and Tippoo was now desirous, as a last indirect resource, of employing the services of the raja of Cochin, as his instrument to effect the same object. On returning from his late visit of inspection, he sent an order to the raja of Cochin to repair to his camp; this raja had obeyed a similar summons in the preceding year, and had seen little cause for aspiring to a repetition of that honour: he accordingly wrote a submissive reply, stating that he paid his pêshcush (tribute) regularly, and was ready to obey any other order, but assigned the best pretences he was able, for intreating to be excused from appearing at court. The Sultaun temporized, and sent an envoy to the raja with a letter acquiescing in his apology, but desiring that he would send his son, or minister, whom he would not detain more than two days, intimating that he wished to purchase from the Dutch the fort of Cochin, and August.

* Vol. i. page 475.

CHAP. XXXIII. 1789. hoped to accomplish it by the raja's means. A second disobedience roused the Sultaun's indignation, and he openly declared, that " if they did not attend his summons, he would come and fetch them by force." But to reach Cochin it was necessary to pass the wall of Travancore, and for the purpose of making intelligible the grounds of the subsequent English war, of which the attack of this wall was the immediate cause, it will be necessary to revert to circumstances within the scope of this work, which have been purposely omitted in the order of their date, and to touch lightly on some earlier occurrences in the revolutions * of Malabar.

The principality of Travancore occupies the southern extremity of the Indian peninsula. Its shores to the eastward of Cape Comorin and opposite to Ceylon, afford an easy communication for small vessels, between that island and the main, with the whole coast of Coromandel. Against the hostility of the southern province of that country, (Tinnevelly), a double line of works, facing from north to north-east, aid the natural defence of the tremendous range of mountains which terminate near the southern cape; but from the period of the occupation of Tinnevelly, by the disjointed authority of Mahommed Ali and the English, and the establishment by that people, of a commercial factory at Anjengo, on the western coast, the relations of amity had been uninterrupted; the raja was acknowledged on various occasions as the ally of the English nation, and was specially so recognized in the treaty of 1769 between Hyder and the English, and in that of

* They would make a curious volume, commencing with Vasco de Gama, and the materials are easily accessible in the Portuguese, Dutch, French, and English authors.

1784, with the Sultaun himself. On the coast of Malabar, the boundaries of Travancore had followed the fluctuations of its fortunes. CHAP. XXXIII. 1789.

In 1662 and 3, the Dutch obtained, in open warfare from the Portugueze, various possessions on the coast of Malabar, among which we find enumerated * Cochin and Cranganore; and of course Ayacotta †, situated on the northern extremity of a narrow stripe of land called the island of Vipeen, extending nearly twenty miles, the whole distance from the estuary of Cranganore, to that of Cochin, and insulated by an inland connexion of those estuaries. In the same year 1663, the Dutch and the raja of Cochin on the one part, concluded a treaty with the raja of *Porca* on the other, by which it is stipulated, that the latter should pull down two hundred cubits of the wall built towards or against the country of Cochin. ‡ Now *Porca* is about forty miles to the southward of Cochin, and we must suppose that distinct principality to have been then interposed between Cochin and Travancore; the Dutch by another treaty, stipulate with the raja of Cochin, to build a fort at Cranganore, (one of the contested points.) Anquetil-de-Peron in 1758, states the bounds of Travancore to have been formerly beyond or south of *Kalicoulan*, (which would have confined the principality to the very apex of the peninsula,) but for some time they had been at *Porca*. In 1759 §, the Samorin of Calicut over-ran the territories of the raja of Cochin, and possessed himself of nearly the whole. In this extremity, the raja had recourse to his south-

* Valentyn.

† Official letters of the Dutch Government of Cochin and Columbo, to the English, in the year 1790.

‡ Valentyn.

§ Manuscript authorities.

ern neighbour, the raja of Travancore, who aided him with an army, under his celebrated General Rama; and after a variety of sanguinary conflicts in 1760 and 1761, the Samorin was completely and finally expelled. As the stipulated price of this important service, the raja of Cochin formarly ceded certain portions of territory to the raja of Travancore, and among others a stripe of land extending from his own recently acquired possessions near the hills, to the branch of an estuary which separates the narrow island of Vipeen from the sea, on which ceded territory and former possession, he immediately commenced the erection of a line of works, as a northern boundary towards Calicut, running east and west from a point of the hills deemed inaccessible, chiefly behind, or south of a river which discharges itself into the estuary. On the southern bank of the entrance of this estuary, was situated the military post of Ayacotta, belonging to the Dutch, and on the northern bank of the same estuary, on a point projecting southward, and about three miles farther up, was the Dutch fort of Cranganore; such is the origin of the lines of Travancore, and such the relative position of the contested points of Cranganore and Ayacotta; and to complete this topographical sketch, it is only necessary to add, that the territory of Cochin extended in front, or to the northward of these lines, from ten to thirty miles, the remaining portion of the principality being in the rear, or to the south of these lines. When Stavorinus visited Cochin in 1776 *, he found the Dutch Company at war with Hyder, and adverts with tolerable accuracy to the nature

* Stavorinus, cap. 12 & 13.

of these transactions, by stating that "the lands of Travancore had from time to time, been suffered to be extended to the eastward, behind the lands of Cochin, as far as the river of Cranganore, so that the King of Cochin has but a little space of ground left to him." We have seen, that on Hyder's re-conquest of Malabar in 1773, he appointed to the Government *Sree Nowas Row Berkêe*, one of his oldest officers, in whose talents and attachment he placed the most implicit reliance, assisted in the military department by *Sirdar Khân*, a name which Stavorinus transforms into *Cha-Dergam.* In 1775, Hyder desiring to possess himself of Travancore, a valuable possession, which would place him as it were on the left flank of his enemy's line of defence, in his meditated invasion of Coromandel, requested of the Dutch company a free passage for his troops through their possessions to Travancore. The refusal of this request, and the delay of a reply to his letter to the Supreme Government of Batavia, enraged him; and Sirdar Khân, with about ten thousand men, ravaged the country with fire and sword, and laid siege to the Dutch fort of Chetwa, about ten miles to the northward of Cranganore; and it was at this time that the raja of Travancore, made an actual purchase from the Dutch, of a stripe of land, near the north point of Vipeen, on which he continued the lines across that island, a breadth of about 1,500 yards, and in the rear of the Dutch Fort at Ayacotta. Reinforcements from Ceylon, in November 1776, induced the Dutch to attempt the relief of Chetwa, which failed: the place fell, and they confined themselves to the strong occupation of Cranganore and

CHAP. XXXIII. 1789. Ayacotta *, *whilst the kings of Cochin and Travancore threw up strong and fortified lines on the opposite side of the river, in order to defend their lands from an irruption on that side.* The lines, if actually commenced fourteen years sooner, were probably now constructed on a new plan, as both parties seem to refer to 1775, as the date of the construction of the works existing in 1789; for the context does not seem to apply to the lines across Vipeen, actually constructed, for the first time, in 1775. After the capture of Chetwa, Hyder's general, considering the attack of the lines as an enterprize beyond his strength, remained inactive; and seemed to be satisfied with the possession of the district of Cochin, situated north of the lines. Mr. Moens, the governor of Cochin, for the purpose of trying the disposition of the two rajas, proposed to them a plan of offensive operations, to which the raja of Travancore gave a distinct negative; declaring that his engagements with Mahommed Ali and the English, assured to him their aid in the defence of his own possessions if attacked by Hyder, but not if he were himself the aggressor. In January, 1777, the letter and presents from Batavia arrived, and Mr. Moens thought it best to send them with an envoy to Hyder, who graciously accepted this advance, and affected to attribute the late hostilities to mutual misapprehension. Stavorinus ascribes this unexpected facility, 1st, to his war with the Mahrattas, 2d, a revolt of the Nairs, as well as Mapillas, and 3d, the *improved state of the Travancore wall*, including in that line of defence the fortifications of Cranganore

* Stavorinus.

and Ayacotta, constituting a system of defensive means, which, in his opinion, Hyder could not attack with much hope of success. The lines however, although very sufficient with regard to the dimensions and construction of the ditch and rampart, were really more imposing than effectual, as throughout the dangerous extent of thirty miles, few points were closed in the rear, and those imperfectly, so that nearly the whole would fall on carrying a single point.

From that period, although no specific question had been raised regarding the lines, and although a special article in the treaty of 1784 included the raja of Travancore (of course as his territory then stood) among the friends of the English, on whom the Sultaun stipulated that he would not make war; he had nevertheless not ceased to appreciate the original policy of his father, nor to undervalue the advantage of a possession which would enable him to make the first step from his own frontiers at once on Tinnevelly and Arcot. The Sultaun's investigation of the routes, and the still more alarming attempt to induce the raja of Cochin, to claim the ground on which the lines were erected, had suggested the fears and the hopes, which in the preceding year, the raja of Travancore had conveyed to the Government of Madras; and Sir Archibald Campbell, in frankly communicating to the Sultaun the representations of the raja, added, that any aggression on that ally, would be considered by the English as a violation of the treaty of 1784, and equivalent to a declaration of war. The answer of the Sultaun was not at that time understood, although it now abundantly unfolds his subsequent pretensions; it stated that the interposition of the territories of his dependent, the raja

CHAP. XXXIII. 1789. of Cochin, prevented the possibility of collision between him and Travancore, and professed, in terms of sufficient courtesy, his desire for the maintenance of the relations of amity with the English state. In fact his measures and preparations were not then sufficiently matured. The character of Sir Archibald Campbell, the first military Governor of Madras, had unquestionably influenced the prudential tenor of his correspondence, and checked the precipitation of his measures; that distinguished officer had returned to England in February 1789, the levies were nearly completed, and independently of his own designs against the English, which were at no time doubtful, he had reasons which we shall endeavour to explain, for apprehending that he might be anticipated by that power.

On the death of Basâlut Jung, the reversionary right of the English Government to the province of Guntoor, was no longer doubtful, and Lord Cornwallis, after some prudential delay, deputed in 1788 a political resident (Sir John Kennaway) to Nizam Ali, for the double purpose of adjusting all accounts regarding the pêshcush of the other circars, and demanding the cession of Guntoor; and the military preparations which accompanied the demand were efficient in securing compliance. Nizam Ali, who had recently obtained sufficient experience of his inferiority to Tippoo Sultaun, and was mortified at the necessity arising from a similar feeling, of ceding Guntoor, which he anxiously wished to retain, determined on sending special embassies, both to Tippoo Sultaun, and the English, with the apparent view of forming, with one or the other, as circumstances might dictate, such an intimate alliance, as should secure him not only against the eventual hostility of the other, but should afford that sort of general protection, which he could not but feel to be necessary to a feeble and declining state. The sacred pledge offered to Tippoo Sultaun, affords strong evidence of his preference to that Mahommedan alliance, and his lofty rejection of the conditions by which that alliance might have been secured, rendered his connection with the English, an affair of necessity rather than of choice. Meer-Abd-ul-Kâsim, the envoy to Lord Cornwallis, opened his negotiation by adverting to the recent demand of the cession of the Guntoor sircar, in virtue of the treaty of 1768, and by demanding the execution of the remaining provisions of that treaty, which it will be recollected, extended the full length of the conquest of Mysoor. By the peace of 1769 with Hyder, the English recognized his sovereignty over the territories he then possessed, and thus virtually abrogated every part of the treaty of 1768, with Nizam Ali, which related to the conquest of these territories. The confederacy of 1780, of which at one time Nizam Ali did not scruple to avow himself to be the author, might be deemed a second abrogation of the spirit of that treaty; and the termination of that contest by the peace of 1784 with Tippoo Sultaun, constituted, on the part of the English, a third abrogation of the treaty of 1768. The act of parliament prohibiting the Governor-General from declaring war, or entering into any treaty for making war, against any native state, except when hostilities had commenced or impended, and the express orders of his sovereign and the India Company to the same effect, were so many arguments in bar to the execution or renewal of the offensive engagements proposed. But in a letter to Nizam Ali, dated the 1st July, 1789, which may be deemed the final result of Abd-ul-Kâsim's mission, and

CHAP. XXXIII. 1789. which is expressly declared to be *equally binding as a* * *treaty*, after reciting these prohibitions, and explaining the grounds of the demands regarding Guntoor, his Lordship proceeds, not to announce the annulment of the treaty of 1768, but to declare his " intentions that it should be carried into full effect;" to explain one of its articles, which regulates the demand of a subsidiary force to be furnished by the Company to Nizam Ali, and to enumerate the powers against whom that force *shall not be employed*, which enumeration recites by name every power of Decan and the South, *with the single exception of Tippoo Sultaun*. The letter further goes on to state that " circumstances have totally prevented the execution of those articles of the treaty of 1768, which relate to the Dewanny of the Carnatic Balagaut; but should it hereafter happen that the Company, with his Highness's assistance, should obtain possession of the countries mentioned in those articles, they will strictly perform the stipulations in favour of his Highness and the Mahrattas." It is highly instructive to observe a statesman justly extolled for moderate and pacific dispositions, thus indirectly violating a law enacted for the enforcement of these virtues, by entering into a very intelligible offensive alliance, which, although the effective revival of the abrogated conditions of an old treaty, was certainly neither a declaration of war, nor that technical instrument named a treaty for making war, executed subsequently to the prohibitory act of parliament; and his Lordship's observations on the same restrictions, written eight months afterwards, in his dispatches to the resident at Poona, not only furnish the

* It was afterwards so pronounced by a resolution of the House of Commons.

the best comment on their inconvenience, but seem to intimate an unconsciousness of the evasion which has been noticed. "Some considerable advantages," his Lordship observes, "have no doubt been experienced by the system of neutrality which the Legislature required of the governments of this country; but it has at the same time been attended with the unavoidable inconvenience of our being constantly exposed to the necessity of commencing a war, without having previously secured the assistance of efficient allies:" "for some years past we have been almost daily obliged to declare to the Mahrattas and the Nizam, that we were precluded, &c. &c. &c." It may not perhaps be necessary to examine, whether the direct violation of that article of the treaty of Mangalore, which most sensibly affected national honour and individual feeling by the brutal detention of native British subjects, as well as the population of Coromandel, were not at all times, since March 1784, not only a legitimate, but an imperious ground of war, of which the time was fairly and honourably in the hands of the British Government; nor is it necessary to recite the innumerable minor insults to which our frontiers had been incessantly exposed, in consequence of experienced impunity; but adverting to the course of transactions which have been described, it was not to be expected that Tippoo Sultaun should view, as a slip of the pen, the exception of his name from the enumeration of friendly powers not to be attacked; or misapprehend the eventual arrangements dependent on the conquest of his dominions. The early occupation of Travancore which he contemplated as an easy achievement, was certainly, the most efficient preparation he could make for such a contest,

CHAP. XXXIII. 1789.

and he commenced his march from Coimbetoor with a* force abundantly sufficient for the service.

In passing the woods of Animallee, he took the diversion of elephant hunting, a field sport sufficiently remote from the objects of history, but forced into that province by the circumstances of characteristic brutality which it developed. The elephant suggests to the mind of the Hindoo, associations which render it in some degree a sacred animal †, and to kill a female elephant is among the worst violations of the law which prohibits the extinction of animal life. It was this very reason that influenced the Sultaun's selection, for the performance of a common military exercise, to prove the temper of the blade, and the skill of the swordsman, which is usually practised on a sheep; the expert swordsman being he who can completely separate the animal into two distinct parts by a single cut across the back. The female elephant was chained to the ground by her four feet, and the chiefs of the army being assembled for that purpose, the Sultaun made the first cut, the example was followed with reluctance even by the Mahommedans; but this barbarian had the cruelty to insist, that even many of the bramins present should cut in their turn; and it is to this enormity that they continue until this day to ascribe his subsequent repulse from the wall of Travancore.

Long before his departure from Coimbetoor, his intentions were of public notoriety, not only in his own army, but in every

* Regular infantry, 20,000; efficient spearmen and matchlock-men, 10,000; horse, 5000; field guns, 20.

† *Gavesa*, represented with an elephant's trunk, corresponds to the *Janus*, and in some respects to the *Terminus* of western mythology.

part of the south; and on his approach, the Dutch governor of Cochin, Mr. Von Anglebec, called on the raja of Travancore, to perform the conditions of a treaty of thirty-four years standing, which obliged him, in the event of an apprehended attack, to reinforce the posts of Cranganore and Ayacotta; which was accordingly done. The Government of Madras, to whom the raja earnestly applied for assistance, did not contemplate these Dutch posts as the left flank of a line, which, if carried, must necessarily be followed by the abandonment of the whole position; and did not propose arrangements to the Dutch, for combining the defensive means in which the two nations were equally interested. An aid of two battalions had been sent in consequence of Sir Archibald Campbell's previous negotiations, but they were now expressly prohibited from being employed on any other than the particular part of that line of defence, which was built on the raja's own territory; while the Sultaun very plausibly argued, that the line actually intersected the country of his tributary, and was built *on his property*, and not on that of Travancore; and that the raja of Travancore had no right to build a wall on the territory of Tippoo Sultaun, nor to exclude him from going to every part of his own territory of Cochin, on either side of that wall. The raja thus terrified, at being refused aid from the Government of Madras, for the protection of his line of defence because one part of it was not his own, renewed a long pending negotiation for the purchase of Cranganore and Ayacotta. A transfer of territory by two parties, which changes the political relations of a third, is certainly liable to be questioned; unless, as in this instance, where the transfer is clearly and indispensably necessary to the political existence of the state; but from the moment of

1789. its occurrence, this transfer was brought into the front of the Sultaun's grievances; he represented to the Government of Madras, that these posts were built on the lands of his tributary the raja of Cochin, for which lands the Dutch paid a rent, in the same manner as any other of his ryots, for the field which they tilled; and Mr. Hollond, the Governor, declared in his reply, that if on investigation these allegations should be substantiated, he would compel the raja of Travancore to return them to the Dutch. The Sultaun was incapable of comprehending the value of truth, even as a virtue of convenience: and the independent possession of those places by the Dutch as a conquest from the Portuguese a century before the existence of his own dynasty, so completely established the absolute falsehood of this assumption as to overturn along with it, the reasonings founded on rigid truth, by which he might have contended with better success for the right of passing to every part of his tributary possessions.

Mr. Hollond took the line of decidedly disapproving these purchases without the previous concurrence of the English Government: the raja broadly affirmed the concurrence of Sir Archibald Campbell, communicated to him through Brigade Major Bannerman, deputed on a political mission to his court in 1788. Mr. Hollond denied the existence of such concurrence, *on the public records*: but did not refer to Major Bannerman for farther information regarding the grounds on which this assertion was supported. In this state of public information regarding the alleged concurrence of Sir A. Campbell, the subject was taken up in the British Parliament; the Court of Directors was required to investigate; a reference was made to Sir A. Campbell, then in England, who did not recollect the existence of such a sanction, and inferred that Major Bannerman must have overstepped his authority if such sanction had been intimated to the raja. The Court of Directors followed up the investigation, by ordering the proper enquiries to be made at Madras. Sir Charles Oakley, when acting as Governor during General Medows's absence in the field, in 1791, demanded from Major Bannerman an explanation of the contested fact; and the following is the result of that correspondence:

It will be recollected, that the only part of the lines really built on the territory of Cochin, was that which crossed the island of Vipeen in the rear of Ayacotta. If the raja of Cochin, or Tippoo, his sovereign, should conquer or purchase from the Dutch the post of Ayacotta in their front, the right of the raja of Travancore to prevent his passing through that part of the lines to the territory of Cochin would at least be questionable, and could only be grounded on the imperious plea of self-preservation. The Dutch had shewn a disposition to part with Ayacotta and Cranganore; and it was feared that they might even sell them to Tippoo, rather than incur the risk and expence of defending them. Major Bannerman, whose mission had a direct reference to the means of defending Travancore, perceiving that in the event of an attack, the raja would have the alternative of defending lines built on the territory of the Sultaun's tributary, or of abandoning their whole extent by laying open their left flank, *strongly urged him to make the purchase of Ayacotta.* The raja entered warmly into the measure, but the negotiation could not be *concluded* without a reference to Batavia; and Major Bannerman, independently of the considerations above stated, deeming Ayacotta beyond competition the most eligible post for the British

CHAP. XXXIII. 1789. troops about to be subsidized by the raja, suggested to Sir Archibald Campbell the expediency of his writing to the Dutch Government to hasten the transfer. In answer to this proposition, Sir Archibald Campbell states his doubts regarding the eligibility of Ayacotta for the intended purpose. "The troops," he adds, "ought to be stationed in the place from whence they could with the greatest ease and expedition invade Tippoo's country; and unless the benefit likely to arise from possessing the island* of Ayacotta should be made to appear greater than I as yet consider it from your description, it would be *unnecessary* for me to apply to the Dutch Government on the subject." † If (as Major Bannerman argues), Sir Archibald Campbell's Government had disapproved the proposed purchase, it was incumbent on them to say so; but Sir Archibald merely declined interference, not because the measure was impolitic in itself, but because he deemed his own interference for its accomplishment to be *unnecessary.* The envoy therefore considered such an answer regarding a measure strongly urged by himself, to do much more than *imply* sanction, and did state that inference to the raja. He goes on to relate, that in July, 1789, after being relieved by Mr. Powney, and on returning to Madras, he did, in repeated conferences with Mr. Hollond, the Governor, distinctly apprize him of the raja's intention to make the purchase; of the steps that had been taken with the Dutch Government, and of the great importance of the measure: that no disapprobation was expressed to him on that occasion, or conveyed

* The island having Ayacotta at its northern extremity, is usually named from *Vipeen,* at its southern end.

† 12th August, 1788.

to Mr. Powney; although the Governor did long afterwards express great disapprobation at the actual completion of the measure thus previously explained. It is therefore clear, that the raja of Travancore stands fully absolved from the charge of making the purchase, without the previous sanction of the British Government; and that Major Bannerman stands equally absolved from the imputation of overstepping his authority in conveying the sanction of his Government, or of erroneous judgment in the importance which he attached to the possession of Ayacotta, which in point of fact was selected as the best position on the coast by the able officer who soon afterwards arrived with reinforcements from Bombay. It is affirmed moreover in this correspondence, that the Sultaun himself recognized the right of sale, by offering to the Dutch double the sum contracted to be paid by the raja.

The protection afforded by the raja of Travancore, to the Sultaun's rebellious subjects, was a branch of complaint which touched more intelligible ground; but this ground was not defended by the Governor of Madras, although rudely assailed by the Sultaun's coarse assertion, that the English chief of Tellicherry had taken bribes for the protection of fugitive Nairs, and for permitting them to embark for Travancore; a permission which would probably have been tacitly accorded by any Englishman, without a bribe: and if the facilities unquestionably afforded to this cruelly oppressed people, might, under other circumstances, be deemed imprudent, the broad fact of Tellicherry having been placed, in all respects, excepting open hostility, in a state of blockade, by a cordon of the Sultaun's troops, during the whole period from the peace of

1789.

1784, till the war of 1790, absolves the public authorities at that place, from every obligation of delicacy, regarding these unhappy fugitives. The charitable aid and protection afforded to them by the raja of Travancore, rather belonged to the class of moral duties, than political rights. The Governor of Madras, however, required him to discontinue the hospitable asylum which the unhappy Nairs had hitherto found in Travancore, and that chief adopted the alternative of disavowing, and endeavouring to conceal a fact which he did not feel to be disgraceful. These discussions were protracted till the month of December; Mr. Hollond had proposed the appointment of commissioners for the investigation and amicable adjustment of all the points in dispute, but the Sultaun had determined on a different issue. His camp was established at about six miles to the northward of the principal gate of the lines; and on the night between the 28th and 29th of December, he ordered the following disposition;

Two cushoons of regular infantry, all the cavalry and irregular infantry, accompanied by the spearmen of the royal retinue, to indicate his own presence, were ordered to manœuvre at day-light in front of the principal gate, and at ten o'clock at night he marched with 14,000 infantry and 500 pioneers, by a circuitous route, discovered to him by a native of the country, to turn the right flank of the lines which terminated at a precipice supposed to be inaccessible. The demonstrations in front drew the attention of the enemy as had been expected; and he found himself soon after day-light in possession of a considerable extent of rampart on the right flank almost without opposition. It was his object to gain the gate about nine miles from the point of entrance; to open it to the division manœuvring in its front, and to establish his whole army within the lines in one day. Although the opposition was feeble, it was near nine o'clock before the whole of the troops had entered, and were prepared to advance in force. After he had advanced between two and three miles, some distant movements were perceived, and the Sultaun thinking it possible that he might not fully accomplish his object on that day, and be obliged to take post and bring up his guns, ordered the pioneers to throw down a certain portion of the rampart into the ditch (about 16 feet wide and 20 feet deep), and to make a wide and solid road, and easy communication with the camp. The pioneers had been marching nearly twelve hours, and were not much disposed to vigorous exertion: the berm as well as the ditch was overgrown with thorny shrubs and bamboos, and the work proceeded very tardily. In the meanwhile the troops advanced in one column along the rampart, the Travancoreans retreating from each successive tower; the resistance at each successively encreasing, until the column approached a building within the works, constituting a square enclosure, made use of as a magazine, storehouse, and barrack. The fugitives knew that support was at hand, but were not as yet in sufficient strength to maintain themselves: they however made a stand at this square, and drew into it a small gun, and some grape from their now useless lines, which did good service against the head of the column; the casualties of the day had fallen heavily on the leading corps; and the Sultaun ordered up a fresh and select one, with orders to carry the building at the point of the bayonet, the corps relieved being directed to fall into the rear. The order, besides being ill-executed, was

CHAP. XXXIII. 1789. misapprehended; and at the moment this corps was about to retire along the flank of the column, a party of about twenty men, which the Travancoreans had sent into the thick cover which here approached within a few yards of the rampart, threw in a regular platoon on the flank, which killed the officer commanding, and threw the corps into inextricable disorder and flight. The relieving corps, aukwardly advancing along the same flank, was met and checked by an impetuous mass of fugitives; the next corps caught the infection, the panic became general, and the confusion irretrievable. The Sultaun, himself, was borne away in the crowd; the rear, now become the front, rushed into the intended road across the ditch, which had been no farther prepared than by cutting down the underwood, and throwing a part of the rampart on the berm; the foremost leaped or were forced into the ditch; and such was the pressure of the succeeding mass, that there was no alternative but to follow. The undermost, of course, were trampled to death; and in a short time the bodies, by which the ditch was nearly filled, enabled the remainder to pass over. The Sultaun was precipitated with the rest, and was only saved by the exertions of some steady and active chêlas, who raised him on their shoulders, and enabled him to ascend the counterscarp, after having twice fallen back in the attempt to clamber up; and the lameness, which occasionally continued until his death, was occasioned by the severe contusions he received on this occasion. His palankeen remained in the ditch, the bearers having been trodden to death, his seals, rings, and personal ornaments, fell as trophies into the hands of the enemy; and the fortune of a day, which was turned by 20 men, cost the Sultaun's army upwards of two thousand. The English dispatches of that period describe the ditch to have been filled with bales of cotton by the Mysoreans, for the purpose of passing in, and that the accidental inflammation of that substance, had compelled them to seek another passage. All the Mysoreans with whom the author has conversed, deny the existence of a bale of cotton in the army ; but all affirm, that the mass of bodies in the ditch were consumed by fire after the retreat ; fuel, as they suppose, having been added for the purpose by the Travancoreans. But when the mass of wood felled for clearing the road, the combustible materials of their dress, and the contents of their cartouch boxes are considered, an accidental spark, near the close of the retreat, may furnish a sufficient explanation of the fact to those who have witnessed similar scenes. *

The Sultaun on clearing the ditch, made the best of his way on foot towards camp, but was soon furnished with the conveyance of a common dooley, to bear him unperceived to his tent. In a mixed paroxysm of rage and humiliation, he swore that he would remain fixed on that encampment until he should carry this contemptible wall. He accordingly ordered the recal of Burhân-u-Deen from Coorg, and of nearly the whole of his detachments for the conversion of the infidels from Malabar. Battering-guns were to be brought from Seringapatam and Bangalore; and three months and a half of ostensible negotiation and real preparation for attack affords a pause, in which we shall first advert to the issue of some prior embassies destined to

* The mass of fugitives who choaked the Mysoor gate of Bangalore, after the assault in 1791, was a horrible example, without any fuel, but the dress and the cartouch boxes.

strengthen his means of aggression, of which his envoys made their personal reports during this interval; and we shall then proceed to relate the influence on the English councils of the abortive attempt which has just been described.

CHAPTER XXXIV.

Mission and subsequent embassy to Constantinople and eventually to Paris — Embassy arrives at Bussora, and after some delay at Constantinople — Negotiation somewhat ludicrous — Fabulous genealogy — The plague — Loss of 565 of the suite — Embark for Alexandria — where they hear of the embassy to France by sea, and prepare to return — by Cairo — Suez — Jedda — Mecca — Medina — Exaction of the Shereef of Mecca, evaded by a singular device of Gholâum Ali — Arrive at Calicut on the day of the Sultaun's repulse from the lines — Out of eleven hundred, bring back sixty-eight — Expence of the embassy — Value received — Joke of the man-eaters — Effect of the intelligence of the attack of the lines of Travancore on the Government of Madras — and Lord Cornwallis — Explicit instructions to Madras, in the preceding November — They animadvert on the orders instead of obeying them — Last and most instructive example of the defective constitution, abolished by the powers committed to Lord Cornwallis — Sultaun's tardy notice of the attack of the lines — Singular history of his own defeat — Resumes the attack by regular approaches — assaults and succeeds — Conduct of the officer commanding the English detachment — Reinforcement under Colonel Hartley — unequal to any but defensive operations — No contact with the Sultaun's troops — Cranganore taken — Tippoo overruns the plain country — Example of mortality from small-pox — Public ceremony on destroying the lines — Visit of Macnamara — who admonishes him regarding the preparations of the English — and receives a letter to Louis the XVI. demanding aid in such event — In fact he was unprepared for war — Explanations — Lord Cornwallis relieved from legislative restraints — negotiates offensive and defensive treaties at Poona and Hyderabad — Nizam Ali professes apprehension of Mahratta treachery — accepts an indirect guarantee — Observations on the character of Lord Cornwallis.

CHAP. XXXIV. 1790.

IN 1784 the Sultaun sent an embassy to Constantinople, under Othmân Khân, formerly his valet, apparently for the purpose

CHAP. XXXIV. 1790.

of obtaining some preliminary information. The intelligence transmitted by this envoy of certain conferences then in progress, between the English embassador, and the Grand Seignor, appears to have hastened the second and principal embassy to that power, consisting, according to the Sultaun's usual spirit of suspicion, of four * persons who departed in 1785; and on their arrival at Constantinople, Othmân Khân returned. The second embassy was instructed, after finishing the business committed to their charge at Constantinople, to proceed on a special mission to the court of France: but the Sultaun, on hearing the personal report of Othmân Khân, changed this resolution, and deputed, by the more expeditious route of a sea-voyage, from Pondicherry, a direct embassy to France, consisting of three † persons including Othmân Khân, in the beginning of 1787; and these envoys, after executing the objects of their mission, had returned and joined him at Coimbetoor. It were superfluous to describe the objects of this embassy, or its courteous reception: or the ridicule and contempt excited by its combination of splendid pretension, miserable avarice, and mean rapacity. The embassadors returned in a state of feud, originally excited on the occasion of receiving some valuable presents by order of Louis XVI. when the two seniors had unfolded the former avocations of their junior colleague, with a view to obtaining the largest shares for themselves; and in retaliation for this secular injury, Mahommed Othmân asuming the fervour of religious zeal, informed

* Gholaum Ali Khân; Lutf Ali Beg; Sha Noor Ullah, and Mahommed Huneef. Sha Noor Ullah had been formerly employed on a mission to Persia.

† Mahommed Derveish Khân, Akbar Ali Khân, and Othman Khân.

against his colleagues, for being indecorously captivated by the beauty of female infidels, and even accepting presents of forbidden liquors; and they were accordingly disgraced. CHAP. XXXIV. 1790.

The probable objects of an embassy to Constantinople are not so obvious as those of the French mission; and similar means do not exist, of checking by European information, facts which may seem too ludicrous to be received without suspicion. Such as they are, they must rest on the memory and authority of Lutf Ali Beg, one of the embassadors, and Seyed Jaffier the secretary, whose journal of the embassy was found in Seringapatam in 1792, and transmitted with other documents to Calcutta, where it is still supposed to be accessible.

This second embassy to Constantinople, embarked in 1785 on four ships, carrying among other presents, four elephants, which all died before their arrival at Bussora, and one of the ships was destroyed by fire in consequence of shewing a blue light when leading up the *Shât-ul-Arab*, the confluence of the Euphrates and Tigris. At Bussora, the envoys were hospitably received by the governor, Soliman Pasha; but were detained nearly three months, until orders should be received regarding the arrangements of their journey to Constantinople; for including the escort, which Tippoo's letters state at upwards of five hundred, the suite of every description, is estimated by the secretary at eleven hundred persons. During their detention at Bussora, the envoys visited the holy shrines of Nejeff and Kerbela: and when leave arrived, they were conveyed by water to Bagdad, and thence overland by Moosul and Diarbeker, to Constantinople, on the route so often trodden by the Roman legions. Some months elapsed after their arrival before they could be presented to the Grand Seignor: he was seated

CHAP. XXXIV. 1790. in a balcony, and they made their obeisance from below. To the question, "Are you well?" addressed in a low tone to an officer near him, and repeated through the medium of three others before it reached the embassadors, the customary answer was returned "praying for your prosperity." "You have sustained much fatigue?" Answer, "It is transformed into delight:" the signal of taking leave instantly succeeded, and they departed after performing the Indian Tusleemât (three low salams, the hand each time touching the ground). After nine months, they had their audience of leave, at which not one word was uttered, and the Tusleemât began and concluded the ceremony. Their first audience of the Vizeer, was of course limited to the delivery of credentials, and a formal speech.

The proceedings of the interview of business are thus described, the Vizeer and Reis Effendi being present, and Ratib the secretary being the interpreter in the Persian language, —*Vizeer*, "Open your business." —*Gholaum Ali*, "Our master is anxious for the establishment of a direct intercourse between the two countries, and offers as a nezer, the fort and territory of Mangalore."—*Vizeer*, "It shall be considered; proceed."—*Gholaum Ali*, "He wishes in return, to be favoured with the port and territory of Bussora."—*Ratib* (before translating to his superior) "Bethink yourselves of where you are, and whom you are addressing, and speak with discretion."—*Sha Noor Ullah*, "Why, what mighty affair is a sea port? When I was on an embassy to Persia, Kurreem Khân, the king, offered me two seaports as a personal present."—*Reis Effendi* (after hearing the interpretation), "And pray, Sir, who may you be? and where have you left your senses? Who is your king Kurreem Khân?

and before whom do you speak? Kurreem Khân was a blackguard." — Gholaum Ali finding that matters were going wrong, interposed to explain away the proposition, into a request for the Sultaun's ships being hospitably received at the port of Bussora. The fate of this first proposition deterred him from adverting to the second in their instructions, as an alternative in the event of the first being rejected, namely, the establishment of a commercial factory at Bussora, with exclusive privileges; and Gholaum Ali proceeded to the third — the demand of permission to dig a canal for the purpose of bringing the waters of the Euphrates to the holy shrine of Nejef. On this proposition being translated, the vizeer smiled, and spoke Turkish to the Reis Effendi, stating (as was understood) that if the thing were proper, it would be effected without the aid of the mighty Tippoo Sultaun, but he had the civility to answer, through the interpreter, that the application must be made to Soliman Pasha. In fact, they had sounded him regarding this proposition while waiting at Bussora; and the Pasha, who appears to have been a man of wit, as well as courtesy, replied with suitable gravity, that the suggestion had once been made in days of yore, but had been forbidden in the dream or revelation of a saint, and that without some communication of assent from the invisible world the project could not be resumed.

There was no other professed interview of business, and this could scarcely be deemed propitious; but during their residence at Constantinople they were treated with courtesy and distinction and entertained with a variety of public spectacles, at one of which they exhibited the evolutions of their sepoy escort; before departing, conversations ensued of a general nature, in which the vizeer made some enquiries regarding the Sultaun's ancestry and

CHAP. XXXIV. 1790.

empire. Whether Gholaum Ali was prepared for such a question is uncertain, but he recited with promptitude and fluency a very plausible genealogy, utterly destitute of truth, which the Sultaun, on the return of the embassy, actually ordered to be inserted in his history, and is the second edition noticed in page 21 of the preface to this work. But the political ills of the mission were greatly exceeded by their physical misfortunes. The plague commenced its ravages, and before their departure from Constantinople five hundred and sixty-five persons had fallen victims to that horrible disease: their orders to proceed to France were unrevoked, but they had expended a large portion of their money, and the funds were insufficient for that ulterior purpose: the plague had alarmed them beyond all discretion, and they desired to be expedited home by whatever route: they accordingly embarked for Alexandria; but the plague continued its effects during the voyage and after their arrival. Here however they received private but certain intelligence of the embassy by sea to France, and took care to note it in their journal as the cause of their return to India. From Alexandria they sailed up the Nile to Cairo and thence crossed to Suez. Gholâum Ali, (afterwards known to the English by the epithet of *silver chair*, from his being carried in a sort of stool covered with that metal,) had some years before lost the use of his lower extremities, and had performed the journey from Bagdad to Constantinople in his palankeen. Of his twelve bearers the plague had left him but one, and he was conveyed across the isthmus in a camel cradle. From Suez they sailed to Jedda, and thence performed the pilgrimage to Mecca and Medina.

While at Mecca, the shereef finding that a portion of the

diplomatic funds still remained untouched, gave a friendly intimation of his requiring a loan to that amount, and Gholâum Ali escaped this robbery by a singular device. He forged a letter which he caused to be brought in by an express camel courier in the night; the messenger was of course stopped by the guards of the shereef, one of whose officers was ordered to accompany him to the quarters of the embassy, and the dispatch was read aloud in his presence. It contained intelligence of a great victory over the last of the Sultaun's enemies in India, and the preparation of a numerous fleet for the purpose of occupying the holy cities with an army capable of renewing the first triumphs of Islâm. Discreet rejoicings ensued at the quarters of the embassy, and secret terrors in the councils of the shereef. The loan was no longer wanted, and the embassy hastened to its port of embarkation, whence it arrived at Calicut, on the very day of the Sultaun's repulse from the lines of Travancore, and shortly afterwards in camp, just five years after taking leave at Seringapatam, bringing back alive to the Sultaun's territory exactly sixty-eight of the eleven hundred who had arrived in safety at Constantinople. The secretary estimated the total expence of this embassy, including the pay of the escort, the value of the ship lost, and the merchandize embezzled at Muscat, at twenty lacs of rupees; and slily observed, that the only value received in return was a firmaun from the Sultaun of Room, and sixty-five half quires * of journal, worth, at the highest estimation of the two articles, in rarity and in waste paper, about five rupees. But the Sultaun attributing no part of

* *Juz*, it is less than half a quire, but that was the nearest translation.

this result to his own folly and ignorance, ascribed the whole to the unskilfulness or dishonesty of Gholâum Ali Khân, who was divested of all his employments, and ordered to confine himself to his house. It was in the course of the investigation which preceded this result, that the Sultaun one evening directed one of the officers in waiting to *call the man-eaters.* The officer stared; and the Sultaun explained, by desiring him to "call the men who had lately returned from Room (Constantinople), after eating their companions." The royal joke became current, and as long as its novelty lasted, the embassadors were distinguished by the nick name of the man-eaters.

The intelligence of the actual assault of the lines of Travancore, had in the mean while produced very different impressions on the Government of Madras, and the Supreme Government of Bengal. At an early period of the correspondence, Lord Cornwallis, influenced by the misapprehensions which have been stated, had expressed his regret and disapprobation of the conduct of the raja of Travancore, in concluding political negotiations without the previous sanction of the power on which he depended for support; but on receiving from Mr. Hollond farther intelligence regarding the raja's purchase of Cranganore and Ayacotta, and Tippoo's claim of sovereignty over these places, which he now intelligibly threatened to enforce, transmitted on the 13th November, 1789, for the guidance of the Government of Madras, a broad and well explained consideration of the serious consequences of war on the one hand, and the fatal policy of a tame submission to insult or injury on the other, with corresponding instructions, which were certainly couched in terms sufficiently explicit. If on investigation it should appear that those places had belonged to the raja of Cochin, subsequently to his becoming a tributary of Mysoor, the raja of Travancore was to be compelled to restore them to their former possessor; if they had not belonged to the raja of Cochin within the specified period, the raja of Travancore was to be supported in the possession, as a legitimate right derived from actual purchase. If Tippoo should be in actual possession of these places, before the arrival of these instructions, a negotiation was to be opened for the purpose of effecting an amicable adjustment on the principles explained; he was not to be forcibly dispossessed without the previous sanction of the Supreme Government, unless he should have attacked also the other territories of Travancore; but in the event of such attack, the Government of Madras was positively ordered to deem it an act of hostility, and the commencement of a war which they were to prosecute with all possible vigour and decision.

The Government of Madras, on the 3d of January, 1790, in reply to an order which they were expected to obey, proceeded to animadvert on the reasonings by which it was supported. As well (say they) might the Dutch dispose of Paliacate and Sadras to the French, without offence to the English, as sell Cranganore and Ayacotta to the raja of Travancore, without offence to Tippoo Sultaun: and reasoning from these parallel cases, they deprecated the policy of committing the honour of Government by taking part in the defence of places furtively obtained; a harsh construction under every possible view of the actual occurrences. The prescribed communication to Tippoo Sultaun, of the fixed determination of the Supreme Government to resist any attack on those places, was made; but a letter, addressed

CHAP. XXXIV. 1790. to the raja of Travancore, even after the attack on his own lines, not only discouraged the expectation of support in the defence of the two contested places; but expressly disclaimed the sanction of Government to a purchase, the validity of which was still undetermined by Lord Cornwallis. The Governor-General in council had ordered the commercial investment to be stopped, and the whole resources of the state to be applied to effective military preparation; but these instructions remained unexecuted. The military preparations were expressly withheld, even after the attack of the lines, for the avowed purpose of saving expence*; and the provision of a large proportion of the commercial investment diverted the public treasure from the objects positively prescribed by superior authority.

This is the last and among the most instructive examples of the influence of that discordant and disjointed constitution of the three presidencies, which more resembled the debating councils of three independent states, than the branches of one consistent government: the Company's servants had been educated in the practice of treating all requisitions from another presidency, as subjects for the exercise of discretion, or the display of talent. Lord Cornwallis was the first possessor of a direct, efficient, and coercive power, over all the presidencies, not only independently of their opinion, but in opposition to the judgment of his own council: and the intellectual habits of youth, and mature age, confessedly the creatures of circumstances, in all but the higher orders of mind, seem, in this instance, to have travelled unconsciously in their accustomed

* Mr. Cassamajor dissented from this improvident economy.

course, without reference to the radical change of constitution, which exacted obedience instead of argument.

The Sultaun's conception of the probable influence of the events of the 29th of December, on the councils of the English Government, was tardily developed and clumsily executed. Seventeen days elapsed before he took any measure: and he then prepared a letter, ante-dated fifteen days, in which he gives a singular account of his own defeat. His troops were employed in searching for fugitives: the raja's people fired, his troops retaliated, and carried the lines; but on the first intimation of the affair, he ordered them to desist and return; and finally, he requests, that the raja may be ordered *to observe the treaty.* In reply to all which, the governor of Madras actually proposed the appointment of commissioners for the adjustment of the points in dispute, and on the occasion of his approaching departure for England, declared to the Governor-General his conviction of Tippoo's amicable intentions. "I think," says Lord Cornwallis, "the late Government of Fort St. George were guilty of a most criminal disobedience of the clear and explicit orders of this government, dated the 29th of August and 13th of November, by not considering themselves to be at war with Tippoo, from the moment that they heard of his attack, &c." "So far am I from giving credit to the late Government for economy in not making the necessary preparations for war, according to the positive orders of the Supreme Government, after having received the most gross insults that could be offered to any nation, I think it very possible that every cash * of that ill-

* *Cash,* or *cass,* is an Indian money of account, of which eighty are equal to twopence-halfpenny.

CHAP. XXXIV 1790. judged saving, may cost the Company a crore of rupees: besides which, I still more sincerely lament, the disgraceful sacrifice which you have made by that delay, of the honour of your country, by tamely suffering an insolent and cruel enemy to overwhelm the dominions of the raja of Travancore, which we were bound by the most sacred ties of friendship and good faith
March. to defend." This letter, written on the 30th March, so far from considering the delusion of Tippoo's amicable intentions to be worthy of an answer, actually anticipates as accomplished, the devastation of Travancore, which did not take place till the ensuing month.

Cannon and equipments of every description, suited to the siege of a regular place of strength, slowly arrived for the reduction of this miserable wall; before the Sultaun would repeat the assault, a series of approaches were carried to the counterscarp, the ditch was filled, and a practicable breach effected nearly three quarters of a mile in extent; the raja attempted to supply by numbers what he wanted in skill and discipline, but these very numbers contributed to spread panic; the resistance was con-
April. temptible; and the Sultaun's army entered Travancore. He next appeared before Cranganore, which the garrison actually abandoned, but were compelled to return by putting to death the leading fugitives. Two battalions of English sepoys sent for the service of Travancore, in consequence of the raja's application for aid, and of Major Bannerman's mission in 1788, had arrived in 1789, shortly before Tippoo's departure to Coimbetoor, and before the transfer of Cranganore and Ayacotta. While Tippoo was in that neighbourhood, in May 1789, sounding the rivers, obtaining intelligence, and even attempting by menaces to induce the

Dutch to surrender Cranganore, Major Bannerman, acting in the spirit of the late governor, by whom he had been originally deputed, ordered the English colours to be planted on a conspicuous part of the lines, and a flag of truce to be sent to the Sultaun's army, to announce the presence of English troops on those lines, to defend them if they should be attacked. We have noticed the impressions produced on the Sultaun's mind, by the change of government: and these impressions had been confirmed by his receiving no similar intimation on his return in October 1789, nor at any subsequent period. The officer commanding those troops, perceiving also that the raja's military means were unworthy of confidence, instead of occupying any particular part of the lines, took a central position of reserve; and finding immediately after the assault, that nothing remained to be supported, crossed over to Ayacotta.

At this critical juncture a force of one regiment of Europeans and two of sepoys under Colonel Hartley, arrived from Bombay, and landed at the same place; but the united corps were unequal to offensive operations, and the fort of Cranganore being deemed untenable, Colonel Hartley withdrew the raja's garrison in the night of the 7th of May, and the place was occupied by the Sultaun on the ensuing morning. The English troops, separated by their insular position, and the Sultaun's disinclination, came for the present into no contact with the troops of Mysoor. Every thing north of the estuary, and all the territory of Travancore and Cochin was now open to the invader; the island of Vipeen was alone untouched, because he had still the confidence of practising on English credulity; the plain country was a scene of merciless devastation; the inhabitants were hunted

May.

and sent in immense numbers to the usual fate of captivity and death. Among the varied enquiries of the author, the circumstantial details were brought to his notice of the fate of a small division of these unhappy beings, namely, eighty young women who were selected for the service of the royal kitchens, to grind corn, and perform other menial offices: one individual of the eighty arrived in safety at Seringapatam, all the rest had died of small-pox: the fact is stated as an example of mortality, and not of the absence of contagion, for they had accompanied the return of the army, and the means of very special separation were of course impracticable.

The Travancoreans had meanwhile retired to their fastnesses, in the south, and independently of the season, which rendered it necessary that the Sultaun's army should leave the coast before the commencement of the monsoon; the military preparations of the English had begun to indicate the design of disturbing his route. Before leaving Travancore, the effectual demolition of the lines was rendered a sort of public ceremony; the whole army off duty was regularly paraded without arms, and marched in divisions to the appointed stations; the Sultaun, placed on an eminence, set the example of striking the first stroke with a pick-axe; the ceremony was repeated by the courtiers and chiefs, the followers of every description, bankers, money-changers, shop-keepers, and the mixed crowd of followers were all ordered to assist the soldiers, and the whole was razed to the ground in six days. Shortly before the Sultaun's departure from Travancore, a French officer named in the Mysorean manuscripts, Macnamara, who is represented as making a tour of inspection of the settlements of that nation in a frigate, touched at this part of the coast, and took the opportunity of paying his personal respects to the Sultaun, by whom he was suitably received. Tippoo affected to treat with levity the serious admonitions of this officer, regarding the formidable preparations of the English, in consequence of his proceedings in Travancore; and invited him to a review of the Assud-Illâhee, who were to drive before them the British grenadiers. Monsieur Macnamara spoke with distinguished courtesy of the appearance and performance of the troops, but it was specially observed by those present, that his politeness did not go the full length of assenting to the Sultaun's proposition. The repeated assurances of this officer, that the English considered the war as actually commenced, somewhat quickened his departure from Travancore, and he took the opportunity of committing to the charge of Monsieur Macnamara, a letter addressed to Louis XVI. stating his confidence of immediate aid, if these apprehensions should be realised.

In plain fact he was unprepared for war. He had calculated ou possessing every part of Travancore in December 1789. If this expectation had been realised, the option would have been in his hands, of a sudden invasion of the southern provinces at once from Travancore, Dindigul, and Caroor, and of being ready by the time an English army could be assembled to commence the war, with the Caveri as his northern frontier towards Coromandel (with the exception perhaps of one or two places), a boundary anxiously and incessantly desired by the ruler of Mysoor since 1751; or if that people should prove humble and acquiescent, he would have the alternative of waiting to consolidate his power in Travancore before he should proceed

CHAP. XXXIV. 1790. May. to ulterior objects. He was disappointed in both of these expectations; it was already May 1790; he had not reduced the whole of Travancore; the English were not humble and acquiescent; his cumbrous train of trophies were still on the road to Seringapatam; he was distant from his regular arsenals, all the equipments of his army required revision, before he should be in a condition to begin an active campaign, and every consideration of prudence or necessity required that he should revisit the capital.

We have seen that so early as 1788, Lord Cornwallis must have contemplated as inevitable an early war with Tippoo Sultaun; and being now relieved by the actual hostile aggressions of that prince on the 29th of December 1789 from the restraints under which he considered himself to be placed by act of parliament, he proceeded without the loss of a single day to issue corresponding instructions to his political residents at the courts of Hyderabad and Poona; the result of these negotiations had long been anticipated by the repeated advances of those courts, and his Lordship was enabled from the first to direct the measures of all the presidencies with a reasonable confidence in their successful issue. The treaty of offensive and defensive alliance concluded with those powers *, provided that measures should be immediately taken to punish Tippoo Sultaun, and deprive him of the means of disturbing the general tranquillity; that each should vigorously prosecute the war; that Nizam Ali, and the Mahrattas should each, if required,

		Executed.		Ratified.
* With the Pêshwa,	-	1st June.	-	5th July, 1790.
—— Nizam Ali,	-	4th July.	-	29th July.

send a contingent of ten thousand horse to act with the English army, and to be paid by that state; and that an English detachment should act in like manner with each of their armies; that an equal division of conquests should be made at the conclusion of the war, with the exception of such forts and territories as should be reduced by the English previously to the commencement of war by the other parties; and that the territories of particular zemindars and poligars named in the * treaty and formerly dependent on the Mahrattas, should, if conquered, be restored to them in full sovereignty by which-ever of the allies they might be reduced; an article, apparently extorted from the unacquaintance of the English with local and historical facts, by which the war commenced with a broad inequality of claim, in the gratuitous cession, without an equivalent of an immense extent of territory acquired by the house of Hyder at successive periods, and by different events, and some of great importance, so far back as 1762. † This treaty was executed by the pêshwa, on the 1st of June; but the reasonable apprehensions of Nizam Ali that the Mahrattas would invade his territories while his army should be absent on service, and his earnest endeavours to introduce in a specific article, the previous guarantee of his own dominions, protracted the final execution of that instrument until the 4th of July. Lord Cornwallis could

* Chittledroog. Kenchengood.
Annagoondy. Cannagherry.
Harponelly. Kittoor.
Bellary. Havanoor.
Raidroog. The district of Abd-ul-Heckeem Khân, the chief of Savanoor.

† See vol. i. page 446.

1790.

not without defeating the objects of the confederacy, proclaim in the act of confederation an offensive suspicion of one of the contracting parties; but, during and subsequent to the negotiations, while he avoided any demonstration which should afford ground of jealousy to the Mahrattas, he desired the resident "to assure Nizam Ali of his disposition, whenever a proper opportunity should offer to take such farther steps for drawing the connexion closer between the two Governments, as may be consistent with good faith, and a due attention to the subsisting engagements with the other allies:" and, these assurances produced the intended effect of a firm confidence in results equivalent to a formal guarantee.

If in the endeavour to trace with accuracy the causes of the impending war, the duties of historical truth have exacted the recital of measures, adopted at an early period by Lord Cornwallis, more calculated to produce a war with Tippoo Sultaun, than an open defensive alliance, for the avowed purpose of limiting his ambition; we have not failed to accompany the recital, with a description of legal impediments, and technical difficulties, which arrested the direct course of his honourable mind; nor have we neglected to revive the recollections confirmed by new evidence in every successive year, of the lawless captivity of our countrymen, and of the national honour prostrated and continuing prostrate since 1784. If the established forms of that international practice usually called the law of nations, which constitutes perhaps rather a code of precedents, than of principles, may be brought to impugn one branch of his Lordship's proceedings, we should, at most, arrive at the conclusion — not that he had ultimately done wrong

—but that he had assumed wrong grounds for doing right; and the opinion of an eminent man* who, at a period when political dissension may be deemed extinct, denied to his revered memory, the character of *a great statesman*, may be left to the judgment of posterity. But whatever may be the decision of that tribunal, with regard to particular *measures*, the praise of a plain, ingenuous, and enlightened conception of the *objects* fit to be attained by a great statesman; of stern rectitude; illustrated, not obscured, by that unaffected kindness, which fixed the attachment of all who approached him—of humanity perhaps too sensitive, which brought the virtues of private life upon the public scene—such praise will not be denied by the future historian, who shall attempt a faithful portrait of this venerable statesman.

* Mr. Fox, on the occasion of voting a testimony to his memory.

CHAPTER XXXV.

Lord Cornwallis's early orders for preparation disobeyed — the season lost — prepares to assume the direction of the war in person — remains at Bengal on hearing of General Medows's appointment — he arrives — takes the command of the army at Trichinopoly — Plan of the campaign — Central force under Colonel Kelly — Letter from General Medows to Tippoo — The Sultaun writes after the army had marched — Singular and instructive contrast — The General's reply — Tippoo unprepared, ascends to his capital — Capture of Caroor — The season — The sick — Imperfect commissariat — Colonel Stuart sent to Palgaut — Ignorance of the seasons — returns with difficulty — detached to Dindegul — Colonel Oldham to Eroad — Colonel Floyd placed in advance towards the ghaut — compels the enemy under Seyed Saheb to ascend the ghaut — Tippoo's anger at this weak measure — Colonel Stuart's siege of Dindegul — assault — repulse — capitulation — ordered to Palgaut — Siege — capitulation — Remarkable resources obtained from the country — Important events during his absence — Description of the line of depôts from Trichinopoly to the ghaut — of the three distant corps into which the army was divided — Topography connected with Colonel Floyd's position — Tippoo descends the ghaut — Colonel Floyd suggests falling back on the head-quarters — ordered to maintain his position — Tippoo crosses the river — Success of the English cavalry does not arrest his approach — Cannonade of the 13th o September — Casualties — Council of War — Retreat — Critical situation — Erroneous belief in the arrival of General Medows, aids in the final repulse of the enemy — He had marched by another route, and was distant twenty miles — Colonel Floyd crosses the country, and after being three days without eating, ultimately forms the junction — General Medows's epigram — Casualties — March to Cheyoor — thence to Coimbetoor — Junction of Colonel Stuart — Advance of the united army — by the Bhavani to Eroad — Proof of its unfitness for a depôt — Tippoo's surprise at the rapid movement of the English army — Capture of Daroporam — General Medows marches to Coimbetoor — thence again to Eroad — Tippoo crosses the Caveri to attack the centre army — General Medows follows.

If in 1788 Lord Cornwallis appeared to have contemplated the strong probability of an early war: if, in his own words*, "we had dissembled our sense of Tippoo's failure in the performance of several stipulations in the last treaty of peace, as well as of many insults and injuries that he has offered to us in the course of the last three or four years;" and if the deliberate judgment of his honourable mind patiently expected the opportunity which should justify to the national authorities efforts "to curb his insolence, and exact signal reparation for the many injuries that we and our allies have sustained from them †;" symptoms of impending war, not to be mistaken, were much augmented in 1789. On the 29th of August of that year his Lordship issued special instructions to the Government of Madras regarding the measures to be adopted by themselves, and the communications to be made to the other presidencies, and to the envoys at Poona and Hyderabad, in the event of being forced into a war; and on the 23d of September those instructions were extended in nearly as ample detail as if the period was fixed for opening the campaign. If these orders, repeated in still more forcible terms in November, had been strictly obeyed by the Government of Fort St. George, immediately on receiving intelligence of the attack of the lines of Travancore on the 29th of December, 1789, a formidable army would have been

CHAP. XXXV.
1790.

* 15th August, 1790.

† Ibid.

CHAP. XXXV. 1790. assembled in the best season for military operations, and allowing sufficient time for the best attainable equipment, that army might (if the Sultaun had chosen to wait their arrival) have been in contact with the rear of his position before the lines, long before he was enabled to carry them. The season was lost, and Lord Cornwallis had prepared to repair these errors in person, when he received intelligence of the appointment to the government of Madras of General Medows, then governor of Bombay, in which situation he was succeeded by General R. Abercromby; the presence of experienced officers to command the resources and lead the armies of those presidencies thus seemed to render unnecessary the execution of his first intentions, and left him more at liberty to draw forth and combine the financial and military means of all the presidencies, for the general and vigorous prosecution of the war.

Feb. 20. General Medows arrived at Madras late in February, when the indignant gloom of reflecting men began to disperse, on perceiving in every direction marks of efficient preparation. A small encampment was formed by the 18th of March, at Conjeveram, which may be deemed the very commencement of efficient military measures.
May 24. On the 24th of May, General Medows took the command of the principal army assembled near Trichinopoly,
26. and on the 26th, made his first march with an army of about fifteen thousand men. The plan of operations resembled in its principal features that in Colonel Fullarton's contemplation in 1783—4. This principal army, after reducing Palgaut and the forts of the province of Coimbetoor, was to ascend by the pass of Gujelhutty; while a force under Colonel Kelly, deemed to be capable of making a respectable defence if neces-

sary against the Sultaun's whole army, and to be formed chiefly of the troops expected from Bengal, was to penetrate from the centre of Coromandel into Bâramahâl, and the operations of the two divisions were to be determined by the future events of the war; but for the reduction of Palgaut as a preliminary measure of the campaign, the season had been thrown away.

Although General Medows had thought it incumbent on the dignity of his station to return no answer to a letter addressed by Tippoo Sultaun to the late Governor, and received the first week in March, repeating in more direct terms his assent to Mr. Hollond's suggestion of appointing commissioners; it appears that on the 5th of April he addressed to the Sultaun one of those letters of form announcing his appointment and arrival, usually written by new governors to the rulers of neighbouring states; a measure sufficiently intelligible, when combined with his silence on other subjects. The Sultaun's reply did not arrive till the army had marched. It was full of pacific professions, and complained of "the representations, contrary to fact, of certain short-sighted persons, which had caused armies to be assembled on both sides, an event improper among those who are mutually at friendship." In answer to Mr. Hollond's proposition for appointing commissioners, after the attack of the lines of Travancore, the Sultaun had haughtily replied, "that he had, himself, ascertained the facts; after this, what was the use of commissioners? Nevertheless, if Mr. Hollond wished it, he might send commissioners to the presence." * His altered tone is remarkable and instructive. On perceiving the adoption of a policy consistent with the

* 7th February, 1790.

CHAP. XXXV. 1790. dignity of a great nation, he asked, with considerable urgency that the General *would receive an envoy from him,* " that the dust which had obscured his upright mind might be removed," and begged that he would *quickly* signify his approval, and order the embassador (a person of rank) to be passed at the frontier. On the day on which the army passed that frontier, General Medows replied, that " the English, equally incapable of offering an insult as of submitting to one, had always looked upon war as declared, from the moment he attacked their ally the king (raja) of Travancore." The Sultaun received this letter at Coimbetoor, and if any evidence were wanting that the united effect of the measures of the late Government, and of his own bad military combinations, found him unprepared for immediate war, that evidence may be traced in his instant departure on the receipt of this letter, with his main army, for the capital.

June 15. It was the 15th of June before the arrangements of the commissariat enabled General Medows to occupy the frontier posts of Caroor, distant only fifty miles from Trichinopoly, which was abandoned without resistance. The south-western monsoon, which at this season pours its torrents on Malabar, sheds a mild and salubrious moisture over the upper countries, and continuing its course over the arid eastern plains, is accelerated by their rarefaction. A powerful wind from the west, raising clouds literally palpable, of pulverized red earth, had utterly obscured the early part of the route, and tainted the respiration with more than the ordinary dust of a camp. In India to open a campaign at a good season, is to enable the troops to sustain the worst; and the disadvantage of commencing operations at this period was evinced by the return of upwards of twelve hundred subjects for the hospital of Caroor before a shot had been fired. The army did not quit this spot before the 3d of July, and after occupying without resistance the weak forts of Aravacourchy and Daraporum, the former was delivered to its primitive Hindoo possessor; the latter was occupied by an English garrison for the reception of a farther body of sick: and leaving in that vicinity a brigade to cover the heavy stores, and some expected convoys, the army marched without impediments, expecting to meet the Sultaun at Coimbetoor at a period when he was actually above the ghauts: and it is perhaps unnecessary to observe farther on the dates recorded in the margin, than to shew that the departments of the army had not yet attained that rare maturity which foresees and provides for all wants before they occur.

1790.

July 3.

5.

10.

17.

22.

An advanced force under Colonel Stuart was immediately detached to prepare for the siege of Palgaut, or receive possession if it should surrender, but there was still much to learn regarding the local influence of the seasons. The town and immediate vicinity of Coimbetoor receiving from the mountains which tower over it to windward, a sprinkling of the south-west monsoon, charged with the temperature of that elevated region, may be deemed comparatively cold, and had received from the Sultaun a sounding name, signifying the abode of health. A traveller passing twenty miles to the east, approaches the burning temperature of Coromandel; Colonel Stuart passing twenty miles to the west, met the full force of the rains of Malabar, and after crossing with difficulty a mountain torrent, and getting entangled between it and another, which placed him for a day in a situation from which he could neither advance nor retreat, was glad to avail himself of the first possibility of returning to head-

23.

CHAP. XXXV. 1790. quarters, after having with great difficulty obeyed the order for summoning the place. The error being thus practically ascertained, the same officer was immediately afterwards detached in
July 31. a retrograde direction for the reduction of the important fort of
Aug. 5. Dindigul, distant one hundred and twelve miles; and another detachment under Colonel Oldham was appointed for the capture of Eroad, in the best line of communication from Caroor to the ghaut.

At the same period that Colonel Stuart had been ordered to Palgaut, Colonel Floyd with the cavalry of the army, afterwards reinforced with a light and efficient brigade of infantry, was advanced in consequence of the appearance of greater numbers, and a better order of cavalry than had yet appeared. These were commanded by the Sultaun's kinsman Seyed Saheb, who had joined him at Coimbetoor with his division from Dindigul, and on the Sultaun's ascent to the capital, was left in command of the Silladar and Pindaree horse, to hang upon the English army and disturb its communications. Colonel Floyd with very inferior numbers, commenced against this corps a series of well-combined and active operations, creditable to his professional address, and to the spirit and energy of the European and native cavalry; and Seyed Saheb, incessantly kept on the alert, found it expedient to place his corps to the northward of the Bahvâny, a river running from west to east, and occasionally fordable at a few points; but finding himself exposed in that situation also to the enterprise of the English troops, and restricted for space between that river and the hills, ultimately ascended for safety above the ghauts. Tippoo was justly enraged at this weak and unskilful proceeding. Seyed

Saheb, as he observed, ought never to have crossed the Bahvâny, but on Colonel Floyd's approach, to have dispersed into small bodies, to have ranged round his rear and flanks, to have occupied in a desultory warfare every detachment on the line of communication with Trichinopoly, and to have straitened the supplies of those appointed to distinct services, and particularly that which afterwards reduced Dindigul and Palgaut, and subsisted exclusively on the country through which it marched; and the Sultaun concluded his angry harangue by declaring that Seyed Saheb had no business with the parade of fighting, and that any one officer under his command would have conducted himself with greater address.

Colonel Stuart arrived before Dindigul, in consequence of these errors, without seeing an enemy, except in some posts of minor importance, which either surrendered to him, or to special detachments. This place erected on the summit of a smooth granite rock of limited extent, had within the last six years been rebuilt with excellent masonry, on a new line of defence, not in conformity to the exact principles of European science, but with a better attention to flanking defence: it mounted fourteen good guns, and one mortar, but its best defence was a rampart of natural precipice, except at one point of ascent. The allotment of ordnance for its reduction was calculated on the expectation of finding the place as it was left in 1784; two 18-pounders, two 12-pounders, and two mortars of the smallest size, constituted the whole battering train, and the equipments for these pieces were more insufficient than their number: two batteries (one of field-pieces chiefly for enfilade and ricochet) opened on the 20th. To add to the insufficiency, two of the embra-

Aug. 16.

20.

CHAP. XXXV. 1790. zures of the breaching battery erected in the preceding night, were found to have been lined out, so as not to bear on the intended breach, and it was necessary to reform them in open day; this being effected the enemy's fire began to slacken after noon, and was silenced before night; by the evening of the 21st, a very indifferent breach was effected, the defences of the works which flanked it being imperfectly taken off, and some of the most important remaining uninjured; but as shot only remained for about two hours firing, and a week would elapse before a fresh supply could arrive, Colonel Stuart, estimating the value of time, and the disadvantage of remain-
Aug. 21. ing passive, determined on risking the assault, on the evening of the same day, under all the disadvantages which have been stated. The slope of the breach, although accessible over the steep ascent of the rock, yet left upwards of ten feet of the interior revetment of rather a thin rampart, quite entire; the ascent by the flanks of the breach was rendered impracticable, and a mass of pikes from the foot of the interior revetment, received every man as he ascended the summit of the breach; the assault was given with spirit, and continued as long as any prospect of success remained, but was ultimately repulsed with loss. Fortunately the cause of this premature attempt was unknown to the garrison, and early the next morning a white flag appeared, and the kelledar capitulated, on the usual conditions of security for persons and property, including under the latter head, an article which would seem strange in European warfare; the pikes and matchlocks of the irregular foot, which like the horse and sword of the Indian cavalry, are the personal property of the individual; but Colonel Stuart had

judiciously ordered the officer charged with negotiating the capitulation, to make no difficulty that should impede for a moment the surrender of the place. CHAP. XXXV. 1790.

After retracing his steps to Coimbetoor, this officer was, without joining head-quarters, ordered with augmented means to proceed to Palgaut. Officers who had served in the siege of 1783, spoke in high terms of the strength of the works, as being composed of long blocks of granite, so built as to present the end instead of the side to the shot, and thus resisting the ordinary means of effecting a breach; the ordnance was therefore prepared on a respectable scale, and placed under the direction of Lieutenant-Colonel Moorhouse, an officer of distinguished reputation. The preparations were made with corresponding care, and at day-light on the 21st of September, two batteries Sept. 21. opened at distances under 500 yards, one for enfilade, and the other for breaching; the latter consisting of eight 18-pounders, dismounted at their first discharge six of the guns opposed to them. In less than two hours the fort was silenced, and before night a practicable breach was effected: the opinion above stated appears to have arisen from attempting a breach in a circular tower, and the reflection of shot from indirect incidence was ascribed to direct resistance. In the present instance, the breach was made in the curtain, and the error was practically discovered. Among the recent improvements was the completion of the ditch across that causeway which led the assailants of 1783 to the gate; but although the covered way had been improved, it was still without palisades, and in a considerable extent immediately opposite to the breach, the glacis was so imperfectly finished as to leave cover immediately under its crest: of these defects the proper advantage was taken the same night. On reconnoitring the covered way, it was found, that the besieged retired every night into the body of the place, drawing after them a rude wooden bridge, which was replaced every morning: the defective spot was immediately seized, a circular place of arms, in a salient angle of the covered way, was next occupied, and its defences reversed; the musquetry, from the crest of the glacis, opposed that of the fort, the gate of the sortie was converted into a battery for two 18-pounders; light mortars were brought up to the position first seized, and were served with decisive effect; the ditch, however, was still to be filled: the advanced position must, on the ensuing day, have remained insulated, until it could be connected, in the usual manner, with the trenches: but all these labours were rendered unnecessary, by the impression produced on the garrison, who, before day-light, called out that they desired to capitulate. The terms were soon adjusted, in conversation across the ditch, and soon after day-light, the rude bridge was launched, which enabled the besiegers to occupy the place; which was found to mount sixty guns, of various calibres. The chief condition of surrender was effective protection against the Nairs, who had joined Colonel Stuart, and were employed in the blockade; but on the fire of the place being silenced, crowded the trenches and batteries, anxious for sanguinary retaliation, which it required vèry exact arrangements to prevent.

Colonel Stuart arrived before Palgaut, with two days' provisions, and without a shilling in his military chest; the sympathy which he evinced for the sufferings of the Nairs, and the rigid enforcement of a protecting discipline, had caused his bazar to assume the appearance of a provincial granary: the fort was ill stored, but, after depositing six months' provisions for the garrison appointed for its defence, he carried back to his Commander-in-chief one month's grain for his whole army: the confidence which his conduct inspired in this short intercourse, having enabled him to pay for these supplies, with written acknowledgments, convertible into cash at the conclusion of the war.

During Colonel Stuart's absence on this service events had occurred of the most serious importance. Sattimungul, on the north bank of the river Bahvâny, had been reduced and occupied by a battalion from Colonel Floyd's corps, whose general operations were confined to the south of that river, looking to that depôt as his main object; and he had been joined, after the reduction of Eroad, by the greater part of the troops appointed for that service under Colonel Oldham. A chain of depôts commencing with Tanjore and Trichinopoly, and including Caroor, Eroad and Sattimungul, were thus in the possession of the English, in a good line for advancing provisions and stores to the pass of Gujelhutty, which General Medows still expected to ascend early in October; but unfortunately, even Caroor could scarcely be deemed a good depot; Eroad was better qualified to contain than protect stores, and Sattimungul was ill adapted to either purpose. Exclusively of minor detachments, and a respectable corps of cavalry and infantry employed, with all the spare carriage, in escorting provisions and stores, to be successively advanced, the army might be considered as separated into three divisions, very different in their composition, but not far from equality in actual strength: the division sixty miles in advance, under Colonel Floyd — the head quarters of the army at Coimbetoor, and the division under Colonel Stuart, thirty miles in the rear, engaged in the siege of Palgaut; making a distance of about ninety miles between the extreme corps.

About fifteen miles farther up the river than Sattimungul, is the fort of Denaickencota, still in the Sultaun's possession. This fort is about seven miles south from Gujelhutty, the foot of the pass, which by the most direct road does not exceed eighteen miles from Sattimungul. About four miles below Denaickencota, is the ford of Poongar, now occasionally practicable; and at a greater distance below Sattimungul, a better ford at Gopalchittypoliam. The river was every where passable in basket-boats, of which a considerable number was collected at Denaickencota and other points. The Sultaun, early in the month
Sept. of September, leaving his heavy stores and baggage at the summit of the ghaut under Poornea, commenced the descent of this most difficult pass of the whole eastern range. The horse, which had last ascended, were first made to descend; and the English cavalry, recognizing their former antagonists, drew no particular inference from their return, but attacked and defeated them wherever they approached a patrole or a detachment. Colonel Floyd, however, had early intelligence of the Sultaun's proceedings: it was indisputably confirmed by the desertion of a native officer, formerly in the English service, who gave a circumstantial account of the number of guns which had descended, and the number still to descend. This successive intelligence, and this individual to be examined, were dispatched, express, to headquarters; with a suggestion founded on the dispersed state of

the army, which has been described, that the advanced corps should fall back upon the head-quarters of the army: but there the intelligence was disbelieved, and the Colonel was ordered to maintain his advanced position. His encampment, consisting of His Majesty's 19th dragoons, of six troops, sixteen troops of native cavalry, His Majesty's 36th foot, and four battalions of sepoys, including the garrison of Sattimungul, and eleven * guns, was exactly opposite that post. CHAP. XXXV. 1790.

Among his arrangements of precaution was a daily examination of the ford of Poongar and its vicinity. On the morning of the 12th, after the return of one of these detachments, Tippoo Sept. 12.
commenced the passage of the river, at the ford, and in basket-boats above it; and before night, had passed a large portion of his army, and encamped some miles to the south of the ford; the remainder was ordered to descend by the north bank, to operate by cannonade across the river, to seize Sattimungul, and eventually to cross by the lower or upper ford, or by boats, according to circumstances. The intelligence and appearances of the two preceding days indicated that the descent had been nearly accomplished; on the 13th, an hour and a half before 13.
day-light, three troops of the 19th were sent in advance, to reconnoitre the ford, and a regiment of native cavalry was ordered out at day-light to support them. There are two roads to the ford, one winding by the river side, and another more direct; the advanced body, after charging and driving into the river some cavalry they had met, returned by the river side; the native regiment was meanwhile moving by the direct road, and had only proceeded a few miles, when it was suddenly met

* Cavalry 1,100; infantry 1,700; total 2,800, and 11 guns.

by larger bodies than had hitherto been observed. The country is intersected by high and generally impenetrable inclosures, chiefly composed of various kinds of euphorbia and opuntia. The regiment instantly charged, and overthrew its immediate opponents, but perceiving heavy bodies of cavalry in every direction, the officer commanding, determined to take post in a favourable spot, which presented itself, formed partly by these fences; and to send intelligence to Colonel Floyd, in order that time might be given for the requisite dispositions, as well as for his own support. It was rather a position for infantry than cavalry, but if he had attempted retreat, the consequences must have been more unfavourable. Nearly an hour elapsed before support arrived, during which time he was surrounded, and hard pressed in every direction; and had expended his carbine ammunition. His earliest support was another regiment of native cavalry, which in the first instance relieved him, in the defensive post, and left his regiment free, to the use of their swords, in conjunction with the 19th, which regiment, including the returning detachment attracted by the firing, and the remaining four troops of native cavalry, immediately followed the supporting regiment.

The Mysoreans in surrounding the regiment which had taken post, had very improvidently entangled themselves among the inclosures; in one of these, from which there was no retreat, between four and five hnndred of the Sultaun's stable horse were charged by two troops of the 19th, and every man put to the sword; in other directions the charges of the European and the native cavalry were perfectly successful; the field was completely cleared of every opponent, and the whole cavalry returned to camp. They had scarcely dismounted, however, before a large body was perceived descending the northern bank of the river, and about ten o'clock, opened some guns on the grand guard, which was immediately ordered to join the line; the Sultaun's columns were at the same time perceived rapidly approaching from the west, in a direction which threatened to turn the left, and a change of front was promptly executed, which placed the infantry in a position difficult to be outflanked, and the cavalry imperfectly covered by a low hill. The Sultaun's army drew up in a corresponding order, seeking but failing to obtain an enfilading fire, and opened a distant, but efficient cannonade from nineteen guns, besides those to the north of the river; this was answered by the English eleven, but not with great vivacity, as well on account of the distance as the limited store of ammunition. At distances much exceeding point blank, a few discharges are generally necessary to ascertain the range; when this was found, every shot carried off a file, and to distract the enemy's aim, the corps frequently receded or advanced a short distance; these movements were executed by the sepoys with the most perfect steadiness. Colonel Floyd in passing along the line when the casualties were most frequent, expressed regret to the native officers, and cheered them with the hope of retaliation in due time: the answer was nearly uniform, "We have eaten the Company's salt; our lives are at their disposal, and God forbid that we should mind a few casualties." The cannonade only terminated with the day.

Of the English guns, two 12-pounders and a six were disabled; the casualties had been serious among the troops, the horses, and the draught oxen; and this last equipment had suffered still more severely in the desertion of most of the drivers during the cannonade. A council of war determined on retreat, and although the two twelves had been restored soon after midnight, by the active and intelligent exertions of an officer of his staff *, the causes which have been noticed, compelled him to leave on the ground one 18-pounder, one 12, and one six. After some blameable delay, in executing the orders for abandoning the untenable post of Sattimungul with its provisions, the battalion crossed in basket-boats, and the whole corps commenced its march at eight in the morning; the infantry and cavalry in separate columns, and the baggage in a third. For about twelve miles, an open country admitted that order of march; but at Oocâra, a country intersected by inclosures, compelled the adoption of a single column, the cavalry with Colonel Floyd leading; and the infantry from that period, entirely conducted by his second, Lieutenant-Colonel Oldham.

Tippoo had, on the preceding night, drawn off his army at the close of day, to a position distant six miles, which he had previously appointed, but the army, overtaken by the night, and by torrents of rain not felt in the English position, unable to find their places in the line, were scattered over the country without order or connexion: if this state of things had been known to Colonel Floyd, there can be no doubt that even with his inferior numbers, and after the fatigues of such a day, he would have attempted and probably succeeded in a decisive enterprise by night. There was no indication of movement until

* "Brigade Major Dallas, who is always active and fertile in expedients, got timber from the fort, &c, &c." Colonel Floyd's letter. He had been foremost in every charge by day, and acted the artificer by night.

the English troops were in actual march; and it was of course between eight and nine before intelligence could reach the Sultaun, whose arrangements were prepared for a renewal of the cannonade with an augmented artillery about noon. He instantly ordered the great drum to be beaten, and verbal orders to be circulated for immediate march, and he hastened with such cavalry as was ready, to reconnoitre, and to send back instructions regarding the route to be pursued. The Sultaun's sepoys had in general fasted a day and night, and were busily employed among the hedges in dressing their food. It was the custom of the army on ordinary occasions to beat two preparatory sounds of the great drum, and march on the third: a portion of the dispersed army was really unacquainted with the orders for *immediate* march, another portion did not choose to understand them; the officers were directed to move without a moment's delay, and did so with whatever men they could collect; but it is supposed that the whole force of every arm really collected for action on that day did not exceed fifteen thousand men *, and certainly did not amount to twenty thousand: they were however flushed with the intelligence of the abandoned guns, and the elation of pursuit, and behaved with considerable firmness and spirit.

It was past two o'clock before Tippoo could bring any of his infantry into action. The column of English infantry marched on the main road, which was now in most places bounded by thick hedges; and the enemy's cavalry, infantry, and guns, bore directly on the rear, and diagonally on both flanks, compelling the column occasionally to halt and return the cannonade with

* The more general estimate is 10,000, but we must consider that it is the calculation of disappointed men.

CHAP. XXXV. 1790.

various success, making as much progress as was consistent with the successive means very skilfully employed, for keeping the pursuers at a distance. In these operations, three more guns were disabled and abandoned, the number remaining being reduced to five six-pounders. About five o'clock, the Sultaun had advanced his whole force so close, as to compel Colonel Oldham to halt, and form the whole infantry in a strong position; a select body of cavalry made a rapid detour, and charged with considerable spirit, the rear of the position, while the infantry in front, was prepared to take advantage of the expected confusion; the English line, only two deep, faced about to receive the cavalry, and repulsed them with great loss, many of the horsemen falling by the bayonet. The English cavalry had by this time advanced near to the village of Shawoor, (or Cheyoor) about two miles in front, the small portion of baggage that remained, was ordered into the village, ground was selected for the encampment, the cavalry had begun to forage, and a troop which had been ordered to examine and make the detour of the village, appeared on its opposite side, on the road leading from Coimbetoor. Some of the followers called out that it was General Medows's personal guard, and the head of his column: and Colonel Floyd, who had at the same moment received from Colonel Oldham a report of his situation, seizing the fortunate error, caused it to be announced to the cavalry, who, throwing down their forage, formed, and returned to the scene of action, proclaiming with three huzzas, the arrival of Medows, which was instantly greeted by a similar cheer, along the infantry ranks. It was almost at the same critical period, that the Sultaun's army had rushed to the close of a fancied triumph, with a general shout, but were checked in the first instance, by the admirable conduct of the infantry, and in the next, by the exulting intelligence of succour; in this state of wavering, they were charged by the British cavalry, who pursued on both flanks of the position, and completely cleared the field. CHAP. XXXV. 1790.

The Sultaun received at once the report of the death of his favourite kinsman Burhân-u-Deen, (who had fallen in a gallant attempt to force one of the fences which have been described,) and of the supposed arrival of the English General: authentic information had placed his division on a different route, but believing for an instant his intelligence to be erroneous, he drew off his army, in disappointment and indignation at the escape Sept. 14. of a prey deemed to be within his grasp. Ascribing this disappointment chiefly to the inclosures which we have mentioned, he some years afterwards ordered them to be entirely levelled over the whole face of the district; and it is a curious fact, that he was materially aided in this operation by an almost invisible agent. The prickly pear or "straight-thorned opuntia*," is the chief material of these fences, and the *Silvester* cochineal insect, introduced into Coromandel shortly after the order had been given, devoured not only the leaves, but the root of that plant with such avidity as nearly to have terminated its existence in the south eastern provinces: while the "Cactus Tuna" or awl-thorned opuntia, remained untouched by the insect.

On the disappearance of the Sultaun's army, Colonel Floyd, about seven o'clock occupied the ground near the village which

* Cactus ficus Indica, Lin.—Ainslie.

he had previously examined. He had, during the action, received a dispatch from head-quarters, dated on the preceding day; it related to promotions and matters of detail; and a postscript was added, stating that the General would march on the 14th for Velladi; a piece of intelligence which he had carefully concealed. This measure appears to have been adopted by the General, on the tardy persuasion that the reiterated intelligence of the Sultaun's descent was not entirely unfounded. Velladi is on the nearest road from the pass by Denaickencota to Coimbetoor, but the direct road to the same place from Sattimungul, fifteen miles lower down the river, is that on which Colonel Floyd was marching, and had been invariably used by every convoy and detachment for the last month. To cross from Cheyoor, his present ground, to Velladi, was nearly twenty miles: the Sultaun, as soon as he had time to examine his intelligence at leisure, caused a report to be circulated, that he had moved to an intermediate position, towards that place; in the hope that Colonel Floyd might be induced to pursue his route to Coimbetoor, and leave General Medows's division without support: but this intelligence had an effect exactly the reverse of that it was intended to produce, by impressing on the mind of Colonel Floyd the absolute necessity of attempting, at all risks, to force the junction, as the only chance for the ultimate preservation of the army; and if the report were true, it afforded the farther hope of entangling the enemy between two fires. He accordingly moved at two o'clock; at day-light he heard and answered three signal guns: General Medows had also heard the firing of the preceding day, and three guns fired at eight at night, to indicate the situation of the detachment; but distant sounds are referred with little accuracy to their true directions, and had not enabled him to determine the situation of his detachment.

Colonel Floyd pursued his march, and arrived at Velladi, at eight at night, without seeing an enemy, the troops having been three days without eating. In the course of the march, however, he had met two native horsemen of the General's body-guard, who, in the anxiety produced by the firing, and the uncertainty of its direction, had been sent as a sort of forlorn hope, on the preceding evening, to endeavour to discover the detachment, and communicate the requisite intelligence. From them he ascertained, that General Medows had marched that morning through Velladi to Denaickencota; and a reciprocal anxiety was excited on his account. The two men and their horses were quite exhausted, it was obvious that no fresh horse or man was to be found in the detachment; but the vital importance was still more obvious of stopping the farther advance of the General; and Brigade-Major Dallas volunteered and executed alone this essential service. He found the army ten miles in advance of Velladi, and reported the existence and the wants of the detachment. The most urgent was that of surgeons for the wounded, (two surgeons having been killed,) and an immediate refreshment of biscuit and spirits for the Europeans, the sepoys being already occupied in dressing the rice which they always carried on their backs; these wants were supplied in the course of the night, and the next morning the General retraced his steps to Velladi. His reception of Colonel Floyd was a noble example of candour: "My dear Colonel! your's is the feat, and mine the defeat." The General was fond of epigram, and it was usually well pointed.

CHAP. XXXV. 1790. The casualties of the 13th and 14th amounted to 436 men killed and wounded, 34 horses, and six guns. Of the killed and wounded, the Europeans, including artillery men, were 128; the
Sept. 16. natives 308. The 16th and 17th were employed in arrangements for the care of the wounded and dispatching them to the hospital at Coimbetoor. On the 18th the united corps made a short
20. march in the direction of Cheyoor, and on the 20th, encamped in its vicinity: the first intention of this movement appears to have been to offer battle to the enemy; but from Cheyoor the General returned to Coimbetoor, where he was joined by Colonel Stuart's division after the capture of Palgaut. The junction of the two corps had in the meanwhile disappointed the Sultaun's expectations, and he retired north of the river, not so much in the expectation of attack, as to be enabled to keep the anniversary of ten days, of the martyrdom of the son of Ali; originally a ceremonial of mourning for that sect exclusively, afterwards of exultation to their opponents, and finally in India, a frantic exhibition without an object in which both unite. Colonel Stuart found the ceremonial observed with the customary phrenzy by the garrison of Palgaut during the siege, and under restriction had even allowed a similar indulgence to the Mahommedans of the besieging force, without the slightest impediment to the operations of the siege.

The army, with the exception of its minor detachments, and the corps appointed to escort the convoys, was now re-united at
29. Coimbetoor, and marched in pursuit of the enemy: the draught and carriage cattle had become well practised, and generally in excellent condition, from the superior forage * of this district.

* Chiefly the Holcus Saccharatus, and Holcus Spicatus.

To restore the condition of cavalry once over-worked, is known to be a slow and difficult process; but the infantry and artillery, with the equipments of the army in every department, were in the best marching order; and with equal intelligence would have forced the enemy to action. In six marches, General Medows, pursuing the route of the enemy, round by the Bahvâny to the Caveri, found Eroad, successively abandoned by his own garrison, and by its captors after emptying the storehouses. Its unfitness for a depôt, was illustrated by the first orders issued after the Sultaun's descent had been fully ascertained, by his attack of the advanced division; the battalion which constituted its garrison, was ordered to retire to Caroor, leaving one company under a native officer, who, on the appearance of the Sultaun's army capitulated, and the condition was actually observed, of permitting the company to march to Caroor.

From Eroad, the Sultaun proceeded due south, closely followed by the English army; measuring its capacity for marching, by his former experience of the tardy movements necessary for protecting convoys, he had on the day the English army left Eroad, marked out his encampment, about sixteen miles from that place, intending to push at the convoy advancing from Caroor, or move to Daraporam or Coimbetoor, according to the direction which might be taken by General Medows. Most of the tents were pitched, and the foragers were out, when his light troops brought intelligence that the English advanced-guard would soon be in sight. The great drum immediately beat, and the army, overtaken at once by the night, and a severe fall of rain, was kept from dispersion by the light of the Sultaun's

Oct.

personal flambeaux. He marched all night, and if the circumstances had been known to General Medows, he could with certainty and advantage, have brought him to action on the ensuing day. He halted however after a short march, to receive his convoy from Caroor, while the Sultaun rapidly pursued his course southward.

It had been his original design to avail himself of an expected delay in the junction of the English convoy from Caroor, to double back upon Coimbetoor, and possess himself of the field hospital, valuable stores, and battering train deposited, not mounted, in that untenable post, and he made his next march in that direction; but the place had been opportunely reinforced by three regular battalions of the Madras establishment, and one corps of Travancoreans, sent by Colonel Hartley, who had arrived at Palgaut, in conformity to the general instructions he had received in September: on receiving this intelligence, the Sultaun took the direction of Daraporam. The garrison of that place was chiefly composed of convalescents, about one hundred Europeans and two hundred sepoys, unprovided with cannon; three batteries erected just beyond musquetry, would level the miserable thin rampart in a few discharges; approaches
Oct. 8. were pushed to the ditch, and the garrison surrendered on a capitulation, which was unexpectedly observed.

15. The General, after receiving his convoy, returned to Coimbetoor: recent events had shewn the expediency of making this weak place more capable of defence, before the departure of the army, and orders to effect the same object, were soon afterwards sent to Caroor and Dindigul. These objects being pro-

vided for at Coimbetoor, to the extent that was practicable, he again put the army in motion to seek the enemy, in the direction of Eroad. Farther stores were wanting from Caroor, and a detachment was made on the route, covered by the march of the army, which waited its arrival at Eroad, whence a supporting corps was sent to meet and facilitate its arrival. On approaching Eroad, a large mass of the Wulsa was met proceeding from the westward of Eroad, whence they had been compelled to depart by the Sultaun's command, in order that no population should remain to give intelligence of his movements, in a country covered by his light cavalry for the same purpose; the object was much canvassed, but not understood in the English army. In the neighbourhood of the camp, the usual straggling scouts were seen, but whenever a patrole was pushed to the westward, it met with increasing numbers. A strong corps under Colonel Floyd was at length sent to force a more extensive reconnoissance, and discovered that the Sultaun's whole army had crossed several days before, above the confluence of the Bahvâny and Caveri, and had proceeded to the northward. General Medows began to cross on the ensuing day, at a ford below Eroad, so deep as to make it necessary for the cattle to swim over, the stores and ammunition to be carried on men's heads, and the tumbrils crossing under water to be opened and dried in the sun on the opposite side, before it could be re-packed. And he followed with all expedition, to check the mischief in the Sultaun's contemplation.

CHAP. XXXV. 1790. Oct. 20. 25. Nov. 2. 7. 8. 10.

Tippoo had heard when last passing Sattimungul of the actual invasion of Bâramahâl, and proceeded with about three-fourths of his army in that direction, leaving the remainder to

1790. watch the motions of General Medows, under the orders of Kummer-u-Deen, now first restored to military command since 1787, by transferring to his charge the elephant and insignia of Seyed Saheb, who was thus tardily disgraced for his flight up the pass of Gujjelhutty.

CHAPTER XXXVI.

English centre army under Colonel Maxwell — composition and strength — enters Báramahâl — movements — cavalry drawn into an ambuscade — Tippoo shews his whole army — draws off at night — Renewed demonstration — Departure in consequence of the approach of General Medows — his movements — mistakes the Sultaun's army for Colonel Maxwell's — Junction — Relative movements — Both point at the pass of Tapoor — Ineffective operations of the English — Tippoo escapes — marches by Caroor to Trichinopoly — followed by General Medows — His opinions and plan of operation — resolves to ascend the ghauts by Caveriporam — Lord Cornwallis determines personally to assume the conduct of the war — General Medows ordered to lead the army to Madras — Striking influence of the seasons — Tippoo's progress into Coromandel — Tiagar — commanded by Flint — beats off two attempts to carry the town or petta — Trinomalee — Negotiations at Pondicherry, and embassy to Louis the XVIth. — English army arrives near Madras — Tippoo's advances to negotiation during the campaign — Results of the campaign — Recurrence to the operations in Malabar — Colonel Hartley's victory over Hussein Aly, and its important consequences — General Abercromby arrives — takes Cannanore, and reduces the whole province — Proceedings of the confederates — engaged in two sieges — Copul and Darwar — Ten thousand horse ready to join Lord Cornwallis — Advantages with which he opened the campaign — Unfavourable anticipations of the Sultaun — Lord Cornwallis's selection of a new line of operations, with its reasons.

CHAP. XXXVI. 1790.

THE respectable corps of native infantry which had made a march of twelve hundred miles from Calcutta, reached Conjeveram on the 1st of August. The exertions recently made in the equipment of the main or southern army had emptied the arsenals, and caused some delay in the equipment of the centre

CHAP. XXXVI. 1790. army, as it was named, which, by the addition of three regiments of European infantry, one regiment of native cavalry, and a formidable artillery, was augmented to nine thousand five hundred men, and assembled at Arnee. Colonel Kelly, its commander, died, and the command devolved on Colonel Maxwell
Sept. 24. on the 24th of September. In conformity to orders from General Medows, that officer entered Bâramahâl on the 24th
Oct. 24. of October, in pursuance of the original plan of the cam-
Nov. 1. paign. On the 1st of November he approached Kistnagherry, the capital and strongest post of the district: the natural strength and improved defences of this tremendous rock rendered it of some importance to determine whether a regular siege should be attempted, and several days were expended in a close and minute examination of its whole circumference. Colonel Maxwell then established his head-quarters near the central position of Càveripatam, intending, as was supposed, by making demonstrations towards the pass and the fort in its vicinity, to return and attempt Kistnagherry by surprise. On
9. the 9th, the presence of considerable bodies of light cavalry
11. indicated the Sultaun's approach, and on the 11th the only regiment of cavalry, allowing themselves to be inveigled in pursuit through a defile, were attacked by about six times their
12. number, and driven back with considerable loss. On the 12th the Sultaun shewed his army in full force, and attempted, by a variety of evolutions, to find the means of attacking Colonel Maxwell with advantage; but the strong position assumed by that officer, his admirable dispositions, and his promptitude in anticipating every design, frustrated these intentions; and the Sultaun drew off at night without any serious attempt. Similar

means on the 13th, varied so as to compel an entire change of position, terminated in the same manner: on the 14th, numbers farther augmented made similar demonstrations, but these were actually intended to conceal his meditated departure on the ensuing day. CHAP. XXXVI. 1790. Nov.

General Medows, as we have seen, had commenced his march from the Caveri on the 10th. On the 14th he encamped at the 14.
southern extremity of the pass of Tapoor, and on the 15th was enabled, by the improvement of the road effected by the Sultaun a few days before, to clear the pass and the range of hills, and encamp on their northern face, on an elevated ground overlooking B.ramahâl, and distant about twenty-nine miles from Colonel Maxwell's position at Caveripatam. On the arrival of 15.
the advanced-guard at the intended ground, a camp was observed gradually to arise, flags to be erected, and troops to take up their ground on the plain, distant about six miles. Nearly three weeks had elapsed since any direct intelligence had been received from Colonel Maxwell. No doubt was entertained that the English army beheld their comrades, and three signal guns were fired to announce the event. In five minutes, every tent was struck, and heavy columns were seen in full march to the west, in the vale of the great pass of Policode.* It was soon understood to be the Sultaun's army. He had drawn off some miles south from Colonel Maxwell's position on the preceding evening, and calculating on General Medows requiring another day to clear the pass, had marked an encampment which he found it prudent to abandon. General Medows moved on the 16th 16.

* Tippoo encamped at Santa Marunhully.

CHAP. XXXIV. 1790. Nov. 17. fifteen miles farther in the direction of Caveripatam; and on the ensuing day the important junction was formed by Colonel Maxwell. The united army was now twenty miles from the head of the pass of Tapoor, and twenty-six from its southern extremity. Kishen Row, the treasurer, was alone admitted to the Sultaun's councils on this occasion. He had no fixed opinion regarding the plan of future operations intended by the English after the disruption of their chain of depôts; but he inferred, that wherever the Sultaun should go, they would follow, and that he ought accordingly to carry the war into their own country, keeping also in view such a line of operation as might enable him to avail himself of any favourable opportunity to recover the places he had lost. If he should be followed up the vale of Policode, the nature of the ground left him no alternative but to ascend the ghaut; and he determined to double back through the pass of Tapoor. His cattle had been much over-worked on the 15th, and it was deemed necessary to give them two complete days' rest. His intelligence stated the intention of the English General to halt on the day ensuing the junction; but if such an intention existed, it had been changed. The two armies were
18. accordingly in motion on the 18th, both pointing to the pass of Tapoor, and both intending to clear it in two easy marches.

As the quarter-master-general's department was preparing, under the protection of the advanced-guard, to mark out the new encampment; they perceived a few tents pitched three or four miles in front of their right; it was Tippoo's Pêsh Khana, or tents always sent on for his personal accommodation with the advanced-guard. The circumstances were reciprocally reported; and the Sultaun, confident in the powers of his equipments, rashly decided on continuing his march through the pass. By the time that the head of the main column of the English army had reached the intended encampment, thick clouds of dust in front, indicated the entrance into the pass of a long and heavy column, while a considerable body of horse made a demonstration on the right, and was supposed to mask a movement of infantry, indicated by columns of dust in the rear of their left, which seemed, however, to accurate observers, to be returning to the westward. The General, with a brigade of infantry and the cavalry, moved out to examine this body, while the head of the column of march was ordered to regulate its advance by that of the corps which the General directed. Colonel Stuart, who commanded the right wing of the army, and led the column, perceiving soon afterwards from a commanding ground the probability of being able by a rapid advance to cut off a considerable body of the Sultaun's infantry, and attack the remainder to advantage, while entangled in the pass, reported his observations and asked permission to attempt it, with his own wing of the southern army, as an advanced corps, to be supported as occasion might require. This proposition was not approved, and the corps on the right under General Medows impeded by ravines was making slow progress. The demonstrations were continued, and the effect of a more rapid advance was sufficiently evinced by the fact of three battalions of infantry of the rear of the main column being intercepted under all these disadvantages of delay, and forced to make a straggling retreat through the ravines and woods in the opposite direction. The remainder of the Sultaun's army, astonished at their good fortune, completely cleared the pass, with the loss of only one tumbril, which had

CHAP. XXXVI. 1790. broken down, and some unimportant articles of military store: the cavalry disappeared about sun-set, a small body taking the route of the pass; and the remainder in a circuitous direction by Pinagra: and the English army, after a tedious march of twenty miles in about fifteen hours, and firing a few shot, encamped at night near the summit of the pass of Tapoor.

On the Sultaun's part, the discovery of the English advanced-guard was made in sufficient time for the baggage, camp equipage, and rear-guard to return, separated from the army by the intervention of the whole of the British forces, and the dust of their retrograde movement contributed to the hesitation of the English General. The Sultaun was personally present with the cavalry which made the demonstration on the right, and went off with a slight escort through the pass shortly before it disappeared. The Pêsh Khana was the only cover in the whole army; and they were equally destitute of provisions, until joined by Kummer-u-Deen and his small bazar two days afterwards. Tippoo however made no delay, his army supplying themselves by the plunder of his own villages; and first pointing to Caroor, and giving out that he would cross the Caveri below that place, he descended by the northern bank of the river, and made no halt until opposite Trichinopoly. Against that place he made various demonstrations, but they had no material result beyond the plunder and devastation of the island of Seringham.

Meanwhile the English General closely following his steps, and for two days having a distant view of the rear of his columns, arrived at the bank of the Caveri, opposite Caroor, on the 27th
Nov. 27. of November; and believing that the Sultaun had passed to the southward, ordered a strong detachment under Colonel Oldham

across the river, with reinforcements for the places which he considered most vulnerable. Deeming the Sultaun's views to be chiefly directed to fixing the seat of war in the low countries, the General declared his opinion *, " that the most determined measure, the likeliest to bring him to action, and drive him out of this country, is boldly to go up the ghauts ourselves, which I mean to do by the Caveriporam pass, and taking post at the head of the Gujelhutty, and opening that of Tambercherry, preserve our communication with Coimbetoor, Policacherry (Palgaut) and the other coast;" a plan of operation which it is not intended seriously to discuss; but which it were scarcely liberal to criticize by the test of posterior information. He added, that he hoped to be able to set out for the Caveriporam pass by the 8th December, and expressed his belief, that if he were once up the ghauts, the enemy would either fight or treat. Before that date, however, he was in full march in the opposite direction, in consequence of the Sultaun's demonstrations before Trichinopoly, which threatened that most important, but weak and extensive depôt, opposite to which the General arrived on the 14th of December.

Dec. 8.

14.

Considerations belonging to illustration of character, to distinguished enterprise, or to results of essential importance, have on various occasions extended our narrative into greater detail than accords with the general plan of this work, and the principal features of the campaign of 1790, have insensibly expanded, for the purpose of illustrating the degree in which they may be supposed to have influenced the Go-

* Letter to the acting Governor in Council at Madras.

 vernor-general, to resume his original design of assuming in person the direction of the war, for motives of great force existed independently of all reference to the conduct of that campaign. "His presence in the scene of action was considered by our allies as a pledge of sincerity, and of our confident hopes of success against the common* enemy." His Lordship arrived at Madras on the 12th of December, having previously dispatched two confidential officers of his staff, to prepare the requisite information regarding a variety of local details.

General Medows appears to have received intelligence of his Lordship's intentions when near Caroor, and now determined to remain in the neighbourhood of Trichinopoly, until he should receive his orders: "but if no orders should be received, or if his Lordship should be prevented by any unforeseen circumstances from taking the command of the army in person, it was still his intention to commence his march for the upper country on the 1st of January." Orders, however, did arrive, in consequence of which he commenced his march to Madras
Dec. 30. on the 30th of December.

The difference of a few days in descending to the eastward from the vicinity of Caroor, had brought the Sultaun's army into the depth of the rains of the north-east monsoon, which usually fall in Coromandel from the 15th of October till near the middle of December, while the English army, placed a little beyond their western verge, entirely escaped their injurious effects; but in following the Sultaun's track they had occasion to observe the

* Minute of Council, Fort William.

havoc it had made among his cattle, and to hear of its serious influence on the troops who were chiefly destitute of cover. On leaving Trichinopoly, Tippoo had proceeded in a northern direction into the heart of Coromandel, marking his route by the accustomed train of plunder, conflagration, and ruin; but perceiving that the military chest would be better replenished by imposing contributions on the towns and villages, he latterly adopted that plan; and, with numerous exceptions where his demands were not satisfied, these places only were destroyed which had been deserted by their inhabitants. On approaching Tiagar, a hill fort with a weak and extensive town at its foot, distant about eighty miles from Trichinopoly, where at length he was joined by the baggage and bazar of his army, he found that the whole of the surrounding population had taken refuge under its protection; attracted by the well known character of its commandant Captain Flint, the defender of Wandewash. The seizure of this multitude would enable him to extort large sums, and he anticipated no difficulty in forcing the town. The demonstrations were made for a regular siege, and the attempt to protect the town incurred from the relative localities the risk of its defenders being cut off from the body of the place. Captain Flint however, confident in his sepoy garrison, and anxiously sympathising with the sufferings of the population, determined that they should not be sacrificed; and beat off with considerable loss two successive attempts to carry the town. Recollections of former years probably contributed to the Sultaun's abstaining from a third.

1791.

The inhabitants of Trinomalee, 35 miles farther north, a town adjoining an ancient temple in a lofty square enclosure, animated

1791. by the intelligence received from the weaker town of Tiagar, collected the arms of the vicinity, and prepared to defend the temple, in the hope of holding out till the arrival of the English army; their behaviour was at first respectable, but batteries erected across the streets of the town, and a position on the neighbouring hill, overlooking the square, induced an unconditional surrender, which was accompanied with circumstances of cruelty and outrage too horrible for description. From this place, the Sultaun, making a circuit of the rich plain country, took the direction of Permacoil, which had been dismantled and blown up in the preceding war. It was kept as a post of observation, with one company and an officer, who had directions to retire on the enemy's approach; but the place being unexpectedly surrounded through the treachery of the native officer, his second in command, retreat became impracticable; and the Sultaun, on its surrender, proceeded nearer to Pondicherry. Zein-ul-ab-u-Deen was deputed to the governor of that place, and was accompanied in his return by a gentleman whom the Mysorean manuscripts, without specifying the name, designate as the second in command. It is stated, that he agreed to undertake the office of the Sultaun's embassador extraordinary to the King of France, on the condition of being reimbursed for the injury done to his private affairs, by his sudden departure from Pondicherry; that this sum was fixed at a lac of Sultâny Pagodas, 48,000l.; that he was furnished with an order to that amount on the revenues of Mangalore; that the payment was delayed on various pretences; that the gentleman was ultimately cheated out of his promised remuneration, and that the embassy produced no result.

But we are indebted to the work of Bertrand de Moleville, for a more distinct account of these transactions. According to that authority the negotiation with M. de Fresne, Governor of Pondicherry, was conducted through the medium of M. Leger, "Administrateur Civil" of France in India, who understood the Persian language, who became himself the envoy to Louis XVI. and who wrote the dispatches dictated by Tippoo relative to this embassy. Tippoo demanded of the King the aid of six thousand French troops; he offered to pay for their transportation, clothing, and maintenance, and with this assistance he engaged to destroy the English army and settlements in India, and ensure their possession to France. M. Leger, on his arrival in Paris, necessarily addressed himself to Bertrand de Moleville, minister of marine, who informed the King of Tippoo's proposals; but notwithstanding their advantages, and although as the minister observes, the insurrection at St. Domingo would furnish a good pretext for the unsuspected embarkation for India of the six thousand men demanded, the natural probity of the King's mind would not permit him to adopt the measure: "This resembles," said he, "the affair of America, which I never think of without regret. My youth was taken advantage of at that time, and we suffer for it now; the lesson is too severe to be forgotten."*

CHAP. XXXVI. 1791.

In the meanwhile, the English army pursuing the Sultaun's route as far as Trinomalee, took the direction of Arnee, where the heavy stores and guns were left under the second in command, Colonel Musgrave, and the remainder of the army pro-

Jan. 12.

* In the midst of his distresses, the King was amused with the shabby finery of Tippoo's miserable presents to himself and the Queen, "trumpery to dress up dolls," which he desired M. Bertrand to give to his little girls.

CHAP. XXXVI. ceeded by Conjeveram to the encampment of Vellout, eighteen miles from Madras, where it arrived on the 27th of January;
1791. Jan. 27. and Lord Cornwallis accompanied by a reinforcement of artillery and native troops, by various important branches of equipment and conveyance, and by a heavy military chest, assumed
29. the command on the 29th.

Some advances to negotiation with the English in the course of the late campaign, are chiefly remarkable for their awkward indirectness, and a deviation from the customary formalities of respect. Early in December, three persons intimating that they were the vakeels formerly nominated to attend General Medows, addressed to him a letter from themselves, stating "the facility of adjusting all differences, if they should be received, and their conviction of their master's assent, if he should be referred to." The General with becoming dignity, ordered the letter to be immediately answered by his aid-de-camp, Captain Macaulay. The unequivocal release of every Englishman in Mysoor, and the possession of some person or place of importance as a cautionary pledge, were stated to be indispensable preliminaries to negotiation. From the neighbourhood of Tiagar, one of these persons addressed a reply to Captain Macaulay, professedly by the Sultaun's command, going over the old ground, and proposing the immediate dispatch of embassadors; and the requisite answer, "that the preliminary measures had not yet been adopted," terminated the correspondence.

Although the operations of this first campaign had not fulfilled the public expectation, objects had been accomplished of great importance to the commencement of a second. Caroor and Dindigul materially facilitated the protection of the southern provinces. Coimbetoor and Palgaut were two additional points of eventual support to the operations of a field corps, and to an intercourse with Malabar; and above all the cattle of the army had received a training, and its departments an organization, which in the absence of previously existing establishments, nothing short of a campaign could have effected.

Colonel Hartley *, deprived of the Madras troops after the fall of Palgaut, was left to operate with a field force of one regiment of Europeans, and two battalions of sepoys, with their usual field artillery, against the Sultaun's troops, left under Hussein Aly in Malabar, which, when collected in the neighbourhood of Calicut, were variously estimated at from six thousand to nine thousand men, besides a large body of Mapillas. The universal hostility of the Nairs prevented the employment of this body in the desultory warfare of detachments which could most effectually frustrate Colonel Hartley's views. Partly therefore from necessity and partly from confidence, Hussein Aly assumed a strong position close to Calicut, and waited the result of a fixed action: this was the exact issue from which the diminutive numbers and superior quality of Colonel Hartley's troops could have any hope of success: the attack was made on the 10th of December, 1790, with distinguished skill and gallantry, and eminent success: the route was complete; Hussein Aly Khân and nine hundred men were taken; the loss in killed and wounded being about a thousand, while the casualties of the English corps amounted to fifty-two. Colonel Hartley lost no time in pursuing the fugitives to the

* He never joined General Medows, as stated in the Annual Register, nor left the province of Malabar in the campaign of 1790.

unfinished fort of Ferrockhee, where 1500 men laid down their arms, but the commandant had made a timely retreat with the public treasure up the pass of Tambercherry.

General Abercromby, the Governor of Bombay had arrived at Tellicherry with a respectable force a few days previous to this action, and on the 14th appeared before Cannanore. The enemy was dislodged with loss from a strong position intended to impede his approach, and retired within their works; but a vigorous and successful attack on the most advanced of these on the ensuing day, caused the unconditional surrender of the remainder. These operations were followed up with spirit and decision by the capture of every remaining possession of the Sultaun's, or his dependents in Malabar; and the unquestioned occupation of the whole province.

The allies on the other hand had cautiously, perhaps judiciously, abstained from any determined irruption from the north into the centre of the Sultaun's possessions; and, however tardy and timid in their proceedings, were at length engaged in two sieges, conducted by the English contingents respectively serving with each. The forces of Nizam Ali against Copul, a tremendous rock a few miles to the north of the Toombuddra, and about twenty miles west of the ancient ruins of Vijeyanuggur; and the Mahrattas against Darwar, a strong fort on the plain, about sixty miles north-west from Copul. Nizam Ali had prepared a body of ten thousand horse ready to act with the English army, and to join at any point that should be indicated. Lord Cornwallis thus opened the second campaign with advantages which nothing short of a first campaign could have achieved, but with none that could be placed in competition with the inestimable advantage now to be exhibited for the first time in the history of British India, of a Commander-in-Chief uniting in his own person the undivided exercise of all the civil and military powers of the state, and the exclusive direction of all the resources of the three Presidencies.

The Sultaun had hitherto failed in his intrigues with the allies for dissolving the confederacy, or even procuring the reception by the English of an envoy to excite in the other confederates the jealousy requisite to his views. He perceived the encreasing means by which he was to be assailed, and the hopelessness of a fortunate issue, without the assistance of the French; and although he was encouraged to indulge the most flattering hopes for the ensuing year, he opened the present campaign without very sanguine expectations.

The plan of a southern campaign was liable to the fundamental objection of separating the seat of war from its great magazine and depôt Fort St. George, and trusting to a new chain of posts, which could not be left for a few days without trembling for their fate. Advanced eighty-eight miles, in a line nearly direct from Madras to the enemy's capital is Vellore, a post which experience had shewn to be well adapted to all the purposes of an intermediate depôt. Amboor, on the same line, was thirty miles farther advanced, and about ninety remained between that post and Bangalore, the place second in importance of the Sultaun's possessions, and distant about seventy-five from Seringapatam; a line of operation which had been rejected in the campaign of 1790, on account of its reputed infertility. To undertake the siege of Bangalore, with the intervention of

1791.

the ghaut, and a distance of ninety miles between the besieging army and its nearest depôt, was an arduous enterprize: but Lord Cornwallis preferred this hazard to that of trusting to a weak intermediate post.

CHAPTER XXXVII.

Lord Cornwallis marches to Arcot — Skilful demonstrations on the direct passes — By an unexpected circuit ascends that of Mooglee without opposition — Unfortunate licentiousness of the first march — Progress of the army — First appearance of the Mysorean horse — Indecision and weakness of Tippoo's measures — Lord Cornwallis arrives without molestation within ten miles of his object — Description of this encampment — Tippoo's presence — Annoyance by night — Able disposition of Lord Cornwallis — Attempt at assassination — Takes up his ground before Bangalore — Reconnoissance covered by Colonel Floyd — Perceives and attacks the rear of Tippoo's army on the march, contrary to instructions — but with a fair prospect of success — till he fell severely wounded — Disorderly retreat — covered by the advance of Major Gowdie, contrary to orders — Observations on this affair — Description of the fort and petta — Attack of the petta — Tippoo's feint for its recovery, did not deceive Lord Cornwallis — Lengthened struggle — Tippoo finally driven out — Colonel Moorhouse — Forage — Grain — First error in the siege — Subsequent operations — Novel and peculiar character of the siege —Operations of the 20th and 21st — determine Lord Cornwallis to give the assault — Description of that operation and its success — Tippoo was distinctly informed of the intended assault, and his whole army was drawn up within a mile and a half — Consequent consternation — Effects on the prospect of the belligerents — Reflections.

CHAP. XXXVII.

1791. Feb. 11.

On the 5th of February Lord Cornwallis commenced his march from Vellout, and on the 11th, the army was concentrated near Vellore. Hitherto every demonstration indicated the intention of ascending by the passes near Amboor, or those of Bâramahâl. The Sultaun had been delayed by his negotiations at Pondicherry, until he heard of Lord Cornwallis's first march, when

CHAP. XXXVII. he proceeded rapidly by the passes of Changama and Palicode, and would have been in time to oppose the ascent of any

1791. of the passes threatened. The demonstrations of the English General were continued till the last moment, by a battalion, apparently the advanced guard, moving up the vale to reinforce Amboor, at the same instant that the first division of the army (followed at a proper interval by the second, on account of the close country to be passed) was in full march to the north, and thence turning to the west, through the easy pass of Mooglee,

Feb. 14. had, in four days, and a circuit of fifty-one miles, completely surmounted every local impediment, and occupied the summit

17. of the pass, with a complete brigade, before it was possible for the Sultaun to have disturbed its ascent. In four days more, the battering train, and every the most minute article of equipment (including sixty-seven elephants from Bengal, which opportunely joined at this place) and provisions for forty-five days, was on the table-land of Mysoor, 90 miles from Bangalore, but still within his own territory, without having fired a shot: a few days more were however occupied in mustering and arranging the departments of store and supply, preparatory to crossing the frontier.

21. The eyes of an army are turned with sharp scrutiny towards a new commander: this early evidence of military skill inspired a just confidence; and the first day's march into the enemy's country gave an unfortunate opportunity for estimating a branch of character equally estimable. The protecting discipline which usually accompanies an English army, is among its national distinctions; one example of its useful effects in the late campaign has already been noticed, and another had occurred more remarks

able for its coincidence, than its value, or its rarity; during the whole of those two days, on which the English batteries at Dindigul were firing for a breach, several ploughs were quietly at work within a thousand yards of the battery, as if to realize those fables of the golden age, which represent the Indian husbandman as uniformly undisturbed by contending armies. The practice was so well understood that a repetition of the usual injunction was deemed unnecessary, but by some unexplained occurrence, a village on one of the flanks was set on fire on the first march; and the ignorant and licentious followers, imagining that retaliation was intended for the outrages practised by the Sultaun, followed the example, and the whole country was quickly in a blaze. The most active exertions failed to arrest the evil on that day, but nine of the most forward incendiaries were selected for execution; and the following short order exhibits an unaffected picture of the habitual feelings of this excellent nobleman. "Lord Cornwallis has too high an opinion of the zeal, honour, and public spirit of the officers of the army, to doubt for a moment that every individual among them felt the same concern and indignation that he did himself, at the shocking and disgraceful outrages that were committed on the last march. His Lordship now calls in the most serious manner for the active assistance of every officer in the army, and particularly those commanding flanking parties, advance and rear guards, to put a stop to this scene of horror; which, if it should be suffered to continue, must defeat all our hopes of success, and blast the British name with infamy." It is scarcely necessary to add that this was the first and the last example; the construction indeed of the villages (walled round, and generally

Feb. 26.

1791. farther protected by a cavalier turret) gave peculiar facility to the arrangements of protection; and a corps was organized for the express purpose of furnishing safe-guards.

No incident occurred worthy of observation, (except the singular conduct of the small garrisons of Colar and Ooscota, who refused to surrender, but made no resistance,) until the 4th of Mar. 4. March, when the cavalry of the Sultaun's army appeared in some force. He had exhibited a strange indecision of character, in suspending every military movement of importance, during his protracted negotiations at Pondicherry, and singular imbecility in permitting the approach of the English army, within ten miles of its object, without the smallest molestation. To have impeded its front, and harrassed its rear in every possible route, was practicable with better dispositions; but in Coromandel, he was absorbed in the contemplation of his six thousand French, and on finding the defence of the ghauts frustrated by Lord Cornwallis's able movement to the north, he was next absorbed by the care of his harem, which, as we have seen, had been lodged in Bangalore soon after his return from Canara in 1784. An escort of five hundred men, with a subordinate agent, would have accomplished the removal of the women and valuables with equal efficacy, but he chose, personally and at the head of his army, to superintend these arrangements, instead of meeting and harrassing Lord Cornwallis, as after all previous procrastination he still might have done, on the day of his entering the territory of Mysoor. On this day's march his cavalry attempted, without the slightest success, to break through the excellent disposition of the columns, for the protection of the immense mass of stores and grain provided for the siege, added to the ordinary camp equipage and baggage, and Lord Cornwallis reached his ground, scarcely deigning to notice their presence.

The encampment rested its left on a broken range of rising grounds, running at right angles with its general direction: beyond that rising ground, and close at its foot, was a swampy but not impassable hollow, and these features extended several miles in the front and rear of the left: the Sultaun's army was reported to be distinctly visible from the height, distant about five miles beyond the hollow, and some time after the camp was pitched, movements were reported, which induced Lord Cornwallis to go out with the cavalry, supported by a body of infantry, to reconnoitre, and he remained out till after dusk; the Sultaun's sole intention was to harrass, and this object, as related to the cavalry, was somewhat inconveniently effected, as we shall have occasion to observe. The same purpose was evinced on the ensuing night, and continued throughout the siege, by adopting a mode resembling that described in the Mahratta campaign of 1786-7. Rocket men crept in silence, to positions within range of the line of encampment, and discharging their missiles, suddenly eluded pursuit, and after an interval, returned to other points; the practice was suited only to the annoyance of an irregular encampment, and after the first attempt, excited little notice in the English army, except when the rockets fell in the cavalry lines, or near the artillery stores.

On the ensuing morning the Sultaun made a demonstration in force which was distinctly penetrated by the English General. Lord Cornwallis drew up in order of battle on the heights fronting the enemy, the portion of his army which was destined to form the rear of his principal column of march, and veiling

CHAP. XXXVII. 1791. his real intention under this demonstration, by a simple and able movement, his columns of troops, heavy ordnance and baggage, favoured by the nature of the ground glided in the rear of this formation, and had made considerable progress towards Bangalore before Tippoo was aware of the deception. The line on the heights, after offering battle for some time, broke into column, soon after the last corps of the column of march had passed its right, and moved on in a parallel direction covering the rear according to the movements of the enemy. A distant cannonade on the rear, (instead of a vigorous attack on the baggage as had been intended by the Sultaun,) terminated the business of the day in that quarter; the efforts of the horse on the front and opposite flank were equally unsuccessful: not one shot was returned by the English, and the army took up its
Mar. 5. ground before Bangalore, late in the day, without the loss of any portion of its stores, and only five casualties, after a simple and masterly movement which fixed the confidence of the army.

During the ineffective cannonade which has been mentioned, and while Lord Cornwallis, accompanied by General Medows and their respective staff, was viewing from a gentle eminence the movements of the Sultaun, three horsemen were seen to approach rather closer than usual; but as these troops are remarkable for their skill and boldness, in examining an enemy's movements, and are usually scattered over the country in all directions, they excited no attention, till they were seen to dash at speed for the person of Lord Cornwallis. Two were killed, and the third, who was secured and spared, appeared stupified, and could give no intelligible account of the enterprize: conjecture was divided between assigning to them the character of ferocious drunkards, or hired assassins. The fact as related in the Mysorean army, appears to be, that on the preceding evening one of them had upbraided the other two with cowardice in the business of the day; after some discussion, they retorted that on the next they would go where he durst not follow, it was agreed that their valour should be put to this issue: each prepared himself with an intoxicating dose of bang *, and the quarrel ended in the frantic attempt which has been noticed.

On the ensuing day Lord Cornwallis moved his encampment to stronger ground, a large portion of the cavalry was employed in the morning, in covering the reconnoissance of the engineers, to the north-east, and at three in the afternoon, the whole cavalry under Colonel Floyd, with the brigade of infantry, attached to the same command, moved for a similar purpose to the south-west. The object was satisfactorily accomplished, and the troops were preparing to return, when a body of less than a thousand horse appeared. Tippoo had on this day made a circuitous march, concealed by the undulatory face of the country, to a position west of Bangalore, his own tent being pitched upon the esplanade of the fort, and his line of encampment marked out at a greater distance to the south-west. He had just alighted: a large part of the army had already taken up their ground, when reports were brought of the approach of the English cavalry, in a direction to intersect the column of march; and the command of Balajee Row, the only part of the cavalry that was not already out foraging, was ordered to check their approach. Colonel Floyd moved at this body with the 19th, supported on his right by a native regiment, and followed by the whole cavalry Mar. 6.

* The leaf of the Cannabis Sativa.

 in columns of regiments; the infantry had been left at a low ground, a continuation of the same swampy hollow mentioned

 in the operations of the 4th and 5th, with orders to wait at that spot the return of the cavalry.

The retreat and pursuit of the horse discovered the rear of the enemy's infantry and guns with large masses of baggage on elephants and camels, and although the orders specially prohibited any enterprise, the temptation was irresistible; in a short period the guns, deserted by their infantry, were passed: the ground became strong and irregular, full of ravines, and rocky hills, the regiment on the right had charged and dislodged a body of infantry, which retired to one of these as deemed inaccessible to cavalry: some other charges were also made on the left, with similar success, and Colonel Floyd, at the head of the 19th, was advancing to dislodge the largest body of the enemy on an eminence, when a musket ball entered his cheek and passed through both jaws; he fell as if struck by a cannon shot, his second in command was on the extreme left, orders could not be immediately received, and a retreat commenced; the native regiment on the right, continuing uninformed of that movement, and actively engaged in advance and on the right. In the meanwhile Colonel Floyd who had been left on the field, supposed to be killed, was remounted by the care of his orderly dragoons, and a troop of the regiment being sent back to escort him, he rejoined it retreating at half speed. At this moment, Brigade Major Dallas who had been with the regiment now left unsupported, perceiving what occurred, came up from the rear to represent the necessity of halting; this was accordingly ordered by Colonel Floyd, who wheeled the 19th towards the enemy; which movement together with the efforts of the skirmishers of the columns of regiments checked the enemy for an instant, but the disorder had become too general to be easily retrieved; the fugitives of the enemy's infantry and rocket men rallied on the different heights; the works of the fort, and the recovered guns, opened a cross fire, the English cavalry retreated precipitately from eminence to eminence across ravines, and the confusion was extreme; when they perceived the brigade of infantry, left under Major Gowdie at the swamp, advanced, with its guns in a position on an eminence, which commanded the only access for retreat or pursuit, and enabled the cavalry to rally in its rear, when he opened a fire which soon cleared the field.

The latter part of these transactions was distinctly visible from the encampment, and Lord Cornwallis was quickly in motion with a division of the army; he proceeded as far as the swamp from which Major Gowdie had advanced without orders, when he met, considerably after dark, the cavalry now formed, followed by the infantry and guns, and the whole returning in perfect order to camp; the casualties in men were not numerous, amounting only to seventy-one, but two hundred and seventy-one horses in the opening of a campaign, was a loss the more serious in the small body attached to the English army, because it was irretrievable; the reader will perceive that this cavalry had been almost constantly mounted for the last three days, and those acquainted with the details of feeding in the south of India, will be aware that the greater portion had within the same period received, some one, and few, indeed, more than two regular feeds. It will therefore excite no surprise, that under the circumstances de-

CHAP. XXXVII. 1791.

scribed, the horses had not strength to clear the ravines, and still less, that the greater portion of those who escaped, were rendered nearly useless for the remainder of the campaign. Men of sound military judgment have questioned the claim of Lord Cornwallis to the praise of understanding the practical use of this arm; but whatever may be the general grounds of such an opinion, a misfortune produced by the disobedience of his orders, is not liberal evidence in its support. Of that disobedience also, the judgment might have been different if Colonel Floyd had not fallen at a critical moment; if the infantry had been ordered up, and if ten guns had been brought in as trophies. Major Gowdie, who was guilty of as distinct a disobedience of orders, received and deserved nothing but praise. Although the affair terminated favourably for the Sultaun, he did not think proper to continue on the ground now known to the enemy. His greatest apprehension was a night attack on his camp, which throughout the siege, was never two successive nights on the same ground. On this night he moved six miles farther west to Kingeri, leaving the garrison of 8,000 men, appointed for the defence of the fort, under the new kelledar* Behauder Khân, and for the petta, 2,000 regular infantry, and 5,000 peons.

The complete examination which had been effected of every part of the fortress to be attacked, determined Lord Cornwallis to commence the siege from the north-east, where he was already encamped. The fort of Bangalore, entirely rebuilt with strong masonry by Hyder and Tippoo, is nearly of an oval form,

* Seyed Peer, the former kelledar had expressed doubts regarding the ultimate result of the siege, and was removed.

with round towers at proper intervals and five powerful cavaliers: a faussebray, a good ditch and covered way without palisades, and some well finished places of arms, but the glacis imperfect in several places: no part was entirely destitute of the support of reciprocal fire, but in no part was there a perfect flanking defence. There were two gateways, one named the Mysoor, the other the Delhi gate; the latter, opposite the petta, overbuilt with the projection of traverses common to Indian forts: the petta or town, of great extent to the north of the fort, was surrounded by an indifferent rampart and excellent ditch, with an intermediate berm, if such it may be called, of near one hundred yards wide, planted with impenetrable and well grown thorns; and this defence was only intermitted exactly opposite the fort, where there was a slight barrier, and an esplanade of insufficient extent: the petta had several gates, protected by a sort of flêche at the end of each sortie outside the ditch. Neither the fort or petta had draw bridges.

The part of the fort opposite the town was certainly not in itself the weakest; but the possession of the town, besides the hope of supplies, would furnish also some security in carrying on the operations of the siege. A disposition was accordingly made for attacking one of the gates with a regiment of Europeans, and one of native infantry, supported by an equal reserve, under Colonel Cockerel, with the usual field artillery and six battering guns under Colonel Moorehouse; for every thing within the ditch was rendered invisible by the thorny defence, and the nature of the point to be attacked was imperfectly understood. The flêche was carried at the point of the bayonet; the winding way, crossing the ditch, and over the planted berm, was scarcely

Mar. 7.

CHAP. XXXVII. 1791.

of sufficient breadth for the column of half companies. The application of a field piece was expected to force the gate, but it was built behind with masonry. Iron eighteen-pounders, prepared for the purpose, were then brought up; and during a very considerable period of resistance, the turrets of the gateway, lined with musquetry and rockets, poured a destructive fire on the column of troops. Two ladders would probably have saved many lives, but there was not one in camp; and after a long delay in making a practicable opening * in the gate, which the troops bore with the greatest steadiness and patience, the place was at length carried: but its great extent, and the difficulty of acquiring sufficient knowledge of all the localities, protracted the occupation of the whole.

The Sultaun astonished and indignant at this event, moved from Kingeri with his whole force, for the recovery of the petta; a long but thin column with numerous guns, moved in sight of the English army, in a direction to turn its right, the cavalry made a concealed detour, to a position where it was well placed to take advantage of any forward movement: but the main strength of the infantry under Kummer-u-Deen, moved by a route concealed from view into the petta, with positive orders to recover its possession at all risks; Tippoo himself being on the western glacis to inspect and animate their exertions.

* General Medows, whose presence on such occasions, always dispelled gloom, watched with anxiety for a sufficient opening; the fragments of the gate were torn open after each discharge, until a small man, (Lieutenant Ayre, of the 86th,) made his way through. "Well done," said the General, "now whiskers, try if you can follow and support the little gentleman;" addressing the grenadiers of the same regiment; a winding sally-port was found from within, by the first whoentered; a respect for the 18-pounders kept clear the direct line of the gate; but neither pikemen nor any other troops had been placed on the flanks of the terreplein to provide against a passage being forced.

Lord Cornwallis was not deceived by the demonstrations which he saw, but distinctly anticipating what he did not see, strongly reinforced the petta, and changed his disposition on the right: a distant cannonade was not returned, but in the meanwhile efforts for the recovery of the petta were made on a great scale, and for some time with considerable spirit. So long as the English troops continued to fire, the Sultaun's were not inferior *; but this mode was soon abandoned, by the Europeans for the never-failing bayonet. In a contest for the possession of streets and roads, this mode could neither be evaded nor withstood, and after a prolonged contest, in which the Mysoreans were successively driven from every quarter of the town in which they took post, and even pursued across a part of the esplanade, with a loss in killed and wounded of upwards of two thousand men, they ultimately evacuated the petta.

The casualties of the English on this day amounted to 131, but no loss made so deep an impression as that of Lieutenant-Colonel Moorehouse, who was killed at the gate. † He had risen from the ranks, but nature herself had made him a gentleman; uneducated, he had made himself a man of science: a career of uninterrupted distinction had commanded general respect; and his amiable character universal attachment: the regret of his

* It may, perhaps, be stated, without exaggeration, that the fire was superior, the musquet balls were cast in molds intersected by two divisions, at right angles with each other, and the shank was left, by which the bullet was fastened to the cartridge; the bullet accordingly separated into five parts, or if very close, a large spreading wound was inflicted; in either case the wounds were difficult of cure, but particularly in the latter.

† He received two wounds, but did not discontinue his animating exertions, till two other musquet balls in the breast terminated his existence.

General, and the respect of his Government were testified by a monument erected at the public expence in the church at Madras.

A hasty attempt had been made with partial success to burn the magazines of forage collected in the petta; the quantity saved prevented the total ruin of the cavalry and cattle, who afterwards prolonged a feeble existence on the sooty thatch of the poorer houses. The most valuable property had been removed on the approach of the English army; but bales of cotton and cloth in every direction indicated a great manufacturing town; and the private hoards of grain of the opulent merchants and inhabitants, could alone have prolonged the existence of the public followers till the termination of the siege.

With the exception of the lamentable error of the engineers in erecting the first battery without previously ascertaining its exact distance, and the loss of inestimable time in discovering its fire to be inefficient, the mere operations of the siege, skilful and highly honourable in all its subsequent progress, present no events within the scope of our general plan. Few sieges have ever been conducted under parallel circumstances: a place not only not invested, but regularly relieved by fresh troops; a besieging army not only not undisturbed by field operations, but incessantly threatened by the whole of the enemy's force.* No day or night elapsed without some new project for frustrating the operations of the siege; and during its continuance, the whole of the besieging army was accoutred, and the cavalry saddled, every night from sun-set to sun-rise. Among the most serious of these projects, was

an unexpected cannonade, within good range, from guns brought CHAP. XXXVII.
to their positions during a thick fog, on the rear of the park of
artillery, containing all the ammunition for the siege: happily 1791.
the steadiness of the artillery-men, and the ready aid of the next corps, enabled them to remove the whole behind the crest of a hill, without a single explosion. By the 20th the Sultaun Mar. 20.
perceived distinct indications of an early assault, and in the morning of the 21st, drew up his army on the heights to the south-west, to protect an advanced body with heavy guns, who had, on the preceding day, been observed opening embrazures in an old embankment, which, resting its left on an unfinished part of the south glacis, extended in a direction, and at a proper distance, to enfilade and destroy the whole of the trenches and open sap, now advanced near the crest of the glacis, and no longer covered by the works of the petta.

On perceiving these preparations, on the clearing up of a fog, about eight o'clock, Lord Cornwallis instantly struck his camp, 21.
and commenced a very imposing demonstration of serious attack on the enemy's right: the guns, nearly prepared to open from the embankment, were soon perceived to be in motion to support the position on the heights, which the Sultaun determined to defend, and Lord Cornwallis had not the slightest intention to attack, unless compelled to it by a resumption of the serious danger which threatened his approaches: the guns did return late in the evening to resume these preparations, and the crisis arising from this and other causes determined Lord Cornwallis to give the assault on the same night, under circumstances not sanctioned by ordinary practice.

The intention was concealed from his own army, until the

last moment, but it was confidentially made known at an early hour to the senior artillery officer on duty, who accumulated every possible means to perfect the breach, and take off the defences of all works which commanded it: the breach intended for the assault was made in the curtain, to the left of the projecting works of the gateway and part of the adjoining tower. The ditch, according to rule, was still to be filled, but a narrow causeway along the bottom of these projecting works, used as a communication by the troops employed in the faussebray had been observed and was trusted to. This however was eventually found to be cut across, but the assailants were provided with ladders of every dimension, and the duties allotted to the several flank companies and corps, were so judiciously arranged as to prevent the possibility of confusion. It was bright moonlight— eleven was the hour appointed, and a whisper along the ranks was the signal appointed for advancing in profound silence: the ladders were nearly planted, not only to ascend the faussebray, but the projecting work on the right, before the garrison took the alarm, and just as the serious struggle commenced on the breach, a narrow and circuitous way along a thin shattered wall, had led a few men to the rampart, on the left flank of its defenders, where they coolly halted to accumulate their numbers, till sufficient to charge with the bayonet. The gallantry of the kelledar who was in an instant at his post, protracted the obstinacy of resistance until he fell; but the energy of the assailants in front and flank at length prevailed. Once established on the ramparts, the flank companies proceeded as told off, by alternate companies to the right and left, where the resistance was every where respectable, until they met over the Mysoor gate: separate columns then descended into the body of the place; and at the expiration of an hour, all opposition had ceased.

On ascending the breach, a heavy column was observed on the left, advancing from the embankment described, to attack the assailants in flank and rear; but this also had been foreseen and provided for, and they were repulsed with great slaughter, by the troops reserved for that special purpose; a similar column lodged in the covered-way on the right, had been dispersed at the commencement of the assault, by a body appointed to scour it, and draw off the enemy's attention from the breach; and at the moment the flank companies had met over the Mysoor gate, another column was perceived advancing along the sortie, to enter and reinforce the garrison; but a few shot from the guns on the ramparts, announced that the place had changed masters. The carnage had been severe, but unavoidable, particularly in the pressure of the fugitives at the Mysoor gate, which at length was completely choaked: upwards of one thousand bodies were buried, but the number of the wounded was not ascertained: the mere casualties of the English army in the whole siege, did not amount to five hundred; but the other consequences of the service, had prepared subjects for a crowded hospital.

With whatever care Lord Cornwallis concealed his intentions, it is certain that they were distinctly known to the Sultaun, who warned the garrison that they were to expect the assault on that night; and with a similar intimation appointed two heavy corps to fall upon both flanks of the assailants. His camp was at a place named Jignee, about six miles to the south-west, and at night-fall he moved his whole army within a mile and a half of the

Mysoor gate, to support the place and avail himself of circumstances. The first circumstance on which he had to exercise his judgment, was the intelligence brought by crowds of fugitives that the place was actually carried: the column which approached the Mysoor gate had been sent to ascertain the fact, and attempt what should be practicable; but on their return in dismay, he remained in silence and stupor on the same spot until the dawn; when he returned to camp, and had leisure to reflect on the causes of this unexpected disaster. He had on every successive day of the siege drawn up an army of very superior numbers to the whole of the besiegers, sometimes in their view, and at others in concealed positions, with the intention, on each successive day, of serious attack; he had as often returned without attempting any thing of importance, on finding every plan foiled, exactly because none of his plans extended to closing in earnest with the enemy; and finally a storming party inferior in numbers to one-fourth of the ordinary garrison had surmounted obstacles deemed impassable, and carried the place in the presence and in spite of the efforts of his whole army fully apprized of the intended enterprise.

If the event were fatal to the Sultaun's hopes, it was of importance no less vital to the prospects of Lord Cornwallis. The forage and grain found in the petta had long been consumed, the neighbouring villages had all been effectually destroyed, and the resource of digging for the roots of grass within the limits of the piquets, had been so exhausted, that scarcely a fibre remained. The draught and carriage cattle were daily dying by hundreds at their piquets; and those intended for food scarcely furnished the unwholesome means of satisfying hunger. Grain, and every other necessary, including ammunition, were at the lowest ebb; and the most favourable result of raising the siege, under such circumstances, would have been the loss of the whole battering train, a retreat upon the depôts of Coromandel pressed by all the energy with which such an event could have inspired the Sultaun's army; and the resumption of offensive operations under such circumstances, balanced even by the advantages enumerated at the close of the campaign of 1790, might well be deemed a more serious undertaking than the actual commencement of a new war, with unbroken resources, whether the alternative be considered as a political or a military question. Past experience had not accumulated sufficient information for the complete guidance of Lord Cornwallis in the arduous enterprise with which he opened the war; and even with more perfect information, it is more easy to shew the existence than the remedy of defective means. But the siege having actually advanced to the point which has been described, it is indisputable that the fate of the campaign, and perhaps of the war, was necessarily cast upon a single chance, and that chance was successful.

CHAPTER XXXVIII.

March from Bangalore northwards — Hostile armies unexpectedly cross diagonally each other's route — Tippoo retires — Lord Cornwallis's object in this movement — A junction with the corps of horse provided by Nizam Ali — Cruel fate of the garrison of Little Balipoor — Junction with Nizam Ali's horse — Sketch of their appearance — and conduct — Character of its commanders — Lord Cornwallis's motives for hastening the attack on Seringapatam — Unusual means of equipment — Influence of the capture of Bangalore on the allies — on Tippoo — Evidence in the latter case — Letter from his mother to the wife of Nizam Ali — Paintings at Seringapatam — Horrible butchery of prisoners — Intercepted letter — Execution of the minister Kishen Row — Lord Cornwallis marches for the capital — Disappearance of the population — Increasing difficulties — Tippoo determines to risk a general action — Battle of the 15th of May — Move to Caniambaddy — Destruction of the battering train — Perilous detachment across the river — Return of General Abercromby to the coast — His loss — Departure of Lord Cornwallis before he knew of his safety — Dreadful state of the army — Unexpected appearance of the Mahratta army on the first march — Description of a Mahratta camp — mercantile police — bazar — trades — tanners — Rejoicings at Seringapatam — United armies move slowly to the north-east — Holioordroog — Incident descriptive of Mahratta Character — Move towards Bangalore — Plan of intermediate operations — English loan to the Mahrattas.

CHAP. XXXVIII. 1791. After this important capture, the most urgent want was that of forage for the preservation of the surviving cattle; but Lord Cornwallis could not quit the vicinity until such temporary repairs had been made at the breaches, as should place the fortress beyond the immediate risk of a coup-de-main. He Mar. 22. moved, however, at day-light on the 22d, from the exhausted and horribly offensive* encampment which he had occupied during the siege, to the west of the fort, near to the scene of operations on the 5th, where it was just possible to affirm, that some patches were not entirely destitute of grass. After effecting the repairs above stated, depositing the battering guns, and organizing an arsenal and artificers' yard to prepare for the siege of Seringapatam; he moved on the 28th, in a northern direction on the route of Deonhully, dispatching on the preceding night, a battalion, to prevent, if possible, the destruction of forage, in the village adjacent to the intended encampment. The Sultaun had moved on the same morning from the ground occupied by the English army on the 4th, in the direction of Great Balipoor; the roads on which the hostile armies were marching, crossed each other diagonally. The battalion had been misguided to a village on the right of the intended route, and at day-break the officer commanding perceived the Sultaun's columns of march crossing his front; he had no alternative but to take post; and the Sultaun, conceiving that he saw the English advanced-guard, quickened his pace to clear it. In the meanwhile, the real advanced-guard, pointing farther to the left, on ascending an eminence, saw the greater part of the Sultaun's army in nearly the same relative position, crossing diagonally at the distance of three miles, and also took post. On ascertaining these circumstances, Lord Cornwallis advanced with all possible expedition. The cattle, reduced to skeletons, were scarcely able to move their own weight; the soldiers, Eu-

CHAP. XXXVIII. 1791.

Mar. 28.

* The best police had been observed in burying the carcasses, but their numbers rendered all precautions ineffectual.

ropean and native, every where spontaneously seized the drag-ropes, and advanced the guns frequently at a run. The Sultaun personally covered his retreat with his horse. The English artillery successively dispersed them at every stand they attempted: the infantry continued the pursuit until the Sultaun was compelled to break into several columns, on different roads, to effect his retreat, losing only one brass nine-pounder and some ammunition; and the English army halted after a march of twenty miles, being double the distance it had been deemed possible to drag the cattle along, and pitched their camp in a situation surrounded with excellent dry forage.

This advantage continued as they advanced to the north, and the oxen recovered with the most surprising rapidity: the physical constitution of the animal prevented a similar improvement in the cavalry, and orders issued at this period for regulating the distribution of forage, were considered by that branch of the army, to have retarded the amendment of their condition. The Sultaun meanwhile collected his scattered columns near Great Balipoor on the same night after a march of twenty-six miles; but not considering his position about eleven miles from the English encampment, to be sufficiently distant, he resumed his march, after a few hours refreshment, towards Sevagunga, in a north-west direction.

The object of Lord Cornwallis's movement was a junction with the corps of cavalry prepared by Nizam Ali, to serve with his army: in passing the forts of Deonhully and Little Balipoor, which surrendered without opposition, the poligars of the latter territory, resuming the military spirit which they had opposed

to Hyder's earlier career, undertook the occupation of the place; a premature and unfortunate determination! for the actual garrison: the place was soon afterwards retaken by surprise and escalade, and the garrison, as rebels, suffered the horrible punishment of amputation of a leg and an arm each. Tippoo's activity against the English army was skilfully displayed in the dissemination of false intelligence: after a march of about seventy miles north, Lord Cornwallis remained stationary for five days; deceived by reports which induced him to abandon the hope of forming the junction, and to move south for the purpose of joining a convoy, April 11.
advancing by the passes near Amboor; but on the evening of his first retrograde march, he received more correct information, which caused him to resume the northern route, and the junction was formed on the second day afterwards, when the united 13.
bodies moved in the direction of the convoy, which was itself escorted by a reinforcement of nearly four thousand men. Tippoo projected a great effort to strike at this convoy, but was foiled in his preparatory movements, by the superior skill of his opponent; and the united bodies moved to Bangalore.

The short period of fifteen days' marching, without any se- 28.
rious occurrence, afforded to the English army a sufficient opportunity for estimating the probable value of their new allies. They were rated at 15,000, and really amounted to ten thousand men, well mounted on horses in excellent condition; and to those who had never before had an opportunity of observing an Indian army, their first appearance was novel and interesting. It is probable that no national or private collection of ancient armour in Europe, contains any weapon or article of personal equipment which might not be traced in this motley crowd; the

Parthian bow and arrow, the iron club of Scythia*, sabres of every age and nation, lances of every length and description, and matchlocks of every form, metallic helmets of every pattern, simple defences of the head, a steel bar descending diagonally as a protection to the face; defences of bars, scales or chain work descending behind or on the shoulders, cuirasses, suits of armour, or detached pieces for the arm, complete coats of mail in chain work, shields, bucklers, and quilted jackets, sabre proof. The ostentatious display of these antique novelties was equally curious in its kind. The free and equal use of two sword arms, the precise and perfect command of a balanced spear 18 feet long, of the club which was to shiver an iron helmet, of the arrow discharged in flight, but above all the total absence of every symptom of order, or obedience, or command, excepting groups collected round their respective flags; every individual an independent warrior, self-impelled, affecting to be the champion whose single arm was to achieve victory; scampering among each other in wild confusion. The whole exhibition presented to the mind an imagery scarcely more allied to previous impressions of reality, than the fictions of an eastern tale, or the picturesque disorder of a dramatic scene.

The impossibility of relying on such a body for the execution of any combined movement was sufficiently obvious; but the most moderate expectations looked to an enlargement of the limits of observation, the relief of the regular cavalry from

* *Gurz*, intended to destroy the defensive armour of the head, a handle like that of a sword, joined to a bar, about two feet long, and surmounted at the end with a globular knob, not entirely solid, but indented by eight or ten deep hollows, leaving a corresponding number of strong angular projections, radiating from an axis in continuation of the bar.

the duties of the light troops, and an extended command over the resources of the country to be traversed: two thousand of the most select were attached to the reserve under Colonel Floyd, and placed under the immediate management of Brigade-Major Dallas, in the hope that his skill, and conciliation, and example, might render them efficient. These fifteen days were sufficient to shew the total disappointment of the most meagre hopes. The enemy practised upon them in every successive day some enterprise or stratagem, always successful. They soon shewed themselves unequal to the protection of their own foragers on ordinary occasions; and after the lapse of a few days from leaving Bangalore, they never stirred beyond the English piquets, consuming forage and grain, and augmenting distress of every kind, without the slightest return of even apparent utility: their prowess was indeed exhibited at an early period, in plundering the villages to which Lord Cornwallis had granted protection; but when it was understood that his Lordship disclaimed such proceedings, but could not controul them, the villagers undertook their own defence; and the march would produce exhibitions of attack and defence, in which the wishes of the army were uniformly adverse to their allies, and an English safeguard would frequently appear protecting their enemies against their friends. The contemptible state of this cavalry may, in some degree, have arisen from the effeminacy and decline which marked the general character of the government to which they belonged; but its more immediate causes were referred to a commander, (Têdjewunt Sing, a Hindoo) of no respectability or military pretension, who was said to have risen to command by court intrigue; and was deemed better

CHAP. XXXVIII. 1791. qualified to render his master a good commercial account of the profits of the subsidy, than a splendid report of military glory. His second in command, Assud Ali, and the ostensible military leader, had some reputation for that precarious valour which depends on interested motives, or animal excitement and depression; but, like his principal, was incapable of command, venal, rapacious, and unfaithful to his trust.

The critical situation of public affairs in Europe, consequent on the portentous events of the French Revolution, added to the powerful motives of local policy and public economy, produced on the mind of the Governor-General an anxiety to hasten the conclusion of the war, by attempting the siege of Seringapatam, at a period which, under other circumstances might be deemed precipitate. The department of carriage for provisions, camp equipage, ordnance and stores, the most embarrassing branch of a General's care, had suffered during the siege of Bangalore, in a degree which required supplies from some of the most distant provinces, through the medium of the public contractors. Individuals had in some degree replaced their losses in the northern movement. To throw the greater part of the camp equipage into Bangalore, was a matter of public regulation; but Lord Cornwallis farther called forth the spontaneous exertions of the officers of the army, in a mode equally honourable to both, by requesting every individual to apply whatever means of carriage he had in his power to command, for the carriage of shot to the place of destination: and exclusively of the greatest practicable sacrifice of the means of conveying personal supplies, which it was obvious would totally cease after advancing from Bangalore, many officers were enabled by their influence among the natives, to hire, on their own account, carriages, which the proprietors would not consent to submit to the control of a public department. Followers of various kinds, chiefly the relations of sepoys, were also prevailed on to undertake, for remuneration, carriage proportioned to their means; even women and boys carrying each an 18 pound shot; and by these extraordinary expedients, the English General, with all his public departments in the most crippled state, was enabled to advance towards his object, with an equipment ample in every respect, excepting the reduced condition of his draught and carriage cattle.

The beneficial influence of the capture of Bangalore on the progress of the confederates, will hereafter be noticed. The agitation produced in the Sultaun's mind, and the guilty terrors by which he was haunted, will best be understood by a simple recital of his measures. After the easy success of an assault on Bangalore, which he had affected to consider as a mad and impracticable enterprise; his first impression was that of fear for the immediate fate of the capital, from a coup de main, without a regular siege; he accordingly dispatched two confidential officers, Kishen Row the treasurer, and Meer Sadik the dewan, to make immediate arrangements for the removal of the treasure, the harem, and the families of his officers, (the uniform pledge exacted by this dynasty) to Chittledroog. As a measure of military policy, if well timed, and judiciously executed, the question of its expediency would be suspended between the certain advantage of a protracted war, and the fatal impression to be produced on the minds of his troops and subjects, by overt demonstrations of despondency; and the latter consideration, strongly represented by his mother,

1791.

whose opinions he habitually respected, induced him to countermand that branch of the orders. The demolition of the bridge over the northern bank of the Cavery, opposite the western angle of the fort, was continued as a measure of prudence under all circumstances; and the leading features of his mean and merciless character, are marked with great precision by his other instructions. We have noticed, but have been restrained by decency from describing the terms of his offensive answers to the ladies of Nizam Ali's family at Adwâni; the impression of altered fortunes is strongly described in a letter which he caused his mother to address to the favourite wife of Nizam Ali, in which she supplicated compassion for an unfortunate Mussulman, her son, who in the pride and intoxication of youth, had given offence to her family, which he sincerely regretted; and the Mysoreans believe in the influence of this application over the measures of the worthless cavalry we have described.

The walls of the houses in the main streets of Seringapatam, had been ornamented by the Sultaun's command, with full length caricatures of the English. In one it was a tiger seizing a trembling Englishman; in another it was a horseman cutting off two English heads at a blow; in a third it was the nabob, Mahommed Ali, brought in with a rope round his waist, prostrating himself before an Englishman, seated on a chair, who placed one foot upon his neck; but the more favourite caricatures are necessarily excluded from decorous narrative. The anticipation must have been acute, which suggested the obliteration of all these favoured triumphs, and a positive order for carefully white-washing the whole of the walls.

The removal of these foolish indications of triumphant hostility and contempt, was perhaps a more conclusive testimony than any other of his considering the capture of the place highly probable; but conscience suggested more serious terrors, in the mass of living evidence at Seringapatam and elsewhere, of his detention of prisoners, in direct violation of the treaty of 1784. Of the English boys, educated as singers and dancers * twenty still remained; a secret order was dispatched for the murder of these unhappy youths as the first victims, and an imperceptible succession of most of the other prisoners of the preceding war. It was difficult to obtain precise information regarding details in which no individual would acknowledge instrumentality, or even ascribe it to another: the bodies were carried out at the first opening of the gates, by the common scavengers, to places of distant sepulture, and the assassination was supposed to be perpetrated by Abyssinian slaves, by the well understood practice of a sudden and violent twist to dislocate the vertebræ of the neck. The orders to the outposts were executed according to local circumstances, and the English army had afterwards direct evidence even to exhumation, of murders so committed, on persons who carried with them the anxious sympathy of the inhabitants; the order was extended to native state prisoners; and the horrible butcheries of this period exemplified, in the most impressive manner, the natural connexion between cruelty and fear.

Although the admirable efficiency of the Mysorean cavalry in the interception of intelligence, had tended to mislead the English General in his northern route, his Lordship, attaching the

* Their instruction, performance, and dress, was precisely that of an Hindostanee dancing girl.

CHAP. XXXVIII. 1791.

highest importance to this branch of the service, had on the first day of his joining the army, given an unlimited command of means to the officer charged with the department of intelligence, who repaid the confidence, by obtaining the best possible information, at the most moderate expence.* One of his emissaries was unfortunately detected at this period, with a letter in the Canarese language, concealed in his hollow bamboo or walking stick. The Sultaun, as we shall hereafter perceive, in reviewing the measures of his reign, had reasonable cause for distrusting all bramins, and such were all his secretaries for the languages of the south. A relation of his own (the brother-in-law of Seyed Saheb) who read the Canarese language, was entrusted with the examination of the letter, and the writer was seized; formerly a bramin, but forcibly circumcised, and now named Mahommed Abbas. The name of Sheshgere Row, brother of the treasurer Kishen Row, was implicated, and before he could be seized, he had heard of the accusation, and fled to his brother at Seringapatam; the treason seemed alarming and extensive, and Tippoo ordered the writer of the letter to be brought into his presence; Abbas perceived his death to be inevitable, and he resolved that it should be exemplary; he denied no part of his own imputed guilt, but boldly declared that no torture should compel him to implicate others. "And how long," said Tippoo, "have you been a traitor?" "From the period," replied he "that you began to circumcise bramins and destroy their temples." He was put to death, by being publicly dragged round the camp,

* Captain William Macleod, who, in 1790, required but the same confidence to have commanded the same success. The whole charge, under Lord Cornwallis, amounted to the incredibly small expenditure of about 200*l.* a month.

at the foot of an elephant; but the treasurer, Kishen Row, with three brothers, including Sheshgere Row, were privately tortured and dispatched. With whatever mystery these affairs were conducted, the acknowledged execution of one of the most able and intelligent officers of the state, could not but excite very general observation, and one half of the community continues under the impression, that as the letter was never submitted to the inspection of a bramin, the imputed participation of Kishen Row in any act of treachery, was a calumny invented by Seyed Saheb, in revenge for retrenchments made some years before, in the accounts of Dindegul.*

May 3.

These executions took place before the departure of Lord Cornwallis from Bangalore. The Sultaun, joined by the division from Gooty of Kuttub-u-Deen, (which had some time before been defeated by Assud Ali, and, according to his gasconade, utterly destroyed,) took a strong position in the main road to Seringapatam, usually named the Cenapatam road, supported by the hill forts of Ramgerry and Sevengherry, where he professed the intention of making a serious stand. — The English General had correct intelligence of the advantages of this position, and of the industry with which forage and grain had been destroyed on that route; and hoped to avoid some of those inconveniences, by adopting the more circuitous route of Caunkanhully nearer the Cavery. It was only on his first march, however, that he benefited by this unexpected determination; from that period forward, not only was every march preceded by a wide confla-

* I could never get Poornea, his colleague, to give an opinion. He kept aloof from enquiry; and of course from interposition, from the natural dread of consequences; and professed to have had no opportunity of forming a judgment.

CHAP. XXXVIII. 1791.

gration, but every human being on the route was so completely removed beyond the reach of the English army, that they appeared to be traversing a country of which the population had been utterly destroyed by some recent convulsion of nature; and in deprecating the cruelty of such measures, we cannot refuse the tribute of extraordinary efficiency to the light troops, who could execute such orders with such precision. It was of great importance to the department of intelligence, that some inhabitants should be found, and twice in the course of this route, detachments were sent in the direction of the river, for food, forage, and information; in the two former, the success was unimportant, but they failed to descry a single human being: in fact they were all collected with their cattle and moveables on the island of Sheven Summooder, the place afterwards so frequently visited by English travellers, on account of the magnificent falls of the Caveri.

The road was much intersected by rivulets and ravines, and the thunder storms in the evening, and by night, were accompanied by torrents of rain. The army marched as usual before daylight, and from local circumstances always by the left; and some idea may be given of the slow progress of a long and heavy train, by stating that the officer commanding the right wing, who had the care of supporting the rear guard, never reached camp until after sun-set. The exhaustion of the cattle daily encreased, and the quantity daily augmented, of stores destroyed, because they could not be carried on, although a large and encreasing proportion was dragged by the troops, and the pressure of the enemy on the rear was rather active than powerful. In this state, the followers, already in the greatest distress for grain, the army reached

Arikera, about nine miles east of Seringapatam on the 13th of May; the quantity of water in the river was already perceived to be discouraging to the prospect of any effective operation against the capital. One of those dams of masonry built across the river for the purposes of irrigation was near the encampment, the passage of the river below the dam was rocky and impracticable, and it was supposed that the rupture of the dam would lower the water and facilitate the passage of the river; but such was the solidity of the work, that the pioneers of the army contributed little to the intended effect, and the object was abandoned, in the expectation of finding a better ford at Caniambaddy, about eight miles above Seringapatam; for in every plan of operation against that capital, a communication was necessary with the army of Bombay under General Abercromby, who had ascended through the friendly territory of the raja of Coorg, and was already in possession of the fort of Periapatam, not forty miles distant from Seringapatam in a western direction.

1791.

May 13.

The Sultaun had not yet, from the commencement of the war in 1790, thought proper to risk a general action with the English army, and he supported the practice by quoting the example of his father, who obtained no advantage by any one of his general actions, but uniformly profited by striking at detachments. It was argued by those whom he admitted to his confidence, that the present leader of the English army pursued a system of measures which afforded little hope of such an opportunity. The example of the capture of Bangalore rendered it inexpedient in every opinion to leave the capital without the army; and under these circumstances there was no hope of striking an effectual blow against General Abercromby, except

CHAP. XXXVIII. 1791.

by a general action with Lord Cornwallis, which should cripple the equipments of that officer, and compel him to return for provisions to Bangalore. The representations of his most faithful officers, and even the remonstrances of his women, deprecated the disreputable effects of allowing his capital to be insulted without an effort; and these united considerations determined him to try the chances of a general action.

On arriving at the ground of encampment near Arikera, Lord Cornwallis perceived a considerable body of the enemy occupying strong ground about six miles in his front, with their right to the river, and their left along a rugged and apparently inaccessible mountain. This was at first considered as a detachment, but certain intelligence was received, during the ensuing night, that although a part only of the Sultaun's army was visible, the whole was present: that his whole front, placed on a continuation of the same strong ground, was strengthened by batteries above, and a swampy ravine below; and as the intermediate ground for the approach of the English army was narrowed by the river on their left, and a steep ridge of hills on their right, to a mile and a half at most, and in approaching the position to less than a mile; he was determined by these favourable circumstances to resist, on his present ground, the nearer approach of the English army to his capital. Lord Cornwallis ascertained, at the same time, that it was practicable to cross the ridge on his right, that after descending on the opposite side, and passing a continuation of the same swampy ravine which ran along the enemy's front, it was possible to ascend the tail of the same range of mountains which formed the Mysorean position, some miles to its left, where the range is crossed by the direct road from Cenapatam to the capital; and he resolved, on that information, to attempt by a night march, to turn the enemy's left flank, and by gaining his rear before day-light to cut off the retreat of the main body of his army to the fort and island of Seringapatam.

Orders were accordingly given with the utmost secrecy, for six regiments of European, and twelve of native infantry, with their field-pieces, and the most effective of the corps of cavalry to march at eleven o'clock; Nizam Ali's horse to follow at day-light; and the intelligence was only communicated at the moment of moving, in order that the plan might not be foiled by treachery. The rest of the army with the camp guards and picquets as they stood, remained to protect the camp, provisions, stores, and heavy artillery under Colonel Duff. Before the appointed hour, one of those heavy storms peculiar to the season set in with more than its accustomed violence. The cattle, scared by the lightning, and shivering under the torrents of rain, could scarcely be made to move. In the contrasted and irregular succession of vivid light and impenetrable darkness, almost every corps lost its way, and was moving in every variety of direction. Lord Cornwallis himself, with the best guides, was found to have advanced between four and five miles, accompanied by no more than one company and one gun: he, of course, halted; and the staff officer who made the discovery, and was confident of being able to find the column, by retracing the marks of the gun wheels, with the aid of the lightning, soon found the tracks completely obliterated by the deluge of rain, and narrowly escaped riding into the enemy's encampment.

Nothing could be done before the dawn, farther than getting

CHAP. XXXVIII. 1791.

the corps into their proper situations; the hope was extinguished of being able then to execute the original plan, or to resume it on the ensuing night, after the indication thus given of the intended movement. Lord Cornwallis therefore determined to persevere in endeavouring to force an action on ground which would probably be less advantageous to the enemy than that which he had chosen; and the consequences of a complete victory might, as his Lordship hoped, relieve many of his distresses, and hasten the conclusion of the war. That the movement had been totally unexpected by the enemy, was evinced by their taking no alarm, until the English army began to descend the heights east of the ravine. Tippoo Sultaun did not decline the meeting, and the praise cannot in justice be denied to him on this occasion, of seeing his ground, and executing his movements with a degree of promptitude and judgment which would have been creditable to any officer. In the rear of his position was the high hill of Carigat, crowned by a redoubt, and terminating abruptly at the Caveri; his own position was a lower branch from the same ridge of hills; and a more direct continuation of the Carigat hill descending northwards, formed a strong rocky ridge between two and three miles to his left, at right angles with the line of the English column descending the eastern hill to cross the same ravine which ran along his front.

A considerable body of çavalry and infantry with eight guns was soon perceived in rapid march to seize this rocky ridge, which was equally the object of the English General, and Tippoo very promptly changed the front of the main body of his army to the left, and afterwards advanced over a series of small hollows and eminences, formed by the annual fall of the waters from the Carigat ridge into the great ravine before described. The detached body completely anticipated the English column in the occupation of the rocky ridge, and opened its first guns just as the first English corps had cleared the hollow and the ravine: between that ravine however and the ridge of rocks thus occupied by the enemy was, first a gradual ascent, and then more level ground broken by large rocks, forming an imperfect ridge, parallel to that occupied by the enemy at the distance of about five hundred yards, but not so elevated; and these broken rocks were used as a support to the subsequent formations. In front of the English column was now a strong position occupied by a powerful corps, and on the left the main body of the enemy's infantry and guns, having changed front, were preparing to advance in line. It was necessary to oppose corresponding arrangements, and a formation was ordered of two unequal fronts united to each other at one and the same right angle. When a considerable part of the column destined to oppose a front to the left had reached its position, and was in the act of wheeling into line, the detached body of select cavalry concealed by the ground until within charging distance, made a respectable but unsuccessful effort to break the line, many horsemen falling on the bayonets. They did not desist on the first repulse, but hovered round, prepared to take advantage of the least disorder; the weak state of the gun bullocks, and the necessity of cautious movement, delayed the formation, and during that period some loss was sustained from the guns on the height opposite the ascending column, and from a well directed though distant fire from the cannon of the main body; each possessing an enfilade more or less perfect of the two lines of formation, if the English had not judiciously availed themselves of the cover afforded by the rocks and broken ground. The rocket, a weapon hitherto held almost in derision, because seen in small numbers it is easily avoided, performed perhaps on this day better service to the Sultaun than any other instrument, because his vicinity to the capital enabled him to discharge, at one and the same moment, flights too numerous to admit of being watched.

The formation of the English army being at length completed, the action commenced with the attack of the position on the rocky ridge, by the smaller of the two fronts, consisting of five battalions under Colonel Maxwell: the instant this was perceived, the eight guns were as usual drawn off, the infantry continuing a good countenance, and a heavy ill-directed fire of musquetry: but Colonel Maxwell, being unincumbered with guns, and having made a disposition for covering both flanks against cavalry, moved with such rapidity, that he not only quickly broke the infantry, but overtook some of the guns in the opposite descent of the hill; the infantry made a creditable struggle to carry them off, but were ultimately obliged to abandon three. The success of this attack was the signal for the advance of the remainder in two lines, against the main body of the enemy; and the action became general along that front. After passing the first of the undulating hollows which have been mentioned, and ascending the next height, the fire of Tippoo's artillery began to relax, but the infantry maintained a respectable countenance, covering the retreat of their cannon according to the uniform practice of the dynasty of Hyder, which never risked guns against the English, to perform their best service with grape. No opportunity had been afforded on this day, of making any effective use of the English artillery, and the first line was only enabled to advance by leaving its guns to the protection of the second, and on their near approach the enemy's infantry began to waver and retreat, making however a stand at each succeeding height.

Colonel Maxwell, who had been ordered, after carrying his first point, to look at once to the security of the right of the advancing line, and to turning the enemy's left, was rapidly succeeding in the latter object, and the Mysorean infantry retired with a more rapid step. At this moment the English cavalry under Colonel Floyd, who had been ordered to keep out of the enemy's range of shot, on the descent of the rising ground beyond the ravine followed by the allied cavalry, and ready to take advantage of any opportunity that might occur, charged the rear guard of the enemy's retreating infantry, which made a determined resistance, and nearly destroyed them. It was like a theatrical exhibition to the first line on ascending one of the swelling eminences described, to see their own cavalry unexpectedly charging the enemy across their front in the hollow below; the operation was executed by the men with perfect gallantry, but it was painful to observe that the exhausted horses were absolutely incapable of striking into a gallop; pursuing the object, they were checked by a heavy body of infantry which had rallied and made a stand, in a strong position of broken rocky ground. Colonel Floyd very properly drew off to leave this position to be forced by the infantry; but Nizam Ali's cavalry who had followed him across the ravine, had now thrown themselves in an unwieldy mass in front of the left wing, and could for some time neither be brought to advance nor recede to the left; the whole line was thus prevented from advancing, and an opportunity was afforded for the escape of the guns and infantry, a large portion of which, must otherwise have been inevitably captured or destroyed. It is asserted by many officers in the Mysorean army, that this impediment was designed, that a horseman with a particular badge, from Assud Ali, was seen at this moment to deliver a message to Tippoo, who was in the rear, anxiously urging the escape of his guns, of which many had been actually abandoned, but were recovered during this delay, and one only fell into the hands of the English in this branch of the attack; and that another messenger attended Tippoo on the same night. The author has since perused the active and treacherous correspondence with the enemy in this campaign, not only of Assud Ali, a person notoriously worthless, but of other officers of fairer fame in the same service, whose names it might be injurious to the English interests in India, to disclose at the present period.

On getting clear of this allied cavalry, the new position of the Mysoreans was quickly forced, and the pursuit was continued, until the works on the island covered the fugitives: the English army lay on their arms, nearly on the ground in which the action terminated, and after the arrival of the tents in the course of the night, encamped just beyond the range of the cannon on the island. The casualties of the English army on this day, did not exceed five hundred men; the Mysorean loss was uncertain, but is estimated by themselves at three or four times that amount.

As a mere evidence of superiority, the victory was complete, and had there been no movement of the cavalry, would have probably been very decisive. But the observation of Sir Eyre

Coote on a parallel occasion, was applied by an old officer to the present, " I would gladly exchange all these trophies, and the reputation of victory, for a few days' rice." The distress was already considerable, and would be felt with a daily-augmented pressure, in every successive day that the army should remain in a country so effectually desolated ; and the admirable efficiency of the Sultaun's light troops, had prevented all communication of General Abercromby's situation, on which Lord Cornwallis's determinations would very materially depend. From the redoubt on the summit of the Carigat hill which terminated the action on the right, a bird's-eye view was obtained of the greater part of the island of Seringapatam, and the eastern face of the fortress. Two successive marches by a circuit of twenty miles to Caniambaddy, gave the means of observing the northern face and western extremity. During the latter part of the march from Bangalore, many of the heavy guns, as well as the field pieces attached to corps, and in these two marches all the battering train, and almost every public cart in the army were dragged by the troops, and the reflection was not pleasant of exhibiting to the enemy, during two tedious successive marches, with an intermediate resting day, evidence so conclusive of the utter failure of all the equipments of the English army.

It appears, however, that it was not until after receiving the official reports of the morning succeeding the last march to Caniambaddy, that Lord Cornwallis saw the impossibility of moving the heavy guns and stores from the spot where they then were, felt the conviction that the accompaniment of this cumbrous impediment at such a season, was from the first a false measure, and saw the necessity of relinquishing entirely the plan of May 20.

CHAP. XXXVIII. the campaign, in which General Abercromby had been instructed to co-operate. The first orders for his return to Mala-
1791. May 21. bar, were accordingly written on the 21st of May, and on the same day considerable bodies of troops were observed, moving
22. towards him from Seringapatam. On the 22d, the destruction took place of the whole of the battering train and heavy equipments, and for the purpose of obviating unfounded impressions, a general order was issued, explaining to every soldier, European and native, the true motives of this measure, dressed in as cheering a garb as circumstances would admit. Still there was no intelligence from General Abercromby, nor of the hostile troops whose march had been observed on the 21st, and on
24. the 24th, his Lordship's anxiety became so great, that he risked the diversion in his favour, of passing three brigades under Colonel Stuart across the river, merely to attract the enemy's attention, but not to move to any distance from the river; a perilous measure which, in the event of its filling, would have placed those troops in a situation truly critical. They returned on the third day without intelligence. It was afterwards ascertained that the orders for the immediate return to the coast, of the army of Bombay had been entirely unexpected, but were carried into immediate execution. Misconceptions regarding the direction of the march, caused the capture of a large portion of the baggage, and an unhappy error in the medical department, the sacrifice of an officer and seventeen sick in the hospital. Four iron 18-pounders, imperfectly destroyed, were left at Periapatam, but the army, burying the remainder of its battering train at the summit of the pass, reached the coast without any farther casualties from the enemy, but with

the destruction of nearly the whole of the cattle from the severity of the season, and a corresponding influence on the health of the troops.

Before receiving any authentic account of General Abercromby's march, Lord Cornwallis experienced the necessity of moving from Caniambaddy. All that had occurred of mortality among the cattle during the siege of Bangalore, fell far short of the horrible scene and pestilential air of this disgusting ground. Among the variety of untried expedients for conveying stores and provisions on leaving Bangalore, that of issuing to the native troops three times the quantity of grain they usually carried, was the least likely to succeed: the experiment was made, in the hope that means would be found by individuals, among their followers and friends, of conveying the surplus quantity of an article on which depended their future subsistence; but the temptations of hunger were paramount to all obligations, and many sepoys were actually without food before half the calculated period had elapsed. The ration of rice to the fighting men had now for some time been necessarily reduced one half; the appearance of the sepoys, of whom a large portion live exclusively on vegetable food, indicated a gradual but very perceptible wasting and prostration of strength; many followers had actually died of hunger, and more were verging in various degrees to the same extremity; the animal food would, under any other circumstances, have been rejected with disgust; some groves of cocoa-nut and areca which had been felled for the substance resembling cabbage found at their summit, had furnished to Europeans a pleasant but most indigestible resource. A bleak wind and continued drizzling rain had more than its usual in-

1791. fluence on constitutions shaken by other causes, and greatly augmented the sufferings of the troops, and particularly of the division which had been without any cover to the south of the river, not one of whom escaped the consequent effects, and one young regiment, on its return to camp, was reported incapable of furnishing the camp guards.

May 26. In a condition thus imperfectly sketched, the army on the 26th commenced its march for Bangalore, by a route to the northward of either of those already mentioned. Every practicable exertion and contrivance was adopted for the conveyance of the sick, and among the most efficient, a regiment of native cavalry paraded in front of each regiment of European infantry that had suffered most, and the dismounted native dragoon led and supported his drooping comrade, as the only possible mode of moving without the abandonment of the sick. When scarcely half of a short march had been accomplished, a body of about two thousand horse, evidently increasing in numbers, made their appearance on the left of the principal column of march near its rear, on the very ground, as was afterwards ascertained, that bounded the field of Chercooli; and although the enemy's army was known to be in the opposite direction, little doubt was entertained from the point at which this body made its appearance, of an immediate attempt on the stores and baggage moving on that flank. Prompt dispositions to frustrate the attack were ordered by Colonel Stuart, who commanded in the rear: and they were not completed, when one of his staff, employed on the left flank, in giving directions regarding the skirmishers, was addressed in a loud voice by one of the horsemen, announcing that he was a Mahratta, and begging that the firing might cease.

Although no suspicion had been entertained of the existence of a Mahratta army within one hundred and fifty miles, the request was complied with. The horseman approached, and the most satisfactory evidence was given of the presence of two Mahratta armies at the distance of a few miles; that of the Poona state, under Hurry Pundit, the Commander-in-chief, and the more efficient army of Purseram Bhow, of which the cavalry in sight was the advanced guard, under his son. Other messengers had taken the direction of the head of the column where the Commander-in-chief was; and before the army reached its ground of encampment, his Lordship received new evidence of the unparalleled excellence of the enemy's light troops; in finding that, not only while distant, every customary means had been employed of transmitting to him distinct intelligence of every successive step in the approach of the Mahratta army, but that in their nearer approach, with an overwhelming and certainly not an inactive cavalry, they were prevented by comparatively a few straggling horsemen, from conveying even the rumour of their approach, until actually in sight.

Lord Cornwallis had certainly reason to complain of the imperfect execution of the promises made by the Mahratta chiefs, but if he had possessed even a few days before, accurate information of their tardy advance, the circumstances of the campaign would probably have assumed a different colour. The relief of hunger was the most urgent want in the English army, in which, perhaps, not one individual had, for the last fortnight, partaken of a wholesome meal; and the inimitable mercantile police of a Mahratta chief, in his own camp, was never more skilfully exhibited than on this occasion, in holding up exorbitant prices until the resources of individuals were exhausted, and gradually adapting the supply to the simple capacity of payment. It was however a spectacle of just retribution, to see the troops of Nizam Ali sharing in the exactions which their own torpor had chiefly contributed to produce: but even the influence of example was inefficient to rouse to energy these stately cavaliers, in all respects singularly contrasted to the mean aspect, and black meagre visage of the common Mahratta horseman, who foraged at large, and effectually commanded the resources of the country.

The bazar of a Mahratta camp presented an exhibition of no ordinary character: and to their famished visitors, exhibited a picture of the spoils of the east, and the industry of the west. From a web of English broad cloth, to a Birmingham pen-knife; from the shawls of Cashmire to the second-hand garment of a Hindoo; from diamonds of the first water, to the silver ear-ring of a poor plundered village maiden; from oxen, sheep, and poultry, to the dried salt fish of Concan: almost every thing was seen that could be presented by the best bazars of the richest towns: but above all, "the tables of the money changers," overspread with the coins of every country of the east, in the open air, and public street of the camp, gave evidence of an extent of mercantile activity, utterly inconceivable in any camp, excepting that of systematic plunderers, by wholesale and retail. Every variety of trade appeared to be exercised with a large competition, and considerable diligence, and among them one apparently the least adapted to a wandering life—*the trade of tanner* was practised with eminent success. A circular hole dug in the earth, a raw hide adapted to it at the bottom and sides, and secured above with a series of skewers run through its edges into the earth, formed the tan-pit: on marching days, the tan-pit with its contents, in the shape of a bag, formed one side of a load for a horse or bullock, and the liquid preparation was either emptied or preserved, according to the length or expected repetition of the march: the best tanning material* is equally accessible and portable, and the English officers obtained from these ambulatory tan-pits, what their own Indian capitals could not then produce, except as European imports — excellent sword belts.

The large convoys of provisions and plunder coming up in the Mahratta rear, rendered it necessary, on consultation with the chiefs, to continue for some time interposed between them and Tippoo's army in the present vicinity. Lord Corwallis was on the 27th relieved by letter from all uneasiness regarding General Abercromby, although on the preceding evening a salute of rejoicing from the ramparts of Seringapatam had created serious uneasiness. As a token of joy for the deliverance of the capital it was entirely unfeigned, but it also pretended to announce a complete victory, with the capture of General Abercromby's battering train, and the unhappy hospital patients were exhibited as authentic evidence of these pretensions. May 27.

Moving slowly to the north-east, the English army passed the vicinity of Hooliordroog, a small impregnable rock with a town at its foot; the town was easily carried, and the garrison capitulated on the usual terms of security for private property, and a special condition of protection against the Mahrattas.

* *Catechu*, a vegetable preparation, long known in Europe by the strange name of Terra Japonica.

CHAP. XXXVIII. 1791.

The condition was religiously observed, and the garrison and inhabitants who had taken refuge on the rock, moved at their own request in the direction of Madoor, under the care of a sufficient English escort; the officer had directions to accompany them the whole distance if required, or until the kelledar should consider himself entirely safe. Not a single Mahratta horseman was seen to hover near, and after marching about half way, no danger being any longer apprehended, the kelledar, with many assurances of gratitude, informed the officer, that he would trouble the escort no farther; and they accordingly parted in opposite directions; but no sooner was the distance sufficient to prevent the possibility of relief, than these unhappy people were surrounded by Mahrattas, and plundered of all their property down to the meanest article of wearing apparel. Considered as an event in the campaign, the plan of this work would pass without notice, an incident productive of no military or political result; but as an illustration of national character the anecdote may hold a fair claim to the space which it occupies. As Hooliordroog, if now held by a garrison of ordinary strength, would necessarily be in a state of siege or blockade until the armies should advance in the ensuing season, the place was dismantled and abandoned, and the united armies proceeded slowly towards Bangalore.

Before reaching that place, the intermediate plan of operations was finally adjusted, of which the first preliminary was a loan of 144,000*l.* to the Mahrattas, who of all the confederates had been personally and nationally most enriched by the war, from the English who had hitherto been personally and nationally impoverished. Lord Cornwallis had not to consider the moral rapacity which dictated the demand, but the political benefit of compliance to prevent their retiring behind the Toombuddra; and the intelligent reader will not fail to remark, that no other Commander-in-chief than the Governor-general of India could possibly have secured this advantage, the sum being realised by a simple order to stop the commercial investment of dollars in its transit from England to China. Purseram Bhow, with his own army, accompanied by the detachment of Bombay troops, proceeded by the vicinity of Sera, for the purpose of operating to the north-west; Assud Ali, with the mass of Nizam Ali's cavalry, relieved Lord Cornwallis from the intolerable burden of their presence, and the forces of that state were to operate to the north-east. Hurry Punt was to remain with Lord Cornwallis as the representative and plenipotentiary of the Mahratta government for political purposes: Têdgewunt remained in his former charge of military commander, for which he was eminently unfit, but was relieved in his diplomatic trust by Meer Aalum, a man of real talent; and each of these representatives of their respective sovereigns was attended by a select body of cavalry, to aid in the general operations of the English army, while their own cavalry should be sent to Coromandel to recover and recruit. It was his Lordship's share of the general plan to interpose his army between the enemy and the Company's possessions for their security, for the convenience of gradually drawing forward his supplies; for reducing such of the intermediate fortresses as were necessary to these ends; and for the further object of establishing an uninterrupted chain of tenable posts from Madras to Seringapatam, by which small convoys or grain merchants might proceed with little or no escort, whenever the season should admit of the armies taking their ultimate ground before the enemy's capital: and in the meanwhile the operations thus allotted to each branch of the confederacy, enabled the whole to subsist, in a great degree, on the resources of the enemy's country.

CHAPTER XXXIX.

Recurrence to the prior operations of the other armies — Army of Bombay — Coorg — its former history — and singular manners — Balance of blood — Raja restores his authority with energy and sagacity — Successful operations against Tippoo's troops — Misfortune of his family — First acquaintance with the English — improved — fixes their attachment by his gallantry and conduct — General Abercromby marches through his country — Mercara, the capital, possessed by the Mysoreans, on the point of surrender — relieved by the raja's express permission — Singular and romantic explanation — General Abercromby's confidence of resuming his former position — Nizam Ali's operations — Number and character of the forces under his personal command — proceeds to Paungul — his army to Rachore — to Capool — Description of the place — siege — surrender — march towards Kurpa — Gungicota — Results — Mahratta operations — Detachment from Bombay under Captain Little — ascends the ghaut of Amba — joins Perseram Bhow — United force moves to Darwar — Awkward and protracted siege — Reinforcement under Colonel Frederic — Misapprehension of wants — Premature assault — Repulse — Chagrin and death of Colonel Frederic — Major Sartorius — Promises of the Mahrattas constantly violated — All operations interrupted and precarious — Place capitulates after six months siege, for want of provisions — Garrison march away — are attacked and destroyed — Reciprocal accusations of violating the capitulation — Perseram Bhow with the English corps, advance to Seringapatam — Hurry Punt by another route — Junction as before described — Result of these operations — Negotiations during the campaign.

CHAP. XXXIX. 1791.

THE convenience of uninterrupted narrative has not permitted us to deviate into the prior history of the several armies which were concentrated near the capital of Mysoor; but the

CHAP. XXXIX. 1791. separation of the allies near to Bangalore, offers a period of natural pause, to look back at the preceding operations, first of the army of Bombay, before it received orders for its temporary return to Malabar; and afterwards, of the allied armies previously to their junction with Lord Cornwallis; but in no farther detail than may be requisite for explaining the nature and extent of General Abercromby's prospects for regaining the position from which he had retired; and conveying a correct impression of the actual progress of each branch of the confederacy towards the ultimate object of the war.

Our last notices of Malabar left General Abercromby the Governor of Bombay, in possession of Cannanore, and the whole province of Malabar, supported, with the exception of the Mapillas (Mahommedans,) by the anxious wishes of the great mass of the population, who rested their only hope of emancipation from the tyranny of the house of Hyder on the success of the English arms. The intermediate country of Coorg, which has frequently occupied our notice, interposes its mountains on the shortest route from Malabar to Seringapatam; and General Abercromby found a still more zealous ally in the extraordinary man who then governed that cruelly depopulated country as its raja.

In the course of those operations which preceded the death of Hyder, the raja of Coorg, with all his numerous family, were taken, and imprisoned in the fort of Cuddoor, on the eastern frontier of Bednore; the raja died, and when Tippoo passed that place in 1783, considering it to be within the reach of enterprise from Bednore, he ordered the family to be removed, by an inexplicable selection, to the fort of Periapatam, on the eastern frontier of the woods of Coorg. Among the prisoners was the raja, of whom we speak, then a youth about fifteen. In this situation, scarcely provided with the necessaries of life, neglected, and unobserved, he had an opportunity of witnessing the sympathy excited in the minds of even the Mysoreans, by the wretched fate of his country, and the barbarous expatriation of his subjects; and his situation on the direct route by which they were driven, like herds of cattle to the shambles, occasionally presented to his direct view, objects to rouse in his youthful and ardent mind, the distant hope of one day avenging their common wrongs.

With the assistance of some faithful friends of the family, who hovered in the woods, and found means of communicating the project they had formed, he escaped from Periapatam in 1788. It was probably after this event, that Tippoo Sultaun ordered the remainder of the family to be removed to Seringapatam; where, after the customary scrutiny, two females, sisters of the raja, were received into the royal harem*; and a third, deemed unworthy of that honour, had a destination of which we shall presently speak. The unhappy raja found his country depopulated, the lands in the possession of strangers, and the few remaining Coorgs prolonging a concealed and precarious existence in the woods, hunted wherever they were heard of, by the troops and new possessors. The young raja placed himself at the head of this remnant of the fortunes of his house, and began to retaliate on his oppressors: he was heard of every where, but seen no where, and with the pretensions of a hero, led the life of a chief of banditti. At a very early period of

* They were restored to the raja, after the capture of Seringapatam.

these adventures, while pursued by encreasing numbers of Mysorean troops, he was deceived by amicable messages, to put himself into the power of his southern neighbour, the raja of Cota Angâree, with whose house there had been an ancient family feud; and repaired to his residence below the ghauts, at a place named Paulee. In the history of every people, a period occurs, when the law of retribution precedes the establishment of regular government; constituting in some degree, the point of honour of that period of society; and our European ancestors scarcely kept a more correct account current, of wrong, and reparation, than is exhibited in the following abstract of this transaction, as related by the raja himself.*

When completely in the power of his host, without the possibility of escape, he received the following proposition. " Your grandfather slew one of my ancestors, I demand a head in return." — *Answer*, " Your ancestor opposed mine in open warfare, one hundred years ago, and was slain. I am here as your guest, trusting to your honour, and your promise; and instead of giving protection, you revive an antiquated claim of blood. I am in your power, and that is my answer." A paper was then produced, and the raja was distinctly told, that he must either make payment with his own head, or terminate the feud by signing the paper. He signed the act, of surrendering as the price of blood, certain of his districts above the ghauts. He was permitted to depart; and the raja of Cota Angâree in person took immediate possession of the districts, which happened to afford a convenient retreat during Tippoo Sultaun's

* In the work noticed in the preface to vol. i. page xix.

active proceedings in the lower countries at this period. But while believing the raja of Coorg to be incapable of collecting fifty men, he found himself unexpectedly surrounded by five hundred, and completely at his mercy: the conversation which ensued completes the history of this singular transaction. — *Raja of Coorg*, " Render an account of your reasons for an hostile ascent of the ghauts." — *Answer*, " You know that you have surrendered this district, as the price of blood, and I am here on my own territory." — *Raja of Coorg*, " Your ancestor was slain by mine in fair battle, upwards of an hundred years ago; no retribution was ever demanded by your house from mine, until, by an unmanly breach of hospitality and faith, you extorted a forcible signature. That was not a convenient time to remind you of what you shall not now forget — the blood of two princes of my house, slain by you in Wynââd. You are now in my power, without a breach of hospitality. Against the head of one of these princes let the head of your ancestor be placed, and your own head shall balance the other." — *Raja of Cota Angâree*, " I admit the statement to be correct; but instead of my head, accept as the balance of the price of blood, the district of Wynââd, as far as Culpâty, a long-contested territory between our houses, to which I shall formally surrender my claim, and cancel the instrument which you signed at Paulee." This proposition was accepted; and in the instrument of transfer (given at length in the raja's life,) the debts and credits, and the adjustment of the balance of blood, are minutely recited. In such a state of society, the casuistry is remarkable, of distinguishing between the validity of an instrument forcibly executed, with or without the occurrence of previous fraud; and that some

1791.

value was annexed to an obligation extorted by mere force, which, among civilized nations, would be considered void, is evident from the corresponding forbearance in shedding blood. The reluctance to increase the balance of revenge, will afford no explanation consistent with the ordinary history of human conduct ; and we can only contemplate as an exception, the rare evidence which will presently appear, that the quality of mercy doubly blessed, was not without its estimation among the chosen spirits of this semi-barbarous race.

During these transactions, the raja had been busily occupied in conveying intelligence of his wishes to the survivors of the dispersed population ; and his numbers gradually but rapidly encreasing, he soon found himself in a situation to dispossess the new occupants. They were of two descriptions, and demanded distinct treatment ; Mahommedans who had accepted establishments as a boon from the Sultaun, and the inhabitants of Adwânee, treacherously swept off at the conclusion of the Mahratta war, and forcibly settled in Coorg. To the latter he afforded such means as he possessed of returning to their native country, the Mahommedans he treated in all respects as enemies, and such as were not slain in the first encounters, quickly abandoned their habitations, to be re-occupied by the Coorgs. The country, however, had profited little from the industry of its new masters, and it was farther injured in the struggles for its re-occupation.

Cattle, implements of husbandry, seed corn, and even the means of immediate subsistence were wanting ; and for all these the raja laid under contribution the territory of his enemy ; along an extensive line of frontier, his incursions skilfully varied, were always successful; and he had the satisfaction of seeing, in the course of that and the succeeding year, a thriving population, hardened by misfortune, and instructed by experience, capable of surrounding him with near four thousand faithful warriors. A detachment passing to Malabar, at the time when he began to shew himself in force, was defeated in its descent of the pass, with the loss of 1,200 men: and the Sultaun upon proceeding to Malabar in 1789, marched a division of his army, under Burhân-u-Deen through Coorg, for the purpose of revictualling the posts; but before he could effect this object, the raja had carried two out of the four, one by a coup-de-main, and the other by encouraging a strong garrison to sally upon apparently inferior numbers, turning upon them with fury, and entering with the fugitives. Burhân-u-Deen effected the provisioning of the two remaining posts with considerable loss. One of these mounting seven guns was soon afterwards reduced, and Mercara alone remained, a post erected by Hyder near the usual residence of the former rajas as the head-quarters of the Mysorean troops in Coorg. In the midst of these successes, however, his enemy the raja of Cota Angâree was not afraid to encrease the balance of revenge, and while the Coorg was engaged in the open encounter of the Sultaun's troops, stole upon the retirement of the raja's family in the woods, and in the affray, two of his wives, a nephew, and many children were killed, and the retreat was plundered of all the domestic valuables, collected by his ancestors, all of which had hitherto escaped the general ruin.

But better fortunes awaited him in another quarter. The accidental mission of a confidential servant to make some purchases at Tellicherry, brought him into communication with Mr. Taylor, the chief of that English establishment. Their common interests and views were quickly understood; authority was received from Bombay, and a system of mutual co-operation was concerted for the invasion of Mysoor, with the inestimable advantages of passing through the country of an ally till within forty miles of the enemy's capital. In direct opposition to ordinary practice, in the country and class of civilization to which he belonged, every promise of this singular man was most sacredly performed, and generally overstepped. To an application for aid in gun bullocks, he correctly replied, that those of Coorg were as unfit for military purposes as the cattle of Malabar; but he immediately made a most hazardous irruption into Mysoor, in which he carried off and sent to the English an acceptable supply of the best quality from the Sultaun's stock, and repeated the enterprise on every favourable opportunity. In provisions, intelligence, and aid of every kind, he anticipated the wishes of his friends, and rivetted their admiration by his frank and romantic gallantry.

In conformity to the plan of operations directed by Lord Cornwallis, General Abercromby commenced his march to the eastward, with four European regiments, five sepoy battalions, and a suitable artillery, in February 1791. He had water conveyance as far as Iliacore, within 26 miles of the ghaut; but the subsequent difficulties required a large exercise of patience and skill, and could not have been surmounted in the face of an enemy; every separate gun being hoisted over a succession of ascents by ropes and tackles. Mercara, the only remaining post occupied by the Mysoreans, had long been invested by the Coorgs, and the raja had given reason to expect, that a few days more would determine its surrender; intelligence however was received of the approach of a convoy of provisions, escorted by a respectable division of the Sultaun's army; and of its being, after a severe action, surrounded by the raja, without the possibility of escape. While General Abercromby was in hourly expectation of learning its surrender, the raja was himself the first to announce, that although the convoy was completely at his mercy, he had allowed it to enter Mercara, and the escort to return in safety. Such a fact, however explained, would, in ordinary cases, be considered as direct evidence of treachery; but the raja's statement, as given in the manuscript, added to his singular character, now sufficiently understood, removed every shadow of suspicion from the mind of General Abercromby.

He explained that during his confinement at Periapatam, the officer commanding, influenced by compassion, (and probably by the interesting character of his young charge,) had been induced to allow of his walking out occasionally on parole, to take the diversion of hunting in the woods. In one of these excursions, he was benighted near a Mysorean post, within the frontiers of Coorg, and the officer commanding, Kâdir Khân Khêshgee, being informed of the circumstance, invited him to his house, and entertained him with hospitality and kindness until the morning: this was the officer who now commanded the escort, and this is the whole extent of obligation stated in the manuscript; but there was another of greater importance, whicn delicacy prevented his relating. On the occasion already noticed, of selecting two of the raja's sisters for the royal harem,

CHAP. XXXIX. 1791.

Kâdir Khân, who was a personal favourite of his sovereign, obtained as a special distinction, the honour of receiving the rejected lady; she was sent to his house, was attended by a person of her own cast, and lodged in a separate apartment, where he never approached her, and availed himself of the first unsuspected opportunity of sending her secretly to her brother's protection.

After the action which has been noticed, in which Kâdir Khân lost above seven hundred men, a disposition was made by the Coorgs, to fall upon the convoy at the dawn of day, with the national broad-bladed instrument, common to this people and to the Nairs; but before commencing the attack, the raja caused proclamation to be made at their outposts, that he acknowledged his obligations to Kâdir Khân, and desired to spare his life. A conference ensued, in which it was pleaded, that the acceptance of individual safety, would cause the destruction of his family, and that his return without executing the service, would be fatal to himself. The raja, with a prodigality of romance, exceeding whatever has been related in the authentic tales of western chivalry, not only allowed the convoy to enter the place, and the escort to return, but at the instance of his friend, extended the courtesy to the kelledar of Mercara, who must have surrendered in a few days to the English army; it was accordingly agreed, that he should eat his provisions as fast as appearances could justify, and then be permitted to capitulate on condition of a safe conduct to Seringapatam; and the raja not only declined the offer of General Abercromby's assistance in the reduction of the place, but supplied the garrison with carriage and safe conduct, and presented them on their departure with a liberal pecuniary donation to supply their future wants *: the walls were then razed to the ground, and he committed himself and his people to the national defence of their courage and their woods. The subsequent incidents connected with our design up to the period of the return of the English army to Malabar, have been already related, and no farther explanation will be necessary to shew the solid grounds of expectation that General Abercromby would be enabled to resume, at the the proper season, from the same advanced position, the part allotted to him in the future operations of the war. We proceed to resume the prior operations of the allies.

The army of Nizam Ali began to assemble in the neighbourhood of Hyderabad, in May 1790, and was joined by the stipulated English detachment of two battalions of sepoys, under Major Montgomery, with the addition of a company of European artillery, for the purpose of the intended siege of Capool. The cavalry individually resembled that under Assud Ali, but were somewhat better commanded; and the infantry under Monsieur Raymond, an intelligent and enterprising Frenchman, was as good as, with indifferent arms and extremely imperfect means of enforcing discipline, he could be expected to make them. A gorgeous mass, numerically sufficient for the conquest of the whole peninsula, moved southwest, at first to Paungul, which was the limit of Nizam Ali's personal campaign, and afterwards, with long and repeated

* After the capture of Seringapatam in 1799, the Raja invited his friend Kâdir Khân to Coorg, where he was received in all respects as a brother of the family. The raja presented him with a large estate, suitably provided with cattle, implements of husbandry and labourers, and on this estate he resided in great affluence until his death, which occurred in 1806.

delays to Rachore, within their own dominions, and there remained until authentic intelligence was received of the descent of Tippoo's army to Coimbetoor in September, when, free from the alarm of interruption, and carrying ruin and devastation in their train, they sat down before Capool on the 28th of October.

A lofty and precipitous rock, surmounted by a rampart, and containing a central citadel commanding the interior area, might enable its defenders to smile at more efficient means. The cannon placed in the batteries were of so bad a quality, that in one week they were disabled by their own fire, a fact of which no previous assurance could convince Nizam Ali's general; and a new battering train, to be brought forward from various points, did not arrive before the middle of January, 1791. The English artillery performed in the most satisfactory manner the duties required by that branch of the service; and the infantry was equally efficient — but the obstinate ignorance of Nizam Ali's commander, rendered their skill and energy of little avail. On the 18th of April, 1791, the place surrendered by capitulation, and Behauder Benda, a similar post about three miles to the northward, acceded to the same terms. Both places were amply garrisoned, and provided with every thing necessary for a much longer resistance; but the unexpected intelligence of the fall of Bangalore, which, correctly viewed, augmented the obligations of defence, had, in the ordinary influence of such events on the human mind, produced a converse operation. Capool had been invested for upwards of five months, and the intelligence which damped the energies of the garrison, furnished them also with a plausible apology for surrender. After the requisite arrangements in that vicinity, the army directed its march to the south-east to regain Kurpa and its dependencies, lost in 1779: Gunjycota surrendered about the time that Lord Cornwallis left Caniambaddy; minor places fell without resistance; but in many instances the fall was merely nominal, it was the submission of poligars who held or had recovered their own places, ever ready to bend to circumstances, and preferring Nizam Ali as a master, only because he could be disobeyed with impunity; with these reservations, however, Goorumconda was the chief place of strength and importance which remained to be reduced in that quarter, and this branch of the confederacy had, with slender merits, accomplished very considerable objects.

The Mahrattas, like Nizam Ali, ostensibly took the field at the same period as the English. The detachment of two battalions of sepoys, with one company of European, and two of native artillery, under Captain Little, destined to act with the army of that state according to treaty, embarked at Bombay, in May, 1790, and entering the river of Jaigur, nearly two degrees to the southward, proceeded in the same boats as far as the river was navigable, and then debarking ascended the ghaut of Amba, in the very depth of the monsoon. On the 26th of June, they joined the army under Perseram Bhow, (Putwurdun) at Coompta, a place about fifty miles south-east from the head of the pass. Meritch, the capital of this chief, is situated near the river Kistna. The removal of an hostile and dangerous frontier, was of the utmost importance to the security of his own possessions; and the virulence of political hostility was aggravated by the personal violation perpetrated on one of his family after the capture of * Neergôond in 1785. The interests of the confederacy in that quarter, could not, therefore, have been committed to Mahratta hands more likely to conduct them with earnestness and zeal; and the force under his command has been rated at 20,000 horse, and 10,000 infantry. The first national object was the recovery of those provinces between the five rivers † obtained by the house of Hyder during the civil war of Ragoba; and of these provinces Darwar was deemed the capital, and principal military depôt, situated on a plain, with the usual annexation of a large fortified town, but both constructed with as much care and strength, as is compatible with an entire ignorance of scientific principles.

Its defence, and the military government of the province, were committed to Budr-u-Zemân Khân, the most respectable officer in the Mysorean service, with a division of five regular cushoons, furnished with a complete field equipment of guns, and an unlimited command over the irregular infantry of the province, a force which Perseram Bhow could not, with any military prudence, leave in his rear. The rivers being full, and the season unfavourable for military operations, he did not commence his march from Coompta until the 3d of August, and arrived before Darwar on the 18th of September. In spite of the opportunity of receiving better counsel, the old Mahratta tactic of firing into the town from a distant eminence during the day, and withdrawing the guns at night, was continued for

* See vol. ii. page 538.

† Kistna, Gutpurba, Malpurba, Werda, Toombuddra.

about forty days. On the 30th of October, Perseram Bhow moved to occupy a more advanced position on a different face of the fort. The actual strength of the garrison at this time was estimated at 7,000 regular firelocks, and 3,000 irregulars, and Budr-u-Zemân Khân, with about 2,000 men and four guns, moved out to an exterior position, to prevent the occupation of the intended ground. He was attacked in this position, and as might be expected, the weight of the service fell on the English detachment; but although Perseram Bhow obstinately refused to adopt the suggestion of commencing the operation by a false attack with his own troops on the flank of the position, he performed, with tolerable accuracy, all that he engaged to execute; and the enemy was dislodged and routed, with considerable loss, and the capture of three of their guns.

The same process of ridiculous annoyance by day, and reciprocal repose by night, was continued until the 13th of December, when an attack by escalade was made on the town, headed of course by the English detachment, whose commander was the first to ascend the ladders, and was wounded. The service was completely executed, and the English returned to their camp; but the Mahrattas who dispersed for plunder, accidentally set fire to the town in several places, and Budr-u-Zemân Khân availing himself of the consequent confusion, sallied, drove them out, and re-occupied the town, the Mahrattas having previously carried off three guns as trophies. It was again carried on the 18th; but in conformity to national practice, even the guns placed in battery in the town, were uniformly withdrawn at night. Captain Little had at a very early period, reported the total inefficiency of the means possessed by Perseram Bhow

CHAP. XXXIX. 1791. for the reduction of Darwar; but the precise nature of that inefficiency either was not accurately understood at Bombay, or was not adequately remedied. A reinforcement was ordered from that place, consisting of one regiment of European infantry, one battalion of sepoys, a considerable augmentation of European artillerymen, *but no cannon or stores*, and three officers of engineers, under the orders of Colonel Frederic, who arrived
Jan. 2. before Darwar on the 2d of January 1791.

Independently of the insufficiency of the cannon furnished by the Mahrattas, so precarious and unskilful were the arrangements of their military departments, that there was frequently a want of ammunition at the most critical periods, and no operation of a siege could be undertaken with the least certainty that any one material required would be ready at the period promised. A deficiency of ammunition, which could not be supplied for a considerable time, induced Colonel Frederic to attempt an assault, at an earlier period than was other-
Feb. 7. wise expedient, on the 7th of February; the arrangements were well advanced, the dry ditch was filled with fascines, and the assailants were on the point of issuing from the advanced cover with the confidence of terminating their labours, when it was found necessary to abandon the attempt. The materials of the fascines were rather dry; the experienced kelledar had sent some trusty men to creep along the ditch and lodge a few lighted portfires among them at the proper time, and before the storming party could have crossed, their fascine causeway was a mass of flame. It was the 1st of March before the expected supply of ammunition arrived, and the regular approaches were resumed; but Colonel Frederic, sinking under

the feelings arising from sacrifice of reputation, in an important command, on which high expectations had been founded, without any of the ordinary means of commanding success, died on the 13th of March, and the command devolved on Major Sartarius of the engineers.

Perseram Bhow had by this time received a few additional heavy guns from Poona; but the same disregard of precision in the performance of a promise, continued to render it equally impracticable to pursue with consistency any fixed series of measures. The approaches, however, continued to advance, disturbed, as during the whole service, by frequent sorties. An extensive lodgment was made on the crest of the glacis by both the Mahrattas and English; but the incessant disappointments regarding every material and every supply, did not inspire any sanguine confidence of early success. Private intelligence, however, indicated an approaching scarcity of provisions in the place; and on the 30th of March, after being invested for six Mar. 30.
months and twelve days, the kelledar proposed to treat for its surrender. The intelligence of the capture of Bangalore on the 21st, had in this, as in every part of the Sultaun's possessions, produced the most powerful influence on public opinion; but the veteran kelledar professed to have been actuated by no motive but the impossibility of retaining the place for want of provisions; and the desire of joining his sovereign with his division, while still capable of efficient service. The last of the garrison, with their arms and ammunition, colours flying, and three field pieces, evacuated the place on the 4th of April. The casualties April 4.
of the English throughout the service, were found to have

CHAP. XXXIX. 1791. amounted to about five hundred; and those of the Mahrattas were computed at three thousand.

Budr-u-Zemân Khân apprehensive of treachery, encamped, and marched his troops in a hollow square, with all the precautions of being surrounded by enemies, and unprotected by the April 8. obligations of public faith; and on the 8th, the British troops, who were unanimous in their admiration of his respectable defence, heard with astonishment and grief, that his corps had been attacked, plundered, and nearly destroyed; and that he himself, covered with wounds, was sent as a prisoner to a Mahratta fort. No official explanation has ever been published of this transaction, and in the prints of the day, it was treated as a simple treachery, perpetrated for the purposes of plunder. The Mahrattas affirm, that Budr-u-Zemân Khân had stipulated to surrender the fort, with its guns and stores in their actual condition: that after the capitulation was settled, he caused the powder in the magazine to be ruined by water, and the stores to be destroyed to the extent that his time and means admitted; and they contend, that they were justified in retaliating the breach of the capitulation. This statement was denied by the party accused; but the author must add, as a tribute of truth, that it was circumstantially related to him by a Mysorean officer, who was wounded on that occasion, and who had (as he affirmed), been personally employed in the destruction of the stores.

The reinforcement from Bombay, which had been conducted to Darwar by Colonel Frederic, commenced its return immediately after the surrender of the place, but before reaching the coast, the native battalion was ordered to return, at the request of Perseram Bhow, and formed a junction near Seringapatam, with the original detachment under Captain Little, now consisting of three battalions, which continued to serve with the Mahrattas, until the conclusion of the war.

The surrender of Darwar was followed by the early possession of every thing north of the Toombuddra, and Lord Cornwallis having communicated to the Mahratta court, his fixed determination to advance against Seringapatam, and his expectation of being joined by their army before that place, Perseram Bhow crossed the Toombuddra, at Hurryhur, and advanced by the direct western road from that place, overcoming the resistance opposed to him at Ramgerry, Meyconda, and other inferior posts early in May; while another army from Poona, under Hurry Punt, proceeded by the more eastern route of Harponelly and Sera, preserving a parallel line, and equal advance, until the junction already described was effected with the English army near the field of Chercooli; an omen which contributed in a degree more important than can readily be conceived in civilized society, to the confidence of that people in a favourable termination of the war. To the north and northwest therefore the Mahrattas had not only recovered their former possessions beyond the Toombuddra, but several places to the south of that river. The garrisons had been withdrawn from the places occupied by Perseram Bhow, on his approach from Hurrygur to Seringapatam, by the western route; but the eastern communication by Harponelly and Sera, on which Hurry Punt had advanced, was strengthened and preserved: and in the course of the intermediate operations before the return of the proper season for concentrating before Seringapatam, the Mah-

May.

rattas would necessarily contract within still narrower bounds the area of the enemy's remaining resources.

In order that we may be enabled, without further retrospect, to proceed in our narrative of the intermediate operations and ultimate concentration of the allies, it will be convenient to notice the advances towards negotiation which had occurred subsequently to Lord Cornwallis's command of the English army.

Tippoo Sultaun's first letter, dated the 13th of February, 1791, was received at Muglee on the 18th, and adverting to the actual distance to be travelled, and to the coincidence of time at which the Sultaun must have discovered all his plans for the defence of the ghauts to be frustrated, a conjecture may fairly be risked that the letter was antedated at least two days. In substance it offered to receive or send an embassador for the adjustment of existing differences. To this letter Lord Cornwallis replied, on the 23d, that the infraction of the treaty was with Tippoo; that if he was willing to make reparation for the insult, and indemnity to the allies, it would be necessary for him to state so in writing, as without the establishment of a basis for negotiation sending an embassador would be useless. On the 3d of March an answer was received from the Sultaun, containing a laboured explanation of the affair of the lines of Travancore, and drawing into prominent notice the misconduct of that raja, in receiving and protecting his rebellious subject the raja of Cochin; disclaiming insult, and repeating his wish for negotiation: this did not seem to require any farther reply.

On the 22d of March Lord Cornwallis wrote a mere letter of courtesy, offering the body of Behauder Khán, the kelledar of

Bangalore, for interment, which was declined with a suitable acknowledgment, and his Lordship directed the funeral to be conducted with due honours by the Mahommedans of his own army.

On the 27th of March, Tippoo renewed the proposition of sending a confidential person, to which Lord Cornwallis, at that time, unaccompanied by any plenipotentiary from either of the allies, answered, that as one of the confederates, he could not receive a confidential person, but if the Sultaun would reduce his propositions to writing, they should be communicated to the allies, and an answer returned.

On the 17th of May, Lord Cornwallis offered the release of the wounded prisoners of the action of the 15th, which Tippoo received with thanks, and renewed the proposal of negotiation. A Mahratta vakeel had joined his Lordship before his departure from Bangalore, and Têdjewunt was present on the part of Nizam Ali. Lord Cornwallis accordingly answered on the 19th, that if he would commit his propositions to writing, a meeting of commissioners might be arranged; *and his Lordship would even consent, if Tippoo should desire it, to a cessation of hostilities.* On the 24th Tippoo answered this letter, *without taking the slightest notice of the last proposition,* but renewed his former ones; and on the same day, (it will be recollected, his Lordship is at Caniambaddy, had destroyed his battering train, and had that morning detached three brigades across the river,) Lord Cornwallis gave up the point of written propositions, and consented that the allies should send deputies to Bangalore. This letter remained four days unanswered; but on the 27th, the day after the junction of the Mahratta advanced guard, the army being in full view of Seringapatam, an episode was attempted, founded on the relaxation of the two last letters from the English General, of establishing an indirect communication, and an ostensible ground of jealousy, by a letter from the Sultaun's secretary to the Persian interpreter, with a present of fruit for his Lordship's use, and a camel, to replace that of the courier of the 17th, which had died at Seringapatam. These demonstrations were witnessed by the whole army, and without entering into all the feelings incident to such a situation, it will be difficult for the reader to comprehend the intense delight, with which on the ensuing morning they beheld the loads of fruit untouched, and the camel unaccepted, returning to Seringapatam.

On the 29th, however, Tippoo replied to Lord Cornwallis's condescending letter of the 24th, and after a series of long and unmeaning explanations, he proposes, that his Lordship should first return to the frontier, and then proceed in the manner suggested in his two last letters.

These abortive communications might have been more rapidly dismissed, but the detail appeared to be of importance, for the purpose of exhibiting an invariable feature of Indian diplomacy, in the exact coincidence of his Lordship's dignified tone, with the Sultaun's humility; and of the Sultaun's gradual ascent in arrogance, with every descending step in his Lordship's concessions.

August. It is probable that a corresponding conviction was impressed on his Lordship's mind; for without being able to state the precise nature of the intermediate advances, we find him early in August consenting to the reception of an envoy "at the warm instances of Hurry Punt," not as it would appear with the expectation of any result, but to obviate the impression of an actual aversion to accommodation, a feeling which was equally contrary to his own disposition and to the interests of his country. The veteran diplomatist, Apajee Ram, once more appeared upon the public scene *: his character was at that time unknown to the British army, and it was only remarked that a mean looking old bramin had arrived, very unlike an embassador, and affording very little promise of the Sultaun's being in earnest. He was attended, at the town of Serjapoor, by an English escort of protection and precaution; but on attempting to proceed to business by arranging the appointment of deputies to meet him on the part of the allies, it was found that he was specially prohibited from negotiating with any intermediate agent, and was ordered to open his business to the direct representatives of the respective confederate powers. Lord Cornwallis deeming his own exalted trust to place him in the situation of a principal, refused to meet, as on equal terms, the deputed servant of Tippoo Sultaun, and Apajee Ram, who was suspected of an incipient intrigue, was accordingly desired to return without delay, and without having the opportunity, in a conference of any description, to combat even these preliminary objections, or to exhibit a force of intellect said to have been still unbroken, and a luxuriance of wit rendered scarcely less playful, but far more caustic by age.

* He was accompanied, as a matter of form, by a Mussulman of rank, ostensibly united in the mission.

CHAPTER XL.

Lord Cornwallis moves from Bangalore, to reduce the intermediate posts to the eastward — Rayacota &c. — recalled by intelligence regarding the Mahrattas — who had been attacked at Mudgerry — Loss not serious — His Lordship resumes his own line of operation — Northern forts — Nundidroog — strength and protracted defence — Irruption of Bâkir Saheb into Bâramahâl — Colonel Maxwell detached to dislodge him — Assault of Pinagra — Unsuccessful attempt on Kistnagherry — Returns — Singular defence of Coimbetoor — Siege raised — Second siege — Attempted relief fails — Intermediate fortresses between Bangalore and Seringapatam – Savendroog — Considerations regarding that place — Colonel Stuart detached for the siege — succeeds — Attack and fall of Ootradroog — Ramgherry — Shevengherry — Holioordroog — taken — Goorumconda — lower fort carried — Skilful expedition for its relief under Futteh Hyder — Facts regarding Hâfiz Jee — Injurious suspicions — Nizam Ali's army returns — retakes the lower fort — and ultimately joins Lord Cornwallis — Grain merchants — System adopted regarding them — Doubtful origin of that people — Professedly wanderers — Language — customs and manners — Note on the manufacture of salt — Observations on the value of these grain merchants — Preparations of General Abercromby — those of Lord Cornwallis – Embarrassing conduct of Perseram Bhow — Consequent delay and its results — his intermediate operations — Private plunder preferred to the success of the campaign — Shameless and unprincipled breach of compact — Meditates the plunder of Bednore — Brilliant services of the English detachment — Hooly Onore — Defeat of Reza Saheb by Captain Little — Perseram Bhow appears before Bednore — hears of Kummer-u-Deen's approach — retires — arrives at Seringapatam after the service was over.

CHAP. XL. 1791.

Lord Cornwallis after the requisite arrangements at Bangalore, where the talents and military skill of Captain Read, had succeeded in bringing forward the most important supplies, without

any loss, although greatly interrupted by the enemy's detachments, moved in a south-eastern direction to Oossoor, which was evacuated, and imperfectly blown up on his approach; fortunately a train laid for the magazine, and intended to explode after the entry of the English troops, did not succeed. Thence he moved July 15.
in the direction of the passes of Policode and Rayacota, for the purpose of reducing the congeries of droogs, which command the access to these passes, from above as well as from below. The possession of these posts would accomplish the double purpose, of opening a free communication for his own supplies from Coromandel, and protecting the Company's possessions, from the inroads of small divisions of cavalry, by occupying all the direct roads from Seringapatam to Bâramahâl. An advanced brigade under Major Gowdie, had some sharp service at Rayacota, the chief of these droogs, garrisoned by 800 men. He forced the lower works shortly before day-light, by blowing open a gate, and 20.
hoped to carry the rock, by entering with the fugitives; he succeeded in carrying several successive gates, but found it imprudent to attempt the summit. He had been instructed to withdraw, in the event of not completely succeeding in his first enterprize; but perceiving a probability of ultimate success, he ventured so far to deviate from his orders, as to hold his ground in an intermediate line of works about half way up the hill, and the place capitulated on the appearance of the army.

The minor posts, all capable of protracted defence, offered 22
various but unsuccessful degrees of resistance; some of them, favoured by local circumstances, stood the assault, and the garrisons escaped by the opposite descent into the woods. His Lordship had it also in contemplation to adopt some arrangement

for blockading Kistnagherry, the capital of Bâramahâl, a place deemed impregnable according to regular means; which, although not commanding any road, was capable, with a large garrison, of interrupting the transit of convoys: but he was called from this vicinity by causes which had not been entirely unforeseen.

In his first interviews with the Mahratta chiefs, he had proposed a systematic plan, of operating in columns at considerable distances with connecting corps, so as to ensure at once extended means of supply and the advantages of reciprocal support; but on farther observation, he found that he should attain no advantage and incur great embarrassment by insisting on such a plan with allies who were incessantly led away by temporary views of private interest, and although sufficiently capable of comprehending, were very unfit to execute any systematic plan. He had therefore yielded with less reluctance to their desire to keep up a complete communication with their respective countries, but had not failed to warn them against the imprudence of dispersing their force. Tippoo Sultaun, as his Lordship had foreseen, availed himself of the first removal of the pressure on his capital to strike at every detachment which should be left exposed, and in pursuance of this plan ordered a powerful corps into Coimbetoor, (to which we shall return,) and moved in person to the northward. It was the danger of Perseram Bhow, from this movement that induced Lord Cornwallis to make a few marches in the same direction, to check the advance of the Sultaun by alarming him for his rear. On arriving at Bangalore he found his apprehensions had been verified to a certain extent. On his route to Sera, Perseram Bhow had thrown a garrison into Great Balipoor, and had left a corps to mask Mudgerry; Kummer-u-Deen, with a superior force, attacked and completely routed this corps, and the garrison of Great Balipoor (800 men) returned in alarm to Bangalore; the loss was not so serious as was apprehended from the first reports; the incident proved useful to Perseram Bhow, by teaching a more prudent use of detachments; and Lord Cornwallis felt himself at liberty to renew his own objects. CHAP. XL. 1791.

With the exception of Kistnagherry, every thing essential to the communication with Coromandel and Bâramahâl to the south-east and east, was already secured, but a considerable number of places, some of them of importance, to the north-east of Bangalore, not only prevented the very important object of commanding the resources of these countries, but were interposed in the line of communication with Goorumconda, and with the army of Nizam Ali. Major Gowdie, reinforced with some battering cannon, was detached on this service, and rapidly succeeded in obtaining possession of all those of minor importance. But Nundidroog was found to require larger reinforcements and more extensive means: he forced the petta, and examined the northern face on the 22d of September, and finding it unassailable in that quarter, made a circuit to the west, and finally sat down before the place on the 27th. Sept. 22. 27.

Every fortified place the English had hitherto seen in Mysoor, exhibited evidence of the extraordinary attention paid by Tippoo Sultaun to the repair and improvement of this important branch of national defence, but the works of Nundidroog, a granite rock of tremendous height, seemed to have engrossed in a peculiar degree his design of rendering it impregnable;

CHAP. XL. 1791. and its defence was committed to Lutf Aly Beg, an officer who had always merited the highest distinction both from Hyder and Tippoo, although by the former he had been condemned to a cruel degradation after the battle of Arnee in 1782 *, and by the latter had but recently been relieved from the disgrace incurred on his return from Constantinople. There was no choice with regard to the face to be attacked, because except in that one direction, the precipice was inaccessible, the comparatively weak point had been strengthened by a double line of ramparts; and the foundation was laid for a third, which ultimately aided the assailants in forming their last lodgement. The defence was highly respectable, the ammunition of the cannon was well served, and the jinjalls, or wall pieces, were served with peculiar steadiness and skill; the labour was excessive, of working regularly up the face of a steep and craggy mountain to breaching distance, and dragging cannon to the batteries; but in twenty-one days two breaches were effected; one in the exterior rampart, and the other in an out-work, and it was resolved to give the assault and form a lodgement for the farther operations against the interior works. The assailants received, however, a particular direction for endeavouring to enter with the fugitives, while the division allotted to forming the lodgement, should be employed in providing cover: and in order that every possible impression might be made on the minds of the garrison, Lord Cornwallis moved the army to the immediate vicinity: some additional flank companies

* Vol. ii. page 388.

were ordered in to lead the assault, and General Medows, with the usual spirit which animated him on such occasions, desired to take the immediate direction of the service.* CHAP. XL. 1791.

The assault was given by clear moon light on the morning of the 19th of October; the arrangements of defence were excellent, and particularly the masses of granite reserved till this period to be rolled down the rock with tremendous effect, but the lodgement was within one hundred yards of the breach, and although the garrison was perfectly alert, the ardour and rapidity of the assailants surmounted every obstacle, and they pressed the fugitives so closely as to prevent their effectually barricading the gate of the inner rampart. It was forced after a sharp conflict, and the place was carried with the loss in the assault of only thirty killed and wounded, chiefly by the stones tumbled down the rock, and in the whole siege one hundred and twenty. Oct. 19.

The communication with Goorumconda, still invested by the troops of Nizam Ali, being thus completely opened, a portion of the battering cannon employed in the siege of Nundidroog was sent to their aid; and Lord Cornwallis was called again to the south-east by an alarm for his communications. A force under Bâkir Saheb, an active young officer, and son of the venerable kelledar of Darwar, had been detached by the route of Coimbetoor and Tapoor into Bâramahâl, with a respectable reinforcement for Kistnagherry, with orders to act on the communications of the English army, and particularly to sweep off in a southern direc-

* Shortly before the assault, while all were waiting the signal in silence, one of the soldiers inadvertently whispered something about a mine. "To be sure there is," said General Medows, "and it is a mine of gold;" a smothered laugh ran along the ranks, and produced the proper impression.

CHAP. XL. 1791. Oct. 21.

tion the population and cattle of the whole district. Colonel Maxwell with a suitable division of the army was detached for the purpose of endeavouring to disperse these intruders, and in descending the ghaut, he received intelligence that a proportion of the enemy had proceeded, in the execution of their barbarous purpose of carrying off the population, to Penagra, a post in the angle formed with the main range of mountains, by the cross chain of Tapoor, whence only a mountain path communicates farther south. He moved with rapidity in that direction, and demanded the surrender of the place by a regular summons; but the enemy, not satisfied with a simple refusal, fired upon the flag. As the appearance of the works justified prompt measures, it was instantly assaulted and carried by escalade, with little loss to the assailants; but of the garrison, two hundred men were killed, before the indignation of the troops could be restrained, and the cavalry escaped by the mountain-paths. The activity of Colonel Maxwell's movements, from the accurate local information he had acquired in the previous campaign, soon induced Bâkir Saheb to withdraw from a country too much bounded for the safe operations of cavalry. He descended by the pass of Changama into Coromandel; but finding, from the presence of the English cavalry under Colonel Floyd, that any enterprise towards Madras would be hazardous, he turned southward, and re-entered the Mysorean dominions by the pass of Ahtoor.

Colonel Maxwell had been ordered, if he found the enterprise advisable, to attempt the destruction of the town, within the lower fort of Kistnagherry, for the purpose of depriving the enemy as much as possible of cover for their predatory arrangements, and after effecting his objects in other parts of the province, he encamped on the 7th of November, within a few miles of the place, without any other demonstration, than that of reascending the pass. He moved at ten at night, in three divisions, and carried the lower fort by escalade: the officers commanding the divisions were instructed, if appearances were favourable, to follow up the blow, and ascend the rock with the fugitives, who had barely time to shut and barricade the gate; and so close was the pursuit, that a standard of the regular troops was taken on the very steps of the gateway. The bearers of the ladders were not so expeditious in their ascent, and the garrison, more numerous than their assailants, began to hurl the dreadful missiles of granite: projections of rock afforded cover to the assailants, and repeated attempts were made during two hours, to apply ladders, which were as often crushed with those who bore them; and Colonel Maxwell at length found it necessary, to desist from the assault with considerable loss: the garrison sallied on their retreat, but it was conducted with so much regularity, that they quickly returned: the English troops, after setting fire to the town, withdrew before day-light; and the detachment soon afterwards returned to head quarters, having moved along the back of the range between the passes of Policode and Pedanaickdurgum, for the purpose of restoring a number of minor posts, to the families of their former Hindoo possessors.

1791. Nov. 7.

Bâkir Saheb had been detached from a corps under Kummer-u-Deen, which took the direction of the capital of Coimbetoor. We have already noticed the employment of a force in that direction, immediately after the Sultaun was relieved from the pressure on his capital in the month of May; and as no service throughout this eventful war, was accompanied by circumstances more remarkable, we shall revert to the proceedings of the first detachment.

It will be recollected that when General Medows followed the Sultaun's course from Bâramahâl to Trichinopoly in 1790, he detached a respectable force under Colonel Oldham, across the river at Caroor. During the early operations of Lord Cornwallis in 1791, his Lordship had ordered this detachment to the north, and it formed the basis of the strong corps which escorted his supplies to the upper country, after his junction with the horse of Nizam Ali. On Colonel Oldham's departure from the south, he left a detachment under the command of Major Cuppage, who, on the concentration of the army of Bombay for the ascent of the ghauts, was charged with the defence of Palgaut and Coimbetoor, and their reciprocal communication. On examining minutely the fort of Coimbetoor, Major Cuppage considering it to be incapable of standing a siege, removed the heavy guns, ammunition, and stores to Palgaut; its possession was indispensable to the fiscal management of the province, and it was deemed capable of resisting any force unprovided with heavy cannon; but on the appearance of a force so provided, the garrison was ordered to fall back to Palgaut. Among the variety of troops employed by the native powers, is a description named *Topasses*, (or persons wearing hats,) originally the descendants of Portuguese of mixed blood, but at that period exhibiting a motley assemblage of various classes and complexions, many of them possessing very distant claims to European descent. A number of these had formerly been entertained in the service of Mahommed Ali; in 1790 a small corps had been collected for the

English service and placed under Lieutenant Chalmers; and general* opinion, not very favourable to their military prowess, was destined to receive a remarkable refutation. CHAP. XL. 1791.

After the removal of every thing valuable from Coimbetoor, Lieutenant Chalmers, on examining the guns deemed unserviceable, found two three-pounders and one four-pounder to stand the proof; means of mounting them were obtained from the fragments of broken carriages: there were also several swivels and jinjalls, and a large quantity of damaged powder; and he prevailed on Major Cuppage to send him five hundred shot for his guns. His corps was reduced by detachments to one hundred and twenty Topasses, and two hundred men from a battalion of Travancoreans, under a young Frenchman named Migot de la Combe, of which number about one half made their escape to the hills when they found they were to stand a siege, and the rest were extremely insubordinate.

The place was invested, on the 13th of June, by about two thousand regular infantry and a considerable mass of irregulars, eight guns, (the largest an eighteen-pounder) a number of jinjall pieces served by irregular infantry, abundance of rockets, and a sufficient body of horse. June 13.

The bad quality of the powder was extremely unfavourable to the efforts of the little garrison, but while endeavouring as far as their limited numbers admitted to repair or scarp the

* The difficulty of determining any measure of state, with regard to the widely encreasing branch of Indian population, growing out of the irregular connexions of, perhaps, thirty thousand Europeans, has hitherto caused an apparent apathy, to a question of momentous political importance. The question must soon force itself on public consideration, and the longer it is postponed, the more difficult will be the decision.

CHAP. XL. 1791. breaches, and place swivels on their flanks in the berm, Lieutenant Chalmers was preparing with greater care the means of repelling the ultimate assault; the powder was sufficiently adapted to the preparation of a contrivance for exploding among the assailants; which was no other than filling with the proper materials a number of small barrels, provided with fuses, to be placed along the banquette in all parts of the fort, and chiefly in proper situations to be rolled down the breaches or over the parapet; and special orders were given that this defence should not be employed until the berm and ditch were crowded by the enemy. It cannot be necessary to enlarge on the coolness and gallantry, under many privations, and under an incessant clamour for surrender from all the Travancoreans, which could prolong such a defence for nearly two months, before the enemy, after repeated summonses, gave the assault. It commenced about two Aug. 11. hours before day-light on the 11th of August, in five columns, each accompanied by ladders, and the ramparts were completely gained at several points. The first struggle was at the post defended by De la Combe, who set an example of great gallantry, but was nearly overpowered by numbers until supported by a reinforcement of Topasses; the period had not only arrived, but had somewhat passed away, for the persons charged with the care of the combustible barrels to execute their orders, not only were the ditch and berm filled with the enemy, but a considerable number was actually on the rampart engaged in close encounter; and the post defended by Lieutenant Chalmers in person, as being the weakest point, was by this time pressed with still greater vivacity than any other; the explosion of a barrel at this moment in a crowded mass of the enemy produced the desired impression, and it was followed up by similar means, by tumbling down large stones prepared along the whole extent of the parapet, and by the redoubled efforts of the garrison to clear the ramparts of the enemy. After a severe conflict of nearly two hours, the efforts of the assailants entirely ceased; the day began to dawn, the enemy was perceived carrying off his killed and wounded, and preparing to evacuate the batteries; while in another direction the distant but cheering sight was observed of an English corps in full march for the place, from Palgaut. At this critical moment, before all the guns were removed, Lieutenant Chalmers ordered De la Combe with a large portion of the garrison to sally; he found the two last and heaviest of the guns limbered, and the bullocks yoked to carry them off, and with the greatest coolness drove them under the immediate protection of the place. To besiegers, who had thus prolonged their operations we can scarcely ascribe an ordinary degree of skill, but the praise of bravery cannot be denied to an enemy who prolonged such a struggle for two hours, and left on the ramparts, and within the limits of the ditch (exclusively of what had been carried away,) a number of bodies, considerably exceeding the whole numerical amount of the garrison.

No efforts for the relief of Coimbetoor could have justified Major Cuppage in compromising the safety of Palgaut; and the detachment with which he marched was somewhat of a motley description: a weak battalion of regular sepoys, one of Travancoreans, 350 poligars, under the direction of an enterprising civil servant, Mr. Macleod, the collector of Madura, the whole not exceeding one thousand men, with four iron four-pounders of Travancore, and the two brass sixes of the regular battalion.

CHAP. XL. 1791. The enemy still continued to occupy the petta after their repulse, for the purpose of covering the retreat of their cannon; but were dislodged from all their posts in the course of the day, and in a subsequent pursuit of two days to the Bawani, lost a considerable quantity of stores. Such a result was calculated to produce in the successful party a degree of confidence exceeding its legitimate grounds. No doubt was entertained that an effort of greater magnitude would be made by Tippoo Sultaun, and Lieutenant Chalmers only requested one additional officer to relieve him in the fatigues of the siege. Lieutenant Nash, with his company of sepoys, was accordingly ordered in; and by means of detachments of various kinds and qualities, the garrison was made to amount to near seven hundred men.

He had scarcely repaired his breaches and mounted his captured guns before the enemy appeared on the 6th of October, with augmented means and a more skilful leader, Kummer-u-Deen, with 14 guns (12 six-pounders and two eighteens), four mortars, 8,000 regular infantry, and a large body of irregulars and of horse. On the 23d, intelligence was received of the approach of Major Cuppage with three regular battalions (at most 1,800 men), two of Travancoreans, and six field pieces. Kummer-u-Deen leaving a strong body in the trenches, marched with the remainder of his force to a distance of about ten miles, to the vicinity of a pass, where the woods of Animally terminate and the plain commences. Unfortunately at this period a large equipment of oxen for General Abercromby's army, were assembled at Palgaut; and Kummer-u-Deen made a decided demonstration of passing to the Major's rear. If he should be enabled to gain the pass, and the uninterrupted access to Palgaut;

by the capture of the oxen, he would strike a blow of infinitely greater importance than the fall of Coimbetoor, and be even in a condition, with his superior numbers, to render precarious the Major's return to Palgaut. The one manœuvred for the pass, the other to prevent its occupation, and a severe action terminated in Major Cuppage's possession of the pass, but also in his return to Palgaut. "I have seen," said Kummer-u-Deen on his return, "the nature of your expected relief; do not persist in throwing away the lives of brave men." He resumed the siege with fresh vigour, and a very respectable degree of skill; a wide breach was in all respects practicable, and the sap was carried to the covered way; the ammunition, originally bad, was nearly expended. Lieutenants Chalmers and Nash were both wounded on the same day, and the bravest of the former defenders of the place urged their commander to accept the repeated offers of an honourable capitulation. Terms similar to those given to Daraporam in the campaign of 1790, were prepared and executed, and it was an explicit condition that the garrison should march to Palgaut; but after the actual surrender of the place, it was pretended that the Sultaun's ratification was necessary; and after a detention of 13 days at Coimbetoor, they were ultimately marched as close * prisoners to Seringapatam, in direct and open violation of public faith, without even a pretext for its infraction, excepting one which was founded on an open violation of truth.

CHAP. XL. 1791. Nov. 3.

We return from these detached events, to the operations of 30.

* My notes do not enable me to say what had become of De la Combe. I rather think that he returned to Coimbetoor after the first siege.

CHAP. XL. 1791.

the main army under Lord Cornwallis, after the junction of Colonel Maxwell, from his expedition to Bâramahâl.

Every thing interposed between Bangalore and Coromandel, was now cleared for the access of supplies; but between that post and Seringapatam, on every possible route, several places of strength remained in the Sultaun's possession, the reduction of which Lord Cornwallis deemed to be of essential importance to the uninterrupted communication with his depôts, during the intended siege. A fresh battering train had been brought forward, and the last and most important convoy, under Colonel Floyd, with the recovered cavalry, was shortly to arrive, but impediments connected with the operations of the allies, to which we shall presently revert, caused an embarrassing delay; and Lord Cornwallis determined to employ the intermediate time, in attempting the reduction of those places, of which the most formidable, and reputed to be the strongest in Mysoor, was Savendroog, a place which at one time he had determined not to attack, from the great improbability of success. This enormous mass of granite, is considerably more elevated than Nundidroog, and stands upon a base at the least eight miles in circumference, every where apparently inaccessible from below, and at the height of about two thirds of its total elevation, separated by a chasm, into two citadels, each independent of the other, and both abundantly supplied with water. Exclusively of the convenient position of this fortress, as the head quarters of a corps, to interrupt the communications, its extraordinary height commanded a view of every convoy that could move on either of the two principal roads. On the return of the army from Caniambaddy, the place had been carefully reconnoitred; it was then deemed to be unassailable, and the discouragement was increased by the reputed insalubrity of the woods and impenetrable thickets by which it is surrounded. The capture since that period of a considerable number of hill forts hitherto deemed impregnable, and particularly of Nundidroog, encouraged the English General in the attempt, which if successful, he expected to be followed by the early surrender of all the others that he desired to possess.

CHAP. XL. 1791.

Colonel Stuart, with two European and three native corps, and a powerful artillery, was detached for the immediate conduct of the siege, and Lord Cornwallis made a disposition of the remainder of the army to watch every avenue from Seringapatam by which the operations of the siege might be disturbed. Colonel Stuart encamped within three miles of the place on the 10th of Dec. 10. December, and immediately commenced the arduous labour of cutting a gun road through the rugged forest to the foot of the rock, a work which, added to the difficulties of dragging iron twenty-four pounders over precipices nearly perpendicular, called for a degree of incessant exertion and fatigue which could scarcely have been exceeded.

The batteries opened on the 17th, and the breach in what was 17. named the lower wall of the rock, although at least fifteen hundred feet higher than its base, was deemed practicable on the 20th. Immediately overlooking it, at a precipitous height, and perfectly well situated for destroying, by the usual artillery of rocks and stones, every thing that should attempt to ascend beyond the breach, was a range of ancient wall. Lord Corn-

CHAP. XL. 1791. wallis had come from the camp, distant seven miles, to witness the assault; the grenadiers were ordered to their stations, and the garrison was seen to be collecting behind this wall. This observation fortunately prevented the assault on that day; the experiment was made of pointing with sufficient elevation by receiving the trail of the gun carriage into an excavation behind the platform. The execution was not only perfect, but the wall was found to be so frail that a few discharges must dislodge its defenders. The arrangements for the ensuing day, were founded on the fact thus opportunely ascertained, the batteries were prepared for the purpose, and in the morning the requisite number of guns were directed against this wall with the most perfect success; every person behind it was dislodged, and the storming party, having been placed without observation, within twenty yards of the breach, the assault commenced by signal at eleven o'clock in the forenoon.

Dec. 21. The defenders had been so unexpectedly dislodged from their appointed positions, that no new disposition had been made. The assailants accordingly ascended the rock without the slightest opposition, clambering up a precipice, which, after the service was over, they were afraid to descend. The eastern citadel was completely carried; and the assailants, on reaching the summit of the rock, had the satisfaction to descry a heavy column of infantry, destined to reinforce the garrison, in full march to enter the place, which would have been effected if the assault had been postponed even for half an hour. A division of the assailants, after ascending considerably above the breach, had been directed to turn to the right along a path which had been observed to be practised by the garrison, leading along the side of the rock to the western citadel. The kelledar of that citadel, observing the defenders of the eastern rock to be driven from their post above the breach, and the assailants to have begun climbing up, sallied with the view of taking them in flank, but was unexpectedly met among the rocks by the division described; and at the same instant, a few well-directed shot from the batteries, fell with great execution among his troops. He retreated in surprise and dismay, followed with great energy by the English troops. At this instant the assailants, who had gained the highest eminence of the eastern rock, obtained a distinct view of the pursuit: they observed the kelledar to fall just as he approached the gate of his citadel, and the pursuers to enter with the fugitives. Every thing was carried within one hour from the commencement of the assault; and an enterprise which had been contemplated by Lord Cornwallis as the most doubtful operation of the war, was thus effected in twelve days from the first arrival of the troops, and five of open batteries, including the day of the assault, with a moderate amount of casualties in the previous operations, and in the assault itself his Lordship had not to regret the loss of a single life.

Colonel Stuart marched on the 23d for the next in strength and importance of the intermediate posts, Ootradroog. This place had been examined and summoned on the return from Caniambaddy; the kelledar had then made a determined reply; but as the recent fall of Savendroog might produce a change in his decision, Colonel Stuart sent forward to offer liberal terms: the flag was escorted to a proper distance, and the garrison beckoned the staff-officer who accompanied it to advance, until within

Dec. 23.

CHAP. XL. 1791. sixty yards of the gate, when a fire of musquetry opened, from which he and the non-commissioned officer who bore the flag were so fortunate as to escape unhurt: the chief engineer (Colonel Ross) accompanied the escort, and an opportu-
Dec 24. nity was afforded of examining the ground, which was favourable to the novel mode of attack adopted on the ensuing day. A proper number of field pieces were run down to the appointed stations, and under cover of their fire the escalade commenced: the side of the rock assaulted was not precipitous, but rose at an angle of perhaps thirty-five degrees, defended by a succession of seven ramparts rising above each other, including that of the petta first stormed, and the place was ill provided with cannon: the artillery officers were ordered, as fast as one wall should be carried, to point their guns over the heads of the assailants against the next in succession, for the purpose of keeping down the fire of the garrison. Some of the gateways were forced by the pioneers, but most of the ramparts were carried by escalade; and such was the astonishment and confusion, that a heavy fire from each successive rampart was actually thrown into the air; and to the surprise of Colonel Stuart, on collecting the returns, the place was found to be carried without the loss of a life, and with a trifling number of wounded.

The forts of Ramgherry and Sevengherry on the central road, surrendered to a detachment under Captain Welsh, with-
27. out much resistance; Holioordroog repaired and re-occupied by the enemy was retaken in advancing, and held, as a post of communication, and nothing intermediate remained, excepting Cabal Droog, which, being on the southern road of Kaunkanhully,

not intended to be used, Lord Cornwallis did not deem of sufficient importance to repay the deviation and loss of time it would involve.

In the meantime the siege of Goorumconda had not proceeded in a prosperous manner. The army of Nizam Ali sat down before the place on the 15th of September, and no progress was made until the arrival, early in November, of the guns dispatched by Lord Cornwallis from Nundidroog. The droog of Goorumconda is of great and deserved reputation, and even the lower fort was of considerable strength. Captain Andrew Read, who had succeeded to the command of the English detachment serving with this army, impatient at their awkward proceedings, offered, on the condition of being permitted the exclusive direction of measures, to put them in possession of the lower fort which commanded the only access to the hill, and would thus complete the blockade which they might then manage in their own way. He made an effectual breach, and the artillerymen volunteered to quit their batteries and lead the assault: it was completely successful, and a large body of Nizam Ali's troops was put in possession, under an officer of reputation, named Hâfiz Fereed-u-Deen, usually called Hâfiz Jee, who was left with an adequate force of infantry and cavalry to continue the blockade; when the main army under the minister, Musheer-ul-Mulk accompanied by the English political resident, Sir John Kennaway, advanced for the siege of Seringapatam.

In order to ensure the safety of the last and most important convoy, proceeding from Coromandel under Colonel Floyd, Lord Cornwallis had requested that this army in its advance, would deviate a little to the eastward, and join Colonel Floyd at the head of the pass; but before they had proceeded thirty miles from Goorumconda, they were recalled by disastrous intelligence, and Colonel Floyd formed the junction without accident. Independently of the ordinary motives which may be supposed to have influenced the Sultaun's mind in desiring to raise the blockade of Goorumconda, it still contained a few of his relations, the family of Meer Saheb; and Hâfiz Fereed-u-Deen was an object of peculiar vengeance. Futteh Hyder, Tippoo's eldest son, then about eighteen, was placed in the nominal command of nearly all the Silledar horse, assisted by Ghâzi Khân, the Sultaun's original military preceptor; and Aly Reza, as a privy counsellor. Their appearance at Goorumconda was totally unexpected; and Hâfiz, supposing the party to be no more than a few plunderers, mounted his elephant for the advantage of a better view, and went out to examine their numbers, followed by no more than twenty horsemen, the rest being ordered to follow. He had not advanced far, when he found himself surrounded by superior numbers, and descended from the elephant to mount a horse, and endeavour to force his way back. While in the act of mounting, he was charged on all sides, and carried off as a prisoner; and the horse, who were coming on in tens and twenties, as they could get ready, were attacked in this state, and cut to pieces; and such was the panic, that the lower fort was evacuated with great loss, and the Mysoreans were at liberty to remove the individuals from the hill, and to afford to the besieged the opportunity of re-occupying the lower fort.

The transactions of the ensuing day are not less remarkable than the first result of this well-conducted enterprise. It will be recollected that Hâfiz Fereed-u-Deen was the embassador sent by Nizam Ali to Tippoo Sultaun in 1789. He had been treated with marked disrespect, and was really more a prisoner than an embassador, when in the course of negotiation, Tippoo was induced to depute Aly Reza to accompany him on his return, and to propose a treaty of marriage. The court of Nizam Ali felt it incumbent on their dignity to retaliate in some degree the disrespect experienced by their own envoy; and the whole was very justly ascribed to Hâfiz Fereed-u-Deen, who affected no concealment of his actual sentiments. When taken, he was plundered of his last garment, and some person had the charity to give him a sort of patch-work quilt, covered with which he was seated at the place of his imprisonment. In this state Aly Reza approached him. "You recollect," said he, "the disrespectful language you employed towards my sovereign and me at Hyderabad on the occasion of the demanded marriage." — "Perfectly well," replied the prisoner, "we were then serving our respective masters: that day is past. If you are here for the purpose of revenge, murder me at once, but do not dishonour me." Aly Reza immediately ordered him to be led out to a concealed situation under cover of a rock, and in his own presence to be cut to pieces in cold blood. On the return of the detachment to Seringapatam, a circumstantial report was made in public durbar of the transaction. Tippoo had the grace to express a slight disapprobation of the death of Hâfiz Fereed-u-Deen, actually commanded by himself; but expressed his satisfaction at the murder of a French officer in Nizam Ali's service, who had been taken at the same time. The military indiscretion of this unfortunate man produced inferences highly unfavourable

Jan.

CHAP. XL. 1792. to his character; and so little were the facts understood even by his own countrymen, that Lord Cornwallis, after receiving all the explanations, publicly ascribed to a treasonable communication with the enemy the inconsiderate act which terminated in his murder.

On the return of Nizam Ali's army to Goorumconda, the English detachment once more put it in possession of the lower fort, and after arranging a more efficient blockade, that army resumed its march to the south, and joined Lord Cornwallis in
Jan. 25. the neighbourhood of Ostradroog, on the 25th of January.

Every thing that related to the eastern line of operation and supply, was not only ready, but the advance had been retarded, not so much by the awkward arrangements of Nizam Ali's army, as by the intentional delays of Perseram Bhow, to which we shall presently advert. All the convoys had joined, and the travelling grain merchants, furnishing to the amount of sixty thousand oxen, many of them formerly attendant on the armies of the house of Hyder, were already in a regular train of communication, and had, for several months past, furnished the English army with grain from various quarters, but chiefly from Coromandel. The granaries there provided for the service of the war were open to all such as brought the requisite certificates; they purchased the grain at cheap rates, and sold it in camp for whatever it would fetch. It was the obvious purpose of Lord Cornwallis, that grain should be plenty, not cheap, for cheapness would check the inducements of the merchant, and diminish the supply; while therefore no limitation of price was attempted, he always ensured to the merchant a fair profit, by purchasing on the public account, whenever it fell below a certain standard, and dispatching the adventurers for a fresh cargo: and by a steady adherence to these simple commercial principles, he secured an abundance which had never before been experienced in any English campaign, and the amount of the supply may be conjectured from the acknowledged fact, that the number of strangers in Mysoor in the campaign of 1792, could not have fallen short of 400,000 persons. Much has been conjectured, and little ascertained regarding this extraordinary class of men, whose habits and history were at that period entirely unknown to the English army. Every man and many of the women were armed with a great variety of weapons, and although moving with their whole train of women and children, who could scarcely be classed among the impediments, proved themselves capable, in several instances, not only of military defence, but of military enterprise, as was particularly evinced in the assault and plunder of the lower fort of Cabal Droog. Farther north they are known by the name of *Brinjâries*, a supposed Persian compound, designating their office with an army; in the south they are called *Lumbânies*, but no conjecture has been hazarded regarding this name, and they have not even a tradition regarding their origin. After a discussion of some length with an assembly of chiefs regarding their descent, and pressing for some traditional account of their original country or home, "That is our country," said the eldest among them, pointing to the tent which covered his grain bags, "and wherever it is pitched is our home, my ancestors never told me of any other;" and nothing can be added of fact or conjecture, except that their language is northern, and apparently a dialect of the Penj-aub-ee. After a

CHAP. XL. 1792. war, in which of course many of their cattle are destroyed, they seek for some forest inhabited only by tigers, worthless to its government, and the terror of the neighbourhood, which they obtain permission to occupy, and enter it fearlessly, waging war with its former inhabitants, until it becomes a safe nursery for the increase of their herds, and affords a few patches for the growth of roots and corn; and detachments go occasionally forth carrying grain or drugs to the sea shore, and bringing a return cargo of salt.* In forming an establishment of this nature to which the author's assent was required, it was particularly stipulated, that they should be governed by their own laws and customs, and punished by their own magistrates, with two reservations, to which in the first instance they strenuously objected; 1st, that no capital execution should take place, without the sanction of the regular judicial authority; and 2d, that they should be punishable for murder: in other respects they were tenants at will, without rent or tax, and governing themselves according to a principle familiar in India, by the customs of

* Salt, of an inferior quality, is manufactured in the interior, by a very simple process, of lixiviating earth impregnated with salt, which discovers itself by an efflorescence on the surface; a reservoir approaching the form of an inverted cone, is formed in a high mound, and lined with viscid clay, perfectly water-tight; from the apex a communication is made by a hollow bamboo tube to the earthen vessel destined to receive the saturated water; and over the tube, in the apex, a rude filter is prepared by crossed twigs and straw; matters being thus adjusted, the reservoir is filled with the impregnated earth, and water added for the purpose of lixiviation. The saturated water, on being received into the separate vessel, is then removed to the boiler, and when sufficiently evaporated, the salt is spread out for its final drying; from the imperfection of the filter, it always contains a quantity of black earth, and its bitter flavour seems to indicate the presence of sulphate of magnesia, and some specimens which deliquesce have probably muriate of magnesia. Many inhabitants prefer it from habit, to the sea-salt of the coast, obtained by solar evaporation.

their cast. The adjacent villages, however, began to claim the land, when it was no longer worthless, and on the whole they were troublesome to the Government. The executions to which they demanded assent, or the murders for which they were called to account, had their invariable origin in witchcraft, or the power of communication with evil spirits. If a child sickened, or a wife was inconstant, the sorcerer was to be discovered and punished; and the traces of belief in a benignant and supreme being, were more faint and obscure in this semi-barbarous community, than among those rude mountaineers who, in every part of India, recede from communication with civilized man. The free command of their own time and means, which the nature of Lord Cornwallis's operations permitted him to allow, rendered them the most efficient branch of his commissariat; and an importance, beyond its value, was attached to their general utility, from overlooking the very unusual circumstances of his situation in the campaign of 1792: but subsequent experience has shewn that the expectation of their accompanying the operations of an active campaign, of which the movements cannot certainly be foreseen, or depending on their supplies, without a perfectly open rear, will always terminate in disappointment.

The preparations of General Abercromby for the campaign of 1792 were well considered and effective. The duties of his government had carried him to Bombay, and he returned to Malabar in November 1791, bringing with him or receiving from Palgaut all the means of a good equipment; and he made his first march from the head of the pass towards Mysoor on the 22d of January with an effective force of eight thousand four hundred men.

Lord Cornwallis was ready at an earlier period, as we have already noticed, with an army, according to the returns, of 22,033 men, a battering train of forty-two pieces, and forty-four field guns, but excluding the artillery-men and pioneers, his effective force, in cavalry and infantry, was 16,721 men. The demonstrations of Tippoo Sultaun to the northward had induced his Lordship to request that Perseram Bhow should advance simultaneously on the direct road from Sera, as well to prevent a detachment towards Goorumconda, which actually occurred, as to form a column on his right to unite at the proper time with General Abercromby: but the general purposes of the war were of secondary consideration in all the movements of this chief: he had a political illness which produced an embarrassing correspondence, and it was the necessity of delay arising from this circumstance which induced Lord Cornwallis to occupy the time intended for advance in the siege of Savendroog, which he had determined to leave in his rear from the great improbability of being able to reduce it; and thus in the actual result the delay was useful.

After separating from Lord Cornwallis on the 8th of July 1791, Perseram Bhow pursued his exclusive object of plunder, in which he was eminently successful, and completed what had been left unaccomplished by Hurry Punt, near Raidroog, of a secure route for its realization in the Mahratta territory. Lord Cornwallis's summons to advance, found him occupied in the neighbourhood of Chittledroog, on which he had formed some abortive designs, to be executed by means of treachery. His supposed illness detained him in that neighbourhood; but in fact, he contemplated the rich plunder of the town and province of Bednore; and to this object, he determined to sacrifice all those interests of the confederacy, which depended on his co-operation in the concerted plan. Well knowing that he could not with safety get entangled in the woods of Bednore, until Lord Cornwallis was actually before Seringapatam, and in conformity to a violation of compact with his friends, as shameless as any that Tippoo had ever practised with his enemies, he not only took no part in the general plan of operation, but did not even arrive at Seringapatam until upwards of a fortnight after the service was finished, and the preliminary articles of peace had been signed.

Perseram Bhow had not sufficiently concealed his purpose from the enemy: it was plainly indicated by his gradual approach on the western line instead of the southern, as demanded by the obvious combinations of any rational plan of campaign; and the Sultaun had strengthened the provincial troops of Bednore by a division under his relation Reza Saheb, which enabled that officer to take the field with a force of about 8000 men, and 10 good field guns.

The English detachment, as usual, bore the prominent brunt of every serious service, and Captain Little who had no alternative but to comply with the requisitions of Purseram Bhow, executed those services in a manner which caused the sordid purposes of the expedition to be forgotten in its brilliant achievements.

Hooly Onore situated near the confluence of the Toom and Buddra was carried by assault, after a siege of only two days on the 21st of December, and the army crossing the Buddra at that place, proceeded south-west towards Simoga, situated on

CHAP. XL. 1792.

the western bank of the Toom or Tunga, which river they crossed on the 26th. It was the purpose of Reza Saheb to wait in the vicinity until the troops should be divided by the operations of the siege, and in that state to attack them unexpectedly in the rear, and by a powerful sortie from the fort. The position which he occupied about ten miles to the southward of the fort so plainly indicated his designs, that it was determined to anticipate them by an attack, which from the strength of his position, he did not expect. His right rested on the river, his front was covered by a deep ravine, and his left by underwood (jungle), deemed impenetrable, a lighter continuation of which in front of the ravine, it was necessary to pass before the position could be correctly examined. On the 29th, Captain Little with only two guns, about a thousand English sepoy firelocks, and five hundred Mahrattas, penetrated the jungle in two columns, and after a severe conflict of upwards of two hours, succeeded in turning the enemy's right by the bank of the river; three guns fell into his immediate possession, the enemy commenced a precipitate retreat, and Captain Little did not abandon the pursuit, on that and the succeeding day, until he had overtaken and captured every gun, and completely dispersed the whole corps; an achievement which, in a fair and combined consideration of judicious design and spirited execution, was certainly not exceeded by any operation of the war.

From this period until the middle of January, the Mahratta army made little change in its head quarters, being too busily employed in realizing plunder, over a large extent of plain country opened to their detachments by this event. In January Perseram Bhow penetrated the woods, and arrived on the 28th before the exterior lines which surrounded the city of Bednore. He was preparing to force them by means of the English troops, when he received intelligence that Kummer-u-Deen had been detached with a large corps of infantry, from Seringapatam, and was rapidly approaching by a route in the woods, which would intercept his retreat. He instantly commenced a retrograde movement, called in his detachments, and commenced his march to the south-east, crossing the Toom, near Simoga on the 10th of February, four days after Lord Cornwallis had stormed the enemy's lines at Seringapatam; and he did not reach the vicinity of that capital until near the middle of March, when general indignation at his faithless and unprincipled conduct had long been merged in greater events.

CHAPTER XLI.

Lord Cornwallis's advance — Considerations — Description of the Sultaun's position — General attack on the night of the 6th February 1792 — Plan of the attack in three columns — Execution — right — centre — left — Tippoo's conduct — Operations of the 7th — Attack on Colonel Stuart in the morning — Admirable defence of the Sultaun's redoubt — Attack on Colonel Stuart in the evening — Advances to negotiation — Tippoo releases the Officers taken at Coimbetoor — Some of them had been liberated in the operations of the 6th — Lord Cornwallis consents to receive the Sultaun's envoy — Discussion of that measure — Attempt to assassinate Lord Cornwallis — Negotiations — Preliminary treaty submitted by Tippoo, to a full meeting of his officers — executed — Delivery of the hostages — Conferences preparatory to the definitive treaty — The Sultaun's rage at the demand of Coorg, as a violation of the preliminaries — discussed — Reciprocal preparations for renewing the war — considered — Tardy decision of Lord Cornwallis — forces the conclusion of the definitive treaty — Territorial cessions described — Motives of Lord Cornwallis's moderation — discussed.

CHAP. XLI. 1792. THE English army under Lord Cornwallis, that of Nizam Ali under one of his sons, Secunder Jah, accompanied by the minister, exhibiting an apparatus more splendid, and a crowd as little efficient as that of the former campaign, together with the small body of Mahrattas under Hurry Punt, a superannuated
Jan. 25. old man, united on the 25th of January, near Savendroog,
Feb. 1. and commenced their march from Hoolioordroog. On the 1st of February every human dwelling was in flames as they ap-
5. proached, and on the 5th, after passing over a high ground which gave a full view of Seringapatam, and of Tippoo's army

encamped under its walls, the confederates encamped about six miles to the northward.

Lord Cornwallis, ascribing to his enemy councils equally dictated by firmness and by wisdom, apprehended that he would leave the defence of the capital to a trusty officer and ample garrison, and keeping aloof with a light and effective army, act on the communications of the besiegers, and dislodge them by the mere force of their own numbers: these apprehensions received additional force, from the absence of the only branch of the confederacy (that under Perseram Bhow) from which his Lordship could expect efficient aid; but the actual presence of the Sultaun's army dissipated all alarms on that account, and promised to realize his best hopes of being enabled to strike a decisive blow before the commencement of the siege. Feb.

A bound hedge, formed of a wide belt of thorny plants, commencing at the bank of the river, about a thousand yards above the island of Seringapatam, runs due north, about three thousand yards, and embracing a commanding eminence, sweeps south-east, in nearly a diagonal direction, until it terminates at the river immediately under the Carigat hill, near the point which terminated the action of the 15th of May 1791; the intention of such belts, is to form a retreat for cattle on the appearance of a superior cavalry, and to be a sort of exterior line of defence. The eminence described, was fortified with a well constructed redoubt, and the Carigat hill had another work not finished; these two works, one within the bound hedge, the other without it, might be considered as advanced works, on the flanks of the position: another interior system of seven powerful redoubts, supported by the fort, and by each other,

CHAP. XLI. 1792. formed the main position of the army, but an eventual retreat was secured by the works of the fort, and by strong lines on the island, along the whole extent of the banks of the river, which formed in itself an additional defence, being in many places not fordable, and in most very rocky and difficult. The guns pointing north in all the works described, were not less than three hundred. The knowledge of the principles of fortification * ascribed to Tippoo Sultaun in some publications, was certainly not discovered in its effects by any of his newly erected fortresses. In the practical erection of redoubts of various construction, he had, on this occasion, been well assisted; their situations had been skilfully chosen with reference to the ground, and he had devoted his whole time and attention to the strengthening of this formidable position from the period of the recession of the allies in June 1791. One detachment of importance only, that of Kummer-u-Deen, was abroad, for a small corps of cavalry, which appeared in the vicinity of Madras, about this period, is no farther worthy of observation, than as it may suggest the true and efficient means which were not employed.

The Sultaun was confident that no decisive enterprise could be undertaken until the junction of the army of Bombay, which had again arrived at Periapatam, and in the intermediate time he expected to finish the important work on the Carigat hill; and although an English corps ascended that hill on the morning of
Feb. 6. the 6th, for the obvious purpose of reconnoissance, while another

* A very handsome case of instruments was found in his tent. In his library, (see Stewart's catalogue,) was a translation of Euclid, and several works of reputation on geometry, mathematics, and astronomy. I have reason to believe, that in the theory or practice of mathematics, nothing could be ascribed to him, except the ambition of being thought to possess this as well as every other science.

examined his right, it is certain that he had no expectation of attack on that night.

Lord Cornwallis, having prepared written instructions to be communicated to officers commanding divisions and corps, the orders were issued immediately after sun-set, and three distinct columns in their appointed order of march, were ready to move about eight o'clock, with a brilliant moonlight; the right hand column preceding the others about half an hour on account of the greater distance, in order that all the attacks might be simultaneous. Until the whole had marched no communication was made to the allies, who were in astonishment and dismay, at hearing of an attack without cannon, and in consternation at Lord Cornwallis's undignified arrangement of going out himself to fight like a common soldier.

The right attack under General Medows was ordered to leave untouched the advanced redoubt on the eminence which was distant from the nearest part of the fort about two miles, and was situated so far to the enemy's left as to be clear of the direct front of their main position. It was intended that this column should penetrate the left of the encampment and line of works about fifteen hundred yards in the rear of the advanced work, and turning to the left carry all the works and overthrow the troops of the enemy's left wing, until it should come into communication with the centre column under Lord Cornwallis and receive his farther directions. The firelocks of this column were 3,300, and the Europeans exceeded in number those of the centre column.

The centre column had no more than 3,700 firelocks, and may be considered as subdivided into three divisions; the front, under Colonel Knox, which was to mix with the fugitives, and pass over into the island; the centre, under Colonel Stuart, which, after penetrating the whole depth of the camp, was to turn to the left, and overthrow the enemy's right wing, after which he was to endeavour to force the works of the island. The rear of the column formed a reserve under Lord Cornwallis, to be joined by the right column under General Medows.

The left column, under Colonel Maxwell, had 1,700 firelocks; it was ordered to force the work on the Carigat hill, to descend and turn the right of the main position, and unite with Colonel Stuart (the senior officer), in forcing the works of the island at that point, or obey such other orders as he should receive from the Commander-in-chief. The whole operation will be most distinctly understood by presenting a summary account of the separate proceedings of each column.

On receiving the several reports of the officers who had examined the position in the morning, two suggestions were discussed regarding the advanced work on the enemy's left; one, to make it the first object of attack; the other, to leave it out of the plan of operations. The last was determined; but there was an ambiguity in the order, and the officer charged with guiding the column, led it to the advanced redoubt, and it was three quarters of an hour later in commencing the attack than either of the other columns. The redoubt mounted eight pieces of cannon, and was supported by three other guns in position which flanked its approach. It was defended with the most obstinate bravery by the troops within, as well as those appointed to support that part of the position. The grenadiers rushed steadily forward, through a heavy fire of grape and musquetry, to escalade the work; but the officer of engineers, who had charge of the scaling ladders, and several of his men being killed in the first attempt, the ladders could not be found, and without them it seemed impossible to get into the redoubt. The last finish had not been given to the work by the construction of a draw-bridge, and a narrow path-way had been left for communication, with a good traverse, which commanded also the gate of the sortie. The gate and traverse were forced; but the enemy determined on resistance to the last, turned one of their guns loaded with grape, and nearly the whole of their musquetry against the gorge. It was stormed; but the fire of the enemy was so well reserved, that nearly the whole party that entered was swept away, and the attack was repulsed, but rallied behind the traverse. The fire of English musquetry, although inferior to that of the enemy, was so well directed through the gorge, that the gun could not be reloaded. A fresh disposition was made for renewing the attack, and the grenadiers ultimately succeeded in closing with the bayonet, and carried the work. Some of its garrison defended themselves to the last; many leaped from the embrasures into the ditch; but scarcely a man escaped being killed or taken. About four hundred men fell in its defence; and the English casualties were ninety-one, of whom eleven were officers. A strong garrison of four companies of Europeans and one battalion of sepoys was left for the defence of this important work, and the column wheeled to the left to execute the remaining part of the order; it was led clear of the left hand redoubt of the main position, (which could now scarcely be deemed tenable), against the next in succession: when the work became distinctly visible, the head of the column was halted for the purpose of closing up, and the

CHAP. XLI. 1792.

great strength and magnitude of the work, combined with the desperate resistance of the first, and the total cessation at this moment of all firing in the centre or left attacks, suggested the idea that they must either have been completely successful, or have been repulsed, in either of which cases it was of greater importance to Lord Cornwallis to be strongly reinforced, than to risk heavier losses for the attainment of works which it was argued must fall of themselves, in consequence of the possession of the commanding work already carried. This reasoning being adopted, the column counter-marched, re-crossed the bound hedge and made a detour to fall in with the route of the centre column, which it did not find until day-break, after the conclusion of the business of the night.

The head of the centre column was discovered about eleven o'clock, by the enemy's advanced posts; the silence previously enjoined, was not broken by a single voice, but without any previous order, every man, as if actuated by a single impulse, lengthened his step, and before the lapse of one minute, the whole column was marching at nearly double its former rate. The advanced division was composed of six flank companies of Europeans, one regiment and one battalion, one battalion company of the regiment preceding the whole, to cover the pioneers; the column penetrated with the bayonet alone, but as the battalion following in its appointed order, was just entering the camp, a galling fire on its flanks, brought down among others, the officer * commanding; he was exceedingly beloved by his men, and his fall produced some agitation, which ended in confusion. Colonel Stuart, whose station was immediately in the rear of

* Captain Archdeacon.

this corps, rode on to rally them, but finding that much time would be lost in the attempt, he ordered up the next corps, the 71st: three companies of the battalion had followed the advanced division, and the remainder of the corps formed in the rear of the 71st, and afterwards behaved with great steadiness.

In order that the direction to mix with the fugitives might be more effectually executed, Lieutenant-Colonel Knox instructed the captains commanding the flank companies, to look more to celerity than solidity of movement, each captain to be exclusively responsible for his own company. The regiment and battalion was directed to follow in compact order, and he passed himself, with the flank companies, through a crowded mass of fugitives, by the main ford close under the guns of the fort. From the circumstances which have been noticed, the flank companies separated in the crowd into two bodies, and continued to penetrate along the glacis, to the south branch of the river, considerably to the eastward of the Mysoor bridge, and contributed by the alarm spread in that direction, to prevent any disturbance to the more serious operations. Three companies, with Lieutenant-Colonel Knox obtained a guide to Shaher Ganjaum, in the centre of the island, and contributed essentially to the success of the centre division, as will presently be seen. The remaining seven companies of the regiment, and three companies of sepoys following in compact order under Captain Hunter, missed the ford, and crossed the river a little below it, into the palace named Deria Dowlut Baug; and Captain Hunter considering himself to be the first that had crossed, took post to wait for farther intelligence or orders; but as day light approached, and neither orders nor intelligence arrived, he perceived that his post, under the immediate fire of the fort, would not be tenable by day light, and most fortunately as we shall find, re-crossed the river, and joined the reserve under Lord Cornwallis.

Lieutenant-Colonel Stuart, with the centre division of the centre column, after calling up the 71st, as has been stated, was proceeding the whole depth of the camp before he should turn to the left, and perceived himself to be close to a strong work (afterwards known to have been named, by way of eminence, the Sultaun's redoubt,) which it was necessary to storm, and a compact mass of cavalry coming forward to charge; a single volley dispersed the cavalry, and the resistance of the redoubt was inconsiderable. Lieutenant-Colonel Stuart left for its defence two companies of Europeans, one of sepoys, and a proportion of artillerymen, and proceeded according to order to overthrow the enemy's right wing. A heavy body of infantry retreated before him, and was supposed to have taken the direction of the river, and to have passed into the island; but when following the direction of the tents as his most certain guide, he had attained nearly the extreme right of the position, he perceived a line of troops drawn up with perfect regularity to oppose him. It was Lieutenant-Colonel Maxwell's division. They reciprocally mistook each other for enemies; and Colonel Stuart had just ordered a volley to be given, and an immediate charge with the bayonet, when the error was most happily discovered. This division had executed with the greatest precision the service allotted to it, by storming the work on the hill; but in descending, in farther prosecution of its objects, was severely galled by an advanced body from the enemy's right, who had availed themselves of the cover of a water-course which winds round its foot, and subsequently by the troops forming the right of the main position. The column, however, surmounted every obstacle, broke the enemy's right, and proceeded until met, as related, by the column under Lieutenant-Colonel Stuart.

Both columns were now near the river, and a heavy fire was opened upon them from the works on the opposite bank. A disposition was made for forcing them; but this first attempt being made where the river was not fordable was beaten back with great loss. Endeavours were now made, at various points, to find a practicable ford: one was found by Lieutenant-Colonel Baird, who lodged a small party under cover on the opposite bank, and sent back a report of his success: the head of the principal column had scarcely half crossed, when the enemy's fire suddenly and totally ceased. It was to the three companies under Lieutenant-Colonel Knox that they were indebted for this unexpected facility: that officer, having waited long and in vain at Gunjaum for the remainder of his division, perceived the heavy fire below him, and distinctly penetrating its cause, ordered the batteries to be stormed in reverse, and thereby ensured a success which might otherwise have been doubtful. The depth of the river where crossed by the united columns, left not a dry cartridge; the bayonet remained as their sole reliance, and Lieutenant-Colonel Stuart, until day-light could give him better means of examining his ground, occupied a position to the eastward of Sheher Gunjaum, with a flank resting on each branch of the river, the right nearly under the Carigat-hill.

In the meanwhile Lord Cornwallis took post with the reserve within the bound hedge where the column had penetrated, with his left towards the Sultaun's redoubt; he received in due time intelligence of complete success in the ultimate and most doubtful object of the whole operation, a firm footing on the island; and took the earliest means in his power to send over by a better ford, which was afterwards discovered, ammunition to enable Lieutenant-Colonel Stuart to maintain it. He was still, however, without tidings of General Medows, and reflected with the utmost anxiety on the profound silence on his right. The enemy was better instructed, and collecting the unbroken forces on the left, with such part of the centre as had retreated in that direction, bore down with the greatest resolution on this reserve: it had consisted of the battalion companies of one regiment, and two complete battalions of sepoys, and had recently been joined by the seven companies of Europeans and three of natives from the Dowlut Baug already mentioned, who had but just replaced their wet ammunition when the attack commenced, about two hours before day-light. "If General Medows be above ground," said his Lordship, "this will bring him." The charge of their venerated Commander-in-chief, assailed by overwhelming numbers, animated every individual, European and native, to the highest stretch of exertion; and he personally gave his own orders with his accustomed coolness and precision: he waited a very near approach before he ordered the charge of the bayonet, which caused a complete but a temporary route: the enemy perceiving his small numbers returned repeatedly, and each time with apparently encreasing vigour, but they were each time met and repelled with augmented energy and cool determination, and it was near daylight before they finally desisted. Lord Cornwallis had, at an early period, been wounded in the hand, but concealed the accident, and the number of casualties in his staff and among the troops was considerable. Still ignorant of General Medows's situation, it was necessary to take a position where his small corps could not be surrounded, and he retired to the Carigat hill, which had been occupied, after being carried by the left column, and at the foot of that hill he at length met General Medows's division. The whole encampment was now brought forward to a nearer position; but before relating the events of the succeeding day, it will be satisfactory to revert to the Sultaun's proceedings during the operations which have been described.

His tent was pitched in the usual place, in the rear of the centre of the position close to the road, by which the head of the centre column penetrated. He had made his evening's meal in the Sultaun's redoubt to the right of that situation, and the garrison which had made way for him and his suite had not time, perhaps not much inclination, to resume their posts when he left it in haste. On the first alarm he mounted, and before he could receive distinct reports of the nature of the combined attack, a mass of fugitives announced that the enemy had penetrated the centre, and the bright moon-light soon discovered to him a lengthened column passing through the camp, and pointing directly to the main ford which would intercept his retreat. He went off with celerity, just in time to pass over before the head of the English column, many of his attendants being killed by the advanced company. He passed in by the sortie of the Bangalore gate, and entered the detached lozenge work at the north-east angle of the fort, whence he issued his orders, and remained until day-light. One of the companies (commanded by the Honourable Captain Lindsay), in passing this sortie, looked in to ascertain whether the gate were open, and could not have been many minutes behind the Sultaun. The day of the 6th had been employed in issuing pay to the troops. It was the routine that on the first day the sum payable to each cushoon should be counted out to the respective buckshees. On the second day they made their detailed payments, and for the custody of the money during the intermediate night, the bags were closed with the seals of the buckshee and the treasurer, and remained in the responsibility of the general treasury or pay-office, till next day. In this state was the charge of Poornea the treasurer when the action commenced. He began immediately to load the treasure on his camels, and in the act of doing so was severely wounded by a musquet ball. He continued however to complete his work, his camels passed over along with the grenadiers, they were particularly noticed by the troops as inconveniently encreasing the crowd, but to no farther extent; and he carried off his whole charge along the foot of the glacis of two faces of the fort, and lodged it at the Mysoor gate without the loss of one rupee. The Ahmedy Chêlas constituted the centre which had given way, and availing themselves of the confusion which ensued, and the open retreat by the Mysoor bridge, nearly the whole body, amounting to 10,000, many accompanied by their wives and children, marched off with their arms to the western woods of Coorg, and thence to their respective homes. Many of the Assud Oollahee availed themselves of the same opportunity; the fugitives and followers of every description passed in crowds over the Mysoor bridge, and many did not stop till they reached Nunjendgode, a distance of twenty-five miles. A number of foreigners who had served both Hyder and Tippoo took advantage of this opportunity to quit a service which they detested, and among them an old man named Blevètte, who had really constructed most of the redoubts, and several of the artificers sent by Louis XVI., who had no other means than flight of returning to their native country. On collecting the reports of the morning, the killed, wounded, and missing, amounted to twenty-three thousand men; and Poornea recommended as the most efficient mode of rallying the missing, to proclaim the farther issue of two lacks of rupees on account, which brought back a much smaller number than he had expected.

Tippoo Sultaun, seated in the detached work, issued his orders for the operations which have been described. During the movements of the advanced portion of the centre column, close under the works, a few guns had been opened by the fort, of which he peremptorily prohibited the repetition, from the apprehension that the troops still in camp might imagine the fort itself to be attacked, and imitate the example of the Chêlas. When clear day-light appeared, it opened without reserve on every thing hostile within its reach. Lord Cornwallis had ascended the Carigat hill for the purpose of commanding a more extensive view. With the exception of that unfinished post, the position on the eastern extremity of the island, the advanced work on the left, and the Sultaun's redoubt, the other detached works continued to be occupied in force by the Mysoreans, scattered parties seemed to be collecting in all directions, but the tents of the

CHAP. XLI.

1792. Feb. 7.

encampment were struck and no semblance remained of an exterior army.

A little after day-light, a body of infantry advanced to dislodge Lieutenant-Colonel Stuart from the provisional position which he had assumed, and finding their fire not returned, (the dry ammunition having not yet arrived,) came forward under cover of walls and houses in considerable numbers. Colonel Stuart had no alternative, but to cover his troops in the best manner he was able, until the enemy should give him an opportunity of using the bayonet; and Lord Cornwallis, who perceived these transactions from the hill, sent a reinforcement with ammunition, which enabled Colonel Stuart to resume the offensive, and drive back the assailants.

The troops on the island were found to be in greater force than the Sultaun had supposed, and before renewing the attack, he deemed it necessary to retake the Sultaun's redoubt, which had a considerable command of the communication between the island and the northern side of the river. This work was nearly of the same construction and strength as the advanced redoubt on the left, but being within range of the fort and island, its gorge was very properly left open, in order that, if carried, it might not be tenable, and there had been no time to reverse its defences, if the rocky ground had admitted the attempt. Under these circumstances, the fire of the fort keeping the army at a distance, the garrison, consisting of one hundred and fifty men, was left to its own resources. A temporary barricade of the gorge, with some broken carriages found in the place, was soon cleared away by the cannon of the fort, and of several field pieces brought into an advanced position; and in the first furious assault, which was repulsed, between ten and eleven, Captain Sibbald, the officer commanding, was killed: Major Skelly, one of Lord Cornwallis's aid-de-camps, who had been sent thither on duty, and found himself unable to return in consequence of its being every where encompassed, had hitherto merely assisted; but now assumed the command; and found, that in this obstinately contested assault, the men had expended nearly the whole of their ammunition: most fortunately, two oxen carrying spare ammunition with the column, and scared in the course of the night, had strayed into the ditch of the work, and were discovered about noon: the men had scarcely filled their cartouch boxes from this resource, when a fresh attempt was made. The Sultaun, on the first repulse, had exclaimed in grief and indignation, "Have I no faithful servants to retrieve my honour?" After some consultation, the cavalry volunteered the enterprise, and a body of two thousand, in compact order, advanced about one o'clock, with a determined countenance, as if to charge at once into the redoubt, but stopping suddenly at musquet range, four hundred dismounted, and rushed with the greatest impetuosity to force the entrance with their sabres. The garrison was perfectly prepared, the gorge was necessarily cleared during the existence of the cannonade, but when it ceased, from the approach of the assailants, the garrison formed across the opening, while the portion of the parapet which bore on the enemy was also fully manned: the fire was so coolly reserved, and deliberately given, that the leading part of the column was completely brought down; and though, after the first hesitation, a disposition to advance was strongly manifested, the steady and

CHAP. XLI. 1792. rapid continuation of the fire threw the enemy into confusion and retreat: two captured guns in front of the right of Colonel Stuart's position had just been tried, and being found to reach the spot at random ricochet range, are said to have produced an unmerited impression: the retreat of the assailants was covered as before by the cannon, and by large bodies of infantry, under the shelter of rocks, firing into the gorge, and the garrison resumed what little cover was afforded by the circular form of the work.

The next and last attack was made by the French European corps, which the garrison awaited with the expectation of a severer effort. The Europeans, however, did not justify this expectation, but went off with a much smaller loss than had been sustained by either of the prior attacks. If the Sultaun found a repugnance in his troops to renew the assault of the redoubt, its defenders were cordially rejoiced to perceive them finally drawing off about four o'clock. In this small work, two officers and nineteen men lay dead; three officers and twenty-two men were wounded, to the extent of being totally disabled, exclusively of the less serious cases. Not a drop of water was procurable throughout the day, for the relief of the wounded; and the sufferings of the unhurt sustained a more severe trial from their friends than from their enemies; but the glory was imperishable, of a number now reduced below one hundred effective men, totally unsupported, having for a whole day, and in circumstances highly unfavourable, defied the efforts of an army acting under the support of the guns of their capital. The inversions of military fact in some European bulletins, have long become the theme of proverbial jest even in their own country; but perhaps none can be quoted so perfect in its kind as a triumphal ode* to commemorate the recapture of the Sultaun's redoubt, by the Sultaun's own hand, composed by his orders, and the most favoured performance of the royal band.

Success against the redoubt being now deemed impracticable, it remained, as a last effort, to attempt to dislodge the troops from the island, where, with the exception of advancing his right to turn some of the enemy's guns against the troops attacking the redoubt, Lieutenant-Colonel Stuart had made no material change in his dispositions. About five o'clock, two heavy columns of infantry entered the town, drove in the advanced posts, and opened a fire on the main position. They were promptly attacked, driven through the town with great loss, and there was time before dark to establish a strong post at the advanced gate nearest the fort. The Sultaun, thus foiled in every effort to dislodge the English troops from any of the positions they had seized, thought proper on the same night to evacuate the whole line of redoubts to the north of the river, and leave them to be occupied by the English, who commenced without a moment's unnecessary delay all the preparatory operations of the siege. †

* The reader may consult the opinion of the late Colonel Kirkpatrick, regarding the merit of the encomiastic odes. — Tippoo's Letters, page 391; and I venture to add, that independently of its veracity, I have never heard a travestie more truly ludicrous, than the song of triumph alluded to in the text, which I heard recited several years afterwards.

† The amount of casualties was less than might have been expected, from 11 p. m. of the 6th, till 7 p. m. of the 7th. Their proportion will shew the degree in which each column had been engaged.

Right column - - - - - - - -	95
Centre - - - - - - - - - - -	342
Left, including its separate and conjoint operations -	98
	535

CHAP. XLI. 1792. Our last notice of an advance to negotiation related to the fruitless mission of Apajee Ram in August 1791. When the long gathering storm was at length ready to burst over his head, the Sultaun, on the 12th of January 1792, made a farther attempt to obtain Lord Cornwallis's reception of an envoy; to which an answer was immediately returned, stating that no negotiation could take place with a person who not only disregarded treaties, but directly violated articles of capitulation. "Send hither," added his Lordship, "the garrison of Coimbetoor, and then we will Feb. 8. listen to what you have to say." On the 8th of February, after all his military efforts had failed, he sent for Lieutenants Chalmers and Nash, who had comparatively not been ill treated, and after addressing himself to the former, to announce their intended release, he asked if he were not a relation of Lord Cornwallis? No. Then he was an officer of considerable rank? No. The Sultaun was incapable of comprehending those sacred obligations which are independent of personal motives. Should he not see Lord Cornwallis on his return to camp? Certainly: he hoped to have that honour. He was then desired to take charge of a letter on the subject of peace, which, as he earnestly affirmed, he had always been anxious to preserve and renew; he solicited Lieutenant Chalmers's assistance in obtaining it, and begged that he would return with an answer to the letter. To all this a suitable reply was made, and the two officers were sent on the ensuing morning to the English camp. The letter affirmed that the terms of the

Of which number there were:

European officers, including those of sepoys -	36
European non-commissioned and private -	267
Natives - - - - - - - -	232
	535

capitulation had been misrepresented, that Kummer-u-Deen had not engaged for the liberation of the garrison of Coimbetoor, but only promised to recommend it; and to cover this gross violation of truth, the Sultaun had caused the counterpart of the articles of capitulation, signed and sealed by Kummer-u-Deen, to be forcibly taken from Lieutenant Chalmers previous to his release. This fact is broadly stated in Lord Cornwallis's reply, as well as the notoriety of the remainder of the garrison being in irons; he nevertheless accepted the release of these two officers, as the indication of a desire to make atonement, and the allies consented to receive his envoy.

In fact a considerable proportion of the prisoners of Coimbetoor, with 27 European captives, and among them several of the Christians, abandoned to barbarian slavery by the grand * officer of an order whose religious vows imposed an opposite obligation, were in prison at Sheher Gunjaum at the time of the assault, and the release of these unhappy sufferers by their comrades and countrymen, was a source of reciprocal joy, more allied to the purest feelings of domestic virtue, than to the lofty agitations of victory. Others of the victims surrendered by the same Suffrein, in 1782, had escaped with some fellow-prisoners from Chittledroog, and received protection from the English corps, serving with the Mahrattas: the information received through these channels, indicated the continued secret disappearance of prisoners †, but testified the existence of many still

* *Bailli* de Suffrein, 1782.

† A considerable number of bankers and other natives, imprisoned at various periods, and falling under various suspicions, were dispatched about this time; among them was a Mussulman, named Mahadee Khân, of whose crime the following account was given me by one of his friends. On the return of Lord Cornwallis to Bangalore, in June, 1791, this person strongly urged his master to make peace, and on

CHAP. XLI. 1792. remaining, contrary to the conditions of the peace of 1784: and independently of the suggestions of moral feeling, the political wisdom might still be questioned, of the slightest relaxation, until the surrender of the last captive; if the murder of the whole, and the fabricated tale of their previous death, might not unhappily have been anticipated as the consequence of persisting in that demand.

A few hours however, before sending for Lieutenant Chalmers, to announce his liberation, Tippoo Sultaun had adopted other, and as he conceived, more efficient measures for the termination of the war, which this concession was intended to promote, by its tendency to remove suspicion. It was observed and reported by the spies, that the head-quarters of the army, well known by its distinguishing flag, was placed in the new ground of encampment, in the rear of the left near the hill, in a situation which exposed it to enterprise, and some officers of the guards, (stable horse) on being consulted, deemed the attempt so feasible, that they volunteered its execution. The whole of the corps was accordingly warned for duty: all the principal officers were admitted to the Sultaun's presence early on the
Feb. 8. morning of the 8th, and were harangued on the importance of the enterprise with which they were charged, and the confident certainty of an early and glorious termination of the war, if they

Tippoo's objecting that the confederates would demand an enormous sum of money, Mahadee answered, that if the requisite powers were committed to him, he would be responsible for raising the money, without touching the treasury, or burdening the country. It was immediately comprehended, that there was no other mode than to lay under contribution those who possessed it; and as his experience enabled him to form very correct estimates on this subject, he was considered by the courtiers as a dangerous adviser; it was only necessary to hint, that he was carrying on a secret correspondence with the English, and his secret murder was immediately ordered.

could only rid him of one individual; the officers all solemnly pledged themselves not to return without executing the service, and received the betel from the Sultaun's own hand; their march down the river excited no other impression than that of a detachment sent to act on the communications, and they were perceived to cross it at Arakerry without any other suspicion. On the 9th they received farther reports from their spies, and at dawn of the morning of the 10th, their selected advanced guard entered in the rear of the left between the camp of Nizam Ali and the English. The enterprises, founded on their exact similarity to each other, had been numerous in the preceding year, and this similarity was the cause of no alarm being excited by seeing a body of horse, supposed to be Nizam Ali's, between the two camps. They lounged on, until they approached the park of artillery, and asked some gun-lascars with apparent indifference, for the tent of the *burra saheb*, or commander. The men, supposing Colonel Duff the commandant of artillery to be meant, pointed without suspicion to his tent, when the horsemen instantly drew their swords and galloped towards it, cutting down the few persons they found in their route: they did not, however, even reach the tent, which they erroneously supposed to be that of Lord Cornwallis; a small body of sepoy drafts for the army of Bombay, encamped in the rear, turned out with alacrity; and opened a fire which dispersed the cavalry without farther alarm, and they escaped with little loss across the hills. The use of bang* or opium among the horsemen of

CHAP. XLI. 1792.

Feb. 10.

* The leaf of the *cannabis sativa*, (hemp,) used in various forms, green and dry, and sold as an intoxicating substance in every bazâr in India. I certainly should

CHAP. XLI. 1792. India, is a familiar preparation for a desperate charge, mischievous at the best, even for that single purpose, but utterly ruinous on any service requiring self-possession; but I am not disposed on enquiry to concur with those who ascribe the failure on this occasion to intoxication. The *morale* of the army (if a term of modern application may be allowed), had sustained a severe shock; and the cool reflection of two days on a desperate enterprise, had not tended to remove the depression. The effect, however, of this evident attempt at assassination, added to the impression of the event formerly related on his approaching Bangalore, induced Lord Cornwallis to listen to the intreaties of his friends for the security of his person. His only guard had hitherto been two sentries, native troopers from his body guard; but from this period, he was prevailed on to permit a captain's guard of Europeans to mount every night over his tent.

Vague accounts had been received of Perseram Bhow's operations; but Lord Cornwallis finally dismissing from his mind all dependence on such an ally, ordered General Abercromby to advance by the route of Eratora, thirty miles above
Feb. 11. Seringapatam, where he crossed the Cavery on the 11th of February. Colonel Floyd, with the English Cavalry and
14. some of the allies, met him at Caniambaddy on the 14th,
16. and on the 16th the junction was formed without material impediment*; the intermediate time between the 7th and 16th, having been industriously employed in the formation of

not state the fact if I supposed public brewers to be ignorant of this article of the *materia venenata*.

* Four regiments and seven battalions, amounting to about 6000 effective men.

materials for the siege, by the reluctant, but indispensable ruin of the extensive and beautiful * garden of the Lâll Baugh. All the arrangements were completed for its active prosecution. Colonel Stuart occupied a more advanced and concentrated position on the island, which he strengthened by field works, in order that he might be enabled to spare troops for the ordinary duties of the trenches. His command included the island, the Sultaun's † redoubt on the north, and another, which he had himself constructed south of the river, to command a ford, and to prevent the occupation of ground which would overlook his position. This position supplied the whole of the materials for the approaches and batteries, and working parties for their preparation. The principal attack was determined against the northern face, near the western angle; and General Abercromby was ordered to pass the river above that angle, to establish the requisite enfilade of the face attacked. There was no regular ford, and the Sultaun supposed the rugged bed of the river to be impracticable for guns; he accordingly evinced particular surprise on finding an advanced guard already in position at day-light on the 19th, and made some active but ineffectual efforts to frustrate the design: but the operation was effected without any material loss.

1792.

Feb. 19.

On the 22d, in connection with the degree of progress made in the trenches of the northern bank, General Abercromby advanced his posts for the purposes of the siege. The Sultaun very properly felt a keen jealousy of every thing attempted on

22.

* Beautiful, according to the ancient taste of our own country, when it had not begun to abhor straight lines, and imitate nature.

† Now called Sibbald's, in honour of the officer who had fallen in its defence.

that side, and Kummer-u-Deen having returned to the vicinity, after having alarmed Perseram Bhow into a retreat from the woods of Bednore, as already related, the Sultaun determined to make a great effort, not only to dislodge the advanced posts, but to compel Lord Cornwallis to abandon altogether the objects to be accomplished by the division south of the river. In the early part of the action, the advanced troops having expended all their ammunition, attempted to retire for a time to better cover, until they could receive a supply, and the Mysoreans rushed forward with a general shout to overwhelm them; the party consisting of no more than three companies of Europeans and two of sepoys, retiring in the most perfect order, unable any longer to tolerate the triumph, suddenly faced about, and reversing the order of pursuit, charged with the bayonet, drove the multitude far beyond their former position, until checked by the fire of the fort, they were obliged to resume it. The enemy reinforced by still greater numbers again advanced, and the party again retired, but were met by a reinforcement and ammunition which enabled them to resume the offensive. Appearances which indicated an attack on General Abercromby's main body, if he should detach too largely, prevented his reinforcing so liberally as he would otherwise have done, and all his dispositions, justly influenced by these considerations, prevented that greater danger; an intermediate corps checked the attempts of a body of horse advancing to fall on the right of the advanced troops, they maintained their ground against the repeated efforts of the enemy throughout the day, and it was near sun-set before the Mysoreans finally desisted from the attack; the English casualties being 104 — those of the enemy greatly more numerous. The corps of

Kummer-u-Deen had advanced from Mysoor on the same morning, the bridge of that name*, under the guns of the fort, was open to the Sultaun's whole army, now encamped on the southern glacis, close to the scene of action; the whole English force south of the river, consisting of three regiments, and six battalions, separated by a rocky river, and a detour of nearly five miles from the main army, might thus be considered as exposed without support to the whole force of the enemy, and great credit is due to the perfect steadiness with which such a situation was maintained. Colonel Stuart's position, although nearer than that of the main army, was now too weak in troops, and too much exposed from contiguity to the fort, to admit of detaching with safety; the distant appearance however of the action, and the obvious alternation of advance and retreat, had caused some anxiety, and he had assembled his flank companies at the ford, ready to attempt a diversion, if farther appearances should seem to demand the risk.

Having noticed the operations which materially influenced the fortune of the war, it is not intended to enter into the detail of the cotemporaneous or subsequent proceedings of the siege.†

In the meanwhile, and in conformity to the acquiescence indicated by Lord Cornwallis in his letter, dated the 11th of February, Tippoo's vakeels had been received in camp on the 14th. For this important service, Gholaum Ali was released from the confinement and disgrace which he had sustained since his return

* More generally called the Periapatam bridge.

† The reader who may desire greater detail, will find the operations of this campaign given with clearness and precision in Major Dirom's narrative, 1 vol. 4to.; and for those of the whole war, he may refer to Mackenzie's Sketch of the War with Tippoo Sultaun, in 2 vols. 4to.

from the embassy to Constantinople, and was associated to Ali Reza, whose infamous proceedings at Goorumconda have been recently discussed. They were met, on behalf of Lord Cornwallis, by Sir John Kennaway, political resident at the court of Nizam Ali, on the part of Secunder Jah, by Meer Aalum, the former envoy to Calcutta, and by a person deputed by Hurry Punt, conversant with the statements of revenue which would form the basis of the ultimate arrangements. Four conferences, lasting nearly the whole day, generally with the intervention of a day for reference and instruction, brought the demands of the
Feb. 22. confederates to a distinct issue; and on the 22d, their ultimatum was sent in to the Sultaun. The operations of the siege were so far advanced as to enable Lord Cornwallis to calculate with certainty on opening his breaching batteries on the 1st of March, at five hundred yards distance, against two points, where an unfinished part of a glacis of masonry towards the river enabled him to see the base of the rampart, with the certainty of forming a practicable breach on the second, if not on the first day, that he should direct his fire to that exclusive object; and frame-work was in preparation to carry the flying sap across the rocky bed of the river, if prudence should seem to require that delay. The action of the 22d had secured the means of corresponding progress on the south. The island and Sibbald's redoubt, with another advantageous point of enfilade on an islet west of the fort, were prepared to take their subsidiary portion of the service, and means were in reserve to set fire to the whole town, if a measure so dreadful to a crowded population should become indispensable. Although a considerable proportion had been sent off, by the route of Mysoor, of the fugitive inhabitants, un-

connected with the army, the families of the officers and soldiers were deemed a necessary pledge. The defective public departments had never re-organized the wreck of the 6th of February. Tumbrils, ammunition and store carts, run in for security on the 7th, remained, blocking up the streets in the utmost disorder; the additional crowd had converted the whole interior into an incipient pest-house, and the carnage in the event of a siege must have been horrible. Grain daily pouring in from the east and from Coorg created an absolute abundance in the camp of the besiegers. A respectable corps of four hundred Europeans and three battalions of sepoys, with field artillery, under Major Cuppage, in Coimbetoor, had reduced the intermediate posts and ascended the Gujelhutty pass, where large supplies were ready to advance; and independently of Perseram Bhow, and the English brigade serving with his army, who however were now positively known to be approaching, means existed of seizing Mysoor and completing the blockade. The opinions therefore which have suggested any doubt of the enemy's capital being at Lord Cornwallis's mercy, appear to have little other ground than the uncertainty of every human event not absolutely accomplished.

On the 23d Tippoo assembled in the great mosque all the principal officers of his army, laid before them the Korân, and adjured them, by its sacred contents, to give him their undisguised advice on the question he was about to propose. He then read to them the ultimatum of the confederates, in the form of five preliminary articles of peace, requiring generally —the cession to the allies from the countries *adjacent* to theirs of one half of the dominions which he possessed before the war, Feb. 23.

CHAP. XLI. 1792. — the payment of three crores * and thirty lacs of rupees, one half immediately, and the remainder in three instalments of four months each; — the release of all prisoners from the time of Hyder Aly, — and the delivery of two of his sons as hostages for the due performance of the conditions. On the mutual execution of these preliminary articles hostilities were to cease, and a definitive treaty was to be adjusted. "You have heard," said the Sultaun, "the conditions of peace, and you have now to hear and answer my question: *shall it be peace or war?*" The officers unanimously replied that they were ready to lay down their own lives in defence of their sovereign and his capital; but with various shades of expression they were in substance equally unanimous, that the troops were disheartened and had become undeserving of confidence. As a mere scene, our settled abhorrence of the principal character cannot entirely extinguish the general impressions of sympathy, resulting from the mournful circumstances of such a meeting, extending to some who were really deserving of compassion: impressions exaggerated perhaps in the author's mind, by finding, in after-times, that few of the members of that assembly could recite its events without tears; but as a mere scene, it also exhibits a singular illustration of the most corrupted mind, and the farthest alienated from truth, being driven by the mere force of adversity to repose its last confidence in truth alone.

Feb. 23. The preliminary articles duly signed and sealed by the Sultaun were sent to Lord Cornwallis on the same day, and although

* The original demand had been six crores, (each crore equal to about a million sterling,) and had been reduced to the sum stated in the text, on the offer of the Sultaun's vakeels *to swear! to the impossibility of paying more than three!*

the terms required that they should be delivered by the hostages in person, he not only consented to a delay of two days in their arrival, but agreed that hostilities should cease on the ensuing morning. The English soldiers received the order with grief, and almost with indignation; independently of the ordinary feelings of the profession, they had long cherished as a moral duty, the hope of liberating with their own hands the survivors of their murdered countrymen; and when for several hours after the cessation, the enemy continued to fire with redoubled animation (a conduct exclusively arising from ignorant and arrogant stupidity), it was difficult to restrain them within the limits of obedience; but about noon the cessation became reciprocal.

1792. Feb. 24.

Every thing that the most delicate consideration could suggest, was observed in the reception and treatment of the hostages; one, a boy of ten, and the other of eight years old; and the observation of Gholaum Ali, that the paternal character was now transferred from Tippoo Sultaun to Lord Cornwallis, ceased to be an Oriental image, if determined by the test of paternal attentions.

The extent of the cessions was of course to be determined by the amount of revenue, and some time, as might be expected, was lost in discussing fictitious statements: when, however, the schedules were prepared for inspection and reference, and in the English share was found the principality of Coorg, the Sultaun became frantic with rage. "To which of the English possessions (he asked) is Coorg adjacent? Why do they not ask for the key of Seringapatam? They know that I would sooner have died in the breach than consent to such a cession, and durst not bring it forwards until they had treacherously obtained possession of my children and my treasure:" (for a crore of rupees had already arrived in camp.) Although there can be no question that the demand of Coorg was unexpected by the Sultaun, there is assuredly as little doubt of the absence of all design of unworthy concealment, on the part of Lord Cornwallis. That his demand, as has been argued, was reasonably chargeable with the character of a departure from his preliminary engagement, is a proposition that can scarcely be maintained. The cession of the principalities of Malabar, adjacent to no English possession but the commercial establishment of Tellicherry, was so far from being questioned as a departure from the preliminary treaty, that the Sultaun and his vakeels openly congratulated themselves on that selection, which was avowed in the conferences even before the conclusion of the preliminary articles. Coorg was a continuation of the same territory without any intervention: no limitation in the length of radius, or form of frontier line, was stipulated by the preliminaries: and that the territory of Coorg was above the ghauts, and in a commanding situation, relatively to the Sultaun's capital, and remaining territories, would be too much to urge as a conclusive objection, in discussing the principles of a treaty, which had for its professed object, to cripple his resources, and render him incapable of farther mischief. But admitting, as was the fact, that the demand was really unexpected by Tippoo Sultaun, it may be affirmed, without the fear of reasonable question, that it ought not to have been unexpected; and that no reflecting mind, acquainted with the principles on which the war had commenced and been conducted, could have expected from Lord Cornwallis the intention of abandoning the only ally who had performed all his obligations with fidelity, efficiency, and honour.

That the surprise of the Sultaun was entirely unaffected, was proved by his having expedited upwards of a crore of rupees to camp, in the confidence of such a selection of territory as accorded with his interpretation of the preliminaries; and immediately after the reception of this demand, immense bodies of men were perceived at work on a strong retrenchment behind the face attacked: a fact which the Sultaun deliberately and repeatedly denied, on receiving remonstrances on the violation of the armistice, although it was distinctly visible to the two armies; while the studied procrastination of the vakeels appeared to indicate a renewal of hostilities, and a desire for obvious reasons, that the rupture should be protracted to the latest possible period. The situation of Lord Cornwallis about the middle of March, was widely different indeed from his condition about three weeks before, at the period of the signature of the preliminary articles. It has been noticed that the only materials for the siege were procured by the destruction of the splendid garden of the Lâll Baugh, they were chiefly of the cypress tree, and from having been long made up were become so dry, brittle, and inflammable, as to be unfit for use; and a new stock of materials must be brought with immense labour from considerable distances. But above all, the army had now been before the place, occupying the late field of action, for upwards of six weeks, under circumstances which materially aggravated the common insalubrity of a standing camp. The precise nature of the climate generating a pestilent endemic

CHAP. XLI. 1792. at this worst season of the year, had until that period been little understood; but the hospitals had for some time been encreasing their numbers in the most alarming degree. Every successive day diminished the powers of the besiegers, and augmented the chances of successful resistance. If hostilities should even be instantly resumed, the delays consequent on the causes described, would in the actual ratio of encreasing sickness, scarcely leave the requisite number of effective men for the ultimate assault; and farther delay would be fatal to every reasonable hope of success; the growth of this state of things had been so slow and imperceptible, every successive evasion had so skilfully consumed * time, that it was made to burst in all its truth on Lord Cornwallis's mind, like a discovery which admitted not a moment's pause. Fair copies of a definitive treaty were prepared and sent to the Sultaun, with the alternative of executing them within a certain number of hours, or finally breaking off the negotiation. The captured guns which had been brought to camp, were sent back to the positions assigned them for the siege, and all other preparatory measures were openly adopted. Perseram Bhow, who had at length appeared, and whose presence might be depended on while there was plunder and not one minute longer, was sent to join General Abercromby †, and commenced his ravages

* It was not known that one of the individuals entrusted with the conduct of the joint negotiation, held a separate correspondence with the Sultaun during the whole period; the individual is no more, but the subject is still too delicate to be farther pursued, with reference to our connexions at the court to which he belonged: the evidence of the fact rests on original documents.

† Lord Cornwallis, in one of his dispatches, explains the reason why he could make no detachment of his allies before the arrival of Perseram Bhow. "It suited neither the health nor inclination of Hurry Punt to go on any detached service, and Nizam Ali's minister, although he with great zeal offered to supply the place

before the armistice was denounced; the vakeels blustered, made some impotent and absurd claims to the liberation of the hostages, and talked of taking their leave, until they found his Lordship's determination to be irrevocably fixed, and then at length announced their master's acquiescence. On an evasion to gain more time, the hostages were moved preparatory to their march to Coromandel, and their guard of Mysoreans were made prisoners. The vakeels entreated with abundant promises, and obtained, that their departure might be suspended for one day; but that day passed over with promises only; a third had nearly elapsed, when they at length appeared with the treaties duly executed; the hostages were restored to their former condition, and on the ensuing day the forms of delivery and interchange of the definitive treaty were publicly concluded.

1792.

Mar. 16.

17.

18.

19.

Where both parties were equally anxious for separation, the matters, chiefly of form, which remained to be adjusted were treated with proper dispatch, but the wisdom of the alternative which brought the question to an immediate issue was evinced, by the indispensable necessity of accepting from the Sultaun a large supply of doolies and bearers, to move the accumulating numbers of sick, who generally experienced a perceptible amendment on the very first march from this horrible ground.

The shameless infraction of the treaty of 1784, with regard to the inhabitants of Coromandel had been daily and constantly evinced during the whole period subsequent to the 6th of

of the Bhow, was so completely ignorant of military affairs, and so total a want of arrangement prevailed in every part of his army, that he was equally unable to put the troops in motion, or to provide for their subsistence, even for a few days, if removed from our army!" Precious allies!

February. In consequence of confidential communications from these unhappy captives, Colonel Stuart had latterly appointed the southern redoubt for their resort by night, and it was an interesting spectacle at the dawn of every morning to see its whole circumference surrounded with men, women, and children, with their cattle and effects, who were passed over to the island before broad day-light, and forwarded by Lord Cornwallis's orders by the first escort, and with such aid as they required; and notwithstanding the mortality which had thinned their numbers, many thousands were in this manner restored to their native homes.

The cessions of the treaty of 1792 may be described in a few words; they were founded on the principle of equal partition to the three confederates, without reference to the gratuitous inequality in the provisions of the offensive and defensive treaties of 1790, or any retrospect to the conditions intended to secure to the earliest in the field, the exclusive benefit of their own efforts. The selections of ceded territory brought the Mahrattas to the river Toombuddra, their frontier in 1779; restored to Nizam Ali his possessions north of that river, and the province of Kurpa to the south, which had been lost about the same period. The English obtained Malabar and Coorg; the province of Dindigul, which had jutted inconveniently into their southern provinces, and Bâramahâl, an iron boundary for Coromandel, which placed her frontier fortress of Rayacota on the table land of Mysoor to the east, as the undisputed cession of Coorg secured a similar advantage to the west.

In whatever degree the wisdom of these measures may have divided public opinion, the moderation of Lord Cornwallis was eminently conspicuous, and universally acknowledged. That the desire of maintaining or establishing a balance of power had, according to the prevalent opinion*, influenced his Lordship's determination, can no where be traced in his official correspondence. The treachery or imbecility of his allies, of whom one (the Mahrattas), had exhibited a total disregard of every obligation necessary to the success of combined measures; and the other, an incapacity to take any effective part in their execution, had undoubtedly rendered him long anxious for an early termination of the war, but constituted no part of the question at issue at the date of the preliminary treaty, when he had only to determine, whether he should be satisfied with any thing short of the extinction of the house of Hyder, which, according to every information and appearance, would have followed the capture of the capital. The approach of Mahdajee Sindea to Poona, with views inimical to the English, might constitute a very important object of future consideration, but did not affect the question, limited to ten or fifteen days, of urging the siege to extremity, or consenting to a smaller sacrifice. Without, therefore, seeking altogether to exclude the influence of these considerations, they are certainly more doubtful than those which remain to be described.

General opinion in England was averse to all war in India, and would censure with peculiar asperity any result which might be tortured into evidence of premeditated conquest. The expediency of the earliest practicable termination of the contest, a proposition self-evident in every war, disputable with reference to

* This opinion is discussed and rejected in Malcolm's India, page 95.

CHAP. XLI. 1792.

conditions alone, and never to the abstract principle, had been strongly impressed on his Lordship's attention by the most recent dispatches from the Court of Directors and the minister for Indian affairs; and the great national importance of being prepared to take any part that the exigency of events might require, in those agitations which were about to convulse the whole European world, was too obvious to be absent from the mind of any statesman. But leaving, as is most candid in every practicable case, the author of a measure to assign his own motives, the decision itself, and the more immediate grounds on which it was formed, are stated with the greatest clearness and simplicity in his official dispatches, before the negotiation, and during its progress. In the first of these documents he declares, "that to allow Tippoo to retain even a considerable portion of his present power and possessions at the conclusion of the war, would only, instead of real peace, give us an armed truce, and he should immediately reject any proposition of this natuie ; but that if such concessions were offered as would put it out of the enemy's power *to disturb the peace of India in future*, his Lordship would suffer no prospects, however brilliant, to postpone for an hour that most desirable event, a general peace."* In the second document, describing the nature of the measure in progress, he states his opinion "that it would be more beneficial to the public than the capture of Seringapatam, and render the final settlement with the allies much more easy;" a most important consideration, which has been overlooked or undervalued in all the discussions on the subject. "Those, (his Lordship adds†,) whose

* Abstract of Lord Cornwallis's correspondence with the Government of Madras, given in their general letter to England, dated 21st February, 1792.

† General letter, 15th March, 1792.

passions were heated, and who were not responsible for consequences, would probably exclaim against leaving the tyrant an inch of territory, but that it was his duty to consult the real interest of the Company and the nation."

Although in the sequel of his communications with the Sultaun, after the conclusion of the peace, his Lordship's natural courtesy disposed him to the most conciliatory conduct, and even to language indicating the direct hope of cordial amity, it is neither just nor necessary, to infer so superficial an estimate of human nature, as should really calculate on friendship as the fruit of deep mortification. No adequate ground had intervened for changing the opinion delivered by his Lordship, in the official letter accompanying the definitive treaty, which describes Tippoo "as a faithless and violent character, on whom no dependence could be placed." It is necessary, therefore, to revert to his Lordship's professed determination to exact "*such conditions as should put it out of the Sultaun's power to disturb the peace of India;*" and it only remains to decide, whether this legitimate purpose, of which the English General had been the acknowledged master, was or was not effectually attained. The evidence of subsequent events will probably be deemed to amount to a negative answer: but candour cannot fail to add, that if, under the political circumstances of the moment, the entire extinction of the Mysorean power were really inexpedient, no farther reduction of that power could have been attempted without the imminent risk of being forced into the extreme alternative.

CHAPTER XLII.

After the departure of the confederates, Tippoo makes arrangements for liquidating the payments — Description — The Sultaun's boasted improvements discussed — Physical science — Barometer — Thermometer — Medical science — General regulations — Coincidence of eastern and western novelties — Military regulations — Infantry — Cavalry — Artillery — Reflections on these changes — Navy — Lords of the Admiralty — Admirals — Ships — Equipments — Commerce — Exports — Imports — Political economy — Black and red pepper — Medical regimen — Connection of commercial and political views — Laborious code — Curious section — Swindling conditions — Suppression of bankers and money changers — Circumstances related — Contrast of particular details with general ignorance — Revenue — True antiquity, and pretended novelty — Innovations not improvements — One improvement — the suppression of drunkenness — of Hindoo temples — Police — Regulations regarding the right and left hand casts — Ethics — from the Korân — and the Greek schools — Truth — Oaths and their systematic violation — Book of regulations all-sufficient — Anecdote — Royal state — The word Tippoo — Tiger — Throne — Intended regulations — Reformation of the calendar — Incidental notices of the intention of a new revelation — Weights and Measures — French — English — Bengal — Ancient Mysoor — Tippoo Sultaun — Measures of internal administration — Erection of an interior rampart to Seringapatam — Means of procuring workmen — Shocking abuses — Siege and capture of Oochingy — Barbarous mutilation — Strange and fraudulent allotment of dwellings to his officers — Return of the hostages — Conversations — Banishment of the Mehâdees — Early history of Dhoondia — Strange history of his connection with the Sultaun — Discontents of the husbandmen — Deceptions practised on the Sultaun — Augmentation of revenue — army — jageers — Ludicrous selection of officers — Death of the raja, and plunder of the palace — Royal nuptials, and previous disappoint-

ments — Reformation of the army — Zumra — Dress — Oaths — Proclamation — Destruction of the lake of Tonoor — Fairy tale — Projected rupture of the dams — Camp bazâr.

CHAP. XLII. 1792.

AFTER the departure of the confederates, Tippoo Sultaun assembled the chiefs of his army and the heads of departments, and announced to them that the three crores and thirty lacs of rupees, by which he had purchased their safety and his own, must be divided into three portions.

1st. From the royal treasury he would give one crore and ten lacs. 2d. The army should contribute, as a nezerâna, (forced gift) sixty lacs: and 3d. The civil officers and inhabitants at large must give a nezerâna of one crore and sixty lacs.

For the contribution of the army it was calculated that ten putties * or monthly payments were, or ought to be, made in the year. This number was ordered to be reduced to seven in the year, and so to continue until the difference should amount to the nezerâna of sixty lacs.

For the remaining crore and sixty lacs, the distribution was prepared by the heads of civil departments, who were most directly interested in lessening the weight to be borne by themselves, and it is notorious that it was not only lessened but entirely removed. The nominal contributions of each were fairly enough computed, and entered in the accounts as paid, but the amount was actually made up by an excess in the contributions of each district, beyond the sum at which it was assessed in the books; and this corruption in the heads of departments, in levying clandestinely the amount of their own contributions, made it necessary for them to connive at similar

* See p. 205. of vol. ii.

CHAP. XLII. 1792.

exactions in the local authorities down to the lowest runner of the most subordinate collector. It is generally believed, that a sum very far exceeding a crore and sixty lacs, was levied on the country; but in the two years, during which the payments to the confederates were protracted, one crore only was carried to the public account, and a balance of nearly sixty lacs remained as a charge against the country till the extinction of the dynasty. This nezerâna, or forced gift, and the horrible tortures inflicted in levying it, caused the most extensive secret emigrations of merchants and others into Bâramahâl, a country under the direct management of the Company's Government; and as every new attempt to realise the balances afforded a cloak for further exactions, these emigrations continued, in various degrees, as long as the existence of the dynasty.

The "incomparable inventions and regulations*," introduced into the administration of affairs by Tippoo Sultaun, constitute the prominent boast of his own memoirs, and have been frequently adverted to in the course of this work. The sudden abstraction of one half of his dominions, imperatively demanded corresponding changes; and this appears to be the most convenient period for taking a general view of his institutions, which are dated at different periods from 1783 to 1799, and underwent the most capricious changes without any adequate motive. No delineation of character can exhibit so authentic a portrait of mind, as these strange aberrations of untutored intellect, purporting to be the spontaneous effusions of superior wisdom: and an abstract sketch of the most remarkable of these

* Preface, p. xxi.

performances, added to some very brief notices of a similar tendency, will not occupy any considerable space. CHAP. XLII.

The Sultaun's acquaintance with physical science may be estimated by two letters addressed to Monsieur Cossigny, governor of Pondicherry; one acknowledging the receipt of "a *barometer*, complete in every respect, excepting the quicksilver, which, owing to its oldness, does not move up and down. It is therefore returned; and you are requested to send a good one, made in the present year." Another letter requests a certain instrument, and a Persian translation of an European treatise on its use; "in which it is written, that at certain times, the quicksilver rises a certain number of degrees; and that, if at such times, a person afflicted with certain disorders, shall, during a paroxysm of the complaint, place his hand on the instrument, the ascent of the quicksilver will mark the height of the disease." * In the first of these letters, the word *barometer* is used; in the second *howanumâu*, literally shewing the air. He appears to have received some obscure idea of the common, or, perhaps, the differential thermometer; and, desired to ascertain its application to medicine, a science in which he affected to be considered as a master, to the extent of frequently commanding, in his official letters, certain prescriptions for the cure of disorders. His system, like that of all Mahommedan physicians, was founded on the distinctions of the Greek schools, into hot, cold, moist, and dry; and among a multitude of absurdities, may be noticed one prescription, perhaps hitherto untried, to prevent hydrophobia, by keeping open the wound for six months. 1792.

* Kirkpatrick's Tippoo's Letters, p. 464.

CHAP. XLII. 1792. The professed and formal regulations for the conduct of affairs had commenced before his departure from Mangalore, with the aid of his great innovator, Zein-ul-ab-u-Deen; and embraced either directly or incidentally every department in the science of government. Regulations military, naval, commercial and fiscal, police, judicature, and ethics, were embraced by the code of this modern Minos, and his reformation of the calendar, and of the system of weights and measures, was to class him with those philosophical statesmen and sovereigns, of whose useful labours the secretary had obtained some obscure intelligence; and it may be convenient to premise regarding the whole, that the *name* of every object was changed: of cycles, years, and months, weights, measures, coins, forts, towns, offices military and civil, the official designations of all persons and things without one exception, * exhibiting a singular coincidence, at nearly one and the same time, and in distant and unconnected quarters of the globe, between the extremes of unbridled democracy, and uncontrolled despotism; in a system of subversion, as sweeping and indiscriminate, as if the axiom were familiarly established, that every thing is wrong because it exists.

A few words will suffice for each subject. The elementary instructions for the infantry contained in a code of *military regulations*, were as well given as could be expected from a person copying European systems, and unacquainted with the elements of mathematical science: the invention of new words of command, would have been a rational improvement, if the instructions had thereby been rendered more intelligible; but the

* Many of these regulations may be referred to in the appendix to Kirkpatrick's Tippoo's Letters; and in an anonymous publication named British India analyzed.

substitution of obsolete Persian * for French or English, gave no facility in the instruction of officers and soldiers, who, speaking of them in mass, may be described as utterly ignorant of the Persian language. The directions for military conduct have a very creditable allusion, (without the name) to the means by which Sir Eyre Coote repeatedly provisioned Vellore in the face of superior armies, and triumphant reference to the fate of Baillie and Brathwaite, in the mode prescribed of attacking the Nazarenes on a plain ; but as a general code of instruction, it is below mediocrity. The organization of companies, battalions, and brigades, was frequently varied, and was sometimes made to include a body of cavalry, and to become a sort of legion, and at other times it changed the proportions of artillery to infantry. Perhaps none of these establishments could be condemned as extremely bad, nor could any be deemed entirely unobjectionable. Previously to 1792, they were all superior to any thing then existing among the native powers, with perhaps a doubtful exception in favour of Sindea's brigades, afterwards so well matured: and the practical effect of the whole system of his infantry was considerable expertness in the use of the musquet, and a respectable degree of facility in the evolutions most commonly required on service.

In the cavalry, besides a formation of regiments never effectually organized, his most remarkable change was the abolition of the martingale, universal among the native powers, which he considered in his instructions as rendering the horse obedient, but cramping his powers. The efficiency of the English cavalry,

* Zein-ul-ab-u-Deen never lost the nickname of *Chep-geer-Dumuc*, his first word of command in the manual exercise.

CHAP. XLII. 1792. in the campaign of 1790, was the true motive for prohibiting an equipment, to the absence of which he was willing exclusively to ascribe the superiority which he thus practically admitted. The general tendency of the changes, effected in the whole of his military establishment, was to increase and improve his infantry and artillery, at the expence of the cavalry. In the artillery practice in particular, the Sultaun affirms, that he had left his masters the Nazarenes at an infinite distance behind him, "although, like the salamander, they pass their lives in fire." There can be no question, that this change in his military establishment was among the causes of that superiority which he attained over his Indian adversaries, in the campaigns of 1786-7, and there is as little doubt, that it became the most decided source of inferiority, in his contest with the English power. The observation is neither new in itself, nor singular in its application; it may be traced in the history of every Indian power, which has prematurely opposed Europeans with their own tactics; and it has received its most recent illustration, in the erroneous counsel and false measures of defence, suggested to the Persians, instead of reading to them, in the history of their ancestors, a better hope of security in the same description of troops, and the same system of warfare, which continued through the lapse of ages, to foil or destroy the flower of the Roman legions, from Crassus to Julian.

The fleet was originally placed by Tippoo under the board of trade. The experience of two wars had shewn that it would always be at the mercy of an European enemy; and it seemed to have been chiefly considered as a protection to the trade against the system of general piracy then practised along the western shores of India, up to the Persian gulf. The loss of a moiety of every resource in 1792, gave a new scope and stimulus to invention; and the absurdity was not perceived of seeking to create a warlike fleet without a commercial navy, or of hoping, literally without means, suddenly to rival England in that department of war, which was represented to be the main source of her power, by the vakeels who accompanied the hostages, and had been specially instructed to study the English institutions. This novel source of hope was not finally organized on paper till 1796, and can scarcely be deemed to have had a practical existence. He began in 1793 with ordering the construction of an hundred ships; but in 1796, he sunk to twenty ships of the line and twenty frigates; eleven commissioners, or Lords of the Admiralty, (*Meer-e-Yem,*) who were not expected to embark; thirty *Meer Buhr*, or Admirals, of whom twenty were to be afloat, and ten *at court* for instruction — a school for seamanship which it is presumed a British Admiral would not entirely approve. A 72-gun ship had thirty 24-pounders, thirty 18-pounders, and 12 nines; a 46-gun frigate had twenty 12-pounders, as many nines, and six 4-pounders; the line-of-battle ships were 72's and 62's; and the men for the forty ships are stated at 10,520. To each ship were appointed four principal officers: the first commanded the ship; the second had charge of the guns, gunners, and ammunition; the third, of the marines and small arms; the fourth, the working and navigation of the ship, the provisions, and stores; and the regulations descend to the most minute particular, from the dock-yard to the running rigging; from the scantlings of the timbers to the dinner of the crew. Without obtruding farther details on the general reader, professional men will probably be enabled to determine the sources of his information. So far as a landsman may presume to conjecture, he had access to tolerably correct authorities in matters of mere detail, which in many cases he rendered ludicrous by a pretended knowledge, and profound ignorance, of the objects to be regulated.

The *commercial regulations* were founded on the basis of making the sovereign, if not the sole, the chief merchant of his dominions; but they underwent the most extraordinary revolutions. On his accession, he seems to have considered all commerce with Europeans, and particularly with the English as pregnant with danger in every direction. Exports were prohibited or discouraged; 1st, because they augmented to his own subjects the price of the article; 2d, because they would afford to his neighbours the means of secret intelligence; and 3d, because they would lift the veil of mystery which obscured the dimensions of his power. Imports were prohibited, because they would lessen the quantity of money, and thereby impoverish the country; propositions which may indicate the extent of his attainments in political economy; and such was the mean adulation by which he was surrounded, that domestic manufactures of every kind were stated to be in consequence rapidly surpassing the foreign, and a turban of Burhânpoor would be exhibited and admired by the unanimous attestation of all around him, as the manufacture of Sheher Gunjaum. The reader would draw an erroneous inference, who should consider these doctrines regarding export and import as belonging to the level of defective knowledge by which he was surrounded. It is not intended to try the opinions of any person from whom he could receive counsel by the test of those profound works which have instructed modern Europe; but at least his treasurer, Poornea, had a sound practical conception of the more simple fundamental truths, connected with the subject; and seldom propounded erroneous opinions, excepting when immediate fiscal profit occasionally obscured his views of prospective advantage. It was under the influence of this utter darkness in commercial and political economy, that in 1784 he ordered the eradication of all the pepper vines of the maritime districts, and merely reserved those of inland growth to trade with the true believers from Arabia. The increase of this article of commerce became some years afterwards an object of particular solicitude, but I could not determine whether the prohibition of growing red pepper or Chili, was to be considered as a commercial regulation to encrease the growth of black pepper, or as a medical regimen, or as a compound of both motives. It is a general opinion in the south of India, that the free use of red pepper has a tendency to generate cutaneous eruptions, and the Sultaun certainly prevented its entering his harem for six months; whether in that period he did not find the ladies improved in the smoothness of their skin, or was influenced by other causes, he withdrew the prohibition of culture about a year after it had been promulgated.

1792.

It was only from the personal reports of the vakeels who accompanied the hostages to Madras, that his attention was called to a proposition however strange, yet stated to be generally admitted among the most enlightened persons at Madras, that the power not only of the English Company, but of the English King, was founded in a material degree on commercial prospe-

CHAP. XLII. 1792.

rity; and the Sultaun devised an extensive plan for a similar increase of power; still however pursuing the principles which he conceived to be sanctioned by the example of the India company, of combining the characters of merchant and sovereign. In a long and laborious code of eight sections, with which the reader shall not be fatigued, he established a royal board of nine commissioners of trade, with seventeen foreign and thirty home factories in the several districts; furnished with extensive instructions for a profitable system of exports and imports, by land and by sea, and a strict theoretical control over the receipts and disbursements; the monopolies however continued to be numerous, and those of tobacco, sandal wood, pepper, and the precious metals, were the most lucrative.

One, however, of the sections of commercial regulation is so perfectly unique that it may afford entertainment. It professes to be framed for the attractive purpose of "regulating commercial deposits, or admitting the people at large to a participation in the benefits to accrue from the trade of the country." Every individual depositing a sum not exceeding five hundred rupees was declared entitled at the end of the year to receive, with his principal, an increase of 50 per cent. For a deposit of from five hundred to five thousand, 25 per cent. Above five thousand 12 per cent. with liberty at all times and in all classes, to receive on demand any part of the deposit together with the proportion of interest * up to the day. These variations of profit, in the inverse ratio of the deposit, were probably intended to shew his consideration for the small capitalist, but a project

* The word *interest* is not employed, usury being at variance with the precepts of the Koràn; *profit* is the term used.

for enticing his subjects into a swindling loan, was too glaring to be misunderstood, although covered with the thin cloak of religion in the following introductory paragraph. "All praise and glory be to the most high God, who, breathing life into a handful of clay, before inanimate, gave it the form of man; and who has raised some chosen individuals to rank and power, riches and rule, in order that they might administer to the feeble, the helpless, and the destitute, and promote the welfare of the people. In pursuance of this duty, it is decreed, &c. &c." At a very early period of his government, he had, in an ebullition of anger, extinguished the business of banker, and monopolized its dependent and most profitable trade of money changer. The circumstances have been related* which in 1779, led to a balance of twenty lacs, charged against this profession; and on Tippoo's demanding payment in 1784, the bankers assented to the gradual liquidation of the demand, on the condition that the revenues should pass through their hands, according to the usual practice of Indian Governments: a direct refusal, and a threat to imprison them all, was deprecated by the intimation, that the business of the money changer would also be at a stand, in the event of their confinement. "I can do without you both," answered the Sultaun in a rage: he ordered the whole to be confined, and issued an ordinance, converting the trade of money changer and broker, into a monopoly for the benefit of Government, furnishing coin for the purpose, from the treasury, to servants paid by regular salaries. In the subsequent year, we find an intelligent person, named Raja Ram Chunder †, reporting

* Vol. ii. page 203.

† Kirkpatrick's Tippoo's Letters, p. 129.

CHAP. XLII. 1792.

that the dealers kept aloof from transactions with the Government shops, that the expences far exceeded the profits, and that it was necessary either to abandon the plan, or to enlarge it, so as to embrace, not only regular banking establishments, but commercial speculations necessary to their prosperity; to all which he could obtain no more satisfactory answer than the following, "There is no regulation issued by us, that does not cost us, in the framing of it, the deliberation of five hundred years — do as you are ordered." A part of the suggested plan was, however, gradually introduced, and the funds in the hands of the money changers, were employed in advantageous loans. Yet with all this parade of being the master of every detail, he was ignorant of the contents of his "tosheck khana" royal warehouse of the capital, to the extent of sending to Poona, on the occasion of a marriage, for a small quantity of gold cloths, of which a ton at the least, was found in store on the capture of the capital.

The regulations of revenue, professing like those for pecuniary deposits to be founded on a tender regard for the benefit of the people, contained little that was new, except that the nomenclature and the institutions of Chick Deo Raj and Hyder were promulgated as the admirable inventions of Tippoo Sultaun, on the same principle that Spanish guns were found ornamented with the tiger stripe and inscriptions, purporting that they were cast at Seringapatam. Among the real novelties in the code of revenue not one improvement can be discovered; as specimens, may be adduced an instruction to seize all Christians and confiscate their property; and directions to individuals for rearing horses, absurd in themselves, and impracticable from the expence. There was indeed one novelty of a ludicrous description; offices requiring an exact knowledge of accounts, and formerly filled by bramins or Hindoos, were ordered to be executed by Mahommedans; and when it was objected to many of the individuals that they could not even write, the Sultaun gravely replied, that they would learn. But in the midst of our disgust at his vices and follies, one improvement occurs not undeserving the modified consideration of western statesmen, who value the health or the morals of the people. He began, at an early period, to restrict the numbers, and regulate the conduct of the shops, for the sale of spirituous liquors, and he finally and effectually abolished the whole, together with the sale of all intoxicating substances, and the destruction, as far as he could effect it, of the white poppy, and the hemp plant, even in private gardens. The large sacrifice of revenue involved in this prohibition was founded on the unforced interpretation of a text of the Korân; "every thing intoxicating is forbidden," and on that fanatical zeal which is deemed to cover, and found to accompany so many deviations from moral rectitude.

The same bigotry led him to the extinction of Hindoo worship, and the confiscated funds of the temples were intended to compensate, and would, if well administered, in a great degree have balanced the tax on intoxicating substances: the measure commenced at an early period of his reign, and the extinction was gradual, but in 1799, the two temples within the fort of Seringapatam, alone remained open throughout the extent of his dominions.

Of his system of *police*, the following extract from his official instructions may suffice. "You must place spies throughout the whole fort and town, in the bazârs, and over the houses of the principal officers, and thus gain intelligence of every person who goes to the dwelling of another, and of what people say, &c. &c." All this Hyder effectually did, and all this Tippoo Sultaun only attempted. No human being was ever worse served, or more easily deceived.

Of his talents for judicature, we must seek for examples, not in a general code to supersede the all-sufficient Korân, but in those occasional edicts which may be thought in some degree to belong to the department of police.

Few persons filling public situations in the south of India, have escaped embarrassment from the feuds and audacious excesses of the right and left-hand casts, and no person, European or native, so far as I am informed, has been able to trace with the slightest probability, the origin of these distinctions. The active leaders of each association belong to the *outcasts*; the Parias being the champions of the right, and the Chucklers, or workers in leather, of the left; and the higher casts of artificers range with one or the other of these generaldivisions. According to the Sultaun, the right hand enumerate eighteen casts in their party, and the left hand twelve in theirs. The loss of lives in the contests arising from their public processions, and the contempt of all authority, in forcibly shutting up the bazârs, and arresting the progress of all business, until the contested flags or distinctions be put down by their opponents, are familiar occurrences; and on one of these occasions the Sultaun applied his profound research and experience to trace the origin of these sects, and to devise the means of preventing future riots.

To the Parias he had already given the new name of *Sâmeree*,

Samaritans, because, as he affirmed, they and the ancient Samaritans, were equally distinguished by skill in magic. The Chucklers were *Chermdôz*, the common Persian designation of their chief employment. " In the language of this country," he adds, " they are called *Yêrè Kei* and *Bul Kei*, that is right and left hand, because these men being the grooms and foragers of the horsemen of Islâm, may be considered as their right and left hands, with reference to the important services which they perform; and such is the origin of the distinction, and of the names: they must accordingly now, as in ancient times, continue obedient to the men of Islâm, and serve no other masters." Then follow some rules for monopolising their services, and for suppressing future riots. The laws of Draco are tender mercies, compared with those which he established. The Yâsa of Chengiz Khân may have been equally summary, and equally careless of human life; but history exhibits no prior example, of a code, perverting all possible purposes of punishment as a public example, combining the terrors of death with cold-blooded irony, filthy ridicule, with obscene mutilation, the pranks of a monkey with the abominations of a monster.

Of eighteen customs or claims, seven liable to become the grounds of contest, were abolished, and the remainder were retained: but the penalties, however characteristic, cannot be exhibited without a veil. *

* 1st, The Sâmeree and Cherm Dôz shall use no flag or standard on pain of the amputation of both hands.

2d, Umbrellas are prohibited to both the divisions of cast; *at si cuipiam adfuerint, testes ejus exsecti in ore suo ponendi sunt.*

3d, The red turban or head-dress is prohibited to both; *at si cuipiam adfuerit, caput amputandum, et super podicem suum ponendum est.*

The best ethical treatises of the Mahommedans, of which the Sultaun's library contained a respectable collection, present beautiful abstracts of the doctrines of the Greek * schools, mixed with abundant darkness, from the metaphysics of the east and the west, to obscure the infidelity which is too obvious to be mistaken, and too dangerous to be avowed. To conjecture that Tippoo Sultaun could not read and understand these perform-

4th, Neither are to wear shoes on pain of having their feet cut off.

5th, They are both required to relinquish the figure of the kite, either on the standard, as formerly, or in any other manner.

6th, Military weapons are prohibited, from the dagger to the firelock. The possession of any instrument besides the small cutting knife, the awl, and the sickle, and such others as may be given by Government, involves the forfeiture of both hands.

7th, The pike with the tinkling circular ornament, is specially forbidden under the same penalties; and the whole of a strangely unconnected regulation, the order of which has only been observed in the seven prohibitions, is closed with the following sweeping clause; *si quis mandata hæc violaverit, palo in imo ventre infosso, crimen suum luet.*

In another regulation we have the following example of uncharitable barbarism; "persons born of slave-women and prostitutes shall not be taught to read or write; if any one shall instruct them, his tongue shall be cut out." "If any person before or after marriage, shall keep a prostitute or female slave, you shall, after ascertaining the fact, *take the slave for government!*"

* It has been affirmed, (in Le Sage's Political Atlas and elsewhere,) that translations of the Greek poets and philosophers were made into Arabic: with regard to the former, I believe the supposition to be entirely erroneous; the mythology, pervading almost every line of Greek poetry, is intolerable to the true believer. The Iliad and the Korân could not co-exist; and this obvious reason rendered impossible the translation of a Greek poet into Arabic. If, in the age of Haroun-ul-Resheed, Homer and Pindar had travelled as freely as Aristotle and Euclid, Europe would have imported back from Arabia, an earlier and a larger portion of civilization and knowledge than she actually received. In a Persian biographical collection, I have seen a life of Homer, in which he is stated to have held the same estimation as a poet among the Greeks, as *Amarilkeis* among the Arabs, but not a line of quotation.

ances, is an inference fairly deducible from the general state of literature in the south. *

But the following extract from the general regulations, affords abundant evidence, that even his theological lore, derived from the impure source of the Korân, furnished a master principle of ethical science; the inversion of which formed the fixed basis of his own conduct. "Falsehood is an offence of the highest nature, against both morality and religion. According to the books *Sherra Wekaya*, and *Tareech Velayet Khorassaun*, &c. offences against the sovereign are of four descriptions; and the punishment ordained for each of them is mentioned in these books. God has also pronounced his curse against liars: — *so heinous a vice is falsehood, that all the other vices on earth are produced by it.*" He then details the punishment of the four-fold offences against the sovereign; which, in other passages, are described by the abbreviated terms of the offences of the hands, the tongue, the eyes, and the ears. The two first are obvious; and the two second relate to the crime of concealing any thing injurious, which is seen or heard. To render more sacred the injunctions to an honest discharge of public duty, the principal public officers, civil and military, were annually assembled from all parts of the country, and each made oath on the Korân, that he had not in the preceding, and would not in the current year, defraud the Government, or suffer it to be defrauded; and had observed, and would maintain fidelity to

* The late Sir Barry Close, a man as extraordinary as he was estimable, who studied, and who mastered, the logic, the ethics, and the metaphysics of Greece, through the medium of the Arabic and Persian languages, sought in vain among the literati of the south of India, for a person who could read and understand the Akhlák è Nâseri.

CHAP. XLII. 1792. the sovereign in every respect. The Mysoreans observe, that every sort of peculation was encreased by the cover of these oaths; and that when subsequently, not content with the oaths of the great officers, he exacted them from every individual in the ranks of the army, and the lowest civil offices of the Government; the lust of plunder became unbridled and unlimited. A person of strict veracity who was present at the examination of an account furnished by a Mahommedan officer, in which the frauds were too obvious to be concealed, related, that the minister, Meer Sâdik could not help noticing it to the Sultaun. In the idiom of the language, when a man has embezzled public money, he is said to have *eaten it.* The Sultaun paused, and meditated for some time. "He is a Mussulman," he gravely replied, "and pronounces the *bismilla** before his meal: if the revenue be diminished, the praise of God is encreased." Whether this particular peculation really remained unpunished, my informant could not positively say; but the extraordinary and notorious facilities for abuses of every description, were too well understood by the rapacious and unprincipled, and only silently deplored by a few honourable and unobtruding individuals.

The code of regulations was ordered to be studied night and day. It was declared to contain "all rules necessary to be observed," but "if any case should occur not provided for, and requiring reference to the resplendent presence, such reference was to be made." An anecdote on this subject enlivened general conversation for many years afterwards. A husbandman came

* Bismilla, *in the name of God,* the commencement, and often the whole, of the grace before eating."

out of breath to tell the aumil* at Kaunkanhully, that a large field of sugar-cane was on fire. "Fetch me the book of regulations; positively I can recollect nothing about a fire in a field of sugar-cane." I will tell you what to do, if I may be permitted, said the astonished husbandman, and with great volubility talked of the village drum summoning every man, woman and child, with each a pot of water. "The book of regulations tells me what to do," said the aumil, "the case is unprovided for, and must be reported and referred." In the meanwhile, the field was destroyed, and the report was made. Rumour was more expeditious than the letter, and every one was full of jest and expectation. The Sultaun heard the dispatch with a vacant stare, which sometimes preceded a laugh, and sometimes a wise reflection. The courtiers misinterpreted the look, and a competition ensued of wit and epigram, at the expence of the unhappy aumil. The royal stare continued for a time, and then dropped into the philosophical preparative. "The man," said the Sultaun, "is a good and an obedient servant; prepare instantly an edict to be added to the regulations, prescribing what is to be done in the event of fire in sugar-fields."

The royal state and title had been assumed in 1786, and the throne found in Seringapatam at the capture of the place, was ordered at the same time to be constructed. In 1789, the period at which his power and arrogance may be deemed to have reached their summit, preparations had been made for the public solemnity of ascending it, but the events of that year interfered with the projected festivities, and the Sultaun never sat upon his

* Aumil, collector of revenue.

throne. The circumstances attending his being named *Tippoo*, and the meaning of that word (tiger), in the Canarese language, have been stated *; the adoption of the tiger stripe in the uniform of the infantry, and as a distinctive ornament in the palaces, in casting guns, and on all the insignia of royalty, was founded on this name. Royal tigers were chained in the court of entrance of the palace, and the construction of the throne was made to conform to the same terrific emblem. A tiger, rather exceeding the full size, of pure gold, and well fashioned, the eyes and teeth of appropriate stones, was the support of the throne; and from a richly ornamented canopy, was suspended over the throne a fluttering *humma*, formed of beautiful precious stones, in conformity to the poetical fancy, that the head on which its shadow falls is destined to be encircled with a crown. One branch of the national festivity was to have been the solemnization of 12,000 marriages on one and the same day, and a separate code was prepared about the same period for regulating domestic manners and morals; among the minutiæ of which one of the secretaries assured me that he saw a draft in the Sultaun's hand-writing to the following effect: " The faithful shall dine on animal food on Thursday † evening, and on no other day of the week: On the same evening and on no other *uxores suas amplexu tenere licet.*"

In the western world *a reformation of the calendar* is uniformly associated with ideas of profound scientific attainment. The era of all Mahommedan nations commences with the Hejira (the flight of Mahommed from Mecca to Medina), but this

* Appendix to chapter 18.

† Which they call *Friday evening*, the night not belonging, as with us, to the preceding, but the ensuing day.

like all other names was to be changed, and the Sultaun adopted the term *mowlood*, the birth, of course signifying regeneration, or being born anew; a figure of speech among Hindoos, originating in the metempsychosis, and of ordinary and familiar application *; but I do not recollect tracing it in any other instance among Mahommedans. The Mowlood is placed about thirteen years before the Hejira, which brings it close to the commencement of Mahommed's mission at the age of forty; and the new calendar consisted in the simple adoption of the Hindoo cycle of sixty years, and the substitution of their year, consisting of twelve lunar months, with an embolismal month at stated periods, to make it correspond with the solar reckoning, for the ordinary lunar year of the Mahommedans, which makes the beginning of every successive year recede eleven days †, and thus make the round of all the seasons. The reader who desires to investigate the Indian cycle of sixty years, may consult the second volume of the Asiatic Researches; each year in the cycle has its appropriate name, and new ones being indispensable, the Sultaun fabricated them from the scheme usually named *Abjud*, the first word of an arbitrary verse, for settling the numerical powers of the letters of the alphabet, and in general use in epitaphs and inscriptions. This was

* A fine bramin boy of about sixteen, a singer and a mendicant, made some ingenious improvisatores, and asked alms. "It is a pity," I said, "that so fine a boy should beg, come with me, and I will make a soldier of you." "That, to be sure, (said he,) would be a transmigration.

† For the purpose of adjusting the odd hours and minutes exceeding 354 in the lunar year, amounting in 30 years to eleven days, the Mahommedans intercalate one day in the 2d, 5th, 7th, 10th, &c. years, adding it to the last month of the year Zihlhedjeh; and the months being alternately of 29 and 30 days, this last month has in the intercalary years, 30 days, and in the others 29 days.

CHAP. XLII. 1792. adopted, ordered, and circulated in 1786, and the very next year he discovered, that it would be an improvement, to adopt another and more simple scheme, by which the power of each letter depends on its place in the alphabet; and the new edict was issued in 1787. The numerical letters composing the name of each year, being added together indicated the place * of that year in the cycle; and the new names of the months were merely ordered so, that the first letter of each should shew its place in the year, as in the alphabet, the twelve first letters of the alphabet, being the initials of the new names of the twelve months; but it was a consideration, which his avocations and studies do not seem to have brought under review, that all chronology is set at defiance, by reckoning from a particular date or era, one part of the series in lunar years, and the remainder, by the solar account.

Before dismissing the subject of the calendar, it may be interesting to observe, that the absurdity of an ambulatory year, making the round of the seasons, was the exclusive work of Mahommed. Before his time, the Arabs, like the ancient Greeks, the Jews, Hindoos, and Chinese, had their embolismal months to reconcile the lunar with the solar year. But of the lunar months, four were held sacred, to the degree of declaring war waged within them to be impious. Mahommed † promulgated a particular revelation, enjoining his followers to attack their enemies in all the months. His enemies, it would seem, had made their embolisms convenient to their own, and injurious to his operations, perhaps because unexpected: it was accordingly declared,

* The letters, for example of the year *Shádáb*, are Sh = 40. a = 1. d = 8. a = 1. and b = 2. total 52; which shews that *Shádáb* is the 52d year of the cycle.

† Korân, chapter 9.

by a pretended revelation, that "the number of months with God is twelve months," and "the transferring of a sacred month to another month, is an additional infidelity." Whether Sale be correct or otherwise *, in ascribing to Prideaux and Golius an error, in supposing this passage to relate to the embolismal month, he admits that this mode of correcting the calendar, was practised by the ancient Arabs, and was prohibited by Mahommed, by the innovation which limited the number to twelve lunar months in one year, and thus subverted the order of nature. The Mahommedans of India necessarily refer to the solar year in their accounts of revenue, and other transactions, which depend on the unalterable order of the seasons, but to the lunar year of 354 days, in their religious festivals, chronology, and military annals. The Sultaun held a consultation of Mahommedan priests (which I have not been able farther to trace) to determine the true date of the Hejira, and probably of the mission of Mahommed; but when in addition to the "incomparable invention" of seventy-two new names, which constituted the amount of real novelty, we find him adopting a reckoning, as the universal standard of all transactions, in direct opposition to the positive injunctions of the Korân, it will be difficult to abstain from combining the new doctrine of a new birth, with those impious pretensions, which he darkly but systematically encouraged, to the prospect of a new revelation, of which he was himself to be the immediate author or minister.

Such is the whole amount of novelty contained in the reformation of the calendar. The new system of weights and measures,

* Sale, Preliminary Disquisition, 198-9.

although the reverse of improvement, is yet connected with some circumstances in the system previously established, which are not entirely destitute of interest. A fixed standard in nature, to which other standards might be practically referred, has been the desideratum of every people, however imperfectly pursued; and previously to the establishment of better principles of science, the merit of these standards ought to be compared rather with each other, than with those subsequently discovered. It is obvious, that a fixed standard, either of weight, capacity, or linear measure, affords very simple and reciprocal means of keeping the others equally invariable. The first and the only scientific standard has been adopted by the French Government, in assuming as their unit of linear measure the ten millionth part of a quadrant of the meridian; and yet this measure, assumed in 1793 as invariable, and deemed to be perfect in general estimation, has been found on subsequent investigation to be full of absurdities * and defects. It has been ascertained that two portions of any one meridian on different sides of the equator, are neither similar nor equal; and that the true measurement of a given portion of such an arc, in any one place, so far from having been practically effected, has terminated in a diversity of results.

An attempt has been made in England, to deduce the measures of length, capacity, and weight, from the measure of time. A pendulum, vibrating seconds under given conditions of temperature and locality, gave the linear measure derived from this invariable standard; and the measures of weight and capacity were deduced by means equally beautiful and simple. A bill

* Article on weights and measures, in the 17th number of the British Review, ascribed to Doctor Gregory.

for the establishment of these standards passed the House of Commons, and was thrown out by the Lords, on account of a variety of acknowledged errors in detail, and of imperfections stated to require a more mature revision. This enlightened age cannot be much longer disgraced by a system, if such it may be called, of weights and measures which has already received its universal condemnation. A reformation of principles does not necessarily involve the subversion, but rather the regulation of existing practice: and as the proposed principle is more sound in theory, and more simple in application than the plausible scheme of our neighbours, it seems probable that we shall also avoid the serious practical inconvenience of their visionary systems. The French revolutionists held it as a principle, *that every thing was to be destroyed, because every thing was to be renewed.* We might hope to approach nearer to a suitable English principle, in affirming, *that every thing is to be preserved, because every thing is to be improved.*

Unfortunately however, the English weights and measures remain in a state little if at all superior to the system of Bengal, as explained in the 5th volume of the Asiatic Researches. This system of northern India like that of England employs one particular kind of grain, to determine the standard of weight, and another to regulate linear measure; and of course leaves both to fluctuate with the quality of the grain, according to the season, and the soil. My attention has but very recently been drawn to the material difference between this system of the north of India, and that which prevails in Mysoor; and as I must trust exclusively to memory for the imperfect account of the latter which I am able to present, it shall be accompanied by such cir-stances as may satisfy the English reader that my recollection is not materially wrong; and may enable the Indian observer to furnish the public with a more accurate description.

A question to a large pecuniary amount, depending on a difference in the measures of capacity, was at issue between persons under the jurisdiction of the government of Mysoor, and others under that of the East India Company at Seringapatam; after some previous communication, the magistrate * of that place was so good as to meet me at the residency for its adjustment; and the minister (Poornea) was requested to be present. The parties attended with their documents and evidence; and the first documents on which the parties were reciprocally agreed, were the texts of the Purànas, which determine the mode of ascertaining the measure of capacity, through the medium of the standard of weight, and these texts were read and collated. Each party brought samples of nine different kinds of grain, sound and well dried; and it was explained, that from the history of their culture, they were necessarily the produce of every variety of soil, and requiring various degrees of moisture or drought; that every variety of season favourable to one would be unfavourable to some other; and that specimens from any one year must necessarily compensate each other, and thus make the average of any one year, equal to the average of any other year; this being premised, one grain of each kind was deposited in a very delicate scale, and the sum of the nine formed the unit of weight. The experiment was verified three or four times, by taking again one grain from

* Colonel Symons.

each of the nine different heaps, and there was not the slightest perceptible inclination of the balance. These units, encreased in the regulated ratio, were then compared with the established weights (which are uniformly the current coins), and carefully verified; and as the result of the whole, a vessel containing a certain weight of these nine kinds of grain, carefully counted, equalized, and well mixed, to fix the specific gravity, was the standard measure of capacity, by which the cause was determined. — The case did not require a reference to the measure of length, and I do not recollect (although I then knew) the manner in which it was deduced. These details will, I trust not appear tiresome, if, as I am disposed to believe, they describe a nearer approach to an invariable standard in nature, than was any where in practice, before the present French system.

The Sultaun simply destroyed * these chances of average accuracy, by referring his standard of weight to poppy grains, accommodated to the old weights in every thing but in name, as is evident from his making one of his established weights 6¼ poppy grains. The measure of capacity, as before, was deduced from the actual coins, but without any allusion to the nine kinds of grain which were to regulate the specific gravity. The standard measure of length was fixed at twenty-four thumbs' breadth,— *because there are twenty-four letters in the confession of faith*; and the breadth of a thumb was ascertained by a certain number of grains of fine rice of a certain weight, or another number and weight of coarse rice, or another of wheat; and

* The ancient system was restored on the re-establishment of the Hindoo dynasty.

CHAP. XLII. 1792.

this, with a new name for every object, constituted the extent of his retrograde march, in this most important branch of public regulation.

A few examples and incidents, selected from a large variety of the "incomparable inventions," on which this strange being sought to found his fame as a legislator and reformer, have been presented with the exclusive view of unfolding a character, inexplicable by any other means: not, however, without apprehension, that a respectable portion of readers may deem the selection too abundant, while another may wish for more ample details.

The digression from which we return, may obviate interruptions to our future narrative, but cannot exclude the farther illustrations of character, with which its progress is inseparably mixed; and in describing the events of the remaining seven years, it may farther contribute to perspicuity, if we endeavour to separate, as far as the subjects shall admit, the measures of internal administration, from those of exterior policy.

The year 1792 was not suffered to elapse without commencing a work intended to secure the capital from the imminent peril which it had recently escaped. The faces of the fort towards the island were already defended by a double line of works. A single line had been deemed sufficient for the northern face, and a small portion of the western works, washed and defended by the river. But the demonstrations made on both these points, and the extraordinary sacrifices to which the Sultaun had submitted, evinced his conviction that both were vulnerable in a dangerous degree. The work now ordered was a second line of rampart and ditch, immediately within, and parallel to the existing single line; together with the improvement and completion of the stone glacis towards the river; and if no other evidence existed regarding his ignorance of the principles of fortification, and of stupid obstinacy in disdaining the instruction which some of his French officers must have been capable of imparting, it would be found in the continuance of all the original defects in the outline of the exterior works.*

The corps of pioneers, maintained at a large expence by Hyder for military purposes in war, and useful labours in peace, had been suffered, by negligence and abuse, to be reduced, at the capital, to a number not exceeding one thousand, and an edict was now issued for collecting twenty thousand men, including masons, simply by a circular order, to seize certain descriptions of men, and their families, and to settle them at Seringapatam until the works should be completed. When collected, they were divided into eighty companies, of two hundred and fifty men each, with officers and accountants; and a guard of peons to each company, to keep them to their work. The guards could not keep perpetual watch over 20,000 persons; the desertions were incessant, and the vacancies as constantly supplied by forcible seizures in the districts, until husbandmen and respectable inhabitants were included in the requisition. A bribe to the officer and accountant at the works, could always

* The well-constructed bastion at the western angle, erected on the rampart, and within the exterior line, the remedy of some of the worst defects of original construction by finishing "*en cremaille*" some of the faces of his towers, and even portions of the covered way; and the construction of very good redoubts, shewed rather a comprehension of mechanical advantage than the slightest approach to scientific principles, and these slight improvements were derived from the French.

CHAP. XLII. 1792. procure for any person *to be returned dead*, and this was converted into a new source of corruption, in which the asophs (civil governors of districts) soon participated: after purchasing this report, and returning to their homes, it was necessary to repeat the bribe to the asoph, to prevent being sent back; a result which would probably verify the report of *dead*, from mental and bodily misery; and the manuscript from which I take this statement, goes on to observe, that "this state of things continued to the end, without any other effect, than the desolation of the country, no part of the works having ever been completed."

During the late war many of the ancient poligars had been restored to their possessions by the confederates, and some had risen and wrested their former strong-holds from the garrisons appointed by the Sultaun for their defence. Among the latter number was Oochingy, a strong hill-fort, situated about twelve or fifteen miles to the north-east of Hurryhur; and at the conclusion of the war the enthusiasm of its ancient possessors induced them to resist the forces of the Sultaun; a strong detachment under one of his best officers, Seyed Ghoffâr,
1793. suffered a severe repulse early in 1793. Kummer-u-Deen, who was seldom employed, excepting in cases of difficulty, was detached with a considerable force in the month of March, and on his report a farther reinforcement, under Khân Jehân Khân *, joined him in April: the defence was prolonged with

* The vicissitudes experienced personally and in his connections, by this brave, able, and interesting man, strongly illustrate the character of the Sultaun's oppressions. He was born a bramin, and was at the age of seventeen a writer in the service of Sheickh Ayâz at Bednore, when it surrendered to General Matthews. On the recapture of that place by Tippoo, every person was sought for who had been

great obstinacy and valour for three months, when the place was carried by two separate and simultaneous assaults; that under the last named officer having alone succeeded. Kummer-u-Deen,

in any respect useful to the fugitive, and this youth was forcibly converted to Islâm, and highly instructed in its doctrines. He was soon distinguished as a soldier, and invested with high command. In 1799, he fell, desperately wounded, in attempting to clear the breach and repel the assault at Seringapatam. He recovered, and was appointed to the command of the raja's infantry, and witnessing the opening of the temples, on the restoration of the Hindoo government, made advances through the minister to be re-admitted to his rank and cast, as a bramin. A select conclave of Gooroos assented to the measure, with certain reservations to mark a distinction between him and those who had incurred no lapse from their original purity; but the khân would have all or none. " I prefer," said he (in conversing with me on the subject) " the faith of my ancestors, but the fellows wanted to shut up my present road to a better world, and would not fairly open the other. I believe that I shall not miss my way, if I perform my duties in this world according to any of the revelations by which the Almighty has deigned to manifest his will to the various classes of mankind; and I feel myself more respectable with the full privileges of a Mussulman, than I should as a half-outcast bramin." Before his forcible conversion he was betrothed, or married in the usual form, and the lady, on arriving at the proper age, sent a message intimating that notwithstanding his change of religion, and marriage with a Mahommedan lady, although she could not be his bramin wife, she could not be the wife of another, and deemed herself bound to regulate her future life according to his commands. After some farther messages, she determined to receive his own immediate protection; a separate quarter of the house was allotted for her exclusive use; when he visited her it was in the braminical costume; and he presented himself to his Mahommedan wife as a true Mussulman. Before I knew him he had married a Mahommedan daughter to a Mussulman, forcibly converted like himself; a Hindoo of the military cast, heir apparent to the ancient chieftainship of Kenchingoad on the Toombuddra, captured when a boy on the fall of the place. On this occasion, his widowed mother had escaped into the woods, and, contrary to the habits of her cast, placed herself at the head of the ancient followers of her house, and continued, during the remainder of Tippoo's reign, to lead the sort of life which has been described in the case of the raja of Coorg. She paid me a visit in 1808, and among other adventures related the following. " Tippoo's aumil, who polluted the mansion of my lost husband and son, wanted iron, and determined to supply himself from the *rut*," (a temple of carved wood fixed on wheels, drawn in procession on public occasions, and requiring many thousand persons to effect its movement.) " It was too much trouble to take

CHAP. XLII. 1793. without any previous intimation (and that alone illustrates the general state of feeling), ordered five handsome boys from among the prisoners as a present to the Sultaun, to be prepared for the future services of the harem, and wrote him a complimentary letter on the occasion. Tippoo was delighted with the hint, and instantly ordered the whole garrison to be treated in the same manner, a command which was actually obeyed.*

The Sultaun had discovered, that among the examples of laxity in the execution of old regulations, while his mind was absorbed in the invention of new, a very small portion indeed of the families of his officers had resided in the fort, a fact which would probably never have reached his knowledge, if desertions had not extended to officers as well as men; and the remedy which he adopted is truly characteristic. The buildings within the fort were divided into ten wards, one of which was allotted

it to pieces, and the wretch burned it in the square of the great tempie, for sake of the iron. On hearing of this abomination, I secretly collected my men, I entered the town by night, I seized him and tied him to a stake, and (bursting into tears, and an agony of exultation) I burned the monster on the spot where he had wantonly insulted and consumed the sacred emblems of my religion." It was on the occasion of the marriage of the khân's own son, that this lady and his connections and relations, of various casts, prevented by the tyranny of their late ruler from the comforts of their customary domestic intercourse, nevertheless assembled for the celebration of the nuptials. Particular days were set apart for braminical festivals, conducted by bramins, others for the khettries, (the family of his son-in-law,) others for Mahommedans; and he was anxious, if I had not dissuaded him, to incur the expence of a great public dinner for the *English, who certainly did not stand lowest in his estimation.*

* *Tribus membris excisis,* i. e. *penitus emasculati, ut mos est alicubi apud Mahommetanos Indicos.* The adults all died: I have seen and conversed with some of the younger survivors. One, not from Oochingy, but from Coorg, personated the Sultaun's eldest son, after the capture of Seringapatam, and attempted an insurrection in Canara.

to the bramins filling public offices, and the rest to the different officers, civil and military, and a price in proportion to its dimension was fixed on each house; not to be paid to the proprietor, for his rights, merged in the higher exigencies of the state, were too unimportant to be considered, but to the Sultaun himself, and it was accordingly stopped by instalments from the pay of the purchaser; the true proprietor being ordered to shift for himself outside. This arrangement commenced in the early part of 1793; but in the subsequent years of pecuniary pressure, he was so shameless as, under the pretext of allotting dwellings more suitable to the rank and dignity of the individuals, to exact the full price of the new dwelling, and to resume the former without compensation. By a perfectly new discovery in finance, he thus effected a perpetually renewable circle of sale, by which, although the property seemed to change masters, the consideration-money always returned to one and the same hand. Some few officers did actually bring their families, but the greater portion merely went through the exterior forms, a deception which, in Hyder's reign, would have been impracticable. The asophs, or civil governors, of districts, were most anxiously included in the arrangement, and messengers were repeatedly sent to expedite the journey of their families from the districts. The messengers were bribed; Meer Sâdik (the minister) was propitiated, a marriage in the family occasioned a delay, the ladies were sick, or pregnant, or confined, or dead; one or two introduced a fictitious harem of slave girls, but not one sent a wife or a child.

The payment of the instalments due to the confederates was protracted by the attempt to pay off the English with more

CHAP. XLII. 1793. than the stipulated promptitude, and to leave the accounts of the other confederates to future adjustment; but Lord Cornwallis had provided in the most honourable and effectual manner against these designs, by ordering that no payment should be accepted by his own nation, until official accounts had arrived of the actual receipt of the corresponding instalment by the other confederates; and this abortive project had no other consequence
1794. than prolonging the detention of the hostages until March 1794. On their approach, accompanied by Captain Doveton, the officer who had been officially appointed to receive them, and pay the proper attentions on behalf of the English Government, the Sultaun proposed as a written question for deliberation, whether he should or should not admit this Englishman to his presence. The counsellors to whom the question was referred represented that the refusal to receive him might excite suspicion, that "he might be amused with professions of friendship, while whatever is in the heart may nevertheless remain there;" the Sultaun accordingly left the capital and moved to a plain in the neighbourhood of Yoosuf-Abad (Deonhully) *, where the hostages were formally restored. On entering their father's tent of audience, accompanied by Captain Doveton, they approached with every demonstration of awe, and when close to the musnud, placed their heads on their father's feet; the Sultaun perfectly silent, and apparently unmoved, touched their necks with his hands;

* One of the new names of places, "the town of Yoosuf,"—Joseph. Flattery and vanity left nothing untouched: Deonhully was the place of the Sultaun's birth. He was the most beautiful of human beings in his time, as Joseph had been the most lovely of antiquity. Yoosuf and Zuleikha, (Potiphar's wife,) are the hackneyed hero and heroine of many beautiful poems, filled with Joseph's irresistible beauty and Zuleikha's unhappy passion.

they arose, and he pointed to their seats, and on receiving Captain Doveton's obeisance, pointed to his seat near to the hostages. In a very courteous reception, he supported with considerable exterior dignity all that related to the intercourse of form, and afterwards entered with great ease and fluency into the topics of the day: the French revolution, the confederacy against that nation which, although formerly pretty equally matched by England alone, seemed to make head against all Europe; the embassy of Lord Macartney to China, with his incredulity at its being limited to commercial objects; his Lordship's former duel with one of his council, and other topics of a general nature, were the chief subjects of conversation. In some subsequent interviews he went the full length of declaring *that he deemed Lord Cornwallis his best friend;* "that he would be governed by his advice to forget the past," and cultivate the friendship of the English nation as the primary object of his policy; and having thus gone through the requisite forms, and literally followed the advice of his counsellors, he gave Captain Doveton his audience of leave, and returned by a circuitous route to Seringapatam.

During the period of about ten days that he had been encamped at Deonhully, an incident occurred, which was raised into importance, and attended with consequences more serious than would otherwise have ensued, from the Sultaun's rage at an indignity offered to his authority, in the presence of his enemies, who in fact were not sufficiently apprized of the circumstances to receive any such impression.

The Korân teaches as one of the signs of the times which are immediately to precede the end of the world, the appearance of an Imaum—*Mehedee* *, who will govern the world for forty years; that *Khyzer* (who drank of the waters of immortality, and by some is identified with Elias) and *Jesus* will descend on earth at the same time, and aid in uniting all mankind in the true religion, the belief and the worship of one God.

In the town of Joanpoor (my notes omit the date) a person appeared, said to be an Arab, named Seyed Mahommed, who professed himself to be the expected *Mehedee*, and obtained many followers. That he was a holy man, all the sects are agreed; those who are not his followers argue, that if he were the expected *Mehedee*, the time has long passed for the termination of the world, and that he must have uttered the words *Ina Mehedee*—*I am Mehedee* (enlightened or instructed by the Almighty, in the right way), without meaning that he was the *Mehedee* who shall precede the dissolution of all things: a numerous class, chiefly of Afghans, contend for the latter doctrine; and it is their distinctive dogma, which they are ready to support with the edge of the sword, "that *Mehedee* has appeared, and has passed away." By the other sects they are represented, perhaps not altogether without ground, as ignorant, ferocious, and treacherous, and cherishing revenge for the slightest offence through successive generations. In all their other tenets, they coalesce with the Sunnites, or sect of Omar; but for the purpose of preventing religious feuds, they are every where excluded from the performance of their rites, within cities, and the body of the camp, from the shout of faith and defiance, offensive to all the other sects, which they put forth

* Instructed in the right way.

together, on a particular night (the 27th) of the Ramazân. On any opposition too, this is their war-whoop, and the signal of resistance, intimating that they will either die or prevail.

The Ramazân occurred while Tippoo Sultaun was at Deonhully, and the *Mehedees* had prepared, *within the camp*, a place for their periodical worship. The Sultaun hearing of this unusual procedure, and highly respecting them as soldiers, sent his Dewan, Meer Sâdik, to remonstrate with their chiefs (men of rank) on the commotion which might ensue; offered them tents, and every sort of facility, in a proper and customary situation, but positively prohibited the performance of the rites within the camp. The chiefs assented to the proposed arrangement, and Meer Sâdik returned with that report to the Sultaun. Yet at the appointed hour of the same night, an assemblage of about three thousand set up their horrid yell. This shout of defiance being distinctly heard in Tippoo's tent, he arose in real alarm, girt on his sword, and ordered a considerable body of troops to be stationed around his tent, for security; but his greatest mortification, was the humiliating reports which would be made of the inefficiency of his government, by the English actually in his camp. I have heard the reports of this religious feud from the conflicting parties, and although misrepresentation is attributed to Meer Sâdik, and the impracticability was affirmed, of removing at so short a notice, it was not even pretended to be customary, that their place of worship should be erected within a camp or a town. For this act of mutiny, the Sultaun, on the ensuing morning, ordered the two chiefs to be confined, and the remainder of the sect (all horsemen) to be

CHAP. XLII. 1794. banished, and knowing their vindictive union, he issued circular orders for banishing all who resided in the several districts.

One person only was exempted from the sentence. Seyed Mahommed Khân, the Sultaun's ancient associate and early preserver, whose appointment to be kelledar of Seringapatam, on his first accession had given an impression of the Sultaun's virtues, which was not confirmed by many incidents of equal promise. The first impulse of this person's mind was to retire from a service whence his religious associates were banished; and in this temper he removed his family to a retired part of the country, with a view to their escape, and proposed to effect their common flight. On reflection, however, he changed this determination. But Tippoo had early intimation of the fact; and on his return to the capital, ordered Seyed Mahommed Khân into confinement, from which he was only released by the capture of the place in 1799.

The two chiefs, named Mehtâb Khân and Aalum Ali Khân, were not released till 1795; and during their confinement, a servant of the former escaped from prison, and was found at the gate of the palace, armed with a dagger. On being seized and interrogated, he avowed that he was there for the purpose of killing his enemy; but declared, in a tone of defiance, that he would answer no farther questions, and it was generally supposed that his object was Meer Sâdik, the person to whose misrepresentations they affected to ascribe their disgrace. However this may be, the Sultaun assigned as a reason for simply remanding him to prison, that if he had ordered his execution, his own assassination would be certain; and no reasonable question has been raised of the accuracy of this opinion, regarding these fit successors of the old man of the mountain.

A person of no ordinary talents, whom subsequent events brought into prominent notice, came into communication with the Sultaun in the course of this year, in a manner which would scarcely be deemed credible, without the previous knowledge of character possessed by the reader. Dhoondee * Wahag, a Mahratta by descent, was born in the territory of Mysoor and the town of Chengerry: his first † military service was performed as a private horseman, under the command of Bistnoo Pundit, in Hyder's invasion of Coromandel in 1780: he was considered by this officer to be brave, active, and intelligent, but eminently dishonest. During the campaign of Lord Cornwallis, he, with a few followers, left the service, carrying off considerable booty, which he had acquired from his enemies, and some which he was accused of purloining from his friends: he proceeded in the first instance to the neighbourhood of Darwar, where, after the conclusion of peace, and the return of the Mahratta armies, he collected a party of freebooters, and levied at first secret, and progressively more open contributions north of the Toombuddra. At a very early period of his new fortunes he sought for conditional protection, and sent

* Sometimes called Dhoondia, and Dhoondajee, Wahag.

† Colonel Kirkpatrick's account of Dhoondee, from a manuscript history of Shânoor, written by Meer Hussein Ali, differs in some respects from the text, which is chiefly founded on the verbal authority of his commanding officer, Bistnoo Pundit, and the historical compilation of Poornea. Colonel Kirkpatrick's work having been published since my departure from India, I had no opportunity of comparing and investigating the circumstances in which they differ; and they are too unimportant to require a discussion of my reasons for adhering to the statement in the text. — Kirkpatrick's Tippoo's Letters. Appendix, p. xxvi.

an agent (an Afghân Mussulman) to represent to the Sultaun, as his ancient master, that with a little secret aid he would engage, on certain conditions, to recover for him the whole principality of Savanoor, without any overt infringement of the treaty of 1792. The Sultaun would give him no direct aid, but exhorted him to prudence and preparation. Dhoondee was too precipitate, and provoked the court of Poona to send an expedition under a chief named Gôckla to destroy him as a robber: he continued however, with great ability, to carry on a desultory warfare with a handful of men, until he was at length so hard pressed as to be obliged to avail himself of the eventual engagement concluded by his Afghân agent to enter into Tippoo's service with his whole party, consisting of about two hundred horse.

He arrived in the neighbourhood of Seringapatam in June 1794, and proceeded to pay his personal respects to the Sultaun. He was accosted in the anti-chamber, by the Sultaun's desire, with the most magnificent promises of promotion, on the condition of his becoming a Mussulman, a proposition to which Dhoondee gave at once the most unqualified negative. He was accordingly ordered into prison, and a detachment was sent to surround the little encampment; and after seizing the horses and valuables, down to the very clothing, the men were set at liberty to seek a new fortune.

On the ensuing day, when the plundered horses were brought to be inspected, Tippoo ordered the Afghân agent into his presence. "It was agreed," said the Sultaun, "that Dhoondee was to become a Mussulman —" the Afghân looked astonished — "What," resumed the Sultaun, "was not that an express condition?" "It may be so," said the Afghán, "I did not hear of it." "What, do I lie?" said the Sultaun, in a rage, "off with his nose and ears." The Afghán was carried out of the presence, and mutilated according to orders; and in a fit of indignation and despair, plunged into the Caveri, and was drowned. A detailed statement of facts, regarding Dhoondee, on which the Sultaun desired the opinion of the four departments of his government, is given * in Colonel Kirkpatrick's work, and occupies upwards of two quarto pages, of very small print; the reader's curiosity may be excited by the information, that in an official document, thus submitted to the consideration of his most confidential advisers, these two pages do not contain two lines of truth. Among the persons required to give an opinion on these false premises, was Bistnoo Pundit, who had himself been robbed by Dhoondee, and who knew him to be both unprincipled and unsafe — he voted for his death — the others for imprisonment. The opinion of the majority prevailed, the captive was forcibly converted, and furnished with a Mahommedan preceptor, and a really liberal maintenance, *in prison and in irons,* from which he only escaped on the day of the ultimate assault and conquest of Seringapatam; when, putting himself at the head of a band of desperate adventurers, who are always to be found on the dissolution of a government, he made the most rapid strides to the establishment of a new and formidable dynasty in the south. He was, however, once more too precipitate, and by seeking, with unparalleled activity, to disorganize all around him, without distinction, ren-

* Appendix, page xxvii.

1794. dered it necessary for the English Government to employ against him the troops of Mysoor, under the Honourable Colonel Wellesley; and after a series of defensive movements, combining distinguished activity and judgment, which protracted his fate for several months, he at length fell in a charge of cavalry, personally led by his opponent.

The adventures of this extraordinary person, terminating in the suppression of an incipient sovereignty, have incidentally led us beyond the limits assigned to this work. The events of the campaign are diminutive, when compared with the subsequent glories of the Duke of Wellington; but they will exhibit to the future historian, a clear developement of those astonishing powers, which have fixed the homage of other nations, and the pride and gratitude of his own.

1794. The unprincipled character of the sovereign has been sufficiently unfolded; and the nature of those gross deceptions, practised by persons who possessed his confidence, will be illustrated in an incident, which led, without previous design, to an important augmentation of resource. It was notorious, that the full extent of extortion practised on the husbandmen was unknown to the Sultaun; and the landholders of an eastern district, not far from the capital, trusting to the authentic evidence of the village accounts, and the plain simplicity of their case, assembled to the number of six thousand persons, accompanied by the village accountants, to submit their grievances to the sovereign. Their spokesmen were admitted to an audience; the account of the sums extorted was indisputable; and Meer Sâdik, the minister, frankly admitted the facts; but affirmed (as was not true), that the whole had been carried to the account of nezerâna, which with the Sultaun was permitted to cover almost any enormity. The minister, however, was not satisfied with simple justification; but in a separate interview with the landholders, gave his own explanation of the nezerâna demanded by the necessity of affairs; represented to them the Sultaun's grief and displeasure, at the ingratitude of his subjects; and pledged himself, that no farther contributions should be levied, if they would consent to an augmentation of thirty per cent. on the fixed revenue; and the amount of the prior exactions may be conjectured, by their gladly agreeing to these moderate terms. He then told them, that he had it in contemplation to relieve them, for a small commutation, from two sources of exaction, which he knew to be severe, the money-changers' shops of the Government, and the monopoly of tobacco.

To the Sultaun he then returned to represent the ill consequence of countenancing groundless complaints, and the admission of the fact which he held in his hand, in the spontaneous assent of the husbandmen to add thirty per cent. to their annual payments, which a deputation at the door was ready to confirm; but that they were particularly anxious for the abolition of the monopoly of the money-changers, and of tobacco, (which the Sultaun knew to be unproductive, and the minister knew to be making the fortune of his personal enemy, Ismael Khân,) and that they would perhaps consent on these conditions to a farther small augmentation.

The Sultaun was delighted with the proposal; and a compromise was made of seven and a half per cent. on these accounts, making the whole augmentation equal to thirty-seven and a half per cent.

CHAP. XLII. 1795.

But Meer Sâdik was not yet satisfied. After obtaining the assent of the landholders to the formal instrument, and presenting it to the Sultaun, he took the opportunity of summing up the facts of the case. That persons who could by their own confession and written agreement afford such an augmentation of their payments, should assemble in a tumultuous manner, to interrupt the ordinary business of the Government, by *a false complaint* against the officers of the revenue, was unpardonable; but that the interests of the Government demanded lenity, and he should only recommend the execution of two of the ringleaders. The chief spokesmen, the most intelligent and active of the potails, were accordingly hanged in the presence of the astonished husbandmen. The whole dispersed. The same exaction was, on the authority of this spontaneous increase, nominally extended to the rest of the country; and no praise was deemed adequate to the merits of a minister, who by an operation so simple had raised the landed revenue in the extraordinary proportion of 37½ per cent.

The army in the meanwhile had received no more than seven months' pay in the year, and began to evince considerable discontent. To reduce the numbers, or touch the efficiency of the instrument, by which alone he could hope to retrieve his affairs, did not enter into the Sultaun's contemplation; but he adopted the project of granting jageers in lieu of one half of the pay, reckoned at ten months' pay in the year, which would leave a balance of five, to be paid in money.

The reader is aware that the receipts of a jageer are simply the transfer of the revenue of the Government; but in collections to be made by those immediately interested in their amount, it was deemed reasonable to reckon the value of the jageer at something more than the common receipts of the Government, and this excess was deemed to be moderate at an estimate of 25*l.* per cent.; but the calculation was made, not on the old rates, but on those recently established, and the actual excess above the ordinary value at which the jageers were estimated to the troops was exactly 71⅞ per cent.* CHAP. XLII. 1795.

It is obvious that such allotments could be made only to corps, troops, or companies, and not to individuals, and the acceptance was very prudently permitted to be optional. The Silledar horse, without exception, embraced the arrangement, and many of the stable horse and infantry. It was Tippoo's wish to extend it to his whole army, but the details of such a measure were complicated, and proceeded but slowly; and such was the disordered state of finance, that the possessors of jageers were alone exempted from frequent and urgent distress.

The annual assembly of the officers of every department to renew their oaths of honesty has been already adverted to, and in the confidence of that obligation on the faithful, who alone were admitted to the new offices of trust, the districts were sub divided, and the number of aumils exceedingly increased, in order that they might be able, by a minute examination of 1796.

* Ancient estimated value	- - -	100
Late augmentation	- - - -	37½
25 per cent. upon 137½	- - -	34⅜
	Total -	171⅞

but as the estimate was made on the gross value, and the expences of collection were saved to the Government, the estimated augmentation of revenue approached one hundred per cent.

every detail, to augment the amount of public revenue. If the claims of talent or recorded service were ostensibly disregarded, corrupt recommendation did not seem to exclude those pretensions in the Sultaun's most extraordinary scheme of selection for these new offices. All candidates for every department were ordered to be admitted and drawn up in line before him, when looking stedfastly at them he would, as if actuated by inspiration, call out in a solemn voice, "Let the third from the left be Asoph of such a district: he with the yellow drawers understands naval affairs, let him be Meer-è-Yem, Lord of the Admiralty: he with the long beard and he with the red turban are but Aumils, let them be promoted," &c. &c. There can be no question that he had studied his lesson for this fraudulent exhibition of oracular wisdom; but it failed in effect from the ludicrous blunders of the scene.

The title of raja of Mysoor, so long excluded from our recollections, will necessarily occupy a brief notice in consequence of the death, by small-pox, of Cham Raj, the father of the present raja, who had been raised to that pageant office, by Hyder, in the year 1772.

Even Tippoo Sultaun in the height of his arrogance had not hitherto omitted the customary form of shewing the raja to his people once a year, at the feast of the Dessera, but now for the first time the ceremony was omitted of even a nominal succession to the musnud. The ancient Ranee, the present raja, then two years old, with the remnant of the family, were removed to a miserable hovel, in which they were found at the capture of Seringapatam, and the palace was rifled of all its contents, and even the individuals of their personal ornaments; the present raja cried bitterly at the attempt to take away his little golden bracelets, and there was still sufficient feeling among the instruments of tyranny, to be touched at the distress of the child, and to abstain from this last violation.*

Among the domestic occurrences of 1796, was the solemnization of the royal nuptials. We have noticed one of the Sultaun's disappointments in a treaty of marriage in 1789, and another had occurred in 1794. In that year, immediately after the return of the hostages, he dispatched a confidential envoy to Calburga, the residence of a saint by hereditary claim, who continued to enjoy a large jageer from Nizam Ali, to demand in marriage a daughter of that family, particularly celebrated for the beauty of its females; a connexion of that description being not unusual among Mahommedan princes. The saint assented to the proposal, on the condition that the Sultaun should either directly or through the medium of the English Government, or in any other manner he should prefer, obtain the sanction of Nizam Ali, without which it was obvious that the family would risk the loss of its jageer; but if the Sultaun could not consent to the application, as circumstances were then unfavourable, and might improve, *when the Sultaun's victorious standard should be erected in Decan*; the saint concluded with an admonition which may sound strangely in an English ear; four wives he observed are allowed to every Mussulman, and peculiarly to Sovereigns; he accordingly exhorted the Sultaun to provide himself with that indispensable requisite, leaving one vacancy for one of his daughters, who

* It was on this occasion that the manuscript was removed, which is described in the preface, page xii. of the 1st volume.

CHAP. XLII. 1796.

would always be at the Sultaun's service, whenever political circumstances should admit: a private envoy from Calburga followed some time afterwards to attempt the removal of these difficulties; but the Sultaun was immoveable on the question of any application to Nizam Ali, and the project was abandoned. The Sultaun, although as little scrupulous as his father in filling his harem, was in fact at this time without a lawful wife. In 1778, Hyder had obtained from Arcot a Nevayet lady *, celebrated for beauty, to be the wife of his heir apparent. During her journey, rumour injurious to her family (not personally to herself) had reached the ears of her destined husband, and although the marriage was solemnized it was never consummated; but at the intercession of Tippoo's mother, who is stated to have received and communicated the first unfavourable reports, another marriage was arranged for him, with the daughter of Lâlla Mea, a near relation of the family, and solemnized at the same time with the other: the daughter of Lâlla Mea became the mother of his only legitimate children †, Mohy-u-Deen and two daughters: this lady died on the day after the storm of the lines in 1792, and the funeral procession to a cemetery without the fort, was observed and respected by the English army. From that period therefore, according to Mahommedan as well as English law, he was a widower, and after the entire failure of his negotiations with Cal-

* Sister to the person who for many years was known at Madras by the name of the Pondicherry Nabob; and pretended, without the slightest foundation, to be the lineal descendant of *Chunda Saheb.*

† Besides these, he had in 1799, *living*, illegitimate 17 + 3 legitimate = 20

Illegitimate, deceased	-	24
Total	-	44

burga, he married in 1796 another relation, the daughter of Seyed Saheb, who, together with a son whom she bore, died about a year and a half afterwards. CHAP. XLII. 1796.

1797. It can scarcely be necessary to state that the various but irregular accessions to the treasury which have been incidentally noticed, continued to be entirely inadequate to meet his disbursements; he looked with increasing impatience to succours from revolutionary France, which should enable him to destroy the English power, and he was anxious that his army should be found in a state of efficiency to perform their part in the expected service. In the letters which he received from his agents at Muscat, successive accounts were received of the rise and progress of the Wahâbees, and he was particularly struck with the account of the assassination of the Turkish general in his own tent by one of that sect, who disdained to escape, and courted the crown of martyrdom, from his confidence in the promised joys which awaited him in paradise, as the reward of the deed. This idea having once entered the Sultaun's imagination, he could speak of nothing but the tribes of Arabia, the *Eels* (tribes) of Persia, and the religious zeal, heroism, and devotion arising from such a bond of union and reciprocal attachment. He accordingly projected the establishment of a tribe, which should be as much devoted to his orders as the Wahâbees to that of their chief, and a considerable portion of this and the succeeding year was devoted to the requisite selection and organization of his own tribe, to which, as it must have a new name, he assigned the appellation of *Kebeela*, one of the many Arabic names for *a tribe.* But tribe and family being in Arabia nearly synonimous, the delicacy affected in speaking of

CHAP. XLII. 1797. women has made it a practice in India to say, *my family* instead of *my wife*; and thus the word *Kebeela*, incorporated into the vernacular language, is universally understood in the south of India to mean *wife* and nothing else. This equivocal term for the Sultaun's elect, became accordingly a source of the most filthy jests throughout the army; and the courtiers were distressed in what manner to apprise him of the ridicule he was exciting. One of the Moonshees (Seyed Hussein — my authority) was at length induced to write on a slip of paper all the synonyms of *Kebeela* in the Arabic and Persian languages, and to take a favourable opportunity of placing it in the Sultaun's view. He immediately recollected the vulgar acceptation of the word *Kebeela*, and changed it to *Zumra*. A general dislocation of corps was the necessary accompaniment of the new organization, and in making the promotions and appointments, he exhibited the same impious pretence to inspiration, which had attracted universal ridicule in his civil appointments. Exterior distinctions were also deemed necessary, for the *Zumra*, as well as the other corps of the army; for the bramins and Hindoos of the different departments were appointed each their appropriate colour for the turban, and patterns for the other articles of dress; and it was upon this occasion that old Butcherow, being questioned by a courtier regarding his dress, made answer — "he may strike off my head, but he shall never put a new turban on it." *

1798. It was on the occasion of closing his arrangements for the

* Related to the author by Butcherow himself. The statement may possibly be heightened, but at least it is evidence of what was passing in his mind. After some severe lessons, we do not yet seem to have learned wisdom on these subjects!!!

organization of the Zumra, that, obscurely anticipating better consequences than actually resulted from his mission to the Isle of France, to be hereafter related, he administered oaths of fidelity to all his officers, civil and military, and to each individual soldier of horse and foot; and caused every Mussulman in his service successively to partake with him of rice and milk, a form of confederation sacred among the Hindoos, but now for the first time introduced into the rites of Islâm.

It was about the same time, and with the same view, that he issued a proclamation, dated 11th of April, 1798 *, fifteen days before the arrival at Mangalore, of his embassadors from the Isle of France. This document, which escaped the diligent researches of the public officers employed in 1799, and did not appear in the printed collection, as evidence of the Sultaun's hostile designs, was painted in large letters on a board, suspended in the great mosque. It was observed in that situation by the author, in the ensuing year †; and the following is the substance of the curious, and not doubtful evidence which it presents. "From the commencement of the year Shâdâb, five benefits are conferred by the God-given Government, upon its servants: — 1st. Of the countries which shall be conquered by the God-given Government, the fourth part of the annual revenue is a donation to the troops.

* The proclamation is ordered to have effect from the commencement of the year Shâdâb, 11th of April, 1798, which would rather indicate its being published at an earlier date, but does not amount to evidence of that fact. The date of the first letter from the embassadors, written on their return to Mangalore, is 9th Bahâry year, 1226 from the birth of Mahommed, which, in the printed copy of the official documents found at Seringapatam, is said to answer to the 26th of April.

† It is probably in the possession of Colonel Marriot.

CHAP. XLII. 1798. 2d. To the widow and children of every man who shall fall in battle, a maintenance equal to a fourth of the share so accruing, and of the pay of the deceased martyr.

3d. The widows and children of men who merely die on service, one quarter of a gold fanam daily (about two and a half rupees a month).

4th. The booty which every individual may acquire shall be his own (meaning that the Government shall demand no share).

5th. Distinctions and honours shall be conferred in proportion to merit and fidelity; in return for all which important benefits, it is incumbent on all the servants of the state to be united and of one heart, in obedience to the command of God and of the Prophet, in laying down their lives to insure the success of the God-given Government in its intended undertakings."

In closing the narrative of such domestic occurrences, from the war of 1792 to the war of 1799, as accord with our general design, it may be proper to notice the nature and objects of a tour at the head of his Zumra and army, after the completion of that arrangement. He had frequently noticed in conversation, that the great lake of Tonoor or Môtee Talâb (the lake of pearls *) had furnished water, and its irrigations forage, at a convenient distance from the capital, to several hostile armies at different periods; and in the war for death or empire which he was resolved to wage, that it ought not to exist, and he took this opportunity of gratifying his army by marching them to the spot, to partake of the diversion of fishing as the water should be drawn off: the project failed in consequence of the breach having suddenly enlarged during the night, and in the

* Vol. i. page 238.

morning the lake was empty. The natural fall of the country caused the waters to flow into the lake of Heroor; and that his army might not be disappointed, he marched thither, broke down this bank also, and feasted them for several days on the sport of the two lakes: that this gratification was the single object of the second operation is evinced, by the order which he gave for the immediate repair of the embankment; and the general intention of the tour has been stated, because far more absurd motives were ascribed to the Sultaun, and had seized the imagination of the credulous soldiery. In the depths of this ancient lake resided every variety of animal, corresponding to the terrestrial kinds, including man, with water nymphs of super-human beauty: a golden rut, (moveable temple) of enormous size, was bound by a talisman at the bottom of the lake, and guarded by this aquatic people. The Sultaun had discovered the charm which was to dissolve the talisman, and the rut would furnish resources for the holy war which was to restore the fortunes of his house, and pour countless wealth into the purses of the soldiery. That Tippoo believed these fairy tales was affirmed by a large majority of his court and army; but the imputation seemed to be either doubted or denied by many among the better informed.

The tour embraced an examination of the dams of the river above and below the capital; and plans for breaking down the old, which chiefly bore the name of Deo Raj, and erecting new ones, with new names, in more judicious situations, in order that Tippoo Sultaun's name might be identified with every monument of peace or war; and that the memory of every other conqueror or benefactor might sink into oblivion. These views, however dark and illiberal in themselves, were magnificent for a sovereign preparing a last desperate effort; and evinced the confidence with which he anticipated a glorious result. The fancy for novelty, which was his ruling passion to the last, found, towards the close of the tour, one remaining object in the regulation of the camp bazâr. The absence from the capital had lasted longer than the bazâr-men had anticipated, and there was a deficiency in the supply of rice. After the feasting which has been described, the foot-soldiers, finding some difficulty in making their requisite purchases, proceeded to seize rice wherever it could be found; and a commotion ensued in the bazâr, which was reported to the Sultaun. He observed, that it was disgraceful for a gentleman soldier to go to the bazâr at all; that they ought to send their servants; and that he would find a remedy on his return to the capital. He accordingly ordered, that the bazârs should be opened but once in seven days; that every person should on that day make his weekly purchases of provisions, which would make a quiet bazâr for the remaining six days. In this fine phrenzy of imaginary reform, he could not condescend to calculate on the vulgar facts, that a variety of perishable articles will not keep for even a second day; that a great proportion of purchasers have not wherewithal to pay for a week's provisions; and that many wants occur which are either not foreseen, or for want of credit, cannot be supplied among those classes who subsist from day to day. The edict, however, was not only issued, but absolutely enforced, for upwards of a month. The most dreadful confusion and distress ensued; and at the expiration of about forty days, the shops gradually opened without orders and without notice.

The balanced alternative of faulty brevity, or uninteresting detail, on which I was unable to satisfy my own judgment, in sketching the strange institutions of the Sultaun's government, has pervaded in a similar degree the selection from a cumbrous mass of matter, for a narrative of domestic transactions, which should convey a just impression of the actual character of his internal administration: a character which, in every despotism, will be frequently found at variance with the principles on which its institutions are *professedly* founded. If the degree in which a suitable medium has been approached, shall divide the opinions of my readers, my expectations will have been accomplished; and leaving the decision to its fate, I return to the measures of exterior policy, subsequently to the peace of 1792.

CHAPTER XLIII.

External affairs since 1792 — Treaty of guarantee anticipated by the confederates in the treaty of 1790, is not accomplished — Causes as regard the Mahrattas — Nana Furnavese — Sindea — Counter project — Nizam Ali's anxiety — charges the English with a violation of faith — his reasoning — Mahrattas prepare to attack him — he solicits protection — it is refused — Discussion of the subject — Proof of the insufficiency of the treaty of 1792 — Death of Mahdajee Sindea — succeeded by Dowlut Row — Mahrattas invade the territory of Nizam Ali — Battle and treaty of Kurdla — Nizam Ali prostrate — relieved by two unexpected events — the rebellion of his son Ali Jah — and the death of the Pêshwa — Augmentation of Raymond's corps — Jageer — gives alarm to Sir John Shore — Cases discussed — terminated by the march of Raymond against Ali Jah — and an application for aid from Nizam Ali to the English — Distractions at Poona — Treaty concluded by Nizam Ali's captive minister — Better dispositions towards the English — Ali Jah's mission to Tippoo of Kâdir Hussein Khân — Conditions — Kâdir sent back to Ali Jah — Diplomatic deception at Hyderabad — Ridiculous collision with the former envoy at that place — Tippoo's various intrigues — Well grounded confidence in their success — Operations of the English against the French and Dutch possessions — Manilla — Cause of the recal of that expedition — Curious consultations at Mysoor regarding its destination — Embassies to Câbul — discussed — Negotiations with France — 1788 — after 1792 — Conviction of the military superiority of revolutionary France — Accidental arrival of a French privateer at Mangalore, commanded by Ripaud — Deception — Consequent plan of Tippoo — Ludicrous loss of his money — Suspicions regarding Ripaud — he is ultimately deputed with others to the Isle of France — Explanation of the bond for the ship, hitherto unintelligible — Embassy arrives at the Isle of France — Public proclamation of this secret mission, by the Governor-General Malartic — his conduct and that of the embassadors discussed — Curious confusion of the Sultaun's mind — Return of the embassadors — and recruits — Tippoo might still have averted war by disavowal — Opposite conduct — Levy of ninety-nine men — Jacobin club — Revolutionary morality of the superior officers — Dubuc deputed to France.

CHAP. XLIII. 1792.

THE 13th article of the treaty of offensive and defensive alliance, between the English, the Mahrattas and Nizam Ali, concluded in 1790, provided that "if after the conclusion of peace with Tippoo, he should molest or attack either of the contracting parties, the others shall join to punish him; the mode and conditions of effecting which, shall be hereafter settled by the three contracting parties:" and Lord Cornwallis, after the conclusion of peace, in the spirit of sincerity and good faith which he had testified from the commencement of the alliance, made an endeavour to reduce this conditional stipulation into the form of an explicit and intelligible treaty of guarantee. But the policy of his Mahratta allies, was in direct and systematic opposition to every thing explicit and definite in its connection with other powers; and the minister, Nana Furnavese, being freed from all immediate apprehension of hostility from the side of Mysoor, was infinitely more anxious for the maintenance of his own influence and power in the Mahratta state, against the designs of Sindea, than for the guarantee of Nizam Ali, whom he contemplated as his earliest prey. For the first of these purposes, he made an early application to Lord Cornwallis to subsidise a British corps, for the declared purpose of enabling the Pêshwa (his nominal master) "to reduce to obedience any dependent which might prove refractory." An obligation thus broad and indefinite, to support the acknowledged head of the Mahratta state, against the dependents of that state, might bring the British subsidiary force into immediate contact with the troops of Sindea, or avert that necessity, as was Nana's true intention, by involving the English Government in an indirect pledge, at variance with the whole spirit of the treaty of Salbey; and Lord Cornwallis very properly rejected the proposition, without any specific reference to the case of Sindea, on those general grounds, which were equally and obviously applicable to all the branches of the Mahratta confederacy.

Sindea possessing no equivocal pretensions to independent power, at the date of the treaty of Salbey, had subsequently been permitted, without even a remonstrance on the part of the English Government, to usurp the whole power of the Mogul empire; and to effect an aggrandisement highly dangerous to his neighbours, and equally perilous to Nana Furnavese, from whom he possessed the power to wrest at pleasure the possession of the Pêshwa — the pageant of a pageant, whom they each desired to employ as the mere instrument of their respective designs. Sindea had even before the war of 1790, made overtures to become a party in the confederacy against Tippoo, and for that purpose to subsidise a British corps, which should accompany him in the first instance to Poona; a curious example of two Mahratta competitors for Mahratta power, reciprocally attempting to render the English Government the instrument of their domestic feuds; but independently of these designs, Sindea desired to impose on the Government of Bengal, not only the obligation of defending his northern possessions during his absence, but a general pledge to aid him in the reduction of the Rajpoot* states in Hindostan, an ancient and honourable people whose preservation and support appears to have been at that and all subsequent times, incumbent on the British Government, on the plain and sound policy of respecting immemorial rights, of preserving a safe counterpoise against the desolating encroachments of the Mahrattas, and of establishing a formidable barrier against foreign invasion from the north.

A scheme of alliance so entirely inadmissible in all its principles, had been rejected by Lord Cornwallis: Sindea had in consequence, moved as we have seen, towards Poona, in the expectation of a much longer continuance of that war, as the most favourable juncture for the accomplishment of his designs on that Government; and with views far from friendly to the English, whom, at its close, he affected to consider as too powerful; and made little secret of his opinion, that Tippoo ought to be supported as an instrument for restraining their dangerous aggrandisement. We accordingly find, in 1793, evidence of an active correspondence between Sindea and the Sultaun, referring to former letters and messages; some probably in 1792, and others of an earlier date.

With a court thus torn by dissension, polluted by intrigue, and governed by a system hostile to fixed rights, there could at no time have existed any reasonable hope of a treaty of guarantee, which should subvert the first principle of Mahratta policy — the plunder of their neighbours. A counter project of

* Malcolm's India, page 101; a work to which I refer with confidence, from my knowledge in most instances, and my conviction in all others, of the authenticity of its facts.

CHAP. XLIII. 1793.

a guarantee treaty, drawn by Nana Furnavese, contained among other anti-social conditions, the recognition of the claim of the Mahrattas, on Tippoo Sultaun, for *choute:* a demand, which appears to have excited the animadversion of the English, from being unauthorised by the stipulations of the treaty of Seringapatam.* But it is to be remembered, that this instrument, which formally recognises the preceding treaties between the house of Hyder and the English Government, is entirely silent with regard to any political relation of a similar nature between Tippoo Sultaun and the other confederates; and, if the Mahrattas had even admitted the practice of European diplomacy, to record in a new treaty, the former engagements intended to be confirmed; the annulment or confirmation of any or every former treaty, left the question of *choute* equally and entirely untouched. They argued, not without reason, that a treaty for terminating a war, implies the restoration of all those relations, not altered by such treaty, which existed before the war; and it is highly probable, that if Lord Cornwallis had attempted in the treaty of 1792, to introduce any limitation to the claim of *choute*, either on Tippoo or Nizam Ali, he would at the least have found an augmentation of his difficulties and delays at Poona.

After a protracted negotiation of more than a year, the hope of obtaining the assent of the Mahrattas to any reasonable treaty of guarantee was finally abandoned: but in the exact proportion of the aversion of the Mahrattas, was the anxiety of Nizam Ali for that bond of union and security; and in his

* Malcolm's India.

anxiety for its completion, he had even demanded as a right already established, the interference of the English in his dispute with Tippoo regarding the tribute of Kurnool. In arguing for the treaty of guarantee, he contended with great appearance of justice, that the failure of one of three parties in the fulfilment of its engagements, was no justification to the other two, for a violation of theirs; and he urged on Lord Cornwallis with the greatest anxiety the conclusion of such a treaty before his departure from India. He could, however, obtain no farther satisfaction from his Lordship, than a declaration that the English Government was satisfied with his verbal acquiescence, and a vague assurance that it would always be ready to act according to existing treaties. On this important subject, historical truth demands the remark, that whatever praise may be assigned to the wisdom and public virtue of Lord Cornwallis's government, the judgment of posterity will probably decide on a few memorable exceptions; and among these will be peculiarly marked, the neglect, before his departure, to regulate by negotiation or otherwise, that degree of reasonable guarantee, for the mere political existence of Nizam Ali, to which he was solemnly pledged by the whole tenor and spirit of the communications which preceded the treaty of 1790, still more than by the letter of that instrument: and whatever animadversions may be excited by the political measures of his non-military successor, towards this declining and dependent power, it must in candour and justice be constantly remembered, that he was left by his military predecessor in a predicament which a liberal candour can scarcely be brought to justify.

Mahdajee Sindea took an active part in the negotiations at

CHAP. XLIII. 1793. Poona, regarding the treaty of guarantee, not only as it regarded the Mahratta state, but that of Nizam Ali, with whose minister he violently and openly remonstrated — against any farther connection with the English power. The Mahrattas, in fact, were preparing, as Nizam Ali well knew, and explicitly declared to the English resident, for the plunder of his dominions, resting on those complex claims of unadjusted account, and arrears of choute, which the reader is aware it would be very unprofitable to discuss. Nizam Ali, sensible of his own weakness, earnestly sought a consolidation of his alliance with the English, and their mediation to avert the extremities which he anticipated from the Mahratta claims; but although it was evident, that unsupported, his destruction was inevitable, to the extent that Mahratta policy might determine, and it was admitted that such event would be injurious to the security as well as to the reputation of the English state; although the improved alliance which Nizam Ali required, would consolidate the English power, without the infraction of any existing engagement; although it was admitted as an established fact in these deliberations, that Tippoo Sultaun was leagued with the Mahrattas against Nizam Ali; and although by the spirit of the 13th article of the treaty of 1790, the English were bound, by no doubtful obligation, to defend the territories of that prince, against the Sultaun's aggressions: these united considerations were deemed by the Governor-general, Sir John Shore, insufficient to balance the hazard of giving offence to the Mahrattas, and the consequent risk of war, * an extremity highly inconvenient to the public

* The reasoning on which this decision was founded, is fully and fairly stated in Malcolm's India, page 153, and the following pages.

finances, and expressly prohibited by act of parliament. To the reproach of justifying his own violation of treaty with Nizam Ali, by the faithlessness of the Mahrattas, he opposed the argument, that the defection of one party from a tripartite alliance, offensive and defensive, and its union with the very power against whom the league was formed, for the purpose of attacking one of the other parties of the alliance, cancelled the obligation of the remaining party, and gave it a right to remain neuter. The refined reasoning brought to establish this abstract right, was expressly declared by Nizam Ali to be at variance with the practical facts of the case; and he earnestly recalled to the remembrance of the English, that he entered into the triple alliance on the avowed and acknowledged conviction of the future treachery and hostility of the M hrattas, and in a full confidence and dependence on the pledged faith and support of the English Government, who now threatened to forfeit that pledge, contrary to their own most obvious interests. Such was the substance of the reasonings on which Nizam Ali was abandoned to a fate which all India saw to be inevitable. Nana Furnavese would have consented with reluctance to any enlargement of the Sultaun's power or dominions, and therefore disliked his co-operation; and Tippoo, from a reciprocal feeling of personal enmity, was somewhat shy in his advances until the expected downfal of that minister should be effected. Sindea pretended to be ready to force the measure either with or without the deposition of Nana; but there is reason to believe that the support of Nizam Ali by the English, instead of his abandonment, would at least have caused Sindea to pause in his designs; and the counter-influence of Nana Furnavese might probably have preserved the

1794. peace of India. Under the actual circumstances, however, Sindea was too good a Mahratta to admit an associate in plunder where the work can be accomplished without assistance; and Tippoo was kept back because the English had made his aid unnecessary. Such then is the earliest test of the insufficiency of the treaty of 1792 for its intended purposes. Tippoo Sultaun, so far from being rendered incapable of disturbing the public peace, was ready and willing to be marshalled by the Mahrattas against Nizam Ali and the English power, if the latter, by the abandonment of its ally, had not left a clear field for the Mahrattas alone.

Mahdajee Sindea died during these discussions, and his nephew and heir Dowlut Row Sindea, not only adhered to the views of his predecessor, but assembled additional forces for their execution. Nizam Ali, abandoned by the English on whom he had confidently leaned for support, sought for such aid as he could obtain from their European rivals. Monsieur Raymond, a person of considerable military talents who had served with his troops in Mysoor, and had been employed after the war, with Lord Cornwallis's sanction, in making a selection from the arsenal at Madras, of a variety of military stores for the service of Nizam Ali, had been skilful and active in forming several corps of infantry, and from the moment of the suspected secession of the English, had been authorised to augment their numbers, and to obtain French officers from Pondicherry and elsewhere: the procrastination of the Mahrattas arising from intestine feuds gave time for the organization of these corps;
1795. and in February 1795, when the Mahrattas approached in force, Monsieur Raymond did not decline the contest with the cele-

brated brigades of Sindea, organized and commanded by officers of his own nation, of which however the best remained at that time in Hindostan for the maintenance of the authority exercised in the name of the imprisoned Mogul.

The better cavalry of the Mahrattas, destitute of all pretensions to tactical discipline, had an interior organization, which enabled the chief to wield and dispose his apparently disordered masses, and admirable arrangements for forage and subsistence. Nizam Ali's cavalry was lamentably deficient in both of these requisites, and particularly the last; but individually, the horses were better, and the men braver, where they could be brought to act; and were animated in this war by the sentiment of defending their means of subsistence and their homes. An action was fought near the frontier on the 11th of March, in which among other Mar. 11.
incidents, a charge of Nizam Ali's cavalry drove Purseram Bhow completely off the field, from which he retreated a day's march, in the full persuasion that the battle was lost; abundance of confusion on both sides occurred in various parts of the field, but Monsieur Raymond manœuvred his troops with great ability, and it would appear, from a plan of the action now before me; sketched by an English officer who was present, that the operations of the day were on the whole most favourable to Nizam Ali. Monsieur Raymond urged him by repeated messages to follow up the advantage gained by the flight of Perseram Bhow, and was in momentary expectation of receiving the requisite orders and support, when at four o'clock in the afternoon, he was stunned by the order to retreat. Nizam Ali in conformity to the absurd practice of his life, was accompanied by his harem, and was actually moved to this fatal order by the fears of the favourite

of the day, who threatened to disgrace him by exposing herself to public view, if he did not instantly retreat to the little fort of Kurdla; a position where nothing short of imbecility could have led him, and where nature aided the efforts of the Mahrattas, in completely enclosing his army, and cutting it off from every source of supply. Hopes infinitely exceeding all that his most sanguine adherents had formed, were thus blasted by the childish compliance of a doating old man, and the sufferings of some weeks in this distressing predicament terminated, as the reader will have anticipated, not in the entire destruction of his power, which would have forced some serious considerations on the English and on Tippoo Sultaun; but in a disgraceful peace, of which many conditions were stipulated to be secret; the public articles being a cession of territory yielding thirty-five lacs of rupees, including the fort of Dowlutabad, the key of Decan, and above all the delivery, as a hostage, of the minister Azeem-ul-Omra, whose councils had led to that dependence on the faith and political support of the English, which had commenced with the negotiation regarding Guntoor in 1788, had been improved in 1790, and seemed according to present appearances to be for ever extinguished.

After the conclusion of this treaty, the Mahrattas retired within their own frontier, but Nizam Ali was clearly and unconditionally prostrate before them, and would probably soon have ceased to exist, as a power, when two events occurred, which in their remote and unexpected consequences, tended to avert his extinction, and restore his political importance. These were the rebellion of his son, Ali Jah, in June, and the death of the Pêshwa, in October, 1795. Immediately after the peace of Kurdla, Nizam Ali, justly sensible of the value of Monsieur Raymond's services, and the importance of augmenting and improving the corps under his command, which, even at Kurdla, had amounted to twenty-three strong battalions, had adopted the most efficient means of accomplishing his object, by assigning to that officer territorial revenues sufficient to ensure their regular payment; the country selected for this purpose was Kurpa, the most convenient to the Government to give, and particularly acceptable to Monsieur Raymond, from its vicinity to the sea-coast, the facilities thereby acquired of recruiting his officers, and the still more important expectation, of uniting with an European corps from revolutionary France, with which he hoped to strengthen the interests of his nation in Decan and the South.

Sir John Shore appears to have felt with acuteness the dangers of this preparatory arrangement, and directed the British Resident to declare that if Monsieur Raymond were not withdrawn from Kurpa he should be under the necessity of advancing a body of English troops in that direction. We have ventured to suggest that any event which should have transferred the dominions of Nizam Ali to the direct possession of the Mahrattas or of Tippoo Sultaun, or both, would have forced upon the English Government a more decided line of policy; and a very obvious illustration of this opinion may be found in the highly probable case of the possession of Kurpa by this very corps which would unquestionably have transferred its allegiance to one of those victorious states; and the merits of that neutral system, which would consider as foreign to the policy of a state, the depression or aggrandizement of its

CHAP. XLIII. 1795.

neighbours, may, in this case, be brought to a tolerably fair test, by examining whether the occupation of Kurpa by a powerful corps in the interest of France, were more safe under the guidance of the hostile states of Poona or Mysoor; or the friendly direction of Nizam Ali; and even this alternative is too favourable to the argument of neutrality, for in the event of an open determination to support Nizam Ali, the danger from Monsieur Raymond's corps would not have existed. The refined arguments in favour of neutrality may be farther illustrated, by anticipating the case which occurred in 1797, of an apprehended invasion of Nizam Ali's territories by Tippoo alone: in this event, the Governor-general deemed himself bound by the implied guarantee to repel the aggression in the first instance, and then to unite with Nizam Ali and the Mahrattas for obtaining redress; whereas in 1794 he deemed the guarantee void, because the Mahrattas had combined in the same expected aggression, and thereby dissolved or suspended the triple alliance. If however the first principle of political duty be recognized in the celebrated charge to the Roman dictator* "to preserve the state from injury of every kind," and if the destruction of this ally were an acknowledged injury to the English state, then the distinction between the cases of 1794 and 1797 would lead to the unfortunate inference that this ally might be defended against a small danger but not against a great one.

The rebellion and flight of Ali Jah terminated the disagreeable discussions on the subject of Raymond's troops, in consequence of the orders given to that officer to march instantly

* Ne quid respublica detrimenti capiat.

against the rebel; and a simultaneous and most urgent application from Nizam Ali to the English government, to aid him with a detachment of troops for the same purpose. Raymond had reduced and captured the rebel just before the arrival of the English corps; but the alacrity with which this request had been complied with, and the efficient celerity of the movement tended to restore better dispositions. The dissensions at Poona regarding the choice of a Pêshwa, between Sindea, who supported the true heir, Bâjee Row, son of the late Ragoba, and Nana Furnavese, who desired to establish as his own pageant Chimnajee, his younger brother, divided * the chiefs of the Mahratta confederacy into two contending factions; and the desire of Nana to employ the aid even of the feeble state of Nizam Ali, facilitated the able machinations of Azeem-ul-Omra, who, as a hostage and a prisoner, contrived to hold at his disposal some of the most powerful Mahratta chiefs; and by concerted demonstrations of the troops of his own state, was enabled to negotiate and conclude a new treaty; softening or omitting the most injurious parts of the treaty of Kurdla; and obtaining his own liberation, which was followed by his reinstatement in the office of prime minister to Nizam Ali. The favourable dispositions towards the English excited by the prompt assistance recently afforded, coincided with the original counsels of this minister, who him-

* In the course of these intrigues, Purseram Bhow, the inveterate personal enemy of Tippoo, was alternately with Nana and with Sindea; after an interregnum of some continuance Nana was himself forcibly expelled, Chimnajee was placed on the musnud with Purseram Bhow as his minister, but this usurpation was of short continuance, Purseram Bhow and his charge fled; Bâjee Row was placed on the musnud, and Nana was recalled, but he also was afterwards made the prisoner of Dowlut Row Sindea.

CHAP. XLIII. 1795. self believing, was enabled to impress the belief on his sovereign, that the treatment he had recently experienced from the English state, constituted no part of their genuine national policy. A spirit of amity was accordingly cherished, of which we shall have occasion to relate some important results, which that sagacious minister had probably foreseen.

The Sultaun was in the meanwhile no careless observer of these transactions; we have seen that an envoy from the Saint at Calburga, was sent to Seringapatam on the return of Tippoo's matrimonial messengers; this envoy was named Kâdir Hussein Khân, and his knowledge of that court had pointed him out to Ali Jah, as a fit agent, to obtain the Sultaun's active and immediate co-operation in the dethronement of his father. The first overture, mostly promptly accepted, was the cession to the Sultaun of every thing south of the Toombuddra and * Kistna. The Sultaun's troops destined for the service, were ordered with as little parade as possible to rendezvous at Gooty, on the pretence of demanding tribute from Kurnool; and Kâdir Hussein Khân, who was received for the purpose into the immediate service of Tippoo, was sent as his envoy to the camp of the rebel, to concert the conjoint operations. He was anticipated by the activity of Monsieur Raymond, who had defeated and taken Ali Jah before his arrival. And the envoy having reason to think that his mission was suspected, and his life in danger; instead of destroying his documents, which would have arrested the career of diplomatic ambition, resolved with great address to provide himself with proofs of innocence. It was at that time

* Original letters of both.

one of the Sultaun's improvements, to seal his letters with wax, instead of the customary Indian process of an impression with ink, and these waxen seals, Kâdir Hussein very dexterously removed from the letters addressed to Ali Jah and his associates, to others of his own composition, addressed to Nizam Ali, to Mumtaz-ul-Omra his relation, who possessed great influence in the absence of the minister, and to other courtiers; and fortified with these documents, he proceeded, after a long pause and considerable hesitation, to Hyderabad, whence he actually dispatched answers to these forgeries, addressed to the Sultaun, who highly approved the ingenuity of the device. There was, however, at Hyderabad, another Mysorean envoy, with whom he came into ridiculous collision: Medina Shah of Kurnool, a saint, whom the Sultaun appears to have addressed * with great humility, in August 1792, as his spiritual superior, whose aid he solicited as a Mussulman, in forwarding the political objects of the faith: the correspondence with Medina Shah, led to his visiting Seringapatam; where the saint, certainly a man of talent, shewed himself to be among the most mean and rapacious of that venal court; and was afterwards deputed as the instrument of all the secret intrigues, which he had already aided in establishing at Hyderabad. I suspect some mistake in the date of the letter of this personage, describing the arrival of Kâdir Hussein in 1797, but the error, if such it be, is of little consequence. Kâdir Hussein, a man of rank and consequence, somewhat ironically magnified, is stated by Medina Shah to have arrived in the suburbs, without a suitable retinue, without orders, and without

* Original draft of his letter.

documents; to have been arrested by the police, to have given a false account of himself, and to be oftener drunk than sober. A singular correspondence ensued between the Sultaun and each of them, in which they were more occupied with reciprocal accusations than political events. He seems alternately to have meditated the recal of each, and at one time had even stopped the allowances of both; but notwithstanding the incessant representations of pecuniary distress, the intrigues were actively continued; and neither of them ever returned to Seringapatam. It would seem, from the negotiations of that period, that Nizam Ali was still ready to conclude arrangements for a perfect union of interests with Tippoo, if the latter had consented to exchange the pledge of a Korân; and the Sultaun's continued rejection of this advance, is a curious example of that intellectual aberration so often observable, which, abandoning every intelligible principle of morality and religion, is yet restrained and chastened by an unimportant form.

Among the complicated intrigues of Hyderabad, at different periods, from 1792 to 1797, was a treaty of marriage with the great niece of Nizam Ali, not only without his consent, but for the purpose of subverting his power; and, after the rebellion of Ali Jah, a treaty of alliance with another son, who meditated rebellion, and who deputed to Seringapatam a person of importance, to concert the means of success, as a permanent embassador. * All the combinations were considered to be so perfectly

* He left Seringapatam before the war of 1799; during that war he was in the suit of Meer Aalum, and was exceedingly alarmed regarding the discoveries which might be made by the examination of the records after the capture of the place. For the reasons already assigned, his name is suppressed.

prepared, that the parties deemed it only necessary to wait a fit opportunity. The Sultaun's own persuasion of success in a project so long and so earnestly pursued, would be insufficient evidence of a speculative fact, in which his judgment was so much biassed; but, the joint opinion of the principal officers of is Government, in a document* intended to dissuade him from a crude and precipitate developement of his general designs, furnishes satisfactory testimony of the maturity of these combinations. The country of Nizam Ali, as they distinctly state, will come into his possession with the greatest facility at the proper time: it is an event which would unite the English and the Mahrattas against him; and, it was therefore necessary to wait with circumspection until he could throw the weight of a French armament into the scale.

1797.

Subsequently to the peace of 1792, and particularly during that state of military preparation, which the complicated intrigues of Hyderabad had rendered necessary to the Sultaun's views; the English Government of Madras had been incessantly engaged in expeditions, rendered necessary by the state of the war in Europe. Pondicherry and the French possessions had been reduced in 1793. In 1795, and 1796, the Dutch settlements in Ceylon and Malacca, and their valuable possessions in Banda and Amboyna, were reduced by armaments equipped at that presidency. An expedition prepared in 1794 against the Isle of France, had been abandoned without any reference to the state of Indian politics; but in consequence of events which had interfered with the expected co-operation

* Seringapatam papers submitted to Parliament; opinion of the five departments on the folly of his connection with Ripaud in 1797.

CHAP. XLIII. from Europe. An armament on a considerable scale intended for the reduction of Manilla, of which the first division had

1797. actually sailed to Penang, was also countermanded in consequence of intelligence received by Lord Hobart the Governor of Madras, of the extraordinary successes of the French army of Italy, the consequent negotiations between General Buonaparte and the Archduke Charles, and the expediency of reserving for defensive measures all the forces of England; which in the judgment of the Governor would be left to sustain alone the pressure of a general war; a fortunate determination with reference to the affairs of India, when we consider the active preparations of the Sultaun, the suspicion of his designs of hostile aggression against the dominions of Nizam Ali, which in 1797, the Governor-general had ordered to be repelled, and the danger to the public interests which would ensue from the absence of so large a portion of the military force. But it is not a little curious to observe, that at the period when the troops destined for Manilla, were on the point of embarking at Madras, the minutes * of a consultation held at Seringapatam shew, that the Sultaun was not without apprehension of its landing at Mangalore, while the principal officers of his Goverment, unanimously declared their disbelief of those reports which referred its destination to that port, or to Mauritius, but think the most probable object to be Manilla, or *stopping up the route by which the French are expected,* without any indication of what that route may be. The same consultation discusses the intelligence from Poona,

* Original documents.

of secret conferences which are rumoured to have for their object the invasion of Mysoor by Sindea. On which the same officers agree, that such invasion is not probable, without the concurrence of the English and Nizam Ali; that each of the three powers are too much occupied with their own affairs and intestine dissensions; that exclusively of these, Sindea has too much ground of uneasiness regarding his affairs at Delhi, to undertake so absurd an expedition; but that if he should come alone, his arrival would rather be a subject of exultation than of fear. The combined result of the documents on both sides thus evince, rather a reciprocal alarm at the preparations of the other, than any matured and definite plan of immediate hostility.

In the boundless variety of schemes, contemplated by the Sultaun for the restoration of his power, and the expulsion of the English from India, he had found means, through his agents at Delhi, of opening a correspondence with the ministers of Zemân Shah, the king of the Afghans; and the Sultaun, early in 1796, sent embassadors to Cabul, who were instructed carefully to conceal their political objects, to proceed by the way of Kutch, where a commercial factory was already established, thence to Kerânchy, in Sinde, on the pretence of establishing another factory; and from that place, on the pretext of a mercantile and religious journey to the holy tombs in Persia, to obtain safe conduct through Belochistân, and make good their way to Cabul. The projected means by which the co-operation of this sovereign was proposed to be rendered available, moved at a more rapid pace than was justified by the sanction of historical experience: the conquest of Delhi, the expulsion of the Mahrattas, and the consolidation of the empire of Hindostân, was to occupy one year: and in the second, an Afghan army was to invade the Mahratta dominions in Decan, from the north, while he should assail them * from the south: these objects effected, the destruction of the remaining infidels would be nothing. Zemân Shah had previously meditated the invasion of Hindostân, and did move for the purpose in the same year, but was recalled by intestine war: the expectation of such an event, however, continued for several years to be viewed by the English Government of Bengal, with serious apprehension, and without speculating on the very improbable event, of an Afghan invasion of Decan, would have constituted a most efficient diversion for the Sultaun, to prevent the resources of Bengal from becoming available in the south: the embassadors accomplished their journey, and appear to have made a suitable impression, and the same persons were again deputed, in January 1799, when the object was not offensive war, but preservation from impending destruction.

Having noticed, to the extent that appeared to be requisite for rendering our narrative intelligible, the most prominent circumstances of those intrigues on the Indian continent, which were intended to restore the Sultaun's affairs; it remains to describe the measures directed to the same end, which he attempted to concert with the French Government. The embassy to Paris, in 1788, terminated in general professions of amity; in assurances of a disposition to promote his views, at

* The original leaves it doubtful, which of the infidels was to be first destroyed; the context seems to indicate the Mahrattas, as the power whom he would necessarily first attack, in achieving the conquest of Delhi.

a proper opportunity, and in explanations of the reasons which prevented the French King from then engaging in an English war. After the humiliating events of 1792, the Sultaun, in his numerous applications for aid, uniformly ascribed his misfortunes to the jealousy of the English at some previous indications of friendship with the state to which he addressed himself; and, in conformity to this general rule, his uniform attachment to the French, and his public embassy to Paris, in 1788, were stated as the efficient and exclusive causes of that confederacy, which the fears and jealousy of the English had contrived for his destruction. The Frenchmen in his service had no difficulty in procuring the means of transmitting these representations; and, it appears, that formal propositions from the Sultaun to the French Government, of which the date is uncertain, but probably in 1795 or 6, were transmitted through the medium of Pierre Moneron; and that numerous communications were made through General Cossigny, who resided in the Isle of France. The remarkable success of the revolutionary armies had enabled the persons of that nation in his service, to impress on his mind the decided superiority by land, of the new French tactics and moral energy, over any possible efforts of the English; and these opinions rendered him not only anxious, but impatient, for the execution of those splendid assurances of the utter expulsion of the English from India, of which he had received the lavish and incessant promise.

While in this frame of mind, in the early part of 1797, a privateer from the Isle of France arrived, dismasted, at the port of Mangalore, and solicited the means of repair. The Meer-

CHAP. XLIII. 1797. è-Yem (Lord of the Admiralty) at that port was Gholaum Ali, one of the former embassadors to France; he had attained a slight acquaintance with the language; he conversed with the master of the vessel named Ripaud, and reported as the result of his examination, that this person called himself the second in command at the Mauritius, and had been specially instructed to touch at Mangalore, for the purpose of ascertaining the Sultaun's wishes regarding the co-operation of a French force which was ready at the Isle of France for the expulsion from India of their common enemy, the English. Gholaum Ali was accordingly desired to conduct this important personage to the presence, where he was admitted to daily interviews and long consultations. The Sultaun, according to his most usual course of action, first made up his own mind, and then proceeded in due form to demand the opinions, in writing, of the principal officers of his Government; not whether negotiations and engagements should be entered into with the French nation, but what those engagements should be, and how they were to be accomplished, stating his own suggestion to receive and retain Ripaud in his pretended capacity of envoy, but ostensibly as a servant: to purchase the ship, lade it with merchandize for the Isle of France, and send confidential agents of his own, with letters from Ripaud to the Government of that island, for the purpose of concerting all that related to the desired armament.

The officers of Tippoo's Government had discovered, through the medium of one of Ripaud's companions, that his assumed rank and political mission was an impudent imposture; and in

1797. Mar. 8.

a joint public document, dated the 8th of March, represented, with a degree of freedom altogether unusual, their conviction of the folly, the peril, and the disrepute of any agency, in which this person should be concerned. " From first to last (they declare, in this remarkable document) the language of this man (whom they afterwards designate rather coarsely as a scoundrel) has been that of self-interest and falsehood, nothing has resulted from this business, and nothing can — the medium of such a low fellow tends to throw discredit on the transaction:" and after stating the facility of possessing the country of Nizam Ali, and the delicacy of any thing which should prematurely combine him again with the English and the Mahrattas; they observe, " the object of this state will be better effected, at a seasonable opportunity, than by relying on the agency of this compound of air and water." * This written instrument, and the verbal representations of its authors to the Sultaun, that he was in the act of disclosing all his designs to the English; and subjecting himself to their immediate hostility, without the prospect of timely succour, were insufficient to divert him from the crude conceptions of his own arrogant mind; he had one uniform remark for all arguments which he could not answer. — " Whatever is the will of God, that will be accomplished." . Ripaud's vessel was accordingly purchased for the sum of seventeen thousand rupees †, and the consideration money was paid and committed to the hands of a Frenchman

* Seringapatam papers submitted to Parliament.

† About 2,125*l.* This seems a small sum, for even a two masted vessel, which the Sultaun states her to have been; and it is possible that the Sultaun's agents might have discovered, on their arrival at the Isle of France, that Ripaud was only authorized to sell his own share of the vessel.

CHAP. XLIII. 1797. named Pernore * who was to pay it at the Isle of France, in conformity to Ripaud's instructions: the officers of the ship were to navigate her on the part of the Sultaun; Ripaud was to remain as French embassador at his court; and four envoys from the Sultaun were appointed to embark in the assumed character of merchants, and after concluding the proper negotiations at the Isle of France, one of them was to return with the fleet and army, and the other three were to proceed as embassadors to the Executive Directory, at Paris. For this purpose, the four embassadors, with their credentials for these several objects, together with *Pernore*, who was also charged with the seventeen thousand rupees of Ripaud, and his letters to the Government of the Isle of France, did accordingly depart, in the month
April. of April, 1797, from Seringapatam, to embark at Mangalore. On the night following their arrival at that port, *Pernore* absconded in a boat, with three other persons, and the seventeen thousand rupees; and, according to the statement of the remaining crew, must have been taken prisoners by the English; an event, of which no traces have been discovered.

On the receipt of this intelligence at Seringapatam, Tippoo appears to have been for a time heartily ashamed of himself, and of Ripaud, who was placed under restraint on the suspicion of collusion, to obtain double payment for the vessel; the affair was too delicate and ridiculous to be tolerated in conversation; but a commencement had been made; the royal will (the identical

* The name was so pronounced by several persons of the late court, with whom I conversed on the subject; but their blunders in European names, are too well known to admit of any thing approaching certainty, and I am aware that the name cannot be as stated in the text.

and only law of the Medes and Persians, which altereth not) had been pronounced, and it was necessary to make some adjustment, in order that the embassy might proceed. If the vessel should arrive at the Isle of France without the consideration money, it is certain that she would be claimed and seized by the owners, among whom it was probable, that Ripaud possessed but a small proprietory share; and to release her and Ripaud, was to abandon the money and the political prospects together. After some consideration, it was determined to restore the vessel to Ripaud, to require his bond for the repayment of the seventeen thousand rupees which he had actually received; and for which the vessel was declared to be a collateral security, and to send him to the Isle of France with the embassadors, now reduced to two, who did not ultimately sail until the month of October. The explanation prefixed to the official documents on this subject, printed by authority in India, ascribes this delay to "the monsoon having set in before the embassy was ready to depart;" and it is probable, not only that the true cause obtained little notoriety, but had been treated with habitual reserve by those who either knew or suspected it; but the complaints and reproaches of Ripaud, after they had sailed, (as stated in the official narrative of the embassadors) of his *having been compelled to give a bond for the ship*, would be unintelligible without the explanations now given.

Ripaud had scarcely got to sea, when, like a true buccaneer, collecting all his Europeans, amounting to five or six, he came up to the envoys in a threatening manner, reproached them for the treatment he had received (for he had been compelled not only to give the bond above mentioned, but to pay for the whole

CHAP. XLIII. 1797. outfit of provisions and stores which the Sultaun promised to furnish), and demanded to *see* the letters addressed to the constituted authorities at the Isle of France; without which, instead of pursuing his voyage thither, he would proceed on a privateering cruize. After some altercation, he forcibly seized and opened the letters, and probably finding that their contents did not confirm the apprehensions he had formed, he steered, without further hesitation, for Port Louis, in the Isle of France,
1798. where he arrived, on the 19th of January * 1798.

The strictest injunctions for the concealment, not only of the object but the existence of a political mission, were contained in their official instructions, and they were furnished for the same purpose with fictitious commercial orders, and a false passport, as merchants; but the Sultaun had not considered that a secret known to the master and crew of a privateer, was not in the train of being rigidly kept. General Malartic, the governor, on being informed of the rank and quality of the persons on board, sent some gentlemen of his suite to wait upon them, and adjust the time for their landing, under suitable honours. The separate report of one of the envoys, states, that the strongest remonstrances were made against this open disclosure of a secret mission; but the other report is silent on the subject: it is obvious that it depended on themselves, positively to resist a public reception, and probable that their vanity, or their avarice, or both, may have contributed to obtain an implied assent, which, to any penetrating or experienced mind, must have been identified with absolute treason to their sovereign.

* The embassadors were not very careful journalists. In their separate reports, one dates their arrival on the 8th.

The Governor, the Admiral, and all the constituted authorities came out to do honour to their public reception, under the customary salutes; and they were conducted in form between a double line of troops to the Government house, where the dispatches were delivered in the same public manner; and after the usual ceremonies, they proceeded to the dwelling appointed by the Government for their residence. The dispatches were found to contain the project of a treaty with the Government of the Isle of France, for fixing the terms and objects of co-operation of a large army supposed to be present, of from five to ten thousand European French, and from twenty to thirty thousand Africans: they were to be joined, at a rendezvous to be fixed, by sixty thousand Mysoreans, and the first object of the war was the conquest of Goa, from the Portuguese, with whom no cause of enmity was assigned: this port and territory were to belong to the Sultaun, and Bombay, when conquered, to the French. The embassadors were instructed to explain, as the next objects of the war, after the adjustment of every thing in the west of India, the reduction and razing of Madras, the subjugation of the Mahrattas and Nizam Ali, and finally the conquest of Bengal.

The embassadors however, on proceeding in the next conference to discuss the business of their mission, found that every part of Ripaud's representations was equally and totally false; and that no armament for the service of the Indian continent had arrived or was expected. Two frigates were dispatched without delay, with the letters in duplicate for the Executive Directory, who, as the envoys were assured, would immediately order the required succour; and in the meanwhile General Malartic had no other means of aiding their views

CHAP. XLIII. than by raising a corps of volunteers in the Isles of France and Bourbon. It was to no purpose for the envoys to represent that they were deputed to bring a large force, and not a small one; that they were not furnished with money to raise a new levy; that the whole proceeding was contrary to their instructions, and "that they would not carry with them the recruits proposed to be raised." * General Malartic, on the second day after their arrival, ordered an advertisement to be

1798.

Jan. 30. published, and on the 30th of January, issued a formal proclamation of similar import, informing the citizens of the two islands (and of course the whole world) that two embassadors had arrived from Tippoo Sultaun with dispatches to his Government, and to the Executive Directory; that the Sultaun desired to form an offensive and defensive alliance with the French, and to maintain, at his charge, the troops which might be sent to him; that he was perfectly prepared, and waited only the arrival of the French, to declare war against the English; whom he ardently desired to expel from India: that as it was impossible for the Governor to spare any regular troops on account of the succours he had lately sent to his allies the Dutch, he invited the citizens who might be disposed, to enter as volunteers, and serve under the banners of Tippoo, and assured them of an advantageous rate of pay, the terms of which would be fixed by the embassadors, who would farther engage, in the name of their Sovereign, for the volunteers being at all times free to return.

* This is the 5th of six distinct written propositions, submitted to General Malartic, as detailed in the narrative of Mahommed Ibrahim, one of the embassadors, in the published documents.

In whatever degree the embassadors at first resisted, or tacitly permitted the publicity of this most unstatesman-like proceeding, it is certain, that they were weak enough to lend themselves to its consequences; to hold publicly the same language which the proclamation contained, regarding their master's designs; to permit the document itself to be publicly distributed at the place of their residence; and without actually enlisting, to encourage men to accompany them, on condition that their pay should be regulated by the Sultaun himself, a point on which some serious dissatisfaction was ultimately expressed by General Malartic, who told them plainly, that having come unsought for, to solicit aid, they ought to submit to such conditions as he thought proper to impose.

The conduct of General Malartic, in frustrating the designs of secrecy, which were so obviously essential to Tippoo's expectations of success, have been ascribed to either inadvertency or design: and neither of these suppositions would increase our respect for his talents as a statesman. It would be difficult to infer inadvertency, when it is considered that, independently of the information he must necessarily have received from the embassadors before their landing, the most inexperienced mind would perceive the demand from one power, for hostile means against another with which it was at peace, to indicate secrecy as the very essence of the transaction. After perusing his dispatches, he must have perceived that the whole mission was founded in the false information of Ripaud, and that the premature publicity in the Isle of France, and of consequence soon afterwards in India, of an open and undisguised plan of hostility against the English and their allies, would inevitably expose the

CHAP. XLIII. 1798. Sultaun to be attacked and overpowered before he could possibly receive assistance from France; and finally he leaves us no room to doubt of his being perfectly apprised of the consequences of his proceedings, by announcing in his letter to the Sultaun that he had laid an embargo on all vessels in Port Louis until after the departure of the embassadors and recruits, "lest the English, our common enemy, should be apprised of the part which you seem determined to adopt with regard to them, and of the supply of men which I have sent to you." If therefore we are to reject the supposition of inadvertency, the alternative, of referring to motives of policy, the crude conception of sacrificing an unsupported ally to the hope of producing a temporary embarrassment to the common enemy, would be equally unfavourable to the sagacity of these public demonstrations: and it may be conjectured, with greater probability, that the obvious disadvantages of precipitating a rupture between Tippoo and the English, were overpowered by the exigencies of his local situation; by the terrors of a furious democracy, which rendered nearly nominal his office of Governor-general of the French possessions in the east; and by the hope of exciting, in a greater degree than he ultimately found practicable, the avarice and enterprise of those perturbed spirits by whom he was surrounded and assailed, and by the expedient of giving a new direction to the lust of plunder, novelty and mischief, for the purpose of effecting his own deliverance from the most worthless and dangerous characters of the colony. The degree in which these several motives may have influenced his conduct, cannot perhaps be determined with accuracy, but no doubt can encompass the proposition, that he unintentionally conferred the most important benefits on the English Government in India, by distinctly, publicly, and officially, unfolding the dangers which it had to avert and retaliate.

Before dismissing the subject of this mission, it is not a little curious to observe an example of the strange wanderings of the Sultaun's mind, in confounding together the events of 1784 and 1792, in the narrative contained in his letters to the constituted French authorities, regarding transactions of which they were perfectly informed, and with which they are first reproached and then forgiven. "During the last war, when he was on the point of conquering the English, an order from Monsieur Bussy compelled the French forces under M. Cossigny to abandon him, and even Lally followed the example, and thus left to his own resources, and abandoned by his allies, he was compelled to make peace, with the loss of half his dominions and three crores and thirty thousand rupees in specie."

Ultimately, the embassadors did embark on the 7th of March, 1798, on the Preneuse frigate, with exactly ninety-nine men, including civil and military officers, for the service of the Sultaun. The capture of two English Indiamen, in the roads of Tellicherry, in consequence of intelligence received on the voyage, detained them but a few days, and they landed at Mangalore, on the 26th of April, 1798. April 26.

In the letter from General Malartic, to Tippoo Sultaun, which accompanied the return of his embassadors, he distinctly announced, that in the event of the Sultaun's disapproving the terms of service which had been conditionally arranged, he had "authorised all the officers, volunteers, and others, to return on

CHAP. XLIII. 1798.

the frigate to the Isle of France:" and, although the embassadors had the imprudence to debark them at Mangalore, without waiting for authority, it was still competent to the Sultaun, after reading the narratives of his embassadors, and ascertaining in them the boundless publicity given to his designs by the official proclamation; and the subsequent enlistment, embarkation, and arrival of men for the expulsion of the English from India, to have still arrested the mischief. He could still have reimbarked, and returned the men without the risk of offence, by representing to the French the impolicy of courting war, before he was prepared; he could still have disavowed to the English, as unauthorised, the whole proceedings of General Malartic, and have announced the return to the Isle of France of his repudiated levy, and he could thus have neutralized the most powerful public grounds on which they justified their preparations for war.

Not the slightest objection however was made to the reception of the troops, nor to any part of the diplomatic proceedings: he evinced the greatest impatience for the arrival at Seringapatam of this motley reinforcement of naval, and military, creole, and European levy, of 99 men; who, soon after their arrival, organized a Jacobin club, on the most approved Parisian models, under the sanction of the Sultaun, whom they distinguished by the fraternal designation of *Citizen Tippoo:* the tree of liberty was planted, surmounted by the cap of equality; the citizens assembled in primary assembly, instructed each other in the enforcement of their new rights, and the abandonment of their old duties: a council of discipline was formed to subvert discipline, by superseding the military authority of the commandant: all emblems of royalty were publicly burned, and the national colours of *the sister republic* were consecrated by *Citizen Tippoo on the public parade*, under a salute of two thousand three hundred pieces of cannon*: all was concluded by the characteristic oath of hatred to royalty, and fidelity to a tyrant, and followed, according to the admission of their own recorded journals, by scenes of the most scandalous disorder and insubordination. Of any comprehension of the purport or tendency of all these proceedings, the Sultaun was so entirely innocent, that he fancied himself to be consolidating one of those associations devoted to his own aggrandizement, by which his imagination had lately been captivated, in the history of the Arabian Wahâbees.

Two persons, Monsieur Chapuis, chef-de-brigade, and Monsieur Dubuc, captain in the navy, commanding the land and the sea forces, seem to have taken little or no share in these mischievous absurdities, although an indication appears of their having imbibed a full portion of the new lights in revolutionary morality. As the time approached for their being presented to the Sultaun, some doubts would seem to have occurred regarding their rank and quality, and the officers of government addressed to them a written requisition for explanations; in answer to which, in a formal instrument under their joint signatures, they declare that they are deputed by General Malartic and Admiral Sercey, not only to serve in their respective professions by

* The number of guns is taken from the proceedings of a Jacobin club found at Seringapatam; the fact is of trifling importance, otherwise than as a test of the absence of veracity.

CHAP. XLIII. 1798. sea and land, but as diplomatic envoys to the Sultaun's court, *with full power and authority, in the name of the French republic and its representatives at the Isle of France*, to treat with him of an alliance to serve as a fundamental basis, and that the treaties con-

June 20. cluded by them would be presented to the national convention, and ratified by the executive power. On which formal and authentic declaration, it is only necessary to observe, that no trace of any such diplomatic delegation is to be found in the dispatches addressed to Tippoo Sultaun, by General Malartic, or Admiral Sercey; or in the proceedings at the Isle of France, or yet in the letter of Captain L'Hermite of the *Preneuse*, announcing his arrival at Mangalore; "with the Sultaun's embassadors, Hussein Ally Khân, and Mahommed Ibrahim, and the Frenchmen whom General Malartic had sent under the orders of M. Chapuis commanding the land, and M. Dubuc commanding the naval forces."

After some conferences with these officers, it was suggested, that although his dispatches had been forwarded to the Executive Directory, it would be expedient to have an accredited minister on the spot to expedite the succours, and furnish the requisite local information; and Monsieur Dubuc was finally associated with two Mahommedan envoys in a joint embassy to the Executive Directory, to embark according to Dubuc's suggestion at the neutral port of Tranquebar, on the coast of Coromandel; and they received their credentials and instructions on the 20th of July, 1798.

While the Sultaun continued, without apparent indication of alarm, to be amused with these revolutionary novelties, and to be occupied with the internal arrangements of his own state, which have already been described, the English government were far from being passive observers of the designs unfolded at the Isle of France, of which they received early and authentic intelligence.

CHAPTER XLIV.

Government of India — Clive — Hastings — Lord Mornington — Relations with the native powers at the time of his arrival — Sindea — his unresisted aggrandisement — Admission of the right to interfere — De Boigne — placed in the situation of a sovereign prince — his successor Perron — Difference of their systems — Perron excludes English officers — French army on the English frontier — Complicated use of the authority of the imprisoned Mogul — Designs of the French — Appeal to the candour of those who thought the case over-stated — State of the Mahratta dissension with reference to the situation of the English — Nizam Ali — Raymond's fine corps of 14,000 *men — His character and conduct — becomes formidable to his superior, Nizam Ali — Governor-general receives authentic intelligence of the events at the Isle of France — Preparation for war — Danger from Raymond's corps — Nizam Ali's fears of both French and English — Dangers accumulated by the English system of neutrality — Negotiation at Hyderabad, for dismissing the French and substituting an English force — Offensive and defensive treaty concluded — Disarming and dismission of the French officers — Wisdom and energy of the measure — Its effect at the native courts — Secret dissatisfaction of the Mahrattas — Sindea's presence at Poona unfavourable — Fluctuating councils — Lord Mornington determines to proceed without them — Tippoo's intrigues at that court — Secret agent — Erroneous conceptions — Friendly disposition of the Pêshwa — Curious evidence of this, in his secret interviews, and excellent advice — Public embassy from Tippoo — Secret agent discovered by Nana, and obliged to return.*

CHAP. XLIV. 1798.

Among the distinguished persons who at different periods presided over the administration of the British interests in India, two men had appeared, whose extraordinary talents and services have assigned to them an eminence in public estimation which had been approached by no other governor ; and the greatest statesmen of the first powers of Europe might have deemed themselves honourably classed with *Clive*, the founder, and *Hastings*, the preserver of that singular empire. A third was now to be added to these illustrious names, on whom nature had bestowed, with a liberal hand, all that could lead to the same eminence ; and the systematic education and practical experience of an European statesman, had conferred advantages which were wanting to the early career of his great predecessors. To these important qualities were superadded the inestimable benefit of early friendship and confidential intercourse with the great statesmen who then directed in England the general interests of the empire, an intimate knowledge of the bearings and influence of all their political views on the complex machinery of the government committed to his charge, and a well-founded confidence of support in every measure which the exigencies of the time might render necessary to strengthen and secure it. A consciousness of his own superior powers rendered Lord Mornington confident in opinions once fixed, and in measures once adopted ; but before determining, the most meagre intellect could not have sought with greater anxiety to be informed and enlightened by previous discussion. No man was so eminently qualified to do every thing for himself, and no man laid under larger contribution the talents of those around him. His own superiority was too marked to admit any mean jealousy of the borrowed credit to be attained by subordinate instruments, whose merits he anxiously and publicly acknowledged and appreciated, sometimes rather above than below their actual value. The same generous feeling prompted him, when he gave confidence, to make it almost unlimited; when he conferred authority, to make it at least commensurate to the occasion; and in guiding the exercise of a delegated discretion, to mark what was well done with applause, and correct what might be better, with a delicacy which almost obliterated the sense of error, or merged it in the confidence of meriting future approbation; and of his penetration in appreciating character, it may be affirmed, without the fear of giving reasonable offence, that of an unprecedented amount of public probity, moral worth, intellectual eminence, and military daring which existed in British India during the period of his administration, the largest and most brilliant portion was drawn forth, and wielded by the master mind of this great statesman.

Lord Mornington arrived at Madras in April, and at the seat of Supreme Government in Bengal in May 1798. In order that we may be enabled to consider with greater accuracy, such events of this wise and brilliant administration as are connected with the scope of our narrative, it will be necessary to take an abstract view of the actual state of those relations with the native powers, which had the most prominent influence on the general security of the British interests in India, at the period of his assuming that important charge.

Of the native powers whose frontier touched that of the British possessions, the most powerful, and looking to future contingencies highly probable, the most dangerous, was Dowlut Row Sindea; but the inordinate ambition which had led him to follow the projects of his uncle and predecessor, for extending over Decan and the south, that unlimited authority which he had established in Hindostân, although it kept him at this period, too much occupied with intrigues at Poona, to excite immediate apprehension for the north-western frontier of Bengal; rendered his actual resources, and ultimate designs, objects of serious consideration for an English Governor-general, who should prefer the manly examination of real danger, to the torpor of a delusive and fallacious security.

We have had occasion to advert to the extensive power possessed by Mahdajee Sindea in Malwâ and Hindostân, at the period of the treaty of Salbey; and without entering into the detail of those important transactions which brought his territories to touch the most vulnerable points of the British frontier in the Doâb, it will be sufficient for the purposes of this work to state that he had been permitted to effect this aggrandisement without even a diplomatic effort to arrest its progress. For the purpose of illustrating the circumstances to which we advert, it will be necessary to explain, that public news-writers are to be found at every Indian Court, who insert in their daily papers of intelligence, exactly what is permitted and no more; that the contents of these papers, together with such secret intelligence as may be obtained, is forwarded by the news-writers of foreign powers whose known functions were generally sanctioned at almost every Court excepting that of Seringapatam; and that these papers, like a more celebrated European journal, were sometimes made the vehicle of feeling the dispositions of their neighbours, to tolerate or resist an intended injury. In July 1792, the news-writer employed by the English Government at Delhi transmitted one of these papers of intelligence, published under Sindea's sanction, which stated "that the Emperor of Delhi had written to the Pêshwa and to Sindea, in-

CHAP. XLIV. 1798. forming them that he hoped through their exertions to obtain some tribute from Bengal" ! ! ! An intimation so very plain could not be overlooked by Lord Cornwallis, and he accordingly, in August 1792, furnished his resident at the court of Sindea, with instructions to represent " that in the present condition of the Mogul (the prisoner of Sindea) he should consider all letters written in his name to be by Sindea's power and authority only, and that the attempt to establish principles of the above description by any power whatever, will be warmly resented by this Government." This it will be observed was the second time in six years, that a similar attempt had been made, once in the direct claim of choute, made in 1786 on Sir John Macpherson, who answered that Sindea must instantly renounce and disavow the claim, or abide the consequences of immediate war; and now in the more cautious advance to the same object with Lord Cornwallis. His Lordship goes on to instruct his political resident,—" You will take care to recal, in the most forcible manner, to his recollection, the spirit of moderation and *forbearance*, that has been manifested by the Government, during the long period in which he has been employed, in extending his conquests in Hindostân, &c. &c." Forbearance necessarily implies, the right to do that from which we abstain; and the English Government would appear, on the face of this record, to have acquiesced in an aggrandisement which it had the right to prevent; a right which perhaps ought not to be forcibly exercised, excepting after timely remonstrance had failed; but in this case even the remonstrance was wanting. It is not intended to exclude from this consideration the question of expediency, on which public opinion was far from being agreed; but the recurrence of the Government to its own past forbearance, when the danger had begun to assume a mature aspect, involves a tacit admission which could scarcely have been expected under the circumstances of the case.

The chief instrument in effecting this aggrandisement, was M. De Boigne, formerly a subaltern officer in the East-India Company's service, on the Madras establishment; who had quitted the trammels of rise by seniority, for a more wide and indefinite field of ambition. The genius and talents of this distinguished officer, had enabled him to organise for Sindea, a regular establishment of infantry and artillery, such as had never before been seen in the service of a native power: and this Mahratta chief, by a liberal, but hazardous policy, assigned to the exclusive management of Mr. De Boigne, territory on the English frontier, yielding a revenue adequate to the maintenance of a regular field force, which in 1803, under his successor, amounted to 43,650 men, and 464 guns; and before that period, was supposed to have been more numerous. Indefinite means of levying or discharging Silledar horse to any amount, with all the apparatus of military, civil, and fiscal establishments, fortresses, arsenals, founderies, and depôts, belonging to actual sovereignty, to which pretension little seemed to be wanting excepting the declaration of independence. In the effective encouragement offered to European officers, the entire freedom of leaving the service, and remitting their property without restraint, was the most novel and attractive. De Boigne, personally availed himself of this liberal conduct, and was succeeded by Monsieur Perron, about 1794. The management of these two officers was, however, in one respect, entirely opposite. De Boigne, received indifferently English and French adventurers as officers; Perron accepted French candidates alone; and, at the period of Lord Mornington's arrival, the number of the English was so very limited in itself, and so systematically discouraged, that the formidable army which we have described, may be considered as officered by Frenchmen, and to constitute a French force on the English frontier. The deposed Mogul Emperor, was made, by a singular contrivance of circuitous mockery, to appoint the Mahratta Pêshwa, his (Vakeel-ul-Mutluk) absolute vicegerent, and the Pêshwa, to appoint Sindea his deputy! an imprisoned sovereign appointed as his absolute vicegerent the usurping minister of another imprisoned sovereign; and that minister was supposed to appoint as his deputy, the actual conqueror of the first named imprisoned pageant; this conqueror being engaged in the design of usurping all the authorities of the very usurping minister, who was feigned to confer this imaginary appointment on himself! These fictions were carried to so great a length, that Monsieur Perron called his army the "*imperial army,*" and himself a servant and subject of the Mogul; and the very plain and intelligible design of rendering the unfortunate Mogul the main instrument of the French for the establishment of their power in Hindostân, was afterwards confirmed by a written projet to that effect, which came into the possession of the English Governor-general.

It has been admitted that this danger, although the greatest, was not the most imminent; and although it be an anticipation of events beyond the scope of this work, it may be submitted to the candour of those statesmen, who condemned the subsequent Mahratta war, and deemed the case of the

French influence to have been overstated, whether they would really have continued to hold that opinion, in the event of this *imperial army* having been left untouched, and in the farther event, soon afterwards expected, of the arrival of a French or Russian army in Persia, or the Penjâb?

To the overgrown power of Sindea in the north, Lord Mornington could not, at this time, have opposed with any effect the party inimical to Sindea's views at Poona, chiefly because their enmity rather related to the interior, than the foreign policy of the Mahratta confederacy. It is true that the young Pêshwa, Bâjeerow, had evinced the greatest anxiety, to be released from the state of insulting thraldom, in which he was kept by Dowlut Row Sindea, and had even secretly solicited the interference of the British Government: but the influence of a state prisoner can seldom be efficient, and there was obvious ground of apprehension, that any pressure or interference from without, might have tended to unite the discordant chiefs. Instead, therefore, of viewing with surprise the subsequent apathy of the Pêshwa's Government, in failing to take its assigned part in the impending war of Mysoor, we shall see abundant cause to admire the skilful management by which the Governor-general was enabled to prevent the Mahratta force from being marshalled against him: and these observations, added to the degree in which our narrative has already attempted to develope the intricate politics of Poona, will be sufficient to afford a general conception of the state of the most important branches of the Mahratta power in 1798.

The ordinary course of our previous narration has sufficiently unfolded the dangerous and hostile designs of Mysoor, together with the means by which an expected invasion from the north under Zemaun Shah, might be made to distract the English councils, to divide their force, and to dissipate their treasure; the state of the war in Europe requires no farther illustration with regard to our immediate object, and the sketch which we proposed to present will be completed by describing the political condition of the court of Hyderabad.

We have had occasion to enter into some detail regarding the origin and progress of the corps of Monsieur Raymond, until the termination of the rebellion of Ali Jah, in the latter part of 1795. Subsequently to that event, this enterprising officer continued to be indefatigable in the organisation, improvement, and augmentation of his corps; which in 1798 amounted to fourteen thousand men, described in the public dispatches of the Governor-general to have "attained a degree of discipline superior in every respect to that of any native infantry in India, excepting the sepoys entertained in the English service;" and their efficiency was supported by a large and well organised train of field artillery. Monsieur Raymond appears to have been deeply imbued with those principles and practices which had been generated by the French revolution, in contempt of the obligations of honour since so familiarly violated in Europe; he had opened a successful correspondence with the officers of his nation, prisoners of war on parole at Pondicherry, for the purpose of obtaining their services; and he was only prevented by the vigilance of Lord Hobart, from being joined by a number * of them, who were apprehended at the moment they meant to effect their escape; but this dis-

* Malcolm's India, page 176.

appointment did not prevent his obtaining a tolerably full proportion of French officers. He had opened a correspondence with Tippoo, which the few documents discovered shew to have been discouraged after the arrival of the party from the Isle of France, by the jealousy of the Frenchmen in the Sultaun's service, of the established reputation and influence of that adventurer. His battalions carried the colours of the French Republic (then at war with England), the staff being surmounted by a spear, transfixing, or supporting, as fancy might interpret, the Mahommedan crescent; the cap of liberty was engraven on the buttons of the clothing; by secret intrigues he encouraged mutiny and desertion (in some instances with success) among the native corps in the English service, who were stationed near the frontier; and every indication, public and private, proceeding from Monsieur Raymond and his officers, evinced (as indeed might reasonably be expected) a spirit of determined hostility against the English Government.

The feeble and indirect effort of introducing English adventurers into the service of Nizam Ali, for the purpose of rivalling the influence and authority of Monsieur Raymond, only served, by its inefficiency, to stimulate the activity and consolidate the power of that chief; and at the period of Lord Mornington's arrival, the most serious alarm for the independence, if not the very existence of the Government, had been excited in the minds of Nizam Ali and his ministers, by the overbearing disposition frequently manifested by the officers of this efficient French force.

Although these considerations occupied the earliest attention of the Governor-general, they acquired a more urgent import-

CHAP. XLIV.

1798. June 18.

ance, on the receipt of *authentic* intelligence of the proceedings consequent to the arrival of the Mysorean mission at the Isle of France, which reached Calcutta on the 18th of June. The necessity of the earliest possible preparations for war with Tippoo Sultaun was too obvious to admit of hesitation, and in contemplating the right arising from his declared designs of aggression, to demand from the members of the confederation of 1790, the execution of the 13th article of that treaty; it was obvious that while an army commanded by Frenchmen, of such principles and views, and of such uncontrouled power, should remain in the service of Nizam Ali, the alliance of that Prince, instead of an accession of strength, would be a source of imminent danger, in a war with Tippoo Sultaun.

Nizam Ali had at no time been insensible to the danger of that increasing power, which disgust at the imputed tergiversation of the English, and the necessity of some resource, had induced him to place in the hands of this French party. Their arrogant and augmenting ascendency, which forced itself with increasing force on the attention of Nizam Ali, and still more on that of his minister Musheer-ul-Mulk, was balanced in the mind of the former, by an apprehension of the consequences of a more intimate connection with the English; which like every unequal alliance, would have a tendency ultimately to reduce him to a state of dependence on that power. This proposition Musheer-ul-Mulk never attempted either to evade or deny, but he met it by a representation of existing danger from his nominal servants; by their insufficiency, without a farther and more dangerous augmentation, which would number the English among his enemies, to save from destruction his avowedly declining state;

by the actual power of the English to protect him from every other enemy; by an appeal to the relative character of the individuals of each nation with whom his long experience had made him acquainted; and by the confidence which he had always endeavoured to inculcate, in the systematic good faith of the English nation, notwithstanding the unfavourable appearances of 1794.

The imperfect sketch which has been attempted will at least enable the reader to understand, that the neutral and pacific system with the states of India, which in the north had preceded the administration of Sir John Shore; and subsequently to the treaty of 1792, had left six years of profound peace in every part of the Indian continent, to recruit the public treasures, had also accumulated abundant necessity for future expenditure; and in the estimation of every person of knowledge and discernment, had left this termination of a period of peace to be any thing but a season of security.

Surrounded on every side with latent dangers, Lord Mornington, in determining to look them successively in the face, and to substitute, by either negotiation or war, substantial and permanent peace, for a precarious and deceitful security, had only the option of selecting that danger which was first to be removed: and the considerations which have been stated, gave an obvious priority to the critical condition of affairs at Hyderabad. The subsidiary force of two English battalions, stipulated by the treaty of 1790, had been dismissed in consequence of the disgust created by the refusal of support demanded in 1794, and recalled at the earnest solicitation of Nizam Ali, chiefly on the early impression of committing his own person to their guard, while

CHAP. XLIV. 1798. the extent was still uncertain, of the defection occasioned by the rebellion of his son Ali Jah: and throughout the vacillating councils of encouragement and augmentation, or distrust and apprehension of the French corps, these two battalions were retained and considered as a resource in every extremity, and had probably diminished his apprehensions of the French party, and thus indirectly contributed to its dangerous growth.

After the previous communication rendered necessary by the
July 8. circumstances of the case, the Governor-general, on the 8th of July 1798, issued his instructions to the resident at Hyderabad, for the negotiation of a new treaty, augmenting the English subsidiary force to six battalions, with a formidable artillery; and stipulating for the dismission of the corps commanded by French officers, in His Highness's service. This treaty, which was signed
Sept. 1. at Hyderabad on the 1st of September, and ratified at Calcutta
18. on the 18th of the same month, declares in its preamble the augmentation to be founded on the express desire of Nizam Ali, and professes the enlarged conditions of the alliance to be founded on the hostile proceedings of Tippoo Sultaun, and the French already described; and the necessity imposed on the confederates of 1790, united in a defensive league, to take immediate measures for the security of their respective possessions; and besides the ordinary conditions, a stipulation for a treaty of triple guarantee, if the Pêshwa shall consent, and if otherwise, binds the English to mediate in any future differences between the two other confederates; and obliges Nizam Ali to acquiesce in their decision; and finally it confirms all subsisting treaties between the English, the Pêshwa, and Nizam Ali; and declares the

free assent of Nizam Ali, to similar subsidiary engagements between the English and the Pêshwa, if the latter should express a desire for such an arrangement.

The first measures adopted in fulfilment of the provisions of this treaty were executed with a degree of celerity and vigour, which was calculated not only to command success, but to produce the most salutary impressions, far beyond the sphere of their immediate operation. The additional four battalions with their artillery, which during the negotiation had been collected on the frontier, marched to Hyderabad, and joined the two battalions already there on the 10th of October. The weak- Oct. 10.
ness of Nizam Ali, as the crisis approached, and the natural timidity of his minister Musheer-ul-Mulk, in contemplating the sanguinary conflict which was apprehended in disarming the French party, added perhaps to the effect of those intrigues at native courts which cannot always be penetrated, disposed the government of Hyderabad to evasion and delay; but after some preliminary discussion, the British resident (Captain J. A. Kirkpatrick) declared, that at this stage of the transaction he could listen to nothing short of the complete and immediate execution of that article of the treaty; and a diplomatic note to this effect, dated on the 21st of October was reinforced by a movement 21.
of the British corps to a position which commanded the French lines, and by a declaration that they would be attacked in the event of farther delay: these decided measures removed the previous hesitation of the court, and produced its active concurrence in the subsequent measures. A proclamation was issued and dispersed in the French lines on the same day, by which the troops were informed that Nizam Ali had dismissed

CHAP. XLIV. 1798. the French officers from his service; that they were released from their obedience to these officers, and that all who supported them should be considered and punished as traitors. The internal divisions in the French party, and some pecuniary balances due to the men, which the officers were unable or unwilling to discharge, added to the menacing position of the British troops produced a serious mutiny in the lines; the men imprisoned their officers, loudly and violently demanding their arrears of pay, and even threatened the lives of their prisoners; and the officer commanding the British troops (Lieutenant-Colonel Roberts) in concert with the resident and the minister, took a judicious advantage of this state of confusion. On the
Oct. 22. morning of the 22d of October, at day-light, the French cantonments were surrounded by a body of horse, belonging to Nizam Ali, and by the British detachment. The men, still in a state of mutiny, were offered full payment of all arrears, and future service under other officers, on condition of laying down their arms; to which terms, after some discussion, they assented *: "and, in a few hours, a corps, whose numbers were nearly fourteen thousand † men, and who had in their possession a train of artillery, and an arsenal filled with every description of military stores, was completely disarmed, without one life having been lost."

As the first step in a series of great political measures, the last mentioned character of the transaction, added an inestimable value to this important event; and, an hostile army transformed

* Malcolm's India, page 244. He was at that period assistant to the resident, and an active and meritorious agent in effecting this important arrangement.

† Including detachments; the number actually disarmed on the 22d of October was eleven thousand.

in one day, and without the effusion of blood, into a friendly force, diffused an impression of wisdom to plan, and energy to execute, which had the most decisive influence at all the native courts.

The apprehension of giving offence to the Mahrattas, which prevented a similar treaty in 1794, was not of inferior importance in 1798. The successful issue of the preliminary measure, in the manner which has been described, contributed, perhaps, to a little salutary caution, in expressing their dissatisfaction; but it is obvious, that the future mediation stipulated by the treaty of Hyderabad, could not fail to be secretly offensive to the power which lived on the plunder of its neighbours. There was, however, no mystery observed in the transaction; the objects of the treaty were communicated to the Pêshwa, both before and after its conclusion; and he was uniformly and earnestly invited to concur in giving effect to the principles of guarantee, contained in the 13th article of the treaty of 1790: but, the councils of Dowlut Row Sindea, which, at that period directed the nominal measures of the Pêshwa, had a reference to interests of his own, distinct from those of the state of Poona. The British Government had a right to remonstrate against that open interference and control which prevented the Pêshwa from performing his engagements as a member of the alliance of 1790, and used the most strenuous endeavours to oblige Sindea to leave Poona. Sindea was perfectly well disposed to unite with Tippoo for the prosecution of his own views in Decan and the South; but he distinctly saw that during the hostile operations of a large portion of his regular army in that quarter, his most valuable possessions in Hindostân were open to a formidable English army, cantoned near the frontier, and that he could not effectually prosecute new conquests without imminent hazard to his actual possessions. Considerable fluctuation, sometimes ostensibly amounting to the prospect of an improved alliance, was manifested at different periods by the Court of Poona; but such demonstrations had no other foundation than the desire to evade and procrastinate. The accession of strength to the English interests, from the events at Hyderabad in October 1798, alarmed Sindea for the double danger which he should incur in the south, and in the north, by a rupture with that state; and although he pertinaciously adhered to the prosecution of his views at Poona, and prevented the Pêshwa from executing the provisions of the triple alliance of 1790, he determined to postpone, to some more favourable opportunity, expected to arise from the events of the war, any active military interference of his own on either side.

While, therefore, Lord Mornington anticipated an unwilling neutrality as the best object he could immediately accomplish at Poona, he continued the intercourse of amity, together with most sincere and reiterated invitations, to participate with the two allies, in the execution of their common engagements, and he accordingly decided on the necessity of pursuing his operations against the Sultaun, without any aid from the Mahrattas, leaving in their present undecided, but not immediately dangerous condition, the state of his political relations with the Pêshwa and Sindea. Before concluding what we have to observe on the actual state of affairs at Poona, it may prevent interruption to our future narrative, if we briefly advert to the state of the Sultaun's secret machinations at that court; which will not only unfold his imperfect conception of the affairs of Poona, but a diplomacy founded as much on personal hatred, as political wisdom; and will aid in exhibiting a more intelligible picture of its confused administration.

On the death of the late Pêshwa, in October 1795, Tippoo dispatched a secret emissary (Balajee Row, from whom this information is derived) to congratulate his successor (Bâjee Row as he concluded), and to concert with him a more intimate political union. On his arrival at Poona, the envoy found Chimnajee on the musnud, Perseram Bhow minister, and Bâjee Row a prisoner in Sindea's army. He soon discovered that this order of things would not last, and found means of getting himself introduced to a secret interview with Bâjee Row, who did not succeed to the musnud till December 1796. The envoy was instructed by the Sultaun, to represent that their respective fathers (Hyder and Ragonaut Row) had been connected by the most intimate political ties: that Nana Furnavese had been the efficient cause of his father's banishment and death, and of placing on the musnud the spurious offspring of a * silversmith; and had equally been the source of Tippoo's misfortunes, by promoting the confederacy of 1790: that the Peshwa ought to consider that minister as a worm secretly consuming the edifice of his government, that he was treacherously leagued with the English, and that his imprisonment or removal was essential to the efficiency of the Pêshwa's rule. To these observations he

* See Hyder's observations on the same subject in 1779, Vol. ii. p. 210. Among the pregnant females shut up with the widow of Narrain Row to insure the appearance of a male infant, the wife of a silver-smith, according to that account, produced the future Pêshwa, *Sewai Mâdoo Row*, who died in 1795.

CHAP. XLIV. 1798. answered, that he was encompassed with various conflicting evils, and would endeavour to extricate himself from them all; he desired the envoy to assure his master of his sense of the important connection between their parents, and his grateful recollection of the pecuniary aid afforded by Hyder to his father in his greatest distress; he expressly prohibited the envoy from any intercourse with his ministers, or relations, and placed with him a confidential agent as a medium of private communication. On the occasion of Musheer-ul-Mulk's departure from Poona, the Pêshwa appears to have entertained a temporary hope of being emancipated both from Sindea and Nana Furnavese, and expressed a desire for military aid; to which Tippoo replied, that his whole army was ready, and recommended, after terminating the domestic feud, an immediate invasion of Nizam Ali's territories from the west, while he should attack it from the south: but although the Sultaun was in secret communication with Sindea, he does not seem to have comprehended that the views of that chief were entirely incompatible with the political emancipation of Bâjee Row, on which expected event the Sultaun unquestionably most relied for giving efficiency to his projected alliance with the state of Poona.

On the occasion of the negotiations opened by the English resident at Poona in consequence of the discovery of the transactions at the Isle of France, the Pêshwa sent for Balajee Row, and informed him of the events at Hyderabad which had established the English ascendancy at that court on the downfal of the French; admonished him that the distracted state of his own Government would compel him to adhere to the stipulations of the treaty of 1790 on the requisition of the two other powers. That his master's intrigues with the French at such a period, were in the last degree imprudent, and would lead to his destruction, without its being possible for the Pêshwa, however well disposed, to avert it; and that as a sincere friend he advised him to drop that connection and conciliate the English by whatever concessions: and it is curious that, among other reasons for temporising, he adverts to the inefficient state of the Sultaun's army, which in general opinion had been exceedingly injured by his late innovations. The Pêshwa was considered both by the envoy and his master to be seriously well disposed to the Sultaun; whose preservation he considered of importance to his own interest, and chiefly in what related to his eventual emancipation from Nana Furnavese; he promised his best efforts to prevent the ultimate march of the Mahratta contingent for the siege of Seringapatam; and the actual ascendency of Sindea being on the same side; the councils of Nana, who really desired the performance of the 13th article of the treaty of 1790, were made to yield to that conjoint influence. Balajee Row however being but a secret agent to the Pêshwa personally, without the knowledge of Nana, had no opportunity of attempting to negotiate with that minister, who had the conduct of the communications with the British resident, and he recommended to the Sultaun a public mission, which accordingly took place near the conclusion of 1798 under Ahmed Khân and Fucker-u-Deen. It was not until April 1799 that Nana Furnavese discovered the existence of this secret mission, when he alarmed the Pêshwa at the consequences of its being known to the English resident, and prevailed on him to dismiss Balajee

CHAP. XLIV. 1798.

Row, which he did with professions of the greatest friendship, charging the envoy to return with all possible expedition, and advise his master to dispel at any sacrifice the storm which was ready to overwhelm him. Before the envoy reached the frontier of Mysoor, he heard of the fate of the capital.

CHAPTER XLV.

Lord Mornington's luminous and instructive discussion of his political relations to the Sultaun — The reduction, not the extinction of his power, desired — Second proof of the insufficiency of the arrangements of 1792 *— Intelligence of the expedition to Egypt — Lord Mornington's letter to the Sultaun on this subject, 4th November,* 1798 *— Friendly reply — 8th November, expostulation and proposal to send an envoy — Sultaun declines to receive him — Vague hopes — Passive fatality — roused by a second letter,* 10*th December — awakened by a third,* 9*th January — Rage, not at his own folly, but that of his agents — Sultaun's eastern apologue — Expected succour from Egypt, founded on the erroneous conceptions of his French officers — contrary to all the facts — Important documents from Constantinople, forwarded to Tippoo by the English — Letter of the Grand Signor — Two answers — one for the perusal of the English, the other the true reply — Curious abstract of European aggression in India — Strange and offensive answer to Lord Mornington's last letter — Consents to receive the envoy too late — Infers his destruction to be intended — Marches against General Stuart— Strength of Tippoo's army.*

Hitherto no direct communication had been made by the British Government to Tippoo Sultaun, regarding their knowledge of his proceedings at the Isle of France, and no remonstrance or explanation had been offered or demanded on either side, regarding those preparations for war which were notoriously in progress; although the usual formalities had taken place on the occasion of Lord Mornington's assuming the Government, and a correspondence had occurred regarding some adjustments of frontier, which were pending at the period of his arrival. The

CHAP. XLV. 1798. Aug. 12.

grounds of this delay are so distinctly unfolded, in a minute of the Governor-general in the secret department, dated the 12th of August 1798, that it were an injustice to this most able and luminous performance, to attempt the abstract of a political lesson so brief and so instructive. " *The rights of states, applicable to every case of contest with foreign powers, are created and limited by the necessity of preserving the public safety*; this necessity is the foundation of the reciprocal claim of all nations, to explanation of suspicious or ambiguous conduct, to reparation for injuries done, and to security against injuries intended.

" In any of these cases, when just satisfaction has been denied, or from the evident nature of circumstances, cannot otherwise be obtained, it is the undoubted right of the injured party, to resort to arms for the vindication of the public safety; and in such a conjuncture, the right of the state becomes the duty of the Government, unless some material consideration of the public interest should forbid the attempt.

" If the conduct of Tippoo Sultaun, had been of a nature which could be termed ambiguous or suspicious; if he had merely increased his force beyond his ordinary establishment, or had stationed it in some position on our confines, or on those of our allies, which might justify jealousy or alarm; if he had renewed his secret intrigues at the courts of Hyderabad, Poona, and Câbul; or even if he had entered into any negotiation with France, of which the object was at all obscure; it might be our duty to resort in the first instance to his construction of proceedings, which being of a doubtful character, might admit of a satisfactory explanation. *But where there is no doubt, there can be no matter for explanation.* The act of Tippoo's embassadors, ratified by himself, and accompanied by the landing of a French force in his country, is a public, unqualified, and unambiguous declaration of war, aggravated by an avowal, that the object of the war is neither explanation, reparation, nor security, but the total destruction of the British government in India.

"To affect to misunderstand an injury or insult of such a complexion, would argue a consciousness either of weakness or of fear. No state in India can misconstrue the conduct of Tippoo; the correspondence of our residents at Hyderabad and Poona, sufficiently manifests the construction which it bears at both those courts; and in so clear and plain a case, our demand of explanation would be justly attributed either to a defect of spirit or of power. The result of such a demand would therefore be, the disgrace of our character and the diminution of our influence and consideration in the eyes of our allies and of every power in India. If the moment should appear favourable to the execution of Tippoo's declared design, he would answer such a demand by an immediate attack; if on the other hand, his preparations should not be sufficiently advanced, he would deny the existence of his engagements with France, would persist in his denial until he had reaped the full benefit of them, and finally, after having completed the improvement of his own army, and received the accession of an additional French force, he would turn the combined strength of both against our possessions, with an alacrity and confidence inspired by our inaction, and with advantages redoubled by our delay. In the present case the idea, therefore, of demanding explanation must be rejected, as being disgraceful in its principle, and frivolous in its object.

" The demand of reparation, in the strict sense of the term, cannot properly be applied to cases of intended injury, excepting in those instances where the nature of the reparation demanded may be essentially connected with security against the injurious intention.

" Where a state has unjustly seized the property, or invaded the territory, or violated the rights of another, reparation may be made, by restoring what has been unjustly taken, or by a subsequent acknowledgment of the right which has been infringed; but the cause of our complaint against Tippoo Sultaun, is not that he has seized a portion of our property which he might restore, or invaded a part of our territory which he might again cede, or violated a right which he might hereafter acknowledge; we complain, that, professing the most amicable disposition, bound by subsisting treaties of peace and friendship, and unprovoked by any offence on our part, he has manifested a design to effect our total destruction; he has prepared the means and instruments of a war of extermination against us; he has solicited and received the aid of our inveterate enemy for the declared purpose of annihilating our empire; and he only waits the arrival of a more effectual succour to strike a blow against our existence.

" That he has not yet received the effectual succour which he has solicited, may be ascribed, either to the weakness of the Government of Mauritius, or to their want of zeal in his cause, or to the rashness and imbecility of his own councils; but neither the measure of his hostility, nor of our right to restrain it, nor of our danger from it, are to be estimated by the amount of the force which he has actually obtained; for we know that his demands of military assistance were unlimited; we know that they were addressed, not merely to the Government of Mauritius, but to that of France, and we cannot ascertain how soon they may be satisfied to the full extent of his acknowledged expectations. This, therefore, is not merely the case of an injury to be repaired, but of the public safety to be secured against the present and future designs of an irreconcilable, desperate, and treacherous enemy. Against an enemy of this description, no effectual security can be obtained, otherwise than by such a reduction of his power, as shall not only defeat his actual preparations, but establish a permanent restraint upon his future means of offence."

Here, then, we find, for the second time, the proof of a proposition, which received abundant intermediate illustrations, that the reduction of the power of Tippoo Sultaun, in 1792, to the degree which was then deemed necessary to render him incapable of mischief, had been sufficient to produce precisely the opposite effect; that in the general confusion of the times, of all the native states of Decan and the south, connected with the political transactions of 1792, his power alone had not only remained unimpaired, but had been anxiously augmented; and finally, that its farther diminution was indispensable to the safety of the English Government. The absolute extinction of Tippoo Sultaun's power was at no period of these preparatory measures in the contemplation of Lord Mornington. He had hoped, through the effective co-operation of his allies, and the successful issue of his preliminary measures, to convince the Sultaun of the fatal tendency to himself of his hostile designs, and to induce his unwilling assent to such arrangements as should render his political existence compatible with the security

CHAP. XLV. 1798. of those great interests committed to an English Governor-general. To have delayed such preparatory measures, or to have apprized Tippoo Sultaun of their object, before it was out of his power to render them abortive, would have involved a degree of imbecility at variance with the whole character of this administration.

During these preparations, however, the danger of French co-operation assumed a more threatening aspect; and although the expedition to Egypt had no immediate connection with the embassy to the Isle of France, it was the result of those previous designs which always reckoned on Tippoo Sultaun, as the efficient instrument of France, for the recovery of their power in the south, as the blind imprisoned monarch of Delhi was to be the ostensible engine of their operations in the north. The existence and position of this approaching danger, whatever might be its previous history, was abundant cause of congratulation to the Governor-general, that he had not delayed those preparations on general grounds, which this particular danger rendered more urgent and indispensable.

A letter to Tippoo Sultaun, dated the 4th of November, announced this unprovoked attack on the Sultaun's Mahommedan ally, and the splendid victory of Aboukir; on which the Sultaun in return offered his congratulations in the language of undisturbed amity; but on the 8th of the same month the Governor-general deemed the proper period to have arrived for announcing his knowledge of the Sultaun's recent negotiations with the French, and proposed to him, in the name of the three powers, to depute an envoy personally known to him (Major Doveton, who had conducted the restoration of the hostages in 1794,) who was authorised to propose the sole means which appeared to be effectual for the removal of distrust, and for the confidence of permanent peace. To this letter he had the temerity to answer, that the existing treaties were a sufficient security, and that he could imagine no other means more effectual; thereby distinctly declining the reception of the envoy. CHAP. XLV. 1798.

The negotiations of the English at Hyderabad and Poona were intimately known to the Sultaun, by the reports of his emissaries at those courts, and the extensive preparations which were in progress, under the presidencies of Madras and Bombay, were too public in their nature, to escape the knowledge of the most careless observer; they were the subject of Tippoo's incessant conversation, and were recounted with a sort of quiescent distress belonging to the fatalist, who rests his hopes on some unknown or improbable event. The English preparations were always tardy, and his allies might be more alert; his embassadors had, in 1789, returned from the Red Sea to Calicut in less time than was necessary for the maturity of the English plans of invasion, and his allies would not abandon him to destruction, without some effort for his deliverance, from France, from the Mauritius, or from Egypt. He would send embassies to Constantinople and to Cabul *, and stir up the faithful to prevent the extinction of the faith; his emissaries at Poona would work on the passions and interests of Sindea, and of Bâjee Row, and the ascendancy of the English at Hyderabad, might again yield to his superior political address. The means alluded to by the Governor-general, could be no other than de-

* These were dispatched, but returned without reaching their destination.

CHAP. XLV. 1798. manding his remaining sea-coast in Canara *; and thereby excluding him from communicating with the French, and from the only possible chance of retrieving his affairs; if his destruction were pre-ordained, let it come! the sooner the† better! but he might still hope that his own efforts would prolong the contest until aid should arrive, and every discussion was terminated by the professedly pious remark, "after all, whatever is the will of God, that will be accomplished:" and this state of passive contemplation, although materially disturbed, was not permanently changed, even by the receipt of the letter from Lord Mornington, dated the 8th of November.

He was somewhat more acutely moved by a second, dated the 10th of December, earnestly impressing on his mind the necessity of giving an early and serious consideration to the subject of the former letter, and announcing the Governor-general's intention of proceeding to Madras, where he hoped to receive satisfactory communications. The Sultaun was still so weak as to believe, that a fabulous version of the history of his embassy, would satisfy Lord Mornington's credulity, and remove his suspicions; but when, early in January 1799, he obtained intelligence of the Governor-General's actual arrival at Madras on the 31st of December, to direct the operations of an immediate war; and soon afterwards received a letter, dated the 9th of January, in answer to his own silly fabrication of a mercantile adventure, on a vessel of two masts, on the return of which a few Frenchmen had taken

* This conjecture was perfectly correct.

† A sort of proverb, "if the evil must arrive to-morrow, let it rather arrive to-day."

their passage to India; when he perused his Lordship's remonstrances against his rejection of the proposed envoy; his recital in detail of the entire amount of the information he possessed, regarding the hostile proceedings at the Isle of France, with a Persian translation of General Malartic's proclamation; his explanation of the necessity imposed on the allies, of seeking relief from this ambiguous state of supposed peace, and hostile negotiation and alliance, and their anxious desire to continue the relations of peace on such terms as should render it safe and permanent; his most serious and solemn admonition to assent to the reception of the intended envoy; his intreaty not to postpone an answer more than one day after the receipt of the letter, and the final and portentous observation, that "dangerous consequences result from the delay of arduous affairs;" when he had finished the perusal of this letter, he appeared to be aroused, as if from a dream, to consider as new facts, all the circumstances which had occupied his discussions for several months before; and at length to be really awake to the full extent and immediate pressure of the danger, and even in a certain degree, to the folly which had produced it.

1798.

Until this period, he had no distinct conception of the gratuitous folly of receiving a military reinforcement of ninety-nine Frenchmen; he had only contemplated their arrival with exultation as the precursors of a more mighty aid; and even now he inveighed, not against his own senseless stupidity in the arrangement of the mission, contrary to the earnest advice of his principal ministers; not against the childish imprudence of receiving, after its arrival at Mangalore, this useless demonstration of hos-

1799.

tility, so entirely disproportioned to his own original expectations and designs; but against the incapacity and disobedience of his envoys, which now for the first time he condescended to discover. One of these, Mahommed Ibrahim, was unhappily a dolt, and knew no better; but for his colleague, Hussein Aly, a man of reputed understanding, no punishment could be too severe. " If," said he, " I were to hang him, his execution would not dispel the storm which is now ready to burst over me. I will send him as an appendage to my embassy to *Room* (Constantinople) that he may perish in the element by which he has conveyed to this country the sources of its impending calamity:" and he was accordingly appointed secretary to that mission.

In his usual volubility of discourse on all subjects by which he was particularly excited, he successively vented his indignation against every person and thing immediately or remotely instrumental in producing his present misfortunes, himself alone excepted, the true, and (with the exception of Monsieur Malartic and the envoys) the exclusive author of his own ruin. In Asiatic conversation, no subject is considered to be gracefully discussed without the introduction of an appropriate tale. The following would, on its own merits, scarcely find a place in a selection of Indian apologues, but it derives an interest from being almost daily recited by the Sultaun to some new hearer, as the most applicable to his own situation.

" A certain king, who was learned in the prophetic and mystical characters formed by the sutures of the human skull, stopped to decypher the fragment of one, which he perceived by the road side; and found the inscription to mean, *this will cause the death of forty persons.* Being desirous of averting the destruction of so many human beings, he ordered the fragment to be preserved, and on his return to his private apartments, pounded it into a fine powder, which he put into a little box and deposited in a secret part of his cabinet, the access to which was prohibited to every other person. In the latter part of this process, he was observed by his favourite wife, who from the king's skill in pharmacy, supposed this powder so carefully preserved, to be some precious medicinal preparation.

"The king soon afterwards departed on a distant expedition, and the favourite wife, disconsolate for his absence, declined in health, and obtained no relief from the united skill of the state physicians. At length it occurred to her to try the effect of the medicine prepared and deposited by the king." The apologue does not stop to explain in what manner this powder of skull obtained or exercised its latent powers, but goes on to say that "the queen became immediately pregnant. The king returns, and is of course enraged: the queen acknowledges her miraculous pregnancy, but pleads innocent of the ordinary means by which it might have been accomplished. The king orders to be tortured and slain, first the chief eunuchs, and then every male thing that could possibly fall under suspicion. At length the queen, reflecting on the possible origin of her disgrace, and anxious, in the expectation of her own death, to confess her unintentional errors, acknowledged that she had violated the secret cabinet, and taken some of the medicine which she had seen deposited by the king in the manner which has been described. The king instantly recollected the circumstances of

CHAP. XLV. 1799.

the deposit. The number of persons put to death was found to be exactly forty, and the mystic prophecy was fulfilled."

The moral, or application, like many annexed to more celebrated apologues, is not particularly obvious; but the Sultaun went on to explain: "a weather-beaten fragment of skull produced the death of forty persons, — the fractured mast of Ripaud's worthless vessel will cause the subversion of an empire."

With this strong conviction on his mind, the Sultaun for some time after the receipt of the letter from Lord Mornington, dated the 9th of January, had nearly made up his mind to throw himself unconditionally on his Lordship's compassion, and to receive the envoy; but, notwithstanding the significant intreaty, to lose not a single day in his reply, he went on with the procrastination naturally belonging to an unpalatable resolve, hesitating from day to day to execute the determination of the last; and the lingering indecision of the fatalist, suggested the hope that, if at the last moment no favourable chance should arise, he might still be in time to submit to an alternative, short of absolute destruction. During that particular period, constant letters were arriving from Dubuc, (who did not finally sail from Tranquebar, until the 7th of February,) assuring Tippoo that the French must actually have embarked on the Red Sea for his assistance, and might be daily expected. Chapuis, and all the French admitted to his presence, reiterated the same assurances; projects of resistance or submission, held their alternate empire, as reason or passion prevailed; and it is believed, by those who had the best opportunities of judging, that the confident assurances of the French officers, were the efficient cause of diverting the Sultaun's mind from the only wise resolution it was then in his power to form, and produced his ultimate destruction.

It is difficult to determine the degree in which these officers may have themselves believed, in the probable realization of the hopes which they excited; but it is certain, that any such belief, so far from being founded on authentic, or even probable intelligence, could only have originated in vague inferences regarding the ultimate objects of the Egyptian expedition, and in an entire ignorance of existing facts. After the destruction of the French fleet, on the 1st of August, 1798, and the universal hostility manifested by the inhabitants of Egypt, in October of the same year, it is certain, that General Buonaparte, so far from being in a condition to meditate distant detachments, had reason to look with anxiety to the mere preservation of his first conquest. His expedition to Acre appears to have been essentially defensive *; and intended to anticipate and destroy the offensive means which Jezzar Pacha was preparing for a formidable Turkish invasion of Egypt. Although Jezzar had previously looked with an eye of jealous hostility to his nominal sovereign, the events of the war shewed that they became cordially united against the common enemy: and, if we even dismiss from our consideration, as a mere pretence, the imputation of offensive preparation on the part of Jezzar, still, the design of occupying a fortress and port, which should place in the hands of its possessor a direct command over the

* Buonaparte's letter to Jezzar Pacha, and the known facts connected with his representations.

CHAP. XLV. 1799.

subsistence of the intermediate country, must, in the actual situation of General Buonaparte, be considered as a wise, defensive precaution.

That General's letter * to Tippoo Sultaun, written in February, 1799, professing the intention of liberating him from the iron yoke of England, distinctly shews the intended execution of that design to be distant, by the wish expressed of previously receiving and conferring with a confidential agent from the Sultaun at Cairo; and if any farther proof were wanting of the absence of every possible intention of an immediate movement to the east, it would be found in the remarkable coincidence of this letter being intercepted at Judda on the very day (the 17th of February) in which he himself crossed the northern frontier of the Egyptian territory for the attack of *El Arish*, a place recently garrisoned by Jezzar, with two thousand men; and in the exactly cotemporary events of the siege of Acre and the siege of Seringapatam.

But the intelligence regarding Egypt was not limited to the representations of the French officers; two documents of a more authentic nature were presented to the Sultaun; a copy of the declaration of war issued by the Porte against the French, in consequence of their invasion of Egypt, transmitted some time before by Lord Clive, Governor of Madras; and on the 16th of

* The words with which the letter begins, "You have already been informed of my arrival on the borders of the Red Sea," may seem to refer to a former letter, which, if sent, is not known to have been received. Intimation was made to me by the person best qualified to know, of a letter or letters addressed by Tippoo to General Buonaparte. I can only say, that in a constant, and generally a daily intercourse for several years with two of Tippoo's secretaries, I never heard of such a letter or letters; and that if its existence had been known to Lord Mornington, I apprehend that it would not have been omitted in his collection of Seringapatam papers.

January, a letter addressed to the Sultaun, by the Grand Signor, dated the 20th of September 1798, transmitted through the English minister at Constantinople, and now forwarded by Lord Mornington, accompanied by a most impressive letter from himself. The letter of the Grand Signor states, that in a time of profound peace with France, and of a neutrality in her wars with other powers of Europe, which those powers even represented as being too partial to their enemy, a French armament under General Buonaparte, suddenly invaded Egypt, without previous complaint, or representation, or notice; pretending that the expedition was exclusively against the Beys, and insinuating that it was undertaken with the consent of the Porte "which is a horrible falsity;" that intercepted letters had discovered their design of *dividing Arabia into various Republics*; and progressively of passing to India, where the French expected to unite with the Sultaun, for the expulsion of the English from that country: that the hostility against all true Mahommedans, proved by the invasion of the *venerated province of Egypt, the granary of the holy cities* Mecca and Medina, ought to unite against them all persons of that faith; that in addition to the ties of religion, the bonds of amity already established between them, afforded reason to hope for his concert in the common cause; that England was united with the Porte in the war against France; and that he made it a particular request, if the Sultaun had harboured any idea of joining the French, that he would lay it aside; and in the event of any subject of complaint against the English, that he would accept the good offices of the Porte for its adjustment.

The fictitious answer to this letter to be transmitted through the English Government, was not written until near a month

CHAP. XLV. 1799. afterwards, and without noticing the offer of mediation, it professes his readiness to unite in all the objects of the Porte for *the prosperity and due ordinance of the faith and its followers*; and acquiesces in the proposition, that the French, by attacking the head of the Church, had rendered themselves the enemies of all true Mussulmans; supporting the doctrine by a somewhat singular text of the Koràn, intended for the perusal of the English —" consider not infidels as friends, consider none such but Mussulmans." The true answer containing his genuine sentiments, to be delivered by his own embassadors, refers to their oral communications for the particular measures in his contemplation, but gives a compendious history of the origin and progress, "the treachery, deceit, and supremacy of the Christians in the regions of Hindostan," which, as a mere literary curiosity, is not unworthy of perusal. In the history, equally of French and English transactions, the mere facts are neither badly narrated, nor more broadly caricatured, than in the early pictures drawn by Englishmen, of the fabulous enormities of their countrymen, in the east: but in the higher colouring of Oriental imagery, the fables are rendered more fabulous; and the supremacy of the English over the French nation, is made as perfect in licentiousness as in power. Twelve hundred French soldiers, in a state of intoxication, in open day, are represented to have entered the houses of the faithful at Hyderabad; to have violated their women, and to have excited general enmity; a fact which, if founded at all, may be supposed to have occurred in a moment of victory, or insubordination. But the English vices are of a more deliberate character, and belong to a more lofty rank, for in the catalogue of their crimes, the sober commission of the same enormity, on the widow of a monarch (the vizier of Oude) is gravely ascribed to an English Governor-general, Lord Teignmouth.

The impressive letter of Lord Mornington, which accompanied the dispatch from the Grand Signor to the Sultaun, certainly produced a considerable effect; but his reply is perhaps the most singular document in these extraordinary transactions; he acknowledges the receipt of the letter from the Grand Signor, whose titles occupy three-fourths of his reply, and without the slightest observation on its contents, this strange epistle abruptly terminates with the following sentence: "Being frequently disposed to make excursions and hunt, I am accordingly proceeding on a hunting excursion; you will be pleased to dispatch Major Doveton, (about whose coming your friendly pen has repeatedly written,) slightly attended (or unattended)." This letter, which must have been written early in February, arrived at Madras on the 13th of that month, and independently of its strange manner was liable to the suspicion of being intended to convey an equivocal sneer; the word (shekâr) hunting, being in the idiom of Mysoor, familiarly applied to military operations *, and without attention to dates, it might seem to indicate his intended attack on General Stuart, which did not occur till about a month afterwards. But I have been assured by those who were near him that the abrupt dictation was the mere effect of chagrin at the necessity of humiliation; that he then really intended and earnestly wished to receive the British envoy, and marched to the Madoor river, upwards of forty miles to the east; General

* When it is intended to speak of an officer as a good partizan with the light troops, he is said to be perfect in *Sawâree Shekâree*.

CHAP. XLV. 1799. Stuart's position being nearly the same distance from Seringapatam, in an opposite direction, from the same motives that in 1794 led him to Deonhully — in order that the state of the capital and its vicinity, might not be exposed to observation. But the same persons, so confident of his humble views at that moment, were equally alarmed for some new caprice, and were satisfied, that if the envoy even had been sent and received, faithless evasions would have imposed on the allies the same ultimate necessity: and it must be added, that his private memoranda, since discovered, strongly evince a still lingering hope of some propitious event. From that eastern encampment, however, he did actually detach an escort as far as Oossoor, with orders to be ready to receive and conduct Major Doveton to his camp. But he had miscalculated the period to which he might venture to procrastinate: he entered his own tents on the 15th of February, and moved on the 20th, and the English army made its first march in advance from the point at which it had concentrated, on the 11th, two days before the receipt at Madras, of the letter which has been described. The declaration of the Governor-general, to be issued on crossing the frontier, and his answer to this extraordinary letter, were coincident in date. In the latter, Lord Mornington expressed his sincere regret, that his urgent representation of the dangers of delay had produced no effect, and that the Sultaun had postponed noticing his admonitions, until the period of the season (for which an appeal was made to his own conviction) rendered the advance of the army necessary to the common security of the allies; that the mission of Major Doveton to him, was no longer expedient, but that General Harris, the Commander-in-chief of the advancing army, had been empowered to receive any embassy which he should dispatch; and the General was directed to issue the Governor-general's declaration, and to dispatch this letter, both dated on the 22d of February, on one and the same day, that on which he should enter the territory of Mysoor. CHAP. XLV. 1799.

The Sultaun, in the meanwhile, kept in constant agitation and suspense regarding the arrival of the envoy; receiving no answer to the letter which conveyed his tardy, ungracious, and insulting assent; and knowing, from the systematic movements of General Harris, that he would necessarily cross the frontier in a few days, drew inferences regarding the determination of the allies more fatal to his own political existence than those which had actually been formed. "All my decisions (he said) must now be desperate. I am but losing precious time in waiting for their embassador, while they are closing in upon me, on either side. I will march and strike a decisive blow." He accordingly left the whole of the Silledar and three thousand of the stable horse under Poornea, with four cushoons of infantry, the whole under Seyed Saheb, to watch the motions of General Harris; and with the remainder of the army proceeded by forced marches by the route of Caniambaddy and Periapatam to attack General Stuart, in whose presence he arrived on the precise day (the 5th of March) that General Harris, after passing the frontier, dispatched to the Sultaun the letter of the Governor-general, dated the 22d of February. But before entering on the narration of military operations, it will be convenient to take a short view of the strength and position of the advancing armies, the circumstances under which they were assembled and advanced, together with the defensive force which the Sultaun possessed to resist this formidable invasion. The latter may be stated, in round numbers, at thirty-three thousand effective *fire-locks*, including the garrison of Seringapatam, but no other garrison, exclusive of officers and of a numerous artillery, which, with drivers and other establishments, amounted to eighteen thousand * more, and about fifteen thousand cavalry and rocket-men, making an effective total, including officers, of about fifty thousand fighting men; of which, at the commencement of hostilities, about five thousand were detached, and eventually not available during the war.

* Kirkpatrick. Appendix, page c. — Beatson, Appendix, page xcii. compared with manuscript information.

CHAPTER XLVI.

View of the strength, advance, and position of the invading armies — Calcutta — Fresh receipt of intelligence — Lord Mornington proposes immediate hostility if possible — Practicability discussed — Short delay judicious and fortunate — Considerations regarding the Egyptian expedition — Remarkable statement of Lord Mornington regarding that armament — Value of Egypt — colonial — commercial — military — discussed — Actual destination of this armament favourable to his views — Hope that the Sultaun would submit without coercion, to the terms required — Lands at Madras — Delicacy towards Lord Clive — Reciprocal feelings of that nobleman — Movements of Zemaun Shah — detain Sir Alured Clarke at Bengal — Command in the south devolves on General Harris — his staff — Early exertions of Nizam Ali — Lord Mornington issues his final instructions for the advance of the army — Wise and liberal authority to the Commander-in-chief — Provisions in the rear — Army of General Stuart — ascends to Coorg — Defensive position attacked by Tippoo, 5th March — Action — repulse — described by the Raja of Coorg — Diplomatic commission under the orders of General Harris — he enters the enemy's country — operations — defects discovered in the first day's march — Abstract of the effects — Slight affair of the 21st March — Intelligence of General Stuart's action — Tippoo's movements — prepares and abandons a fine position at the Madoor river — Battle of Malvilly — results — General Harris's unexpected movement across the Caveri, frustrates the Sultaun's plans — motives for this movement — Tippoo's disappointment and dismay — Gloomy and affecting consultation of the Sultaun and his officers — determine on a desperate battle on chosen ground — which the English army passed at the distance of three miles — Fresh disappointment regarding their intentions — Average progress of the English army under five miles a day — Ultimate encampment for the siege.

CHAP. XLVI.

Rumours of the proceedings at the Isle of France reached Calcutta on the 8th of June, 1798, and on the 18th a regularly 1799.

CHAP. XLVI. 1799. authenticated copy of Monsieur Malartic's proclamation was received in a letter from Earl Macartney, governor of the Cape of Good Hope, dated the 28th of March, and this unquestionable intelligence was confirmed and explained by the attestation of several respectable individuals who had personally witnessed in the Isle of France the transactions to which that document referred.

The evidence of meditated hostility was complete: the time and the means of receiving a French force sufficient for its execution remained uncertain; it was the business of a wise and vigorous policy, if possible, to anticipate the blow; and an energy was certainly displayed, in all respects, proportioned to a just estimation of the value of time. On the second day, after the receipt of this intelligence, Lord Mornington issued his final orders for assembling, without delay, the English armies on the coasts of Coromandel and Malabar, with the view of making an attack on the Sultaun, instantaneous, if possible, or at the earliest possible period that it could be made with effect. The coincidence of date is very remarkable between the receipt of this intelligence by the Governor-general, and a letter addressed to him by the secret committee of the Court of Directors, 18th of October, 1798, (in concurrence with His Majesty's ministers), noticing the armament of Toulon, and the proclamation of Monsieur Malartic, and recommending that anticipation of the meditated attack which Lord Mornington was in the act of ordering at Calcutta at the moment of the signature in London of authority to that effect. The expediency of early and active preparation was incontestable; but an immediate movement on an adequate scale, was found to be impracticable on various accounts, on consulting with General Harris, at that time Commander-in-chief and provisional governor at Fort St. George.

The arsenal of Madras, and the resources of its government, were to furnish, not only the great body of the invading army, with its field equipments, but the whole of the battering train, the stores and provisions, and the means of transporting to a distant object, this enormous and unwieldy mass. Motives of economy had prevented the existence of any regular establishment of draught or carriage cattle, and the experience of every war had shewn the difficulty of collecting, and the still greater difficulty of giving an efficient training to the requisite numbers of wild and unpractised animals. Even in the war of 1790—1792, when the authority and resources of the state under Lord Cornwallis, were made to bear with all their energy on the means of efficient equipment; officers of observation had deemed one of the most important results of the inconclusive campaign of 1790, to be the training and organization of this most essential branch of military equipment, for the better conducted operations of 1791, and 1792; and the practical force of these remarks, which it requires experience and candour to appreciate, may be conceived from the following, among numerous facts; that Lord Cornwallis's army with a battering train, even after the exhausting effects of the siege of Bangalore in 1791, marched in *two* days more than General Harris on the same route, was able to perform with every possible exertion in *five**, while he had yet scarcely seen an

* Beatson, page 67; ascribed by the author to abuses among the natives in that department, and a spirit of opposition to their reformation; this is the chief impediment always experienced in organizing that department in every first campaign, on a large scale.

enemy. Those who were disposed to undervalue these impediments, quoted as a parallel instance, a case far removed from similarity, the sufficiency of the preparations made by early exertion for the siege of Pondicherry in 1793, when the trained equipments discharged in 1792, were ready and anxious for employment, and thousands were solicitous to hire their cattle and drivers for a simple transport of stores, to a fixed domestic point in Coromandel, on whom no inducement could prevail to undertake an active foreign campaign; and it can scarcely be deemed a speculative proposition, not only that no large army in the south of India ever has been, but that no army ever will be perfectly efficient in its movements, in the early part of a first campaign, without a proper establishment of oxen previously trained.

To this most essential obstacle to immediate movement, was added at the time, the dispersed state of the military establishment of Fort St. George; partly arising from the permanently vicious administration of the nabob of Carnatic, aggravated at this period by the large detachments made for the expeditions against Ceylon, and the Eastern Islands, recently captured from the Dutch.

To a conjoint movement from the side of Malabar, the season opposed an insuperable obstacle, experience having shewn, that no equipment can surmount these western hills, and retain its efficiency at an earlier period than December: man is the only animal who braves the seasons with success.

It may perhaps be deemed fortunate, with reference to other considerations of a collateral nature, that the impediments to immediate movement, were of so decided a character: the masterly transactions at Hyderabad, had in the intermediate time, doubled the efficiency of that alliance, by the whole amount of the danger removed, and the force rendered disposable for the war; the preparations of the two governments of Madras and Bombay, were better matured, the eventual and probable expence was saved, of a second campaign, and the danger was averted, of an enlarged scope to the critical intrigues of Poona; while with the ample means of every description, which this comparatively short delay afforded the opportunity to provide, the Governor-general was enabled to form the brilliant conception, of finishing the war, not only in a single campaign, but by one operation, to which undivided object, every effort from every quarter should be exclusively directed. Looking, therefore, with all the advantages derived from subsequent experience, to the determination which Lord Mornington ultimately formed, on a full discussion of these combined considerations, it is probable that, in determining to commence the war as soon as should be practicable, after the conclusion of the monsoon of Malabar, no time was really lost; the truest economy was consulted, by bringing forward the whole force of the state for one great and efficient effort, instead of conducting less effective operations at a protracted and ultimately enlarged expence: and in the actual event, the intrigues at Poona were anticipated and foiled, before their authors had begun to reduce them to a definite shape.

The first authentic information of the invasion of Egypt by the French, was received at Calcutta, on the 18th of October: previous intelligence of the preparations making in the Mediterranean had arrived in the beginning of August. "Various cir-

CHAP. XLVI. 1799. cumstances attending the equipment of the armament at Toulon, had inclined the Governor-general to apprehend, that at least a part of it might be destined for an expedition to India, although he could not believe that the attempt would be made through Egypt;" and Rear-Admiral Rainier had, with his accustomed zeal and ability, concurred in the expediency suggested by Lord Mornington, of proceeding with the fleet to the coast of Malabar, instead of Malacca, as he had previously intended. It is remarkable that Lord Mornington's statement, that he could not believe, in August 1798, that the attempt in India would be made by the French through Egypt, is dated in March 1799, many months posterior to his knowledge of their actual occupation of the country, with that ulterior view. Ordinary minds are contented that results should seem to correspond with their supposed anticipations; and this spontaneous admission of being disappointed by the event, ought probably to be viewed as the tacit dissent of a great statesman, from the political wisdom of the measures of his adversary. Doubts have occurred to less competent observers, regarding the soundness of either of the three avowed motives, for undertaking this celebrated expedition: — 1st, the attainment of a valuable colonial possession; 2d, commercial advantages to arise from opening the canal of the Ptolemies across the Isthmus of Suez, and thus placing in the hands of the possessors of Egypt, a superiority in the Indian trade over those nations who should continue to double the Cape of Good Hope; and finally the military facilities afforded to the French for the attack of the English possessions in India.

As a colonial possession, all the facts which have hitherto been developed, seem to shew that its advantages could at no period be made to equal the expence of its maintenance; or if such a period should ever arrive, it must be posterior to an entire dislocation in the present relations of the world; in which revolution must among other events be involved, the destruction of that government "whose moon is in its wane," according to the prophetic denunciation of every historian, and whose fall has often been predicted, without being as yet followed by any serious symptom of immediate accomplishment.

At the apprehension of commercial rivalry it is presumed, that no London merchant would be alarmed who should compare the single expence and hazard of the longer voyage, with the endless repetition of risk, damage, and embezzlement, exclusively of actual disbursement, which would accompany the more complex operation; shorter in mere geographical distance alone; even admitting what, might perhaps be questioned, the assumed facility of opening a really practicable communication between the Red Sea and the Nile.

The military facilities are more obvious to a transient than to a close observation. The power possessed of naval superiority, might always and easily render impracticable the communication by the narrow mouth of the Red Sea; and with regard to the plans indicated in the intercepted letters, of dividing unconquered Arabia into various republics, as the *via sacra* of democracy from Paris to Calcutta, the wonders really accomplished by the efforts of revolutionary France cannot restrain a smile, at this projected extension of fraternity among the defenders and the religious plunderers of the holy cities: a march through the inheritance

CHAP. XLVI. 1799.

of the robbers of the desart; or at best through a region depending on foreign countries for its own food, to reach the sister republic of Citizen Tippoo.

It is not intended to conjecture in what degree the disbelief of the Governor-general was founded, on any of these considerations, but it may be suggested with greater confidence, that his knowledge of the actual invasion of Egypt, by the whole of the armament prepared at Toulon, relieved him from the apprehension of immediate interruption from that quarter, during the probable continuance of the war in Mysoor. The motives for urging his preparations for the purpose of shortening, by every practicable means, the duration of the impending war, were sufficiently powerful, independently of all reference to the Egyptian expedition; and his greatest apprehension continued to apply, not to the force amply occupied, and after the 1st of August, locked up in that country, but to an additional armament which might have proceeded by the ordinary passage, round the Cape of Good Hope, to co-operate in its farther objects. On the second day after receiving the intelligence from Egypt, (the 21st of October,) he issued peremptory orders to the Government of Fort St. George for completing the equipments in every department, and advancing the battering train and all the heavy stores to the most eligible situation on the western frontier; and announced his intention of reinforcing their native army with three thousand volunteers from Bengal, and with the most ample supplies of treasure. The brilliant victory of Aboukir, of which information was received at the close of the same month, materially augmented the improbability of interruption from any armament which had not previously sailed; and the Governor-general opened the correspondence with Tippoo Sultaun which has been recited, and determined to proceed to Madras for the purpose of conducting the expected negotiation; in the hope that the prosperous events in India already detailed, combined with this recent intelligence, and with the progress of his military preparations on both coasts, would dispose the Sultaun's haughty mind to a just estimate of his actual danger, and render unnecessary these formidable means of ultimate coercion.

On the last day of the year 1798, Lord Mornington landed, as we have seen, at Madras, where the son of the great Clive had succeeded to the Government in the preceding August. The provisions of the law required that the authority of the Governor in Council at Fort St. George should be vested in the hands of the Governor-general during his residence at that Presidency; and the public acts and proceedings of that Government must necessarily pass in his name; but on first assuming his seat in council, Lord Mornington declared that his power of superintendence on the spot, should not exceed its ordinary exercise at the seat of the Supreme Government at Fort William, and he requested Lord Clive to conduct all the ordinary details of the Government, and especially those which related to patronage, according to the principles which had been observed by his Lordship since his arrival in India, while his own attention should be chiefly devoted to the general interests of all the Presidencies. The delicacy of this proceeding was calculated to excite a continuance of that energy and vigour in forwarding the public service, which had already obtained the recorded testimony of his unqualified approbation; no de-

CHAP. XLVI. 1799.

clarations, however, could entirely divest his Lordship's presence at Madras of the ostensible interception of that credit, which the subordinate Government might otherwise hope to claim, from the independent exercise of its own energies, in the important crisis in which it was placed, or subdue in ordinary minds the smothered jealousy produced by a necessary supercession. But a genuine purity and nobleness of mind, elevated far above the access of every such unworthy feeling, was evinced by Lord Clive, in public exertions, if possible, augmented by the presence of the Governor-general; in efforts to insure success, as anxious as if they tended to his own exclusive honour; and in a manly and honourable support of his superior, on public principle, as warm and cordial as if it had been the undivided result of personal attachment.

The continued apprehension of an invasion of Hindostân by Zemaun Shah, who was stated to have crossed the Indus, rendered it necessary to place the army of Bengal in a state of preparation; and it was ultimately determined, that combining these circumstances with the intended absence of the Governor-general, Sir Alured Clarke, Commander-in-chief in India, should remain to direct the military operations in that quarter; and that the immediate command of the army assembled at Madras, and the general conduct of the southern war should devolve on Lieutenant-General Harris, the local Commander-in-chief of the troops of that presidency. To the benefit of various military experience, General Harris added the inestimable advantage of a personal knowledge of every locality, connected with the operations of the impending service, obtained during the campaigns of 1790, 1791, and 1792; and an intimate acquaintance then acquired, and recently improved, (while exercising the powers of Commander-in-chief and provisional governor,) with the personal character, and varied qualifications of every individual whom he might find it necessary to employ; and the penetration with which this knowledge was exercised, may be appreciated by the universal admission, that in estimating the acknowledged merit of every branch of military preparation for the campaign of 1799, none was more perfect, perhaps none so efficient, as the admirable selection of the principal staff of Lieutenant-General Harris.

The happy consequences of the recent changes effected at Hyderabad, were manifested in the timely march and actual arrival at the appointed rendezvous before General Harris was ready to move, of the whole subsidiary force, and a selected body from the late French battalions, amounting together to ten thousand infantry with their guns, and a better chosen, though not so numerous a body of cavalry as that which had accompanied and incumbered Lord Cornwallis. The appointment to the general control and direction of Nizam Ali's contingent, of Captain Malcolm, who in his capacity of assistant to the Resident, had himself materially contributed to the political and military arrangements which secured their services, was an important branch of the new organization. His personal acquaintance with the chiefs, and his conciliatory and animated manners, gave a new tone to their proceedings; and the energy and efficiency of the troops of Nizam Ali in 1799, formed a remarkable contrast with their conduct in 1791 and 1792. On the 3d of February, Lord Mornington issued his final instructions for the advance of the army, and the first movement was made on the 11th. Feb. 3. 11.

CHAP. XLVI. 1799.

Although the strength of the army above the ghauts, in 1792, exceeded in number, by upwards of six thousand men, that which was destined for the campaign of 1799, and nearly ten thousand, if the corps of Nizam Ali be excluded *; yet, in the former war, a number exceeding that difference, was employed in the fortresses on the lines of communication; and, as all the means of every description for the reduction of the enemy's capital, was now to accompany the army for terminating the war by a single blow; the plan of the campaign excluded the occupation of intermediate posts, and rendered disposable about an equal number of troops. The amount of those equip-

		Total.	
* European cavalry - - -	884		
Native ditto - - -	1751		
		2635	
European artillerymen - - -		608	
European infantry - - -	4381		
Native ditto - -	10,695		
		15,076	
Gun lascars - - -	1483		
Pioneers - - - - - -	1000		
		2483	
			20,802
Subsidiary force serving with Nizam Ali		6536	
His infantry, formerly French - -		3621	
			10,157
			30,959
Bombay army -			6,000
Grand Total -			36,959

Battering guns * - - -	40
Field ordnance - - -	57
Howitzers - - -	7

besides the field train, with the contingent of Nizam Ali, and besides his regular and irregular horse, about 6000.

Army of 1792 - - - 43,113.

ments, described by the modern technical designation of *materiel*, had never been equalled on any former occasion; and, if there were any question regarding their efficiency, it arose, in a great degree, from their abundance. The powers of the Commander-in-chief were co-extensive with the resources which he might find it necessary to command; and his authority was ordered to be obeyed, without reference, by all officers, civil and military, to whom he might find it necessary to issue his commands. The energies of the state, exercised in their most important and critical form, were cramped by no restrictive suspicions of imaginary abuse. The jealous taint which on former occasions we have seen embodied in the fear of weakening power by delegation, was now contrasted with the generous and masterly conviction, that ample authority, and broad discretion, wisely conferred, are more precious to the giver, than the receiver: and, in the energetic language of the author of this liberal policy: "when Lieutenant-General Harris took the field, I thought it my duty to invest him with the most extensive powers, which it was possible for me to delegate; and he has carried with him to the gates of Seringapatam, the full vigour and energy of your Supreme Government."

An adequate corps, under Lieutenant-Colonel Read, who exercised the civil and military authority in the province of Bàramahâl, was destined to collect, arrange and eventually escort further supplies of provisions to the army in advance. A similar corps, under Lieutenant-Colonel Brown, was appointed for a corresponding service in Coimbetoor, and finally the important army * of Bombay had ascended into Coorg, and

* 6420 fighting men, artillery and infantry, European and native.

CHAP. XLVI. 1799. agreeably to instructions waited the orders of Lieutenant-General Harris for their further guidance. This army was commanded by Lieutenant-General James Stuart, the same excellent and estimable officer who commanded the right wing of the army under Lord Cornwallis in the preceding war, and brought into the present campaign every advantage of local information which could give efficiency to his military experience.

General Stuart, after assembling his army at Cannanore, finally marched from that station on the 21st of April. He arrived at the top of the Poodicherrum ghaut on the 25th of the same month, and proceeded, in obedience to his instructions, to assume a defensive position close to the frontier of Mysoor. The nature of the country, every where covered with thick woods, in most places nearly impenetrable, made it impossible to occupy a regular defensive position, and compelled him to place his troops in several divisions, so disposed, as to be capable of affording reciprocal support: the most advanced of these was the height of Sedaseer, indispensable with reference to an early junction, as being the only spot from which the signals, established between the two armies, could be observed.

Mar. 5. On the morning of the 5th of March, the very day on which General Harris crossed the frontier, a few tents were descried from the hill of Sedaseer, about nine o'clock, and gradually the pitching of an extensive encampment in advance of Periapatam, and little more than six miles distant, and on further observation, a green tent of large dimensions was perceived, indicating the presence of the Sultaun. The ground at Sedaseer was occupied by a brigade of three native battalions, under Lieutenant-Colonel

Montresor, and although the information of trust-worthy spies recently returned from Seringapatam, gave reasonable assurance that the Sultaun, at the time of their departure was still at the Madoor river, and that a detachment under Mahommed Reza, usually called the Binky * Nabob constituted the only force west of the river Cavery; General Stuart thought it prudent to send forward another battalion to a convenient position for reinforcing, if it should be necessary the advanced brigade at Sedaseer.

Early on the morning of the 6th, Major-General Hartley, the second in command, went forward to reconnoitre the enemy's army, which was discovered to be in motion; but their movements were so well concealed by the closeness of the country, that it was impossible to ascertain their precise object, until between the hours of nine and ten, when a simultaneous attack was made on the front and rear of the position; and the battalion destined to reinforce it, was prevented from joining by the intervention of two columns from the right and left, which united in the rear, at the instant of the commencement of the attack in front. March 6.

Before the enemy had accomplished this purpose, Major-General Hartley had time to apprise General Stuart of their attack, and remained himself to give any assistance that might be necessary. The best position was immediately assumed, the brigade was completely surrounded on every side, and had to contend with a vast disparity of numbers; the troops were aware that many hours must elapse before they could receive efficient support, but they were also animated by the conviction that aid

* This word signifies *fire*, and the title was a sort of nickname given to this officer, from his being peculiarly expert at that species of devastation in an enemy's country.

CHAP. XLVI. 1799. would ultimately arrive; and maintained their ground with so much cool resolution, that the utmost efforts of the Sultaun's best officers and troops were unable to make any serious impression on these three sepoy battalions.

As soon as General Stuart received intelligence of the perilous situation of his advanced corps, he marched without a moment's hesitation, with the two flank companies of His Majesty's 75th, and the whole of the 77th under Lieutenant-Colonel Dunlop. It was half past two before he arrived with this small but most efficient body in sight of the enemy's divisions, which had penetrated to the rear and possessed themselves of the great road leading to Sedaseer. The energy of the attack rendered it of short duration; less than half an hour was sufficient to accomplish the precipitate flight of the Mysoreans through the woods, to join the division which still continued the attack in front. On arriving at Lieutenant-Colonel Montresor's post, General Stuart found his men exhausted with fatigue, and their ammunition almost expended. At twenty minutes past three, the enemy retreated in all directions, and left General Stuart to admire the immoveable steadiness of the native troops in a protracted encounter of nearly six hours, and the energy of the Europeans whom he had led to their aid. The success was materially enhanced in value, by finding on collecting the reports of corps, that his loss was considerably smaller than might have been expected; amounting only to one hundred and forty-three men, while that of the enemy was unusually severe, amounting according to credible reports to upwards of two thousand; a difference, to be ascribed chiefly to a judicious occupation of ground, and a cool reservation of fire in the defensive position; and in the reinforcement, to the effective consequences of a rapid and vigorous encounter.

The raja of Coorg personally accompanied General Stuart, and witnessed for the first time the conduct of European troops in the presence of an enemy. There was a chivalrous air in all that proceeded from this extraordinary man, and some passages of his letter to the Governor-General, giving an account of the operations of this day are tinged with his peculiar character. "General Stuart marched with two regiments of Europeans, keeping the remainder of the army in the plain of Kanydygood; on approaching, he ordered the two regiments to attack the enemy. A severe action ensued, in which I was present. To describe the battle which General Stuart fought with these two regiments of Europeans; the discipline, valour, strength, and magnanimity of the troops, the courageous attack upon the army of Tippoo, surpasses all example in this world. In our Shasters, and Purânas, the battles fought by Allered and Maharut have been much celebrated, but they are unequal to this battle; it exceeds my ability to describe this action at length to your Lordship." After reciting the flight of the Sultaun's troops, the relief of the advanced post, and the ultimate retreat of the enemy, he concludes,—"In this manner General Stuart, before my eyes, while I was looking on, having chastised my enemy, has provided great happiness for me, and all the subjects of my country. General Stuart has in this manner achieved a glorious deed."

The first impression on the Sultaun's mind, was to renew the attack on the ensuing day, with augmented numbers, but in

CHAP. XLVI. 1799. the mean while General Stuart had changed all his dispositions. The chief object for which this advanced post had been occupied, must necessarily cease to exist, during the presence in its front of the Sultaun's main army; and the security of the abundant depôt of provisions in the rear, accessible by other routes, rendered necessary a new and more concentrated disposition of the troops: and the evacuation of the post of Sedaseer, afforded to the Sultaun the faint colour of describing as a victory what every officer in his army felt to be an ignominious repulse. "Having (in the language of the raja of Coorg) brought disgrace upon himself, he employed all his art and knowledge to recover his lost reputation; and having in this manner considered for five days, but not having taken up resolution to attack the Bombay army again, he marched on the sixth (the
Mar. 11. 11th of March) to Seringapatam;" and thence, with no favourable anticipations, to oppose the progress from the east, of the more formidable army of General Harris, to which our narrative must return.

In order that General Harris might be enabled to give his undivided attention to military operations, he was assisted by a political and diplomatic commission, to act not only in communication, but in *obedience to his orders*, and the mere recital of the names, will be sufficient to announce its importance and efficiency. The Honourable Colonel Wellesley, (now Duke of Wellington,) Lieutenant-Colonel Close, (afterwards Sir Barry Close,) Lieutenant-Colonel Agnew, and Captain Malcolm, with Captain Macaulay as their Secretary. The winding route of the army under General Harris, from the vicinity of Arcot, was continued through the vale of Amboor, and the province of Bârama-hâl, whence it ascended the ghauts, and encamped within the English frontier, near Rayacota, on the 4th of March. 1799. Mar. 4.

After entering the enemy's country on the 5th, with one of 5.
the divisions, some days were necessarily occupied in reducing that portion of the congeries of hill-forts in the vicinity of Rayacota, which the treaty of 1792 had left in possession of the Sultaun; and on the 7th, the head-quarters were established at 7.
Kellumungulum, about sixteen miles within the territory of Mysoor: on the 9th, the whole army was collected on that 9.
ground, and made its first united movement on the enemy's country on the 10th, the day which General Harris had indicated 10.
to General Stuart, as the latest to which, if possible, his arrival before the enemy's capital ought to be protracted.

The contingent of Hyderabad, consisting altogether of about ten thousand infantry with their field guns, strengthened by His Majesty's 33d foot, and followed by the largest portion of Nizam Ali's cavalry, was placed under the separate command of the Honourable Colonel Wellesley; and although the order of march varied with the nature of the ground, this strong and important corps usually formed a distinct column parallel to that of the main army, for the protection of the intermediate columns of the battering train and its regular stores, together with the more irregular masses of the departments of grain and the general baggage. Corps detached from each column, moved in the front and rear of the intermediate space, and afforded an effectual protection to the whole of this enormous mass.

Although every resource of the state had been applied by the Governor-general, to perfect the equipments of the army;

CHAP. XLVI. 1799. although, every energy of the Commander-in-chief, and an experienced and enlightened staff, had been applied to the organization of that undisciplined crowd of persons, not military, employed with upwards of sixty thousand oxen, chiefly untrained, in the regular branches of the commissariat; besides, a countless amount of brinjaries, and grain and provision merchants; the defects and counteractions to be surmounted, in the introduction of order among men, whose habits and interests equally tended to confusion, began to shew themselves on the first march. The
Mar. 11. 12. army halted on the 11th; moved on the 12th, and again halted,
13. 14. from the same cause on the 13th, and marched on the 14th to an encampment within sight of Bangalore, and distant from it about nine miles.

It will be recollected, that from this fortress (now dismantled), to Seringapatam, there is a choice of three routes; the central, and the shortest, by Cenapatam; the more northern, by Holiordroog, used by Lord Cornwallis, in 1792, and the most southern, by Caunkanhully, in 1791. It was, of course, of the greatest importance, that the enemy should be kept in ignorance of the intended route; and without attempting the shorter mountain road, by which the English commissioners were led, and their animals crippled in 1783, it was necessary to advance to the ground now occupied, before either of these routes could be entered with advantage. The movement, however, and all the corresponding demonstrations, produced, as was intended, the impression, that Bangalore was to be restored and occupied; and, that the army would advance by the route of Cenapatam. The Sultaun, on his return from Coorg, had himself made his first march on that road, and the corps under Seyed Saheb,

and Poornea, who had hitherto accompanied and harrassed CHAP. XLVI.
every march, now took the same direction, first destroying all
the dry forage in Bangalore and its vicinity, which was distinctly 1799.
seen from the camp, in a widely-extended blaze. Mar. 14.

The same mortification and from the same cause, was experienced in a third day's halt on this ground, where a selection was made of every store, which could by any possibility be dispensed with, to be destroyed, for the purpose of
increasing the available carriage. On the 16th the army en- 16.
tered the road of Kaunkanhully, and on the 18th again halted 18.
a fourth day: "the loss of powder, shot, and other military stores had already been so considerable as to excite some degree of alarm at this early period of the campaign." * Historical truth, which even in feeble hands may transmit the lessons of experience, has made it necessary to dwell on the inevitable imperfections of this great equipment, which no wisdom could repair, and no liberality remove; and for the purpose of obviating the necessity of recurrence to the same subject, it may be sufficient here to explain, that a fifth halting day occurred on the 31st, and on the last eighteen marching days from the 16th of March, the day on which the army entered the road of Kaunkanhully, till the 5th of April, when it entered its ultimate encampment before Seringapatam, the average length of each day's march did not quite amount to five miles and two-thirds.

With the exception of a company of native infantry, destroyed by a charge of cavalry on the flank, in consequence of the inexperience of the young officer who commanded, in not

* Beatson, page 65.

CHAP. XLVI. 1799. Mar. 21. reserving his fire, no unusual events occurred in this tedious march, until the 21st, when the army encamped at Kaunkanhully. The destruction of the intermediate tanks at Achel, between this place and Sultanpet, had compelled Lord Cornwallis, in 1791, to make the longer march, the injurious effects of which, on his exhausted cattle, were sensibly and severely felt during the remainder of the campaign. The anxious and active reconnoisance of the deputy quarter-master-general*, enabled him to ascertain, in the course of the day, without being himself observed, that the tanks were still full, and that it was just possible to avert consequences still more injurious than those experienced in 1791: a detachment sent forwards at ten at night, arrived in time to fill up the breaches which had just been opened, and to remove the milk† hedge, intended to poison the residue of the water. The body of Mysorean troops left to cover this work of destruction, although not surprised, were attacked at rather an earlier moment than was expected, and suffered a more serious loss than was supposed or reported by the assailants; the leading division of the army followed at daylight, and the head quarters were established on that ground
22. on the 22d.

24. On the 24th, while in the act of crossing the Madoor river, whence the Sultaun had marched for the attack of General Stuart; a letter was received from that officer which removed the uneasiness occasioned by vague and contradictory reports, and gave the first authentic account of his success and unimpaired efficiency. The Sultaun who left Periapatam on the

* Major Allan.

† Euphorbia Tiraculli.

11th, remained for some days in the vicinity of the capital to refit; his first movement was in the direction of Cenapatam, but learning on the 16th, that General Harris had entered the southern road, he deviated by his right to Malvilly, and marched to the Madoor river, where he encamped on the 18th, and was joined by Seyed Saheb and Poornea, who had also crossed from the central road. The southern road from this river to the point where General Harris first entered it, presented numerous situations, where the advance of the English army might have been obstructed, and at least materially delayed by steady troops, without any risk of disaster to themselves; but it was a close woody country, and we have had occasion to observe, that after some early experience of disadvantage, it had become the fixed system of Hyder, as well as Tippoo, to prefer an open field; and although, on his arrival at the river, he opened several roads through the woods which indicated an intention of departing from this general rule, he not only abstained from any effectual attempt, but even, after examining and occupying the finest imaginable position for opposing the passage of the river in front, and placing beyond it a strong corps to operate at the same time on the enemy's right flank, from very advantageous ground, with an open rear and a secure retreat from both positions; he abandoned the intention of giving battle on this ground, as strongly recommended to him by Monsieur Chapuis, and his own best officers, because the plan of defence necessarily involved the risk of a few guns; and he determined to fight on ground which he had examined about two miles to the westward of the fort and village of Malvilly; which, among other advantages gratuitously bestowed on his enemy, gave them, during the intended action, the most convenient cover for their unwieldy impediments.

1799. Mar. 27. On the 27th, the English army, on preparing to take up its ground of encampment to the westward of Malvilly, distinctly perceived the Sultaun's army drawn up on a height little exceeding two miles from the intended encampment. The great object of the English General was, to escort in safety to the spot on which they were to be used, the effective means of reducing the capital, and not to seek for serious action until that object should be attained. He accordingly ordered the ground of encampment to be marked, and the troops to continue their march, in such order as should admit either of encampment or action, the principal division under his own orders being destined to form the right, and the column under the Honourable Colonel Wellesley the extreme left, and eventually to turn the enemy's right. The troops intended for the advanced pickets under Colonel Sherbrooke moved out as usual to examine their ground, and they were soon threatened by large bodies of the enemy; after some manœuvring they took post with their right to a village, and the support of these troops eventually brought on the action. The column of the principal division, or right wing of the army, successively deployed into line on the left of the pickets, and when formed, advanced on the enemy. An interval between two brigades caused by the nature of the ground, seemed to present an opportunity for an effort of cavalry, which the Sultaun himself directed and accompanied, till in the very act to charge. The charge was prepared with deliberate coolness, and executed with great spirit; it was purposely directed against the Europeans, and although many horsemen fell on the bayonets, was completely repelled without causing the slightest disorder in the ranks, and the advance of the line being continued in a direction outflanking the enemy's left, the Sultaun's guns began soon afterwards to be withdrawn from the heights.

In the meanwhile, the division under Colonel Wellesley moved in echellon of corps, to turn the enemy's right, supported on his right by a brigade of cavalry under Colonel Floyd; the English centre being entirely refused, and Colonel Floyd being prepared to act with either attack, as circumstances might require: the remainder of the cavalry was on the right, keeping in check a body of horse, which threatened by a circuitous route to attack the baggage. As Colonel Wellesley approached his object, the Sultaun's cushoons advanced in very creditable style, in front of their guns, against the 33d, which was the leading corps, giving their fire, and receiving that of the 33d, together with a discharge of grape, till within sixty yards, when the regiment continuing to advance with a quickened step, they gave way; and Colonel Floyd, availing himself of the critical instant, charged and destroyed them to a man. The guns now began to be withdrawn from this flank also, and an appearance of making a stand on another height occupied by the second line of the Mysoreans, was only intended to cover their retreat.

The result to the Sultaun of this injudicious affair, was the loss of upwards of a thousand men, and to the English of sixty-nine only: and the superiority of the Mysorean equipments rendering farther pursuit unavailing, General Harris returned to occupy the encampment marked out in the morning.

The Sultaun had appointed as his rendezvous in the event of defeat, a ground about twelve miles to the westward; and the

CHAP. XLVI. 1799. corps moved, each independent of the other, with a degree of confusion and despondency which could scarcely be imagined from the English accounts.

Mar. 28. From this western ground the Sultaun, on the 28th, moved in a
29. direction exactly north; and on the 29th nearly S. E. with the view of placing his whole army in General Harris's rear during the remainder of his march to Seringapatam, by the expected route of 1791, which had been so totally destroyed under his own inspection, that not a particle of dry forage, and scarcely a pile of grass, was left unconsumed.

General Harris, however, had taken an unexpected direction, and during the execution of this detour was actually south of the Cavery.

28. A short march on the 28th, brought the army to the point from which it had long been secretly determined to deviate to the south, if, on examining the ford at Sosilla, about a mile above the confluence of the Cavery and Caupani, and about fifteen miles east of Seringapatam, it should be found to answer the description given by native reporters; the distance from this encampment somewhat exceeded twelve miles, and the escort to cover the reconnoisance, under the deputy quarter-master-general, reached the vicinity of the ford, just at dark, without seeing an enemy, and conducted themselves so adroitly, as to excite no apprehension in the inhabitants of a movement in that direction by the English army, and they took, therefore, no steps to remove their property; the escort returned to camp at mid-
29. night, and on the 29th, the leading division was across the river, and found both there and on the route, a profusion of forage and cattle. The battering train, and the last of the

army, were over on the 30th, and the whole halted on the 31st, to benefit by an abundance so grateful and important. CHAP. XLVI. 1799. Mar. 31.

The inducements to this judicious and well concealed movement, had long engaged the most serious consideration. It was foreseen, that by whatever route the army should advance, the forage and provisions would be destroyed or removed, and that the nearer approach to the capital, would be rendered a perfect desert; an unexpected change of route, which should secure even one day's abundant forage, would, under such circumstances, be in that single view, a most important advantage; and a southern movement was recommended by the farther consideration, of rendering fruitless the preparations the Sultaun might have made on the northern bank, and compelling him to change his line of operations. The forage and pasture on that bank, was known to be systematically destroyed, while that on the opposite, was reserved for his own army; and some portion of it at least would, by this movement, be secured for the allies. An ultimate position for the siege, to the south of the Cavery, would facilitate the junction of General Stuart from Coorg, and of the supplies from Coimbetoor, under Lieutenant-Colonel Brown; and finally, the best opinions inclined to prefer an attack on the capital from the S. W., if on inspecting its present state, known to be in many respects materially altered since 1792, no forcible reason should appear for changing that design.

No advantages anticipated by the English General from this unexpected movement, could approach the corresponding impressions of astonishment, disappointment, and dismay, produced on the mind of Tippoo Sultaun, when he arrived near Malvilly, on discovering that all his intermediate plans of defence, coun-

CHAP. XLVI. 1799.

teraction, and annoyance, had been rendered absolutely nugatory, and that he was even too late for disturbing the passage of the Cavery. His march was continued in the direction of the bad ford of Arakerry, to Bennoor, where reflecting on the disastrous issue of his two first efforts at Sedaseer and at Malvilly, and on the able movement by which his next preparatory measures had been foiled, he sunk into absolute despondency, and in this state he received the whole of his principal officers. "We have arrived (said he) at our last stage (intimating that there was no hope), what is your determination?" "To die along with you," was the universal reply. After some gloomy consultation, it was the prevailing opinion that the English General would cross over to the island of Seringapatam by the southern fords, and then assume his ultimate position for the siege. The determination was accordingly formed at this council, to anticipate his movement, as was easily practicable with their efficient equipments, by crossing at the ford of Arakerry, and assuming a strong position on General Harris's supposed route. The intended position was near the village of Chendgâl, south of the island from which the principal ford takes its name, and there it was determined to give battle, with the solemn and unanimous resolve to make a last and desperate effort, with no alternative but death or victory. Every person present was deeply affected by the solemn air and visible distress of their sovereign; and one of the chiefs, with a heart too full for ordinary self-command, on taking leave prostrated himself at the Sultaun's feet and embraced them, the ceremony usual among Hindoos and Mahommedans on taking leave for a long absence. The Sultaun dissolved into tears: the whole assembly caught the infection: all followed the example, and reiterated the voice of the first chief; and the ceremonial and declarations of the day indicated a reciprocal adieu for the last time in this world. Meer Sâdik was dispatched to superintend the destruction of all the buildings on the esplanade, on the side of the expected attack, and such of those in Sheker Gunjaum as had not already been destroyed. The Sultaun's two eldest sons, who were present with the army, were sent to Seringapatam, with orders to make a proper defence in the event of their father's death, and the army crossed on the ensuing day to examine and prepare the position at Chendgâl, from which there was a safe retreat, within a new exterior line on the island, commanded by the guns of the fort, which had been constructed since 1792; and the encampment was pitched within these lines, which were little more than an hour's march from the intended field of action.

On the 2d and 3d of April, the troops were under arms in their appointed stations, concealed as much as practicable from observation, and the Sultaun anxiously examined, from the adjacent high grounds, the slow progress of the English army, in order that the action might commence at the proper moment after the columns should point to the Island. He had, however entirely misapprehended the General's intentions, and found that on his arrival at the point of expected deviation to the right, he made a detour to the left, for the purpose of avoiding the intermediate low grounds, and reaching by a more level but circuitous route, the position occupied by General Abercromby, in 1792, to the south-west of the western angle of the capital. April 2. 3.

The dispositions which had been made by the Sultaun, for an action expected to be, at least in the first instance defensive,

CHAP. XLVI. 1799. were inapplicable to offensive movements, and the nature of the ground offered no advantage for such an operation. The English army was accordingly permitted to pass at the distance of three miles from the main position, without the slightest attempt to execute the desperate resolutions which had been formed at Bennoor.

Twenty-five days later than the time which General Harris had announced in his original instructions to General Stuart, as the most advanced period of the season, to which his arrival at Seringapatam could be safely protracted, he took up his ground
Mar. 5. for the siege of that capital, exactly one month from the first advanced movement, into the territory of Mysoor, and after a march of one hundred and fifty-three miles and a half, which distance being divided by twenty-three, the number of marching days, gives 6⅔ miles as the average of each day's march within the enemy's territory, and divided by the whole number of days employed in effecting the arrival of the army at its object, gives for its average progress, under five miles a day.

To men unused to the practical observation of the departments of an army, or accustomed to departments previously organised, it cannot be easy at once to comprehend a scene, in which elementary training, and military operation, is one and the same process, in which the raw material, instead of the manufactured instrument, is put into the master's hand. The first impression, without such explanations, would be that of surprise, perhaps of censure, at the tardy progress. Men of experience and reflection viewed the conjuncture with far other feelings, which cannot perhaps be expressed in a more authentic form, than is exhibited in an original letter now before me, written to a private and confidential friend, by one of the most accomplished officers of the staff, five days after the arrival of the army. " We have here, in despite of all the accumulated difficulties which daily attended and impeded our march, an adequate battering train complete, with twelve hundred rounds for the cannon, and a good proportion for the howitzers, thirty-three days provision for our fighting men, (capable of lasting much longer if necessary,) and every reasonable expectation of farther supplies. I can hardly believe, when I look at the mass of men and matter collected here, that it is possible we should have moved it from Rayacotta to this ground in one month. On the 13th we expect the united force of Stuart and Floyd to join us: and if no untoward accident occurs to mar our plans, the campaign, hitherto so apparently tardy, will be the most extraordinarily rapid that has ever been recorded. A direct move to the capital of an enemy, one hundred and fifty miles from your frontier, without occupying a single intermediate post! The Governor-General is bold in his plans, and I think, bold as they are, they will be attended with complete success: and that unless something approaching the miraculous should interpose to save the place, it will be ours about the end of this month:" and whatever anxiety might have been felt in the previous contemplation of these difficulties, or during the period which was occupied in surmounting them, the confidence expressed by this officer, was now the universal sentiment of the army.

CHAPTER XLVII.

Attack of the enemy's posts on the 5th March fails — succeeds on the 6th — General Floyd's march to bring up the Bombay army — Detachment under Kummer-u-Deen well commanded — Ineffectual efforts — Junction formed — General Stuart crosses to the north — Second departure of General Floyd, to bring up the provisions from the rear — Unexplained failure of provisions — how relieved — Subject still under discussion — Sultaun's anticipation and present opinion, regarding the point of attack — Two plans submitted to General Harris — he decides on that which involves crossing the river in the act of assault — Commencement of the siege — Northern attack — Southern — on the 17th — Second parallel on the 20th — Tippoo proposes negotiation — General Harris sends him his ultimatum — rejected with disdain — Sortie on the 22d — Batteries open 23d — Arduous operation of establishing the third parallel, 26th and 27th — Another advance to negotiation — answered by still offering the same ultimatum — Sultaun's despondency — Breaching batteries — directed to the true breach, 2d May — Breach practicable on the 3d — Arrangements for assault on the 4th — Intermediate proceedings of the Sultaun — Flatteries — Seyed Ghoffâr — Astrology — Incantations — Roused by the assault.

CHAP. XLVII.

1799.

The front of the encampment was distant about three thousand five hundred yards from the works of the fort: an aqueduct, branching from the Cavery, a few miles to the westward, and passing in a winding and irregular course, and varying distance along the front, was occupied, at all its strong points, by the Mysorean troops, and some intermediate cover enabled the rocket men towards evening, to project those dangerous missiles into most parts of the camp, and to occasion some disquietude for the safety of the park of artillery stores: an attack was accordingly ordered soon after sun-set in two columns, under the direction of the Honourable Colonel Wellesley and Lieutenant-Colonel Shaw, for the purpose of establishing advanced posts nearly in the positions contested with General Abercromby in 1792. The object failed on the right from the darkness of the night, and from the unexpected impediment of a succession of deep trenches in a grove; and on the left it was not wholly attained. The loss from these circumstances fell somewhat heavy; but on the morning of the 6th the attack was renewed, April 6. under the same officers, on an enlarged scale, better proportioned to the numbers to be dislodged, and completely succeeded. The Mysoreans were forced to retire with precipitation, and strong advanced posts were established within eighteen hundred yards of the fort, with their left on the river and their right at Sultaunpet; including, within the latter extremity, extensive plantations, which furnished a most important and abundant store of materials for the batteries and approaches.

On the same day, Major-General Floyd, with four regiments of cavalry, and the greater part of the left wing of the army, marched on Periapatam, for the purpose of strengthening the Bombay army, under Lieutenant-General Stuart, and enabling it to form the ultimate junction for the siege of the capital. Nearly the whole of the Mysorean cavalry, and a considerable body of infantry, regular and irregular, under the command of Kummer-u-Deen, were immediately detached with orders, if possible, to prevent the junction, or in every event to cripple the equipments. The Sultaun's cavalry had on no occasion been so well commanded, or held themselves so effectually prepared, at a moment's warning, to profit by the slightest irregularity or error, and strike a decisive blow, as throughout the whole of this march to and from Periapatam; but the only result was to compel their opponents to corresponding vigilance and care, and of course to retard their movements. The raja of Coorg continued to accompany General Stuart to Periapatam, but at that place took his leave, to return for the arrangement of those measures of supply which might eventually be necessary. His romantic character rendered him an object of peculiar interest to General Floyd, and the officers of the division from the eastward; and a squadron of the 19th dragoons sent as an escort, with the staff officer who first communicated with General Stuart (the first European cavalry the raja had ever seen) was a novelty at which he expressed his admiration, with that natural and extravagant energy, which the habits of civilized life, have a tendency to restrain. He accepted with enthusiasm the invitation to see the line of the eastern division under arms, and was received with suitable honours. He expressed a just approbation of every thing he saw, but continued after his return to General Floyd's tent, to testify his particular and unwearied admiration of the 19th regiment, intimating a wish to procure at a proper time for his own personal use, one of the dragoon's swords; he was informed in general terms that he would be gratified, and on his rising to take his leave, General Floyd unclasped his own sword, and, in a few words judiciously suited to the occasion, begged that he might be permitted to present it for the raja's use; the offer and the acceptance were appropriate and impressive, and the raja continued in after times to exhibit this valued gift to his European visitors, as one of his most precious memorials, and to recount with animation when, and by whom, it had been worn, and how, and on what occasion conferred. CHAP. XLVII. 1799.

The united corps formed their ultimate junction with General Harris before Seringapatam on the 14th, and on the ensuing day April 14.
the Bombay army crossed the river to the north, and occupied 15.
ground on a continuation of the line of General Harris, and to the westward of Lord Cornwallis's right in 1792, for the general purposes of the siege, and with a more special view to the enfilade of the face to be attacked, and of the exterior trenches or field works, constructed for impeding the future progress of the approaches from the south.

On the 19th, Major-General Floyd again marched with the 19.
whole of the regular cavalry, a brigade of infantry, and all Nizam Ali's cavalry, by the route of Mysoor and Nunjendgode, to the head of the Caveriporam pass, for the purpose of bringing forward the convoy of provisions under Lieutenant-Colonel Brown from Coimbetoor, together with that collected by Lieutenant-Colonel Read in Bâramahâl; the junction of the troops under these officers, would give Major-General Floyd sufficient strength to cover the whole returning convoy; the cattle of the public departments and all the brinjaries accompanied this division, for the three-fold purpose of augmenting the means of bringing forward the expected supplies, refreshing the cattle with good forage, and relieving the army from the insalubrity of the deaths which must have occurred if they had remained, the ground being already thickly strewed with dead cattle. The departure of all followers, really superfluous, gave also the important advantage of lessening the consumption of food, a subject which had now become the source of most painful anxiety

and alarm. The circumstance is thus stated in *Beatson's View of the War with Tippoo Sultaun* *, published in 1800. "On the 16th of April it was discovered upon measuring the bags which contained the rice, in order to ascertain the exact quantity remaining in camp, that our stock was much diminished, and that there was only sufficient remaining for eighteen days' consumption for the fighting men of the army. The cause of this alarming and unexpected deficiency had not been satisfactorily explained; but such was the actual pressure of our situation at the moment we were about to commence the siege. Happily, from this alarm the Commander-in-Chief was soon afterwards effectually relieved, by a tender, for the public service, of twelve hundred bullock loads of rice," &c. &c.: and it appears that this tender was made on the 22d, three days after the march of Major-General Floyd. †

After a lapse of eighteen years, this transaction still continues to be an unfit subject for historical disquisition. The constituted authorities in England, are still at public variance on the justice, the wisdom, and consistency of their own respective proceedings: and, the author feels the propriety of remitting to the future historian, the issue of a case deemed to be still undecided.

Before the arrival of General Harris, the Sultaun inclined to the expectation of an attack, either on the northern face, at the point intended by Lord Cornwallis, or on the north-eastern angle, which general rumour had then indicated as one of the projects which his Lordship had considered. On finding

* Pages 99, 100.

† General Floyd returned with his convoy on the 11th of May.

that the army passed on to a western encampment, it was the general impression, among his best officers, that the attack would be made on the south-western, and not on the western angle. They had a strong confidence, that the siege could not be sufficiently advanced to give the assault, before at least, the occasional rise of the river, which always precedes its steady periodical filling, should render too precarious for such a risk, any plan of operations, which should involve crossing the river in the act of assault; although, on General Harris taking up his ground, they made active defensive preparations on the south bank of the river, near the western angle, where some lines, *en crémaille*, had already been constructed. They rather suspected all the demonstrations on that point to be intended as a feint; and were at least as anxiously occupied on the south-western angle, and the southern face, in contemplation of an attempt from the English to establish themselves on the island; and this persuasion was not shaken, until General Stuart, by crossing to the northern bank on the 15th, and taking all the preparatory measures for the permanent occupation of his ground, forced the conviction, that the assault would be prepared to cross the river, from one or both attacks on the western angle, and its vicinity: the passage of both branches being practicable, while the river was dry, as had been sufficiently ascertained before the commencement of the actual operations of the siege.

The alternative of two plans of attack was submitted to the Commander-in-Chief by the chief engineer about the 12th. It is not intended to deviate from the usual plan of this work by entering into the detailed operations of this siege, however

CHAP. XLVII. 1799. interesting in their nature, and important in their consequences, and little beyond those general views which the reader has been accustomed to expect, shall be attempted, in recounting its most prominent events.

Independently of several subordinate considerations, the practicability of carrying on the siege, even after the filling of the river, was the chief recommendation of an attack on the south-western angle, and the risk of being obliged to abandon the enterprise if it should, from any unforeseen contingency, be protracted until the same periodical event, was the main disadvantage of that on the western angle, which left the bed of the river interposed. In every other respect, the vicinity of the western angle was the weakest part of the fort; capable of being breached for the ultimate assault by one operation; furnishing the opportunity of a perfect enfilade of the northern and south-western * faces; and the option of assaulting from either or both banks; but the chief engineer added as a disadvantage of this plan, independently of the intervention of the river, that the western extremity of the fort, from the circumstance of its gradually narrowing to a point, offered greater facilities than any other which could be attacked, for a retrenchment to cut off the whole space attacked, and to protract the operations of the siege. †

The Commander-in-Chief, after giving a deliberate consideration to this important alternative, decided on ultimately storm-

* It fronted about W. S. W. for about five hundred yards, and from a work at that point, took a direction which fronted nearly S. S. W.

† The reader who may wish for details, will find them stated with minute accuracy in "Beaston's View of the Origin and Conduct of the War with Tippoo Sultaun."

ing across the river, confident in the ample means he possessed of bringing the contest to that issue, before the filling of the river, and trusting for the rest to the approved excellence and tried valour of his officers and men.

The period which was permitted to elapse before the commencement of decisive operations, did not include one hour of lost time. Every moment had been improved in collecting and making up such a stock of materials as should insure an uninterrupted progress, whenever the siege should commence; an event which may most correctly be dated on the 17th of April; when an attempt of the enemy to establish a redoubt on the northern bank, on ground commanding that intended for General Stuart's approaches and batteries, rendered it necessary to dislodge them without loss of time. This operation, covered by all the fire from the southern bank which could be brought to bear on the requisite points, was conducted with great gallantry by Colonel Hart, under a severe cannonade from the fort; the troops were ultimately established in good cover within 1,000 yards of the western angle of the fort, and this advanced post was afterwards connected with those previously established, in such a manner as to give great security to the subsequent operations.

April 17.

At the proper moment after the enemy's attention had been seriously drawn to the north, the southern operations also commenced; the bed of a water-course, forming, with little farther labour, a parallel one thousand yards from the fort, was occupied without much opposition by a proper number of troops under Major Macdonald, and connected during the night by a regular approach from the former less advanced positions; while on the

CHAP. XLVII. northern branch, work was in progress for the erection of the first batteries.

1799.

Some misapprehensions in the engineer department caused

April 20. the loss of a day ; but on the 20th a battery from the northern bank opened with good effect on the enfilade of the south-western face, and of the entrenchment occupied by the enemy south of the river. Two guns were brought to a covered position on the enfilade of the left of those entrenchments. An advanced position near an old powder-mill was occupied in force upwards of four hundred yards in advance of the general line of the enemy's other field-works. From this it was necessary in the first instance to dislodge them, and the attack was made at six o'clock in the evening, under the direction of Colonel Sherbrooke, in three columns, led by himself and by Colonels St. John and Moneypenny, with such judgment and energy, that two thousand of the enemy were dislodged with a loss of two hundred and fifty men ; while the English casualties amounted to one man killed and four wounded : and the possession of this entrenched position enabled the English to establish, in the course of the night, a parallel at the distance of seven hundred and eighty yards from the fort, and four hundred and forty from the enemy's remaining entrenchments.

This system, ultimately the most rapid, of safe and gradual advance almost literally without loss, made a more serious impression on the Sultaun's mind than could have been effected by precipitate measures, and produced a disposition to negotiate. On the 9th he had merely made an advance, by affecting to desire an explanation of the cause of hostilities, for which General Harris, with proper brevity, referred him to the letters which he had received from Lord Mornington. On the present occasion, the Sultaun noticed the powers announced by Lord Mornington, to be vested in General Harris, and requested to be informed of his pleasure, regarding a conference between proper persons to be appointed on both parts: the General's reply took an abstract view of the anxious and repeated efforts of the Governor-general to avert war by negotiation, and the Sultaun's rejection of the means proposed, until the lateness of the season had left no alternative but the advance of the armies: but as the Sultaun now desired to know his pleasure regarding the points at issue, and it was hoped that the request was made in sincerity, he enclosed the draft of a preliminary treaty, containing the conditions on which alone any negotiation could be founded. The main conditions were, the cession of one half the territory possessed by the Sultaun before the war — the payment of two crores of rupees, one immediately, and the other within six months — and the delivery as hostages, of four of his sons, and four of his principal officers, to be selected by General Harris; and the General added, that unless his acceptance of these terms under his seal and signature, were returned to the English camp within twenty-four hours, and the hostages and specie, in twenty-four hours more, the allies reserved to themselves an extension of their demands for security, even to the possession of the fort of Seringapatam, until a definitive treaty could be arranged, and its stipulations carried into effect.

If, as the best information gives reason to conclude, the Sultaun's judgment had not yet risen to a just conception of his danger, it is still more evident, that his spirit had not yet sunk to the level of his fortunes. He raved at the arrogance and

CHAP. XLVII. 1799. tyranny of the conditions, talked of the pre-ordained decrees of fate which might still invert the relative condition of the belligerents; in the short span of human life, it was of little importance, whether an inevitable event should arrive a few days or years sooner or later, and it was better to die like a soldier, than to live a miserable dependent on the infidels, in the list of their pensioned rajas and nabobs; and he declared his disdain of returning any reply to such propositions.

April 22. Indications of erecting an additional battery on the northern bank, produced a vigorous and well-conducted sortie upon all the out-posts and advanced works of that attack: it commenced by a demonstration on the rear, about half past two in the morning, which was immediately followed by a serious assault on the front, with about six thousand infantry, including the French corps who led the principal attack, and behaved with great spirit, some of them having fallen within the entrenchment upon the English bayonets, and others quite close to it. The attack was continued or renewed for several hours, but it was every where received and repulsed with such perfect steadiness, that it was at length abandoned, with the loss of near seven hundred men. The English loss was comparatively small, and the chief injury of the attack arose from the suspension of the intended work.

23. On the 23d the enlarged batteries of both attacks opened with great effect; silenced every gun opposed to them, and had so perfect an enfilade that it appeared impossible, without new means, for any troops to remain for the defence of the curtains. The usual operations of taking off the defences and advancing the approaches were carried on till the 26th, when it became

necessary to dislodge the enemy from their last exterior intrenchment, distant three hundred and eighty yards from the fort, covered on their right by a redoubt, and on the left by a small circular work open in the rear; works which, added to the serpentine direction of the intrenchment, and in some places to regular masonry en cremaille, protected them, in a considerable degree, from the enfilade of the northern batteries, and afforded an imperfect flanking defence.

April 26. The Honourable Colonel Wellesley, who commanded in the trenches, was charged with the direction of the attacks for dislodging them. A little after sun-set, and shortly before the period appointed for the relief of the troops in the trenches, the attack was made in two columns, under Colonel Moneypenny and Major Skelly on the enemy's right and centre; both succeeded, and the united columns turning to their right, pursued the enemy, who continued firing as they retreated; the assailants however being severely galled from the fire of the fort, and having in a great degree accomplished the main object of the attack, took post in an aqueduct which had formed the ditch of the enemy's entrenchment, and was now destined to be the third parallel of the besiegers. The circular work still occupied by the enemy on their left, was however found to have a greater command than was expected over the water-course, the enemy had collected in great numbers at this important point, and the situation of the troops who had taken post was considerably exposed. Lieutenant-Colonel Campbell of the 74th, arriving at this moment with a part of the relief for the trenches, and the importance being urgent, of instantly dislodging the enemy from the circular work, he proceeded, and with no more than one hundred and twenty men, not only charged and dislodged an enemy amounting to thousands, but favoured by the night, pursued them across the Periapatam bridge, entered the right of the enemy's camp on the island, spiked some of their guns, and making use of the most skilful means to conceal his numbers and secure his retreat, returned in perfect order under cover of the confusion he had created. In the fort and on the island, a recollection pervaded every mind of the events of the 6th of February 1792, and a general impression prevailed that the assault of the fort had commenced. The projection of fire-balls had not yet superseded in Seringapatam the ancient practice of India, to favour the assailants more than the defenders, by blue lights on the ramparts; and a general and beautiful illumination of the whole fort was followed by a furious random discharge of artillery. The Sultaun's second son commanded at the southern face, and ordered with the utmost consternation the Mysoor gates to be shut; the proper persons were not to be found for upwards of half an hour. The remainder of the night was employed by the English in connecting the acquisitions of the day with the former approaches, and on account of the advanced position and imperfect cover, the troops who, according to ordinary detail, would have returned to camp, remained as a double guard to the trenches.

The circular work however alternately gained and lost had not been retained by the besiegers, and during the night was re-occupied in great force by the enemy. From this work, and from some ruins and other cover in the vicinity, and under its protection, the flanking musquetry of the enemy became so galling at day-break of the 27th, that it became a serious question whether the English troops would be able to maintain a position which had already cost so many brave men to acquire. The Commander-in-Chief, who had a distinct view of the whole from the more elevated ground, and perceived at once the critical situation of the troops, and the essential importance of holding the position, gave peremptory orders that it should be held to the last extremity, and that the enemy should, at whatever risk, be instantly dislodged from the circular work, and ruined buildings; an operation which must necessarily be performed under the whole fire of the fort, distant only three hundred and eighty yards, as well as of the exterior musquetry and rockets. Colonel Wallace was charged with the execution of this most critical and dangerous service, which he performed with distinguished gallantry and success. After seizing the circular work, and effecting a lodgment behind it, he found his position still annoyed from the ruins; and detached Major Skelly to dislodge the enemy, and establish himself in the cover which they afforded; this operation was effected with similar decision and success; both of the posts were formed on the ensuing night into strong and regular posts, and the advanced parallel was now perfectly secured against all ordinary molestation from its right, and the progress in every other quarter enabled General Harris to look with renewed confidence to the farther operations of the siege.

It was impossible that the dark obstinacy of the Sultaun's mind, the flattery of juvenile expectants, by whom he loved to be surrounded, in preference to the experienced and the brave, or even the apathy of the fatalist, could be any longer blind to the rapid approach of the last moment, in which negotiation could avail. The religion which he revered, as well as that which he had cruelly persecuted, were equally invoked; the moolla and the bramin were equally bribed to interpose their prayers for his deliverance, his own attendance at the mosque was frequent, and his devotions impressive, and he intreated the fervent *amen* of his attendants to his earnest and reiterated prayers; the vain science of every sect was put in requisition, to examine the influence of the planets, and interpret their imaginary decision. To all, the period for delusion appeared to have ceased, and all announced extremity of peril.

Driven on the 27th from his last exterior line of defence, the Sultaun appears for a moment to have perceived the true character of the approaching crisis; and with a mind half reconciled to terms which he hoped would be less humiliating than those announced on the 22d, and a still more anxious desire for deception and delay, he addressed a letter to General Harris, stating, that he was about to send embassadors to adjust the points at issue: to which the General immediately replied, that however justified by his non-compliance with the terms offered on the 22d, and by the subsequent change of circumstances, in extending those demands, the allies were disposed to evince their moderation, by still adhering to the conditions of that date, but that he would receive no embassadors, unless accompanied by the hostages and the treasure; and finally, that these conditions were open to his assent, under his seal and signature, until three o'clock on the morrow, and no longer: under the condition also that the hostages and treasure should reach the English camp before noon on the ensuing day.

After the Sultaun's perusal of this reply, mixed indications rather of grief than rage, finally subsided into a silent stupor, from which he seldom seemed to wake, except for the purpose of affecting a confidence, by which no one was deceived, that the capital could not be taken. But no trace was evinced of those active energies of mind and body, by which alone such a confidence could be reasonably supported: the enemy had sufficiently indicated, not indeed the precise spot, but the near vicinity of the spot in which their breaches would be effected, and the most judicious of his officers had suggested to him the obvious operation of cutting off the whole angle, by a retrenchment of easy execution. He listened in silence while it was contended by the flatterers, that there was every where a second rampart, to which the enemy could not ascend, and that it would be impracticable for them to pass along the exterior rampart, while the interior should be lined with musquetry: it was rejoined, that the interior rampart could not singly be relied on, from its being completely enfiladed; that the proposed retrenchment would check the heads of the assailing columns, and support whatever flanking fire could be brought into operation, and that it did not diminish, but encrease the means of defence on which the opposite party relied, besides providing for subsequent resistance in the event of the two ramparts being carried. But it was all deliberation and no decision; this essential work was not attempted, and the Sultaun even relaxed in that personal inspection which he had hitherto practised, as if desirous to hide from his own observation, the extent and imminence of his danger.

In the meanwhile, the approaches and breaching batteries of the besiegers were rapidly advancing; and when completed, the true point of attack being concealed till the latest possible moment, the fire was chiefly directed against those works which had the power of flanking the future breach, and the passage of the river. A stone glacis, affording very imperfect cover, which ran along the northern face, extended round the western extremity, but terminated at the south-western face of the angle bastion; whence there was no other cover than the mere retaining wall of the counterscarp which was much lower than the crest of the glacis, and afforded a full view of the fausse braye and rampart. Over the angular bastion towered a large cavalier, which had been long silenced, but appeared to contain a small interior retrenchment, where a few men were occasionally observed.

May 2. It was not until the morning of the 2d of May that the batteries, after having previously destroyed the shoulder of the angle bastion, began to form the breach about sixty yards to the south-east of that work. On that day the fausse braye was com-
3. pletely breached, and on the 3d the rampart was in the same condition; the breach was reported practicable; the river had been forded in the night; it was ascertained that the descent into the ditch from the retaining wall of the counterscarp was only seven feet: that the ditch itself was fordable; that the rubbish of the rampart and fausse braye formed an irregular but continued slope from the ditch to the summit of the rampart; and means to accompany the assault were provided for the descent from the counterscarp into the ditch.

The troops destined for the assault were placed in the trenches before day-break on the 4th; the command of the assault was committed to Major-General Baird, and the troops were disposed into two columns, the right under Colonel Sherbrooke, and the left under Colonel Dunlop, which were to issue together from the trenches, and after surmounting the breach to wheel to the right and left, and after carrying the rampart, and occupying such works as might be expedient, were to meet on the eastern face of the rampart, and there be guided by circumstances. The Honourable Colonel Wellesley commanded a powerful reserve. All these arrangements having been previously directed, the troops, amounting to 4376 men, silently took their appointed stations in the trench.

The intermediate military conduct of the Sultaun may furnish some aid to a just estimation of his character. On the day of General Harris's ultimate encampment before the place, the Sultaun caused a small tent to be pitched for his personal accommodation, on a large cavalier, on the south face, whence he directed the early operations, which have been described; when General Stuart passed the river to the northward, the Sultaun moved his head-quarters (where all reports were ordered to be made), to the western angle, whence he superintended the efforts made to dislodge that army from its northern position. On the opening of the first batteries, he removed from this exposed situation, and fixed his head-quarters in the northern face (on which, from its construction, the enfilade was less extensive than on the south western), in an apartment formed by an old gateway, which had for some years been closed by an exterior revetment. The troops on duty at the several works, were regularly relieved; but the general charge of the angle attacked was committed to Seyed Saheb, assisted by Seyed Ghoffâr, an officer of a provincial corps of English sepoys, taken with Colonel Brathwaite, who subsequently entered into the Sultaun's army, and became a zealous and able servant of his new master. The large cavalier behind the angle

CHAP. XLVII. 1799.

bastion, was committed to Monsieur Chapuis. The Sultaun's eldest son, with Poornea, commanded a detached corps to disturb the northern attack; his second son commanded the Mysoor gate, and southern face; and Kummer-u-Deen was absent, watching General Floyd. Among his own personal staff and attendants, it has been observed, that there was not one man of professional character. He fancied, the attachment of men raised by his own favour, to be more genuine and sincere, than the support of persons possessing established character and high pretensions; and whenever a report was made of the alarming progress of the besiegers, these ignorant sycophants affected to ascribe it to fear. Seyed Ghoffàr was early in the siege wounded in the hand, but did not confine himself. He saw distinctly what was to happen; "he is surrounded (said this excellent officer) by boys and flatterers, who will not even let him see with his own eyes. I do not wish to survive the result. I am going about in search of death, and cannot find it." In the forenoon of the 4th of May, he saw in common with other experienced observers, that the trenches were unusually crowded, and concluded that the assault was about to be given; nothing could persuade the Sultaun and his flatterers, that the enemy would dare the attempt by day-light, and the kelledar, Nedeem, one of the new men, was so grossly ignorant and destitute of all reflection, as to make an issue of pay to some of the troops on duty, which caused their absence at the moment of assault; the Sultaun, however, in reply to the report from Seyed Ghoffâr, said it was proper to be alert, but that the assault would be given at night; meanwhile that officer had satisfied himself by farther observation, that an hour would not elapse before it should commence, and in a state of rage and despair hurried towards the Sultaun: "I will go (said he) and drag him to the breach, and make him see by what a set of wretches he is surrounded; I will compel him to exert himself at this last moment." He was going, and met a party of pioneers, whom he had long looked for in vain, to cut off the approach by the southern rampart, "I must first (said he) shew these people the work they have to do," and in the act of giving his instructions, was killed by a cannon shot.

In the meanwhile, Tippoo, as if despairing of human aid, was seeking those delusive means of penetrating into futurity, so familiar in the history of every country, and of even engaging supernatural aid, through the incantations of the bramins, from whom he had merited the most earnest prayers for his destruction. The Jebbum, at an enormous expence, was in progress; and the learning and sanctity of the high-priest at Cenapatam, was farther propitiated by costly offerings. The Sultaun, in his early youth, treated with derision the science of astrology, and various statements are given regarding the completion of the particular prediction, which made him a convert to its reality; but it must have preceded the marriage of his son to the daughter of the Bebee of Cannanore, and his discoveries at Coimbetoor, in 1789, which he relates with considerable ostentation of his own proficiency in the science. Either from chance, or from right judgment respecting objects more real than those of their pretended science, the astrologers had exhibited to the Sultaun a set of diagrams from which they gravely inferred, that as long as Mars should remain within a particular circle, the fort would hold out; he would touch the limit on the last day of the lunar month, the 4th of May, and on that day they dared only to recommend, that the Sultaun should present the prescribed oblations, for averting a calamity: which oblations were ordered to be prepared on the 3d of May. On the morning of the 4th, about nine o'clock, he proceeded to the palace, bathed, and presented the oblation, through the high-priest above-mentioned, with the customary formalities; and with the farther solemnity of attempting to ascertain the aspect of his fortunes by the form of his face reflected from the surface of a jar of oil, which constituted a part of the oblation; a result depending on mechanical causes, by which the reflection of any face may be formed to any fortune.

Having finished these ceremonies about the hour of noon, he returned to his accustomed station, and shortly afterwards ordered his usual mid-day repast, when intelligence was brought of the death of Seyed Ghoffâr: he was greatly agitated at this event, but gave the proper orders in consequence; and sat down to his repast, which he had scarcely finished when a report was made to him of the actual assault, and he hastened to the breach along the northern rampart.

CHAPTER XLVIII.

Selection of the hour of assault — Awful expectation — Brilliant opening — Breach carried — Right column succeeds rapidly — Left more slowly — The Sultaun in person — retires to the interior fort — Motives uncertain — Falls — Seyed Saheb — Proceedings at the palace — Major Allan — The princes — received by General Baird — sent to camp — Sultaun's fate still unknown — found at length — identified — Funeral solemnities — General Orders — Lieutenant-Colonel Close — Fall of the Sultaun, a relief from some embarrassing questions — Eldest son surrenders — all the principal officers — Poornea — Dhoondia — General Harris marches to the northward — Peaceable submission of the whole country — Characters of Hyder and Tippoo contrasted — Commission for the affairs of Mysoor — Principles which guided their decisions – Right of conquest — Claims of humanity — Suggestions of policy — Central government to be formed — Conflicting claims of the ancient and late family — discussed — Determination to restore the ancient Hindoo house of Mysoor — Relation of the new state to the British Government — distinguished from all preceding arrangements — The experiment successful — Wisdom of considering its farther application.

CHAP. XLVIII. 1799.

Although General Harris had ordered the troops destined for the assault to be placed in their appointed stations before daylight on the 4th of May, this arrangement was made for the purpose of eluding observation. The breach was reported to be perfectly practicable on the evening of the 3d, but he was desirous that the forenoon should be employed in extending its breadth; in taking off any remaining defences; and in destroying any repairs which the besieged might have effected during the night; and he was farther induced to fix on the hour of one, as that at which, from the known habits of the natives regarding refreshment and repose, they would be the least prepared to expect him.

The state of silent and awful expectation, in the trenches, and throughout the army, as the expected hour approached, may be more easily imagined than described. The distinguished officer appointed to lead the assault beheld those walls, within which he had himself been immured in irons, during a tedious imprisonment of nearly four years; the faithless captivity and secret massacre of his countrymen were unhappily known to him from no borrowed sources, and the prospect of avenging the wrongs which he had witnessed and partaken, and of terminating, in one short hour, the future possibility of every similar outrage, formed a mass of reflections and of motives capable of rousing to the highest pitch of animation, a less ardent spirit than that of Major-General Baird. Within a few minutes of one, he sent round to the corps composing the assault, to be ready at an instant's warning, and when the precise moment had arrived, he ascended the parapet of the trench, in full view of both armies; a military figure suited to such an occasion; and with an energy and animation not to be surpassed, drawing his sword, and addressing the soldiers in a tone which thrilled along the trenches, he desired them to "follow him, and prove themselves worthy of the name of British soldiers." A small but gallant band of Mysoreans met the forlorn hope on the slope of the breach, the greater portion of both fell in the struggle; but in less than seven minutes from the period of issuing from the trenches, the British colours were planted on the summit of the breach. To the great surprise of the assailants, a deep and apparently impassable ditch was interposed, between the rampart they had surmounted, and the great cavalier which overlooked the breach, and formed a portion of the interior line of defence; and two discharges of grape from the retrenchment in that work, had fallen heavily among the approaching columns: but the opposition ceased on their farther progress.

As soon as the assailants had ascended in sufficient force they wheeled in obedience to orders, to the right and left; General Baird himself accompanying the right attack. Three cavaliers, from which serious resistance, was apprehended, were fortunately abandoned, as the column proceeded along the rampart, from the apprehension of their retreat being cut off: a subaltern of the Scotch brigade, Lieutenant Molle, having peculiarly distinguished himself by preceding the head of the column, at the distance of several yards, pressing, with the utmost animation for the first of the cavaliers, and singly displaying to the assailants, and to the whole army, the actual possession of that important work. General Baird, after occupying these and other necessary points; arrived without much serious loss, after surmounting the breach, in less than an hour at the portion of the rampart, over the eastern gateway.

The left hand column had not been so rapid in its progress. Lieutenant-Colonel Dunlop was seriously wounded in a personal conflict with one of the Mysorean chiefs at the summit of the breach; and as the column advanced, a succession of well-constructed traverses along the northern rampart, presented the most formidable resistance. It was the Sultaun himself who animated their exertions, and had passed the nearest traverse just as the left column began to advance from the breach, the resistance in front was most powerfully seconded by the flanking musquetry of the inner rampart. All the commissioned officers attached to the leading companies, were soon either killed or disabled. Lieutenant Farquhar, of the pioneers, attempted to lead them ,and was instantly killed. Captain Lambton, Brigade-Major to Major-General Baird, next placed himself at their head; and at that moment obtained a support which facilitated all the subsequent operations.

On reaching the summit of the breach, and discovering the ditch interposed between the exterior and interior ramparts; General Baird had ordered every possible effort to be made for effecting the passage; a narrow strip of the terreplein, left for the passage of the workmen, employed in the excavation of the ditch, was discovered by a detachment of the 12th. The passage of the ditch, and the ascent of the inner rampart of the south-western face, were effected by mere climbing, without material opposition; that face of the inner rampart having to the last moment been scoured by a perfect and destructive enfilade, which had greatly facilitated the operations of the right attack. On reaching the summit of the inner rampart, this detachment turned to the left, got possession of the western cavalier, and then proceeded to attack in flank the defenders of the interior northern rampart, who fled before them. At the instant of Brigade-Major Lambton's putting himself at the head of the left attack, this detachment of the 12th pushing along the inner rampart, were approaching the flank of the traverse, defended by the Sultaun; and the defenders, instead of the assailants now became exposed to the destructive effects of a flanking fire. Brigade-

Major Lambton, thus supported, urged the attack with the greatest animation; the two parallel columns on the outer and inner ramparts, preserving their proper relative positions, rapidly gained ground, and the Mysoreans reluctantly abandoned every successive traverse, until in addition to the front and flanking fire which has been described, they arrived at a part of the rampart whence they distinctly perceived the troops of the right attack already arrived over the eastern gateway, and ready if necessary to fall on their rear; from that moment all confidence was lost, and the confusion became irreparable. A principal passage was near, from the outer to the inner rampart, and through a regular gateway in that work to the body of the place; the troops began to escape, some in that direction, some over the ramparts, and a large portion by the water-gate which led to the river. The Sultaun had received a slight wound and mounted his horse a few minutes before this occurrence; if an attempt at flight had been his object, the water-gate was near, and his escape was more than possible; he took the direction of the body of the place through the gateway of the interior work, with intentions, which can only be conjectured, and were not perhaps distinctly formed in his own mind; the most sanguine hope could only have led to an honourable capitulation in the palace; to close the gate of the interior rampart, if practicable, would have been unavailing for the purpose of defending the inner fort; for these works were no longer defensible after General Baird had passed the point of their junction: and the rampart which he now occupied was itself a part of the interior work. Among the conjectures of those who were chiefly admitted to the Sultaun's intimacy, in the last days of his existence was one founded on obscure hints which had escaped him, of the intention to destroy certain papers, to put to death his principal women, and to die in defence of the palace. He was destined to a fall more obscure and unnoticed; no individual among the assailants was aware of his presence on the northern rampart, and he was entirely undistinguished in the ultimate mass of fugitives: before he reached the gate, he had received a second wound, but did not fall. Fugitives from the body of the place, as well as the exterior rampart were crowding in opposite directions, and with various intentions towards this gate; the detachment of the 12th had descended into the body of the place, for the purpose of arresting the progress of the great mass passing through the gate from the exterior works, to the interior of the place; and the two columns of the assailants were now directing a destructive fire by regular platoons, into each side of the arch. In attempting to pass through, the Sultaun received a third wound from the interior detachment, his horse was at the same instant brought down, and his faithful attendants perceiving his situation, placed him in his palankeen, but the space became so crowded, and choaked up by the dead and dying, that it was impossible to remove him; and he appeared to have afterwards moved out of the palankeen. While in this situation, some English soldiers entered the gateway, and a personal attendant proposed that he should make himself known for the preservation of his life. The Sultaun either suspected an opposite result from such a disclosure, or determined not to be so preserved; and peremptorily forbad it; but one of the soldiers attempting to seize his sword belt, the Sultaun almost fainting from his wounds, seized a sword which lay near him, and made a desperate cut at the soldier, who shot him through the temple, and he instantly expired.

Major Lambton, with the left attack, had meanwhile, in obedience to the general instructions of the day, proceeded without farther opposition along the northern rampart, and joined Major-General Baird over the eastern gate-way. No intelligence had been received of the Sultaun, nor was any suspicion entertained of his actual fate. Three officers of the general staff, Majors Allan, Beatson, and Dallas, observed as they passed along the rampart, two men lying desperately wounded near the inner ditch, one of whom, by his dress and complexion, appeared to be of distinction; and they descended for the purpose of more particular examination. It was not the Sultaun; but Major Dallas recognised and addressed him by his name — *Seyed Saheb.* He was supported in his attempt to rise, and clung round Major Dallas's knees in the most affecting manner, imploring compassion for himself, and for the honour of his family. The officers were in the act of placing him in his palankeen, which had tumbled into the ditch, and had sent for a surgeon to dress his wounds, when a renewal of a heavy fire of musquetry compelled them to attend to other duties, and he soon afterwards expired.

The same officers, proceeding along the southern works, ascended a cavalier, which overlooked some part of the interior area of the palace, and perceived indications which induced them to infer the presence of the Sultaun, which Seyed Saheb had previously assured them to be probable; and reported these observations to General Baird, who had also received similar information, and had halted to refresh the troops, and complete all his dispositions on the ramparts, before he should proceed to summon the palace. These preparatory measures being effected, he requested Major Allan, Deputy Quarter-master-general, to undertake the important charge of proceeding with a flag of truce to the palace, to offer protection to Tippoo Sultaun, and every person within it, on the condition of immediate and unconditional surrender, and to declare, that in the event of the slightest resistance, they must all abide the worst consequences of an assault. A part of the 33d was already drawn up before the gate of the palace, and Major Allan was accompanied by a portion of the 12th, and a battalion of sepoys, while General Baird prepared the flank companies, now somewhat recovered from their fatigues, and the heat of a most oppressive day, to execute, if it should be necessary, the final alternative which he had announced.

Major Allan executed the delicate charge committed to his discretion with distinguished humanity and judgment. He found the attendants of the palace exhibiting from a front balcony, marks of the utmost consternation; and on his invitation, some of them descended by an unfinished part of the wall. There was an obvious wish for delay, which Major Allan strongly deprecated as pregnant with inevitable destruction. He insisted on returning with them, and giving personally to the Sultaun the assurances with which he was charged; and he ascended, accompanied by two officers * only. Before entering the palace, he explained that the flag which he held in his hand was a pledge of security; and farther to conciliate their confidence, he took off his sword and insisted on committing it to the charge of the Kel-

* Captain Hastings Fraser and Captain Schohey.

ledar, who was one of the persons that had descended. The aspect of many hundred troops in the courts which he afterwards passed, rendered the situation critical; but neither encreased nor diminished the danger arising from one person out of three being unarmed. After many hesitations, which had nearly exhausted his patience, he was at length conducted to an apartment, where he was received by two of the Sultaun's sons, one of whom he recognised as one of the hostages of 1792. After such assurances of personal safety and protection to every person within the walls, as the feelings of an honourable and humane mind suggested on such an occasion, his great object was to impress on their attention as the sole means of preserving their father's life, whose escape was impossible, the necessity of his immediate surrender. They assured him that the Sultaun was not in the palace; many unnecessary impediments were made to the opening of the gate; and their objection of not daring to sanction the measure, without their father's order, seems to indicate their belief at that moment that he was still alive. They were at length convinced that the measure was necessary to their own security, and gave a fearful assent.

Major Allan on opening the gate found a large body of troops drawn up, with General Baird at their head; that officer had in the intermediate time received unquestionable information of the secret massacre of every European prisoner taken during the siege*; his indignation was raised to the highest pitch; the soldiers in the ranks, half frantic with rage, and burning to exact a memorable retribution, could in their present tem-

* On the ensuing day the fact was ascertained beyond all question by the exhumation of the bodies.

CHAP. XLVIII. 1799.

per, scarcely have been admitted with safety within tne gates of the palace; and General Baird, instead of immediately entering, ordered the princes to be brought out to him; this also was attended with many terrors and considerable delay, but every feeling of indignation subsided on their appearance, he was sensibly affected at their approach, and his gallantry during the assault, was not more distinguished than the humanity and kindness which he displayed on this occasion. He ordered that they should be conveyed under a proper escort, with suitable honours from the troops, to the Commander-in-chief: and no intelligence having yet been received of the Sultaun, General Baird proceeded, properly attended, to search the palace, (which had been surrounded to prevent escape) avoiding of course, the apartments of the women. All search being found unavailing, the kelledar was apprised of the serious consequences to himself, which might ensue, in the event of his any longer refusing to disclose the place of the Sultaun's concealment. At what period he was himself informed, has not been distinctly ascertained, but he at length described the spot where he understood him to have fallen, wounded only as he then supposed. General Baird personally proceeded to the gateway, which exhibited a horrible picture; it was already night, but the political importance of ascertaining the fact, rendered it necessary to cause the bodies, heaped in mass over each other, to be separately removed for examination by torch-light; the only man alive in the gateway, saved from suffocation by getting under the palankeen, was the personal attendant to whom we have already adverted, and on being informed of the object of search, he pointed out the spot where the Sultaun lay. The body on being brought out, was immediately recognised by the kelledar and several others, and being placed in a palankeen, was conveyed to the palace, where its identity was satisfactorily ascertained by the unanimous testimony of all the domestics.

The Sultaun's second son who commanded the southern face, had escaped by the Mysoor gate in the confusion of the storm, and surrendered himself on the ensuing morning. He, as well as the younger brothers, were received with distinguished consideration by General Harris, and the motives for their first removal no longer existing, they were invited to return to their respective apartments in the palace: the brutal apathy of the elder, on viewing his father's body, and the affecting indications of grief exhibited by the two younger sons, marked a singular contrast of character; but both added to the evidence, if any had still been wanting, of the unquestionable identity of the body; and orders were immediately given for its interment on the same evening, at the particular request of his sons, and under the immediate direction of the Cauzee of Seringapatam. May 5.

His remains were deposited near those of his father, in the superb mausoleum of the Lâll Baug, with all the splendour and distinction which the religious observance of Mahommedan rites, and the military honours of European sepulture could bestow. Peals of thunder terrific * and extraordinary even † in this district, burst over the Island of Seringapatam immediately after

* Two officers and several men were killed in camp.

† I have repeatedly marked, from the adjacent heights, the course of the thunder clouds; there seemed to be a distinct tendency to burst over the island of Seringapatam and its immediate vicinity; and I do not think that imagination had any thing to do with this remark.

CHAP. XLVIII. 1799. the funeral; and the wanderings of a pious imagination might innocently deem this awful close intended to mark the termination of the ceremony, and the memory of the scene.

The general orders and official reports of the Commander-in-Chief, and the recorded applause of the Governor-General on the occasion of this memorable conquest, constitute at once the most authentic and interesting evidence of the personal merit which was deemed most worthy of applause. These documents are subjoined in an Appendix for the satisfaction of the reader *, who will not fail to remark the prominent place assigned in this distinguished list to the Adjutant-General of the army, Lieutenant-Colonel Close †, whose eulogium echoed the feelings of every heart, for his extraordinary services had been obvious to the daily and hourly notice of every officer and soldier.

The fall of the Sultaun relieved the Governor-General from the embarrassment of determining the future treatment to be assigned to his expected prisoner; of reconciling compassion to the fallen, with indignation against recent and wanton murder; and, of forgetting the crimes of his captive, in the sense of what he owed to his own dignity. General Harris was equally relieved from every immediate care, excepting the security and consolidation of his conquest and its dependencies, by the surrender of Poornea, Kummer-u-Deen, and Futteh Hyder, the Sultaun's eldest son; with nearly all the principal officers, civil

May 14.

* Appendix at the end of the volume.

† Afterwards Major-General Sir Barry Close, now unhappily no more!

and military; and by the useful aid derived from the first of these persons, in suggesting a variety of practical details, for the proper disposal of the wreck of Tippoo Sultaun's army. Dhoondia, the prisoner, whose singular history has already been noticed, had, in a few days, already collected a band of desperate freebooters, troublesome, rather than formidable, except as regarded their encreasing numbers; and General Harris, after making a proper provision for the care of the capital, and committing its command to the Honourable Colonel Wellesley, found it expedient to move the army to the northward, whence these audacious banditti were dislodged, after considerable resistance; the principal posts were occupied in an adequate manner; and the territories of the fallen Sultaun peaceably submitted to the future decision of the victors.

Thus terminated a dynasty composed only of two Sovereigns, the first of whom had risen from obscurity to imperial power, and the last, educated as a Prince, had fallen in the defence of an hereditary crown: resembling in some of the circumstances of its close, the fate of the Roman capital of the Eastern empire: substituting, like that catastrophe, in place of the fallen dynasty, not only the power of a new Sovereign, but the influence of a new race; yet exhibiting the marked contrast, of kindling, not quenching in its fall, the lights of science and civilization.

The characters of Hyder and Tippoo have been developed in the narrative of their conduct with a degree of detail which might have rendered a distinct delineation unnecessary, but a sketch of both, for the purposes of recapitulation and contrast, may still be acceptable and useful.

Hyder Aly Khân was born in 1722, and died in 1782, having

lived nearly sixty-one years, and reigned near twenty-two. In person he was tall and robust ; his neck was long, and his shoulders were broad : in his youth he was peculiarly active, in later years disposed to corpulence : for a native of Ìndia, inclining to a complexion fair and florid. With a prominent and rather aquiline nose, and small eyes, there was in his countenance a mixture of sternness and gentleness ; but the leading impression on the minds of those who describe it, was that of terror ; an inference resulting perhaps as much from experience as from physiognomy. His voice was mellow and musical, and on ordinary occasions, he spoke in a subdued tone. In dress he exhibited rather an extravagant mixture of the soldier and the fop ; a turban of brilliant scarlet, projecting by means of a cane frame, and almost overshadowing his shoulders, was the great peculiarity of his dress ; and it has been stated, perhaps without much exaggeration, that one hundred cubits of fine turban* web were rolled up in its various involutions. The other parts of his dress were (excepting in the field) studiously splendid, and he delighted to see his public officers magnificently attired. His toilet was performed in the manner of the bramins, his eyebrows and whiskers being shaved away, or the hairs pulled out, so as to leave a line scarcely visible.

He was fond of show and parade, and on great occasions was attended by a retinue of one thousand spearmen splendidly clothed and armed, preceded by bards, who sung his exploits in the Canarese language.

He was a bold and skilful horseman, and delighted chiefly in that simple mode of conveyance. His efficiency as a swordsman

* Dustár è sed dusta ber ser è mobâric mê bust. A phrase found in two or three of the manuscript histories of Hyder.

was highly estimated in his youth; and as a marksman he was perhaps unrivalled. It was scarcely ever known that his ball missed the mark; and volunteers engaged in single combat with the royal tiger in the public shews, confident of being preserved in the last extremity by the fusil of Hyder, from the balcony.

He could neither read nor write any language; but exclusively of Hindostanee, his mother tongue, he spoke with entire fluency the Canarese, Mahratta, Telegoo, and Tamul languages. Of the Persic or Arabic he had no knowledge whatever; and the sum of his literary attainments consisted in learning to write the initial of his own name, *H.*, to serve as his signature on public occasions; but either from inaptitude to learn, or for the purpose of originality, he inverted its form ʒ instead of ح Unlearned, in the ordinary acceptation of the term, he formed his mind upon a broad experience and sagacious observation of mankind, whom, in the actual scene on which he moved, he generally trusted as they deserved, to the precise extent to which they could not deceive; with ostensible frankness, and perpetual suspicion: and in the few instances of a more liberal confidence, his penetration was once, and but once, deceived, in Kundè Row.

He possessed the talent ascribed to some other eminent men, and perhaps to all with some exaggeration, of attending to several subjects at once; dictating to a moonshee, hearing and answering the report of a spy, and following the recital of a complex account, at one and the same time, and giving to each individual his appropriate instruction.

A harem of six hundred women might seem to constitute in itself evidence of the absence of particular attachment; if numerous examples, and among others, that of Nizam Ali, had not exhibited the mental thraldom exacted by an individual of the groupe. But Hyder, in his intercourse with the harem, had no feeling distinct from animal instinct. To a person who should exclusively have observed this part of his character, his whole soul would have seemed absorbed in a passion to which he brought no portion of mind; the animal, not the man, was sunk in sensuality; the mind was never permitted to wander from the most rigid attention to public business; every thing was examined both in abstract and detail, and no business was ever delayed from the indolence or self-indulgence of the sovereign. From sun-rise till past the noon, he was occupied in public durbar; he then made his first meal, and retired to rest for an hour or two. In the evening, he either rode out, or returned to business, in which he continued to be engaged till near midnight, when he made his second meal; sometimes drank largely, but secretly, of European liquors, and retired to rest.

Of his temper as of his countenance, he possessed the most disciplined command; his apparent bursts of anger were not the effect of mental disturbance, but of the alleged necessity of ruling with a sceptre of iron; and keeping for ever present the terror of his power. In an humble sphere, he would probably have been deemed a man of wit, but he tempered a natural facetiousness with the gravity belonging to his exalted station; and though reserved from a sense of propriety and from habit, no person could relax more agreeably in social intercourse, and even in public audience; but on ordinary occasions, the principle of terror was ever predominant; and he sunk from dignity to inspire fear. On occasions apparently trivial, he would pour forth a torrent of that obscene abuse, in which he excelled, on persons of whatever rank; and there were, moreover, in his whole court, perhaps, not six persons who had not, on some one occasion, sustained the actual lash of the côrla (long whip.) The same use of the tongue and whip in his subordinate officers, recommended them to his notice as zealous servants, exercising an efficient command; and it was a common trick of Aboo Mahommed, his chief chôbdâr, when his master appeared displeased at some supposed relaxation, (or as he chose to interpret, was in ill temper,) to bring him into good humour, by the sound of the côrla at the gate, and the cries of an innocent sufferer, seized casually in the street for the purpose. On the conquest of a new country, it was his invariable habit to inflict some memorable severities, not only for the purpose of extorting money, but with the avowed object of impressing his new subjects with a salutary terror of his name. On the same avowed principle, of inspiring terror into all descriptions of men, whether absent or present, he availed himself of a police too horribly perfect, to punish with boundless cruelty, the slightest levity of observation, made in the confidence and seclusion of domestic intercourse, that had any reference to his public or private conduct: and thus, where it was worse than death to blame, unqualified applause became the necessary habit of public and of private life.

In spite of this reputation, and the notorious system of exaction and torture applied to every individual who had to render an account; men of almost every country were attracted to his court and standard, by brilliant prospects of advancement and wealth; but a person, once engaged in his service, and deemed to be worth keeping, was a prisoner for life; he would hear of

CHAP. XLVIII. 1799. no home but his own standard, and suffered no return; but the summary severity, cruelty, and injustice of his character were directed rather to the instruments than the objects of his rule; official men had cause to tremble; but the mass of the population felt that the vigour of the government compensated for many ills, and rendered their condition comparatively safe.

In action, Hyder was cool and deliberate, but enterprising and brave when the occasion demanded. In his early career, and in his wars with the native powers, he was far from sparing of his person, but opposed to Europeans, it was observed that he never personally encountered the heat of action. His military pretensions are more favourably viewed in the conduct of a campaign than of a battle; and if the distinction can be allowed, in the political, than in the military conduct of a war. In the attack and defence of places he and his son were equally unskilled; because in that branch of war, no experience can compensate for want of science.

In council he had no adviser, and no confidant; he encouraged, on all occasions, a free discussion of every measure suggested by himself or by others, but no person knew at its close, what measures he would adopt in consequence.

Hyder was of all Mahommedan princes the most tolerant, if, indeed, he is himself to be considered as a Mussulman. He neither practised, nor had ever been instructed how to practise, the usual forms of prayer, the fasts, and other observances. He had a small rosary, on which he had been taught to enumerate a few of the attributes of God, and this was the whole of his exterior religion. It was his avowed and public opinion, that all religions proceed from God, and are all equal in the sight of

God; and it is certain, that the mediatory power represented by *Runga Sawmey*, the great idol in the temple of Seringapatam, had as much, if not more of his respect, than all the Imaums, with Mahommed at their head. CHAP. XLVIII. 1799.

In common with all Sovereigns who have risen from obscurity to a throne, Hyder waded through crimes to his object; but they never exceeded the removal of real impediments, and he never achieved through blood what fraud was capable of effecting. He fixed his stedfast view upon the end, and considered simply the efficiency, and never the moral tendency of the means. If he was cruel and unfeeling, it was for the promotion of his objects, and never for the gratification of anger or revenge. If he was ever liberal, it was because liberality exalted his character and augmented his power; if he was ever merciful, it was in those cases where the reputation of mercy promoted future submission. His European prisoners were in irons, because they were otherwise deemed unmanageable; they were scantily fed, because that was economical; there was little distinction of rank, because that would have been expensive: but beyond these simply interested views, there was by his authority no wanton severity; there was no compassion, but there was no resentment; it was a political expenditure, for a political purpose, and there was no passion, good or bad, to disturb the balance of the account. He carried merciless devastation into an enemy's country, and even to his own, but never beyond the reputed utility of the case: he sent the inhabitants into captivity, because it injured the enemy's country, and benefited his own. The misery of the individuals was no part of the consideration, and the death of the greater portion still left a residue, to swell a scanty population. With an equal absence of feeling, he caused forcible emigrations from one province to another, because he deemed it the best cure for rebellion; and he converted the male children into military slaves, because he expected them to improve the quality of his army. He gave fair, and occasionally brilliant encouragement, to the active and aspiring among his servants, so long as liberality proved an incitement to exertion, and he robbed and tortured them, without gratitude or compunction, when no farther services were expected: it was on account of profit and loss, and a calculation whether it were most beneficial to employ or to plunder them.

Those brilliant and equivocal virtues which gild the crimes of other conquerors, were utterly unknown to the breast of Hyder. No admiration of bravery in resistance, or of fortitude in the fallen, ever excited sympathy, or softened the cold calculating decision of their fate. No contempt for unmanly submission ever aggravated the treatment of the abject and the mean. Every thing was weighed in the balance of utility, and no grain of human feeling, no breath of virtue or of vice was permitted to incline the beam.

There was one solitary example of feelings incident to our nature, affection for an unworthy son, whom he nominated to be his successor, while uniformly, earnestly, and broadly predicting, that this son would lose the empire which he himself had gained.

Tippoo Sultaun was born in 1753 *, and died in 1799, in his

* It is singular that there should be any doubt regarding his age, at the time of his death. By a genealogical tree, in my possession, prepared, as I conclude, from the records of the palace, by the English officer charged with the immediate care of the family, he was fifty and a quarter years by the Girrà, at the time

forty-seventh year, having reigned seventeen years and four months. In person, he was neither so tall nor so robust as his father, and had a short pursy neck; the large limbs, small eyes, aquiline nose, and fair complexion of Hyder, marked the Arabic character derived from his mother. Tippoo's singularly small and delicate hands and feet, his large and full eyes, a nose, less prominent, and a much darker complexion, were all national characteristics of the Indian form. There was in the first view of his countenance, an appearance of dignity which wore off on farther observation; and his subjects did not feel that it inspired the terror or respect, which in common with his father, he desired to command. Hyder's lapse from dignity into low and vulgar scolding, was among the few points of imitation or resemblance, but in one it inspired fear, in the other ridicule. In most instances exhibiting a contrast to the character and manners of his father, he spoke in a loud and unharmonious tone of voice: he was extremely garrulous, and, on superficial subjects, delivered his sentiments with plausibility. In exterior appearance, he affected the soldier; in his toilet, the distinctive habits of the Mussulman; he thought hardiness to be indicated by a plain unincumbered attire, which he equally exacted from those around him, and the long robe and trailing

of his death; of course lunar, as are all accounts so kept; this would make his age by the solar reckoning about forty-eight years and nine months, and the date of his birth about July 1750. Butcherow repeated to me the Canarese verse, recording his birth, in the year *Angeera*, 17th of the month *Margêser*, which would date his birth about January 1753, and his age at the time of his death, (as Butcherow, a confidential public officer, positively affirmed,) forty-six years and four months, solar reckoning. The first of these accounts can scarcely be correct; Hyder married, or was betrothed to the mother of Tippoo, in Coromandel, in 1750. Tippoo was certainly born at Deonhully, and Hyder did not return thither till 1751.

CHAP. XLVIII. 1799.

drawers were banished from his court. He had heard that some of the monarchs of antiquity marched on foot at the head of their armies, and he would sometimes affect a similar exhibition, with his musquet on his shoulder. But he was usually mounted, and attached great importance to horsemanship, in which he was considered to excel. The conveyance in a palankeen he derided, and in a great degree prohibited, even to the aged and infirm; but in all this tendency, there was as much of avarice as of taste. He was a minute reformer in every department, to the extent of abridging, with other expences of the palace, the fare of his own table, to the pleasures of which he was constitutionally indifferent; and even in the dress of his menial servants, he deemed respectable attire, to be a mark of unnecessary extravagance.

Of the vernacular languages, he spoke no other than Hindostanee and Canarese; but from a smattering in Persian literature, he considered himself as the first philosopher of the age. He spoke that language with fluency; but although the pen was for ever in his hand, he never attained either elegance or accuracy of style. The leading features of his character were vanity and arrogance; no human being was ever so handsome, so wise, so learned, or so brave as himself. Resting on the shallow instructions of his scanty reading, he neglected the practical study of mankind. No man had ever less penetration into character; and accordingly no prince was ever so ill served; the army alone remained faithful, in spite of all his efforts for the subversion of discipline and allegiance. Hyder delegated to his instruments a large portion of his own power, as the best means for its preservation. Tippoo seemed to feel every exercise of delegated authority as an usurpation of his own. He would familiarly say to the soldiers, if your officer gives you one word of abuse, return him two. The revolutionary doctrine of equality imported from France, scarcely appeared to be a novelty. No person ought to be of importance in a state but the Sovereign alone; all *other* men ought to be equal; the murder of the Sovereign was not an extraordinary incident in the history of any nation, and probably arose from laxity in command.

From constitutional or incidental * causes, he was less addicted than his father to the pleasures of the harem, which, however, contained at his death about one hundred persons.

From sun-rise until midnight he devoted his whole time to public affairs, with the interruptions necessary for meals, and for occasional exercise, seldom imitating his father's practice of a short repose in the heat of the day. But his occupation was not business: he was engaged in the invention of new machinery never finished, while the old was suffered to decay. His application was intense and incessant; he affected to do the whole of his own business, and to write with his own hand the foul draft of almost every dispatch, however unimportant; and he suffered the fate familiarly known to attach to that absurd pretension: the machine stood still, because the master would not let it work. A secret emissary had been sent to Poona, he reported, and reported, and represented that his cash was expended: after the lapse of several months, Tippoo delivered a foul draft to a secretary — let this be dispatched to A B, at Poona. Here I am said the emissary! he had returned for some weeks from

* Obstructio in urethra. One of the "vitia obscœnarum partium," which a medical friend tells me was unknown to Hippocrates, Galen, or Celsus.

CHAP. XLVIII. 1799. mere necessity: he had presented himself daily at the durbar, and could never before attract notice. The Sultaun for once hung down his head.

The ruling passion for innovation absorbed the proper hours for current business: and failures of experiment, obvious to the whole world, were the topics of his incessant boast as the highest efforts of human wisdom. Hyder was an improving monarch, and exhibited few innovations. Tippoo was an innovating monarch, and made no improvements. One had a sagacious and powerful mind; the other a feeble and unsteady intellect. "There was (says one of my manuscripts *) nothing of permanency in his views, no solidity in his councils, and no confidence on the part of the governed: all was innovation on his part, and the fear of farther novelty on the part of others; and the order of to-day was expected to be reversed by the invention of to-morrow. It may be affirmed of his principal measures however specious, that all had a direct tendency to injure the finances, undermine the Government, and oppress the people. All the world was puzzled what distinct character should be assigned to a sovereign who was never the same. He could neither be truly characterized as liberal or parsimonious; as tyrannical or benevolent; as a man of talents, or as destitute of parts. By turns, he assumed the character of each, In one object alone he appeared to be consistent, having perpetually on his tongue the projects of jehâd — holy war. The most intelligent and sincere well-wishers of the house concurred in the

* By the venerable Seyed Hussein, who, with most of the native authorities, mentioned in the preface to the first volume, have paid the debt of nature since I left Mysoor.

opinion of his father, that his heart and head were both defective, however covered by a plausible and imposing flow of words; and they were not always without suspicions of mental aberration."

Tippoo, like his father, admitted no associate in his councils: but, contrary to his father, he first determined, and then discussed; and all deviation from the opinion which he announced, or was known to favour, was stigmatised as obstinacy or incapacity.

As a statesman, Tippoo was incapable of those abstract views, and that large compass of thought, embraced by his father's mind. His talents as a soldier, exhibited the same contrast. He was unable to grasp the plan of a campaign, or the conduct of a war; although, he gave some examples of skill in marshaling a battle. Unlike his father, whose moderation was ever most conspicuous in success, whose equanimity was uniform in every aspect of fortune, and, who generally extracted some advantage from every discomfiture, Tippoo was intoxicated with success, and desponding in adversity. His mental energy failed with the decline of fortune; but it were unjust to question his physical courage. He fell in the defence of his capital; but, he fell, performing the duties of a common soldier, not of a general. The improvement in his infantry and artillery, would have been considerable, had it not been marred by incessant dislocations, and unmerited promotions: but, his army, as a whole, gradually declined in efficiency, as it departed from the admirable organization received from his father. The success of the campaign of 1786, may, in part, be ascribed to the remains of that organization. His failure against the English, arose from the false policy of neglecting his most efficient arm — the cavalry.

During the life of Hyder, it was the fashion to indulge in high expectations of the qualities of the heir apparent, but it was the homage of disappointed, uninformed, and generally of unworthy men. Hyder in his life-time was stigmatized as a tyrant; comparison made him almost seem merciful: the English prisoners hailed the intelligence of Tippoo's accession; and they learned to mourn for the death of Hyder.

The tolerant spirit of Hyder, reconciled to his usurpation the members of every sect: appropriate talents regulated his choice of instruments, to the entire exclusion of religious preference; and it may be affirmed that he was served with equal zeal by men of every persuasion. Hyder was seldom wrong, and Tippoo seldom right in his estimate of character: and it is quoted as a marked example, that Hyder knew Seyed Saheb to be a tolerably good man of business, but neither a brave nor a sagacious soldier; and, accordingly, never employed him in an important military trust. Tippoo in the campaign of 1790, had himself degraded him for incapacity, but in 1799, committed the post of danger, and the fate of empire, to the same incompetent hands. A dark and intolerant bigotry excluded from Tippoo's choice all but the true believers; and unlimited persecution united in detestation of his rule every Hindoo in his dominions. In the Hindoo no degree of merit was a passport to favour; in the Mussulman no crime could ensure displeasure.

In one solitary instance, the suppression of drunkenness, he promoted morals without the merit of virtuous intention: bigotry exacted the literal version of a text generally interpreted with laxity: arrogance suggested that he was the only true commentator: and the ruling passion whispered that the measure was new. Both sovereigns were equally unprincipled; but Hyder had a clear undisturbed view of the interests of ambition: in Tippoo that view was incessantly obscured and perverted by the meanest passions. He murdered his English prisoners, by a selection of the best, because he hated their valour: he oppressed and insulted his Hindoo subjects, because he hated a religion which, if protected, would have been the best support of his throne; and he fawned, in his last extremity, on this injured people, when he vainly hoped that their incantations might influence his fate: he persecuted contrary to his interest; and hoped, in opposition to his belief. Hyder, with all his faults, might be deemed a model of toleration, by the professor of any religion. Tippoo, in an age when persecution only survived in history, renewed its worst terrors; and was the last Mahommedan prince, after a long interval of better feeling, who propagated that religion by the edge of the sword. Hyder's vices invariably promoted his political interests; Tippoo's more frequently defeated them. If Hyder's punishments were barbarous, they were at least efficient to their purpose. Tippoo's court and army was one vast scene of unpunished peculation, notorious even to himself. He was barbarous where severity was vice, and indulgent where it was virtue. If he had qualities fitted for empire, they were strangely equivocal; the disqualifications were obvious and unquestionable; and the decision of history will not be far removed from the observation almost proverbial in Mysoor, "that Hyder was born to create an empire, Tippoo to lose one."

1799. Hyder might have been rendered, in the early part of his career, a firm and efficient ally of the English government; and a clear view of his own interests would probably have rendered him faithful, if treated with fidelity. The unhappy ascendancy of Mahommed Ali made him their inveterate enemy, and he transmitted that sentiment to his son, who had at no period either the inclination or the sagacity to become a faithful ally. The English Government had uniform and incessant grounds of dissatisfaction with the conduct of Tippoo. Hyder had just grounds to complain of the English Government.

June 4. So soon as the willing submission of the whole country of Mysoor had been fully ascertained, the Governor-general with the special concurrence of Nizam Ali, appointed a commission * to conduct and order, for the common benefit of the allies, the ultimate arrangement of the conquest.

The East India Company and Nizam Ali derived an undoubted right to the disposal of the dominions conquered by their united arms; the cession of any portion of it to any other party might be a consideration of policy or humanity, but could not be claimed on any ground of justice or right. The Mahrattas had obviously forfeited every pretension to participate; the progeny of Tippoo Sultaun could claim no title which had not been superseded by the right of conquest; and in estimating their claims it was impossible to forget the usurpation of Hyder, and the sufferings of the family expelled by his crimes. A descendant of that family existed at Seringapatam, but although he might have

* General Harris, Honourable Colonel Wellesley, Honourable Henry Wellesley, Lieutenant-Colonel W. Kirkpatrick, Lieutenant-Colonel Barry Close.

much to hope from the humanity of the conquerors, he could assert no right to any share of the conquered territory.

To the free and uncontrolled exercise of the right of conquest no obstacle existed in the internal state of the country: the people had manifested the most anxious desire for a new settlement; all the Mahommedan officers of the late government were in Seringapatam, at the discretion of the allies, and from the uniform policy of the late dynasty, never possessed any influence in the country capable of disturbing such a plan of internal government as should be deemed just and expedient.

In regulating therefore the right of conquest, no principle could be more justly assumed than that indemnification and security, the original objects of the war, should constitute the basis of the peace.

To have divided the whole territory equally between the Company and Nizam Ali, would have afforded strong grounds of jealousy to the Mahrattas; and by injudiciously enlarging the dominions of Nizam Ali, who was incompetent to manage what he already possessed, and thus placing many of the strong fortresses on the northern frontier of Mysoor in his possession, that important barrier would be in a situation to endanger, not to strengthen, the British possessions.

The establishment of a central government in Mysoor, under the protection of the English state, would obviate many of these objections ; and the admission of the Mahrattas, however destitute of every claim of right, to a limited participation in the division of the conquered territory, (on the express condition, however, of a new treaty calculated to preserve the general tranquillity of India,) was, after a full consideration of various plans, that which appeared best calculated to reconcile the interests of all parties, and to secure to the English Government a less invidious and more efficient share of financial, commercial, and military strength. The future distribution of territory on these principles having been calculated, on a fair consideration of the convenience of the parties, to whom it should be allotted, the delicate and important question remained, of determining in what hands the new government of Mysoor should be placed; and although no positive right existed, the choice would naturally fall on either the family of Tippoo Sultaun, or the ancient house of the rajas of Mysoor.

The claims of humanity on both sides rendered the decision a painful and ungracious task. The usurpation, although comparatively modern, had yet subsisted a sufficient time to have extinguished the hopes of the ancient family, and accustomed them to the humility of their fortune; while the sons of Tippoo Sultaun, educated with the proudest expectations, would be deeply sensible to the disappointment of their hopes.

The heir of Tippoo Sultaun, if placed on the throne, must be subjected to the same diminution of power and territory, which had formed a leading object of the war against his father: and, educated in the same principles and prejudices, would have felt such a condition to be little short of the most abject and humiliating degradation. In the most narrow view of the subject, the son of Tippoo Sultaun must have felt a perpetual interest in the subversion of a settlement, founded on the partition of his father's dominions. The foundation of such a settlement would have been laid in the principle of its own dissolution. The interests, the habits, the prejudices and passions, the vices, and even the virtues of such a prince, must have concurred to cherish an aversion to the English name and power, and an eager desire to abet the cause of their enemies. A hostile power would have been weakened, not destroyed: and a point of union for every hostile machination would have remained in the centre of the English possessions.

The restoration of the descendant of the ancient rajas of Mysoor, was recommended by the same course of reasoning which excluded the heir of the usurpation. The kingdom of Mysoor, so long the source of calamity and alarm, would become a barrier of defence, and an accession of strength; and, in addition to these motives of policy, every moral consideration, and every sentiment of generosity, favoured the restoration of the Hindoo family of Mysoor. Such is the brief statement, imperfectly abstracted from the public records, of the principles which guided Lord Mornington in determining to re-establish that ancient family in the government of Mysoor; and, to soften the decision to the heirs and adherents of the usurpation, he granted to the families of Hyder Ali and Tippoo Sultaun, a more munificent maintenance, than they had enjoyed during the late reign; and to the Mahommedan officers, and chiefs of the state, who had survived the Sultaun, pensions founded on the same truly economical views of wise liberality.

The delicacy was observed of removing from Seringapatam to their future residence at Vellore, the families of the late dynasty, before the commissioners should hold any intercourse with the family of the raja of Mysoor: but on the departure of the principal branches, they paid a visit to the future raja, whom they found with others of his persecuted family, in a condition

CHAP. XLVIII. 1799.

of poverty and humiliation which excited the strongest sensations of compassion. The future raja himself was a child of five years of age, but the widow of that raja from whom Hyder usurped the Government, still remained, to confer with the commissioners, and to regulate with distinguished propriety the renewed honours of her house.

The adjustment of the treaty of partition, and of the subsidiary treaty of Mysoor, followed as the necessary consequences of those principles which have been stated: the portion of territory conditionally reserved for the Mahrattas was ultimately divided between the other allies, because no inducements were sufficient to procure from that people an assent to conditions which involved some relaxation of their pretensions to universal plunder. The subsidiary treaty of Mysoor was founded on principles which established the most perfect community of interests between the English Government and the new state: the English Government was charged with the duties of external defence, the new state with those of internal administration, including the extent of military police required in a country composed of the re-union of a multitude of petty principalities. The raja was installed at the seat of his ancestors, in the presence of an immense multitude of Hindoos, who testified the most unfeigned delight at a spectacle which revived the long extinguished hope of perpetual emancipation from Mahommedan tyranny. The practical efficiency of the Government was secured by the uncommon talents of Poornea in the office of minister to the new raja, and that efficiency was directed to proper objects, by the controul reserved to the English Government in the provisions of the treaty; and by the happy selection of Lieutenant-Colonel Close to be political resident at the new court, a man whose eminent talents, extensive experience, and conciliatory manners, enabled him to guide the new minister, without permitting him to feel the existence of control. A large portion of the wreck of the infantry was employed under the new Government; and by a supplemental treaty, concluded after the experience of a few years, a respectable part of the excellent cavalry of Mysoor, who in the intermediate time had been employed with distinguished credit under Colonel Wellesley, in Decan, were reserved for the service of the state, and prevented from swelling the numbers of that confederation of disbanded armies which, under the designation of Pindarees, is in the year 1817 opposing to the English prosperity in India, a more embarrassing necessity for incessant and extensive preparation, than they have hitherto experienced from long established Governments; the Mahommedans of the nineteenth century retracing the steps of Sevajee in the seventeenth.

Among the inconveniences of that singular and generally beneficial government, established by the British nation in India, is the practice of committing the higher offices of the army and the state, and almost all situations of trust and emolument to Europeans; and thereby excluding the natives of the country from every object of honourable ambition. The settlement of Mysoor was distinguished from all preceding measures of British policy, was quoted with applause in the remotest párts of India, and was acknowledged with unlimited gratitude by the people to be governed, by leaving every office civil and military to be filled by the natives themselves, with the single guard of those powers of interposition in the internal affairs of the government which were reserved by a special provision of the treaty. It is obvious that any ostensible exercise of such a power by the British political resident, would have a direct tendency to weaken and subvert the authority of the native government, and that such an interposition, to be efficient to its true purposes, must be delicate, silent, and unobserved; the experiment was new, and with relation to its remote consequences of momentous importance; the eminent talents of the minister and resident were supported by the cordial co-operation, in the military command, of the Honourable Colonel Wellesley, a name which no epithet can exalt; and Lord Wellesley had the satisfaction of being enabled to declare at the close of his memorable administration in India, that the actual success of the arrangement of Mysoor had fulfilled his most sanguine expectations.

It is not intended to suggest that the exclusive employment of native agency is an example fit for imitation in the more extended scale of our national administration in India; but the general success of this experiment, and the practice (where discretionary power has been allowed) of the most efficient public officers in the south of India, have established the wisdom, the safety, and may we add the justice, of committing to the governed, a larger interest in the prosperity of the government; of securing fidelity by opening to their hopes a field of moderate and legitimate ambition; and thus temperately regulating that system of exclusion which, in its present state, no humility can otherwise contemplate than as the brand of national degradation.

APPENDIX.

No. I.

G. O. BY THE COMMANDER-IN-CHIEF.

" *Camp at Seringapatam, 5th May*, 1799.

" THE Commander-in-Chief congratulates the gallant army, which he has the honour to command, on the conquest of yesterday: The effects arising from the attainment of such an acquisition, as far exceeds the present limits of detail, as the unremitting zeal, labour, and unparalleled valour of the troops, surpass his power of praise. For services so incalculable in their consequences, he must consider the army as well entitled to the applause and gratitude of their country at large.

" While Lieutenant-General Harris sincerely laments the loss sustained in the valuable officers and men who fell in the assault, he cannot omit to return his thanks, in the warmest terms, to Major-General Baird, for the decided and able manner in which he conducted the assault, and for the humane measures which he subsequently adopted, for preserving order and regularity in the place. He requests that Major-General Baird will communicate to the officers and men, who on that great occasion acted under his command, the high sense he must entertain of their achieveвластьment sand merits.

" The Commander-in-Chief requests that Colonel Gent, and the corps of engineers under his orders, will accept his thanks for their unremitting exertions in conducting the duties of that very important department; and his best acknowledgments are due to Major Beatson, for the essential assistance given to this branch of the service, by the constant exertion of his ability and zeal.

" The merits of the artillery corps, are so strongly expressed by the effects of their fire, that the Commander-in-Chief can only desire Colonel Smith, to assure the officers and men of the excellent corps under his command, that he feels most fully their claim to approbation.

" In thus publicly expressing his sense of their good conduct, the Commander-in-Chief feels himself called upon to notice, in a most particular manner, the exertion of Captain Dowse and his corps of pioneers, which, during the present service, have been equally marked by unremitting labour, and the ability with which that labour was applied.

" On referring to the progress of the siege, so many occasions have occurred for applause to the troops, that it is difficult to particularize individual merit; but the gallant manner in which Lieutenant-Colonel Shaw, the Honourable Colonel Wellesley, Lieutenant-Colonel Moneypenny, the Honourable Lieutenant-Colonel St. John, Major Macdonald, Major Skelly, and Lieutenant-Colonel Wallace, conducted the attacks on the several outworks and posts of the enemy, demands to be recorded. And the very spirited attack led by Lieutenant-Colonel Campbell of His Majesty's 74th regiment, which tended so greatly to secure the position our troops had attained in the enemy's works, on the

26th ultimo, claims the strongest approbation of the Commander-in-Chief.

" The important part taken by the Bombay army, since the commencement of the siege, in all the operations which led to its honourable conclusion, has been such, as well sustains its long established reputation. The gallant manner in which the post, at the village of Agrar, was seized by the force under Colonel Hart, the ability displayed in directing the fire of the batteries established there, the vigour with which every attack of the enemy on the out-posts of that army was repulsed, and the spirit shewn in the assault of the breach, by the corps led by Lieutenant-Colonel Dunlop, are points of particular notice, for which the Commander-in-Chief requests Lieutenant-General Stuart will offer his best thanks to the officers and troops employed.

" Lieutenant-General Harris trusts, that Lieutenant-General Stuart will excuse his thus publicly expressing his sense of the cordial co-operation and assistance received from him during the present service; in the course of which he has ever found it difficult to separate the sentiments of his public duty from the warmest feelings of private friendship."

EXTRACT FROM GENERAL ORDERS.

Dated Seringapatam, 8th May, 1799.

" Lieutenant-General Harris has particular pleasure in publishing to the army the following extract of a report transmitted to him yesterday, by Major-General Baird, as it places, in a distinguished point of view, the merit of an officer on the very important occasion referred to, whose general gallantry [illegible] conduct, since he has served with his army, have not failed to recommend him strongly to the Commander-in-Chief.

" If, where all behaved nobly, it is proper to mention individual merit, I know no man so justly entitled to praise as Colonel Sherbrooke, to whose exertions I feel myself much indebted for the success of the attack.

True Copies,

(*Signed*) P. A. Agnew,

Military-Secretary."

No. II.

G. O. BY GOVERNMENT.

"*Fort St. George*, 15*th May*, 1799.

" The Right Honourable the Governor-General in Council, having this day received from the Commander-in-Chief of the allied army in the field, the official details of the glorious and decisive victory obtained at Seringapatam, on the 4th of May, offers his cordial thanks and sincere congratulations to the Commander-in-Chief, and to all the officers and men composing the gallant army, which achieved the conquest of the capital of Mysore on that memorable day.

" His Lordship views with admiration the consummate judgment with which the assault was planned; the unequalled rapidity, animation, and skill with which it was executed, and the humanity which distinguished its final success.

"Under the favour of Providence, and the justice of our cause, the established character of the army had inspired an early confidence, that the war in which we were engaged would be brought to a speedy, prosperous, and honourable issue.

"But the events of the 4th of May, while they have surpassed even the sanguine expectations of the Governor-General in council, have raised the reputation of the British arms in India to a degree of splendour and glory, unrivalled in the military history of this quarter of the globe, and seldom approached in any part of the world.

"The lustre of this victory can be equalled only by the substantial advantages which it promises to establish, by restoring the peace and safety of the British possessions in India on a durable foundation of genuine security.

"The Governor-General in council reflects with pride, satisfaction, and gratitude, that in this arduous crisis the spirit and exertion of our Indian army have kept pace with those of our countrymen at home; and that in India, as in Europe, Great Britain has found, in the malevolent designs of her enemies, an increasing source of her own prosperity, fame and power.

"By order of the Right Honourable the Governor-General in council.

(*Signed*) J. WEBBE,

Secretary to the Government."

No. III.

G. O. BY GOVERNMENT.

" *Fort St. George, 24th May,* 1799.

" The Right Honourable the Governor-General in Council is pleased to publish in General Orders the following copy of a letter from the Commander-in-Chief.

" My Lord,

" I have forwarded to your Lordship, by various hircarrahs, an account of the success of the army in the assault of Seringapatam, with copies of the orders issued on that occasion : in those orders I expressed my approbation of the conduct of the troops in general, and my sense of the merits of those officers whose behaviour had attracted particular notice.

" It remains for me to state what is in justice due to others, whom, for obvious reasons, I could not present in the same manner to your Lordship's notice ; these are officers on the general staff, in my family, and others whose zeal induced them to forward the public service by the exertion of their abilities in aid of departments to which they were not officially attached.

" In every point of view I must call your Lordship's particular attention to the Adjutant-General of the army. His general character as an officer is too well established, by a long and distinguished course of the most meritorious service, to require my testimony; but the particular exertion of his talents on the present service, in directing, regulating, and assisting, the progress of our departments, when embarrassed by all the difficulties attending a deficiency of conveyance for an uncommonly extensive equipment, during the advance of the army; and the ability, zeal, and energy, displayed by him in superintending the various operations of an arduous siege, where he was ever present, stimulating the exertions of others, or assisting their judgment and labour with his own, claim from me to be stated to your Lordship in the most forcible terms. It is my earnest wish that my sentiments on this subject may be publicly recorded, and it is my firm opinion, that if the success of this army has been of importance to the British interests, that success is to be attributed, in a very considerable degree, to Lieutenant-Colonel Close.

" From the officers more immediately in my family I have derived all the assistance in the conduct of the public service, which I had reason to expect from their experience; and I am highly indebted to your Lordship for the indulgence with which you attended to my wishes in the selection of Lieutenant-Colonel Agnew and Captain Macaulay as my confidential staff.

" Major Dallas has strong claims to be particularly recommended to your Lordship's notice: the readiness with which he came forward to exert his personal influence with the principal natives in the bullock department, at a period when it seemed scarcely possible to move forward the public stores; the effectual aid which he gave to the store department, by his personal assistance in its arrangements, and the duty, equally important and laborious, which he voluntarily took upon himself, of seeking and securing forage for the public cattle during the marches of the army, are amongst the many instances in which his zeal has been distinguished, and which entitle him to the attention of Government.

"In the department of the quarter-master-general, the conduct of Lieutenant-Colonel Richardson and Major Allan has been very satisfactory to me: Captain Turing has ably assisted Lieutenant-Colonel Close in the adjutant-general's office; and Captain Orr of the guides has merited great praise, by his judgment, diligence, and activity in conducting the marches of the army, and of all the detachments of importance, which, since our encampment here, it has been necessary to make under Major-General Floyd.

"Captain Macleod, of the intelligence department, has been employed in the management of the bazars of the army, in the arrangement of the banjarries, and on a variety of services not specially the duty of any regularly established office, but which required a perfect knowledge of the customs of India, and the strictest integrity in the person charged with their execution. I have on all such occasions given my full confidence to Captain Macleod, and his conduct has shewn him deserving of the trust.

"I have thought it a necessary part of my public duty to make this report to your Lordship, for the information of Government, and have the honour to be, &c. &c. &c.

(*Signed*) GEORGE HARRIS.

"*Seringapatam, May* 13*th* 1799."

"The Right Honourable the Governor-General in council directs the Commander-in-Chief of the allied army in the field to assure the officers on the general staff of the army, those composing the confidential staff of the Commander-in-Chief, and those whose zeal, ability and exertion have been distinguished in aid of the departments to which they were not officially attached, that his Lordship entertains the highest sense of their several eminent services during the late glorious campaign in Mysore.

"The conduct of the Adjutant-General, Lieutenant-Colonel Close, has amply justified the implicit confidence reposed by the Governor-General in council in his extensive knowledge, approved experience, superior talents, ardent valour, and indefatigable activity.

"The uniform zeal, perseverance, and fortitude with which Lieutenant-Colonel Close has exerted all these great qualities, in every trial of difficulty and danger, entitle him to the praise, respect and esteem of the Governor-General in council. His Lordship feels himself bound by every obligation of justice and public duty to recommend the extraordinary merits of Lieutenant-Colonel Close to the particular approbation of the Honourable the Court of Directors, and to the applause and gratitude of his country.

"The selection which the Commander-in-Chief had so judiciously made of Lieutenant-Colonel Agnew and Captain Macaulay, for his confidential staff, was confirmed by the

Governor-General in council, with a just expectation that His Excellency would derive considerable advantage to the public service from their able assistance.

"The Governor-General in council is happy to record a public acknowledgment of the distinguished conduct of Major Dallas, and to assure that officer that his Lordship has a just sense of the important services which he has rendered in his successful superintendence of the laborious departments under his charge.

"It is very satisfactory to his Lordship to remark, that the conduct of the quarter-master-general's department, under Lieutenant-Colonel Richardson and Major Allan, and that of the department of the guides under Captain Orr, has met with the approbation of the Commander-in-Chief; his Lordship desires that his public thanks may be conveyed to those officers, and on this occasion his Lordship thinks it proper to publish to the army the particular thanks which he had already directed the Commander-in-Chief to convey to Major Allan and Captain Orr, for the essential services rendered by them on the 22d March last, after the battle of Mallavelly.

"His Lordship is also happy to concur in the honourable testimony borne by the Commander-in-Chief to the merits of Captain Turing and of Captain Macleod, and directs that his thanks may be conveyed to those meritorious officers.

"In all ranks and departments of the allied army his Lordship has observed, with sincere pleasure, a general spirit of harmony and concord, which (under the happy auspices of the Commander-in-Chief) has united every heart, head, and hand, in the common cause, signalized each progressive operation of the campaign, with a peculiar character of alacrity and ardour, and crowned its early conclusion with victory, triumph and renown.

"By order of the Right Honourable the Governor-General in council,

J. Webbe, *Secretary to Government.*"

N. B. The name of Captain Malcolm was inadvertently omitted in these communications, but General Harris paid a just and ample tribute to his services with Nizam Ali's troops, in an official letter addressed to the Governor-General.

GENERAL INDEX

OF

NAMES AND SUBJECTS.

A.

C

D

F

H

8

I

J

L

O

P

Q

R

T

U

V

W

Y

Z

THE END.

ERRATA. Vol. III.

Page 32, line 5, for "formarly" read "formally."
40, Note, for "Gavesa" read "Ganesa."
43, There is an error in the reasoning regarding the lines across Vipeen, from my having omitted to modify the passage to conform to the fact of the purchase stated in page 33; which was ascertained, and in that page corrected after the narrative had been written.
114, last, for "remarks" read "remark-.'
190, 13, for "served" read "reserved."
199, Note, for "Coimbetoor" read "Travancore."
208, 10, for "Ostradroog" read "Ootradroog."
218, 9, for "by" read "on."
223, 15, for "and" read "one."
351, 12 from the bottom, for the "period" read "a semicolon."
358, 6 from the bottom, after "conditions" read "contains."
392, 10, for "in India" read "on India."
415, 6, for "Sheker," read "Sheher."
459, Add to the end of the note, *He was again in Coromandel in 1752, whence his wife was probably sent to Deonhully on the occasion of her pregnancy, for he himself remained in Coromandel till 1755.*

In both volumes I perceive the occasional omission of the *de* which ought to precede the names of Bussy and Suffrein, and I have probably committed the same unintentional error with other French names.

Musheer ul Mulk and Azeem ul Omra, titles of the same person at different periods are sometimes misapplied.